LOMA LINDA UNIVERSITY

School of Medicine

MORNING ROUNDS
DAILY DEVOTIONAL STORIES

A Collection of Stories, Essays, & Insights

by

Students, Alumni, Faculty, & Friends

of

Loma Linda University School of Medicine

Submitted to Commemorate the School's Centennial

1909-2009

Edited by Donna R. Hadley

Volunteer Chair, Centennial Celebration Planning Committee

Published by
Loma Linda University Press
Office of Academic Publications
Loma Linda University
Loma Linda, CA 92350
Printed in the United States of America

Copies may be ordered from
Loma Linda University Campus Store
11161 Anderson Street, Suite 110
Loma Linda, CA 92354
Tel: (909) 558-4567
Email: campusstore@llu.edu
www.lomalindamarket.com

Publisher: Loma Linda University Press
Cover concept: JD Sevilla
Cover designer: Scott Guptill
Front cover photo credits:
    Hasan Syed (left) and Lorelei Harbour (right)
    Photographer: Danny Wongworawat
Back cover photo credits:
    Aidan Gustafsson (left) and Astrid von-Walter (right)
    Photographer: Kenneth Larsen
Compiler and production editor: Donna Hadley
Project manager: Alice Wongworawat
Copy editor: Duane Fike
Research editor and indexer: Michael Weismeyer
Printer: Sinclair Printing Company, Los Angeles, CA
Compositor: Loma Linda University Printing Services
Typeface: Adobe Jenson Pro

This book is printed on acid-free paper.

Library of Congress Cataloging-in-Publication Data

Morning rounds : daily devotional stories.
    p. cm.
Prepared for the centennial of Loma Linda University School of Medicine in 2009.
Includes indexes.
ISBN 978-59410-014-4 (paperback) (alk. paper)
1. Physicians—Prayers and devotions. 2. Medical students—Prayers and devotions. 3. Loma Linda University. School of Medicine—Faculty—Prayers and devotions. 4. Loma Linda University. School of Medicine—Students—Prayers and devotions. 5. Devotional calendars— Seventh-Day Adventists. I. Loma Linda University. School of Medicine.
BV4596.P5M67 2008
242'.68—dc22
2008049785

Copyrights

Abbreviations

The following abbreviations are used throughout the book

Loma Linda University Entities

CME	College of Medical Evangelists (now Loma Linda University)
LLU	Loma Linda University
LLUAHSC	Loma Linda University Adventist Health Sciences Center
LLUBMC	Loma Linda University Behavioral Medicine Center
LLUCH	Loma Linda University Children's Hospital
LLUHC	Loma Linda University Health Care
LLUHS	Loma Linda University Health Services
LLUMC	Loma Linda University Medical Center
LLUSAHP	Loma Linda University School of Allied Health Professions
LLUSD	Loma Linda University School of Dentistry
LLUSM	Loma Linda University School of Medicine
LLUSN	Loma Linda University School of Nursing
LLUSP	Loma Linda University School of Pharmacy
LLUSPH	Loma Linda University School of Public Health
LLUSR	Loma Linda University School of Religion

Degrees

BA	Bachelor of Arts
BS	Bachelor of Science
BSc	Bachelor of Science
JD	Juris Doctor
DD	Doctor of Divinity
DMin	Doctor of Ministry
DrPH	Doctor of Public Health
DTh	Doctor of Theology
EdD	Doctor of Education
EdS	Specialist in Education
MA	Master of Arts
MBA	Master of Business Administration
MD	Doctor of Medicine
MDiv	Master of Divinity
MHA	Master of Health Administration
MHIS	Master in Health Information Services
MPH	Master of Public Health
MS	Master of Science
PhD	Doctor of Philosophy
PsyD	Doctor of Psychology
RelD	Doctor of Religion

Foreword

The devotional dated October 23 by Richard A. Schaefer recounts the following incident:

In the late fall of 1911, Nathan P. Colwell, MD, secretary of the Council on Medical Education, visited the College of Medical Evangelists to make a preliminary assessment of its standing with the American Medical Association . . . [He] asked, "Why are you starting a new school, when there are already 150 medical schools in the United States?" . . . [John] Burden [the business manager for CME] then described the unique physical, mental, and spiritual emphasis of the church's international missionary program. He added, "Will you tell me, doctor, to what school can we send our young people to equip them for this world mission work with this threefold preparation?"

Colwell replied, "There is no such school in existence . . . . Mr. Burden, when I took my medical course, it was to become a medical missionary. . . . The medical got me, and the mission lost out."

Since its inception, Loma Linda University School of Medicine has consciously strived to remain true to its medical mission. Of the school's more than 9,500 graduates to date, approximately 736 have served overseas for at least a year with 25 currently serving overseas. In an age of technology and affluence, our medical students are signing up in record numbers to serve the underserved at home and abroad. Mission electives are an integral part of the training of our students as they go out into the global classroom. Based on their reports upon their return, they have learned life lessons that are impossible to teach within the confines of four walls. In addition, there has been a renewed interest in our deferred mission appointment program—in which sixty-eight students are currently enrolled.

As we began preparing to celebrate the centennial of the School of Medicine in 2009, there was a desire to include as many students, alumni, faculty, and friends of the school as possible in this significant milestone. The proposal of a devotional book seemed to be ideal for this purpose. But would 365 authors actually submit their stories and insights? The response was better than anyone on the Centennial Planning Committee dared hope! An added bonus was the level of enthusiasm displayed for the project by contributors of all ages, in all stages of their medical practice, with varying backgrounds, and from all around the globe. Collectively, they tell the very personal side of our centennial journey.

The stories that are included in this book are indicative of our success in keeping the "medical" united with the "mission"—both globally and locally. I think you will agree . . . it is, perhaps, the most important reason for the School of Medicine's existence.

May God continue to bless you; and in return, may you be a blessing to others. Remember to include God in your *Morning Rounds* . . . no matter what your life's work.

H. Roger Hadley, MD
Dean, LLU School of Medicine

Prologue

Early in 2008, an invitation went out to those affiliated with the School of Medicine to submit "stories" of times when "an incident occurred, a situation evolved, or something noteworthy happened that gave pause to think of its spiritual implications." This request for submissions further articulated, "Maybe it inspired you, or provided insight about life's lessons, or was just a good learning experience." Understandably, we were unsure as to what kinds of responses we would receive. What you hold in your hands represents a selection from those who replied.

The beauty of having 365 different authors is that their stories are as wide-ranging as the individuals who wrote them. This collective group of authors represents a diversity of ages, life experiences, geographic locations, religions, cultures, and races. Many of their essays vary greatly as they tell of unanswered prayers, answers to simple prayers, and even answers to prayers for the seemingly impossible. How you, the reader, view these reflections will be individualized as well. It is important to note that what these writers have in common is a connection with the School of Medicine in some way, and a real love for and trust in God. What is shared individually by each of them is very personal indeed.

Our prayer is that you will find those passages that speak directly to you—that give you hope, inspiration, comfort, new insights, and perhaps a deeper appreciation for this medical school and God's leading of it for the past 100 years. If you are successful in finding any or all of these things within the following pages, then our purpose for compiling this book will have been achieved.

The Editor

The information provided in the authors' bios is accurate as of the date of publication.

Dedicated to

All LLUSM students, graduates, & faculty . . .

You are the history of our school.

Acknowledgments

Alice Wongworawat—my highly capable executive assistant, whose compulsion to meet deadlines, along with her strict attention to minutiae, kept this project moving forward.

Duane Fike—a gifted copy editor, who volunteered hundreds of hours to this project and whose recommendations and advice were invaluable.

Carol Weismeyer—from the office of student affairs in the dean's office, whose proof-reading skills are *par excellence* and whose dedication to this project went "above and beyond."

Michael Weismeyer—the doctoral student looking for summer work, whose vast fund of knowledge and expertise as writer, researcher, and indexer contributed to the project in ways that cannot be measured or duly praised.

Audrey Howard, Flint Jonston and Eppie Manalo—the staff of Academic Publication and University Press, for their helpful editorial suggestions and assistance with the "housekeeping" details of publishing.

Medical Editors—the group of physicians from various disciplines who assisted with the glossary and made this book medically sound.

Editorial Review Board—those individuals from varied backgrounds who helped decide the direction, tenor, and validity of this book.

School of Medicine dean's office—Carletta Bender, whose assistance with the authors' bios helped tell "the rest of the story": JD Sevilla, the talented graphic designer who developed the design concept for the front and back covers; and Lenoa Edwards, Henry Lamberton, Treva Webster, and Lynn Wilkemeyer, who willingly assisted with so many aspects of this book in addition to their daily "routines."

Scott Guptill—graphic designer from the design department of Loma Linda University Printing Services, who designed the cover and dust jacket, formatted the pages, and patiently and skillfully facilitated the countless revisions.

Dennis Park—executive director of LLUSM Alumni Association, who shared the stories and histories of many alumni.

Tamara Thomas—associate dean for faculty development who, when asked if she had any ideas for the title quickly responded, "Morning Rounds." How perfect.

Donna Hadley—my lovely wife, who conceived the idea for this book and volunteered her time to bring this project to fruition; her warmth and tenacity sold the idea to hundreds of contributors.

And to each of the authors, who allowed us glimpses into their worlds. With a broad spectrum of styles, voices, and backgrounds, you have shown us a very personal side of medicine and life. They have helped write the centennial story of Loma Linda University School of Medicine. My profound thanks to each one.

H. Roger Hadley, MD
Dean, LLU School of Medicine

MORNING ROUNDS
DAILY DEVOTIONAL STORIES

A Prayer for Morning Rounds

LORD, through your mercy, wisdom, and power,

You heal the sick when all other help has failed.

And You promise them the hope of eternal life

after their life on earth is done.

I pray that You will touch my heart

with deep compassion for my patients' sufferings,

and light my mind with a thorough knowledge

of Your way for their many ills.

When I stretch out my hand to minister to the sick,

touch them through me with an increasing portion

of Your mercy, wisdom, and power.

And whether or not they are to be healed,

LORD, let me lead them to a deeper faith,

and to rest in Your gracious love.

Gayle R. Wilson, LLUSM class of 1973-B, is a family practitioner in Dallas, Oregon.

January 1

Give instruction to the wise, and they will become wiser still; teach the righteous and they will gain in learning. Proverbs 9:9, NRSV

Most of what I have learned about life comes from my studying the life of Jesus. The rest I observed from the experiences of others. The following reflects some of these lessons.

You can do something in an instant that will give you heartache for life.

You should always leave loved ones with loving words. It may be the last time you see them.

You can keep going long after you can't.

Either you control your attitude or it controls you.

Regardless of how hot and steamy a relationship is at first, the passion fades and there had better be something else to take its place.

Heroes are the people who do what has to be done when it needs to be done, regardless of the consequences.

Money is a lousy way of keeping score.

My best friend and I can do anything or nothing and have the best time.

Sometimes the people you expect to kick you when you're down will be the ones to help you get back up.

Sometimes when I'm angry I have the right to be angry, but that doesn't give me the right to be cruel.

True friendship continues to grow, even over the longest distance. Same goes for true love.

Just because someone doesn't love you the way you want them to doesn't mean they don't love you with all they have.

Maturity has more to do with what types of experiences you've had and what you've learned from them, and less to do with how many birthdays you've celebrated.

Your family won't always be there for you. It may seem funny, but people you aren't related to can take care of you and love you and teach you to trust people again. Families aren't always biological.

No matter how good a friend is, they're going to hurt you every once in a while and you must forgive them for that.

Sometimes you have to learn to forgive yourself.

No matter how bad your heart is broken, the world doesn't stop for your grief.

Our background and circumstances may influence who we are, but we are responsible for who we become.

Just because two people argue, it doesn't mean they don't love each other. And just because they don't argue, it doesn't mean they do.

We don't have to change friends if we understand that friends change.

You shouldn't be so eager to find out a secret. It could change your life forever.

Your life can be changed in a matter of hours by people who don't even know you.

Even when you think you have no more to give, when a friend cries out to you, you will find the strength to help.

The people you care about most in life are taken from you way too soon.

Wil Alexander is professor in LLUSM department of family medicine and is emeritus professor of relational studies in LLUSR. He received a PhD degree from Michigan State University in East Lansing, Michigan, in 1962. He was founding director of LLU Center for Spiritual Life and Wholeness. In 1990, he received the LLU Distinguished Service Award.

January 2

Jesus said to him, "If I will that he remain till I come, what is that to you? You follow me." John 21:22, NKJV

We all have people we have admired during our lifetime. I want to honor Mervyn Hardinge, LLUSM class of 1942, who graduated from medical school the year I was born. He taught in the anatomy department, and later headed the pharmacology department before becoming dean of LLU School of Public Health.

I liked his devotionals before his lectures, particularly his reflection on the closing verses of John when Peter asked, "What about this man?" Jesus said to him, "If I will that he remain till I come, what is that to you. You follow me" (John 21:21-22, NKJV).

God's calling of others is not our business or worry, and what they get in compensation is not our concern. Our part is to be faithful in what He asks us to do. Dr. Hardinge was that way. I appreciated his help as a sponsor of the medical evangelism seminar that met on Friday evenings to study God's plan for Loma Linda. And though his desk was piled with work, he always found time to talk if I stopped by with a concern.

It was after Dr. Hardinge became dean of the School of Public Health that he pointed out the misnomer of "healthcare" that so commonly refers to what doctors, nurses, or hospitals do. His definition of healthcare was more in line with the remedies listed by Ellen G. White: "pure air, sunlight, abstemiousness, rest, exercise, proper diet, the use of water, trust in divine power" (*The Ministry of Healing*, p. 127). "This book [the Bible] contains the wisdom of the Great Physician" (*Testimonies for the Church*, vol. 9, p. 71). Thus, in a secondary sense, my honoring here is a tribute to Ellen G. White, without whom Loma Linda University and Medical Center would not exist.

For all this dedication to good health, we now have national recognition. We can be proud that Loma Linda was honored in *National Geographic's* cover story on longevity, November 2005. And without the principles on which Loma Linda University and Medical Center were founded, many of us would find old age a pain or burden.

Yet, there is more we must do. With adverse drug reactions becoming a leading cause of death (*JAMA*, April 15, 1998) and with a 2.7-fold increase from 1998 to 2005 in deaths related to those reactions (*Archives of Internal Medicine*, September 10, 2007), we should review our role as healers. Thankfully, God designed the body for self-healing—as we see with cuts, burns, and breaks. If people will bring their health habits into harmony with basic principles, even heart disease and other major conditions are reversible (*U.S. News & World Report*, August 6, 1990).

We are deeply indebted to Dr. Hardinge, Ellen G. White, and many others. They have helped us understand the gospel of good health. Interestingly, in Hebrew, the word for health and for salvation is the same. Christ understood this relationship, and He did not separate them in His ministry. Should we?

Richard Ruhling, LLUSM class of 1966, also has an MPH degree. He is an internist in Takoma Park, Maryland.

Be very careful, then, how you live—not as unwise but as wise, making the most of every opportunity, because the days are evil. Therefore do not be foolish, but understand what the Lord's will is. Ephesians 5:15-17, NIV

Someone once said: "The main thing is to keep the main thing, the main thing." In other words, keep on target with your primary goal, not being sidetracked by the multitudes of other duties competing for your focused attention. Nothing is truer in the life of the Christian medical student, resident, or physician, who is constantly inundated with a myriad of demands, drawing him or her away from the main goal: continuing the teaching and healing ministry of Jesus Christ. In the Gospel of Matthew, we see that His ministry was threefold—teaching, preaching the good news, and healing. "Jesus went through all the towns and villages, teaching in their synagogues, preaching the good news of the kingdom and healing every disease and sickness" (Matthew 9:35, NIV).

As a surgical resident on-call, I was asked to see a patient in the emergency room. An unfortunate elderly man, who had a recurrent spinal tumor re-excised, had now returned with a gaping wound dehiscence, the size of his head, on his upper back. This series of events had left him in despair; so I was triggered to ask him my favorite spiritual care question: "What is your source of strength?" He said he didn't know; so I shared with him that I found my strength in my Lord and Savior, Jesus Christ.

He was intrigued by that concept, but I was called away to other duties. I promised him I would return, but it was 11:00 p.m. before things finally quieted down. In his room, we returned to this topic. After sharing with him some verses from the "Roman Road" (Romans 3:23, 5:8, 6:23, and 10:9), we actually prayed a prayer for him to receive Christ. I wasn't sure how much he understood but was surprised when I asked him, "So where is Christ now?" and he answered, "In my heart."

In Ephesians, Paul reminds us that we are living in days of evil. The "god of this age," Satan, will continually distract us from our focus on Christ. Now at the end of my residency, I see that without constant reminders, especially from other like-minded believers at work, I would have easily lost the focus to practice spiritual care and witness. Therefore, we need to make a conscious effort to live daily for Christ, looking for every opportunity to care for, minister to, and even share the gospel with those we meet. Let this be our resolution together as we begin this new year!

Bob Wu, LLUSM class of 2003, completed a residency in general surgery at Mary Imogene Bassett Hospital in Cooperstown, New York, and is currently in a laparoscopic fellowship at University of Southern California in Los Angeles, California. In 2003, he received the Wil Alexander Whole-Person Care Award.

January 4

And walk in love, as Christ also has loved us and given Himself for us, an offering and a sacrifice to God for a sweet-smelling aroma. Ephesians 5:2, NKJV

It is not always in the exceptional, the unusual, that we find our meaning or purpose. The everyday occurrences sometimes so poignantly define how Christ would use us—what He wants us to do for Him. The following is just such a course of events that the Lord used to speak to me of His purposes that are working in my life.

Every two years, my state medical license needs to be renewed. So, in early December about a year ago, I sent the application with some hundreds of dollars. My new license arrived later that month; and, in the busyness of the holidays, I put it in my purse and forgot to send needed copies to the administrative departments at my workplace.

When I remembered in early January, I took the license from my purse and noticed half of the license was moistened—stained with something. I passed it in front of my nose. What was that familiar sweet smell? Anointing oil? The vial of spikenard-scented oil that I keep in my purse, for anointing the sick or the sent out, had slowly leaked a bit onto the license. My mind thought, "What is this, Lord? What does it mean?"

Reflecting over the weeks since that day, my Lord and Savior, Jesus Christ, has shown me that my faith is now a vital part of my medical practice. God's truth directs the way I conduct myself. His wisdom is the wisdom that I share with my patients. And, if there is opportunity to pray with my patients and co-workers, there is His wonderful working and healing in our lives.

It was not always this way. Early in my career, I separated my newfound faith from my work; I compartmentalized it. Also, I was afraid to get too close or too involved with patients and co-workers—fearing their needs would overwhelm me or drain me, and fearing that I would not know how to balance my needs with their demands. I was relying on myself; and I did not yet know the wonderful power of God and His love to fill and overflow to others.

A change, however, occurred somewhere. When I realized His great love for me—when I truly felt it in my heart—it filled me; and that love and power were there to share with others. His great Word is a love letter to each of us. It is filled with wisdom that brings healing, wholeness, and great lasting joy. As you will discover, the world does not so much need a physical healing as it desperately needs His great love. Live it, love others, and be joyful. Anointed for ministry; He has put His seal of ministry upon me. Will you let Him put His seal upon you?

Jennifer Dorsey Boyd, an LLU graduate in the physicians' assistant program in 1981, has been practicing for twenty-seven years. She resides in Murrieta, California. January 4 is the date this incident occurred.

But I fear, lest by any means, as the serpent beguiled Eve through his subtilty, so your minds should be corrupted from the simplicity that is in Christ.
2 Corinthians 11:3, KJV

My husband and I are privileged to operate a home-health retreat in picturesque southeastern Minnesota. Our Mercy Valley Farm is nestled along wooded limestone bluffs bordered by glimmering trout streams. Nearby Amish farms dot the gently rolling landscape. The Amish in our area are practical and industrious—but poor. Because of their religious beliefs, they do not carry health insurance or accept government aid.

As a result of their stand, they are readily receptive to simple home remedies. My faith, and my trust in God's effective healing methods, has been substantially strengthened by my working with the Amish. The following story illustrates how they have helped me, too.

One cold January evening, as my husband and I were settled in by our cozy wood stove, the phone rang. The call was from one of our Amish neighbors. Their 6-year-old daughter had developed a skin infection, which had rapidly spread within the past twenty-four hours from her ankles up to the knees. The parents had tried a few home remedies; but as the short winter day turned into dusk, their hopes faded into despair.

They asked if I would please come to see what else could be done. Quickly, I packed my medical bag with poultice materials and herbal teas. Cautiously driving over the narrow, snow-covered gravel road, I headed for their old weathered farmhouse.

I found the little girl sleeping on a small cot in the middle of the dimly lit room. A worn blanket covered her shoulders, leaving both lower legs exposed, as even the weight of a thin sheet on the sore limbs would have been unbearable. Her little legs were swollen to nearly twice their normal size. Clear fluid was seeping through the pores of the taut, reddened skin.

I stood there for a moment, assessing the scene—the exhausted pain-weary child, the anxious faces of the parents, and the solemn siblings hovering around the small, quiet form. I silently sent up an urgent request for heavenly wisdom to meet this challenging situation. Then we went to work.

The parents were instructed to fill two large buckets, one with hot water and the other with cold water. The infected legs and feet were to be immersed alternately in hot then cold water for a total of seven changes. This contrast bath was to be given four times during the day. After each water treatment, a charcoal or herbal poultice was to be applied to the infected area. We prepared garlic and other infection-fighting herbal teas for her to drink throughout the day. I also prescribed plenty of pure drinking water and a nutritious plant-based diet—free of sugar, grease, and lard.

When I left the home later that night, the house seemed warmer and brighter. The family was filled with new hope and courage. When I returned the next morning, the father and mother happily reported that the pain in their daughter's infected legs had definitely diminished. The family members faithfully gave water treatments, applied poultices, prepared teas, and strictly adhered to the dietary plan. The pain, redness, and swelling gradually disappeared without a single visit to the doctor's office. This household was truly grateful for God's wonderfully simple healing ways!

Mary Ann Kimmel-McNeilus, LLUSM class of 1972, is a family practitioner in Lanesboro, Minnesota. This incident occurred in January.

January 6

Each of you should look not only to your own interests, but also to the interests of others. Philippians 2:4, NIV

I was a medical student on a clinical rotation in orthopaedic surgery when I met James Shook, LLUSM class of 1977-A. Others had warned me that he worked long hours as a pediatric and spine specialist, and that he would expect extra effort from each of us. He pushed us to take a thorough history and to really get to know our patients and their families. I was struck by how he greeted by name family members of patients, years after they had been in his office. And he always remembered some detail of their lives that made them laugh or smile.

His practice had many challenging patients, especially those with severe neuromuscular disorders that other physicians seemed to be too busy for (which was ironic, since nobody was busier than Dr. Shook). His love of these deformed children was undeniable; with a grin he would tell us that they were "his people."

Late one hectic office day, a well-dressed couple brought in their wheelchair-bound child, with disabling cerebral palsy. He had severe mental retardation and could not speak or even communicate from his drooling, deformed body. The visibly frustrated mother finally broke down; and through her tears she asked Dr. Shook what use all her effort was in taking care of this barely conscious boy who could not appreciate the huge sacrifice.

The situation was clearly impacting this family in an overwhelming way. Dr. Shook touched her shoulder, and, with his reassuring smile, told her that her son would someday thank her in eternity. He would one day hold her and say, "Thanks, Mom, for taking care of me all those years when I couldn't do it myself."

When the family had gone, Dr. Shook told me that this was a wealthy, driven couple that had focused entirely on their own status and achievement before this child forever altered their lives. They were now forced to constantly focus on someone other than themselves. He said that they didn't realize it yet, but someday, in eternity, they would thank their boy for their own salvation.

My journey to becoming an orthopaedic spine surgeon was greatly influenced by that one day with Jim Shook.

Gerald Alexander, LLUSM class of 1993, is an orthopaedic surgeon in Fullerton, California.

January 7

So they set out and went from village to village, preaching the gospel and healing people everywhere. Luke 9:6, NIV

My first patient on my internal medicine rotation was exquisitely bald, somewhat listless, and unquestionably tooth-free. He had been admitted for vomiting and abdominal pain and was subsequently found to have a small-bowel obstruction. Because he was 80 years old and not a good surgical candidate, the only course of action was to place a nasogastric tube and wait. Four days had passed when I appeared on the scene—fresh from Christmas vacation—and he became my patient.

A shockingly bright quilt adorned his bed; as I approached, he cracked open an eyelid. After the obligatory introduction, "Hi, I'm a student doctor, and I'll be taking care of you while you're here," I began to examine him. His abdomen was fairly distended and as I percussed, I commented: "Your belly sounds like a drum." "A drum?!?" he exclaimed and chuckled gleefully.

Each morning—whether he was nauseated or hungry, in pain or not—we would discuss his "drum" and laugh. Even though there was no magical solution to take away his discomfort, when he was given something to laugh about, he nonetheless became cheerful and optimistic. Tapping into the humor of his discouraging situation made the wait-and-see game a little more bearable for both of us.

So many times in medicine, in life, we become so inextricably entrapped in healing, working, or improving that we lose sight of the big picture. The blood pressure is controlled, but we forget to ask about the patient's new grandbaby. The cancer is in remission, but the patient is still depressed because her hair has fallen out. The bills are paid, but the breadwinner is too exhausted to enjoy family game night.

"To make man whole," the motto of Loma Linda University, suggests that our job is not only to treat the disease, but also, and ultimately more importantly, to treat the person in whom the disease has taken up residence. Too often it takes a situation in which our hands are tied to remind us that life on earth is not about the way it ends; it's about what we do on the road we take to get there. Unless we care for the entire person—body, mind, and soul—then medicine and life are just work.

My patient's bowel obstruction was ultimately resolved, and most likely would have been, whether or not his distention was likened to a drum. However, without the "drum," I would have missed out on the smiles, the laughs, and the wink he gave as he shuffled, still chuckling, out the door.

Lisal Folsom, LLUSM class of 2009—for which she was junior class co-social vice president and senior-year community service co-chair for LLUSM senate—grew up in Centerville, Ohio, and attended Walla Walla College (now Walla Walla University) in College Place, Washington, where she majored in vocal music and met her husband, Nathan. January 7 is the day she met the inspiring patient featured in this story.

January 8

I long to see you so that I may impart to you some spiritual gift to make you strong—that is, that you and I may be mutually encouraged by each other's faith.
Romans 1:11-12, NIV

The faith of students I work with continually encourages me. Among many examples are those of two recent graduates who have given me permission to share their stories. I became acquainted with Belen and Greg shortly after each had started their freshman year at Loma Linda. At the time, I realized they were each experiencing some initial challenges in managing the workload.

When I talked with Belen, I learned that she was commuting to Sacramento, California, twice a month to help her mother manage her business. Like many immigrant families who depend on their children for tasks that require fluency in English, Belen's family had relied upon her from the time she turned 18 to fill the role of administrator in their adult-care home. Before she started medical school, her parents separated; and she and her mother were unable to find a new administrator.

I seriously questioned whether Belen could continue her work in Sacramento and succeed academically, but she did both tasks during her first year-and-a-half of medical school. Her faith in God and her commitment to be a medical missionary sustained her. Belen married her medical school classmate, Jason Lohr, both LLUSM class of 2001, and they are now living out their faith at our mission hospital in Ile Ife, Nigeria.

Greg, LLUSM class of 1999, and Audrey Shank, LLUSM class of 2001, also met when they were medical students at Loma Linda. Greg started school with the vision of becoming a missionary surgeon. But he struggled with the volume of material he was required to master. He literally studied nearly every waking moment. While in the shower and during breakfast, he reviewed notes he had covered with plastic. Then, after his personal worship, he would head to class. After classes and labs, he would study through supper and until he went to bed, taking just a thirty-minute break for exercise and friends. But he still had difficulty.

After following a recommendation that he be evaluated, it was confirmed that he had dyslexia. Taking advantage of the help that was available for students who have learning differences he persevered. His diligence produced results, and he was accepted into a surgical residency (for which he gives all glory to God). He finished it while Audrey completed a residency in family practice. (Tomorrow's devotional, written by Audrey, reminds us that dyslexia does not mean a lack of ability or skill.) Today, Greg and Audrey operate a remote mission hospital in the northern African country of Cameroon.

The faith of these students demonstrates how God works through obstacles and human limitations to accomplish His purposes. Today, if you are facing obstacles or are disheartened by your sense of insufficiency or weakness, I hope you will remember the stories of these students. And I hope that you will be strengthened by the promise of God that strengthened them: "My grace is sufficient for you, for my power is made perfect in weakness" (2 Corinthians 12:9, NIV).

Henry Lamberton is associate dean for student affairs for LLUSM, and is associate professor both in LLUSM department of psychiatry and in LLUSR. He received an MDiv degree from Andrews University in Berrien Springs, in 1974; and a PsyD degree from Fuller Theological Seminary in Pasadena, California, in 1992.

January 9

Whatever your hand finds to do, do it with all your might. Ecclesiastes 9:10, NIV

The longer we are at Koza Adventist Hospital in Cameroon, the more the job description of my husband, Greg Shank, LLUSM class of 1999—besides surgeon and hospital director—expands. For instance, when a 35-year-old man comes to the hospital with a painful inguinal hernia, my husband is a general surgeon. But when a pregnant woman comes in need of a cesarean section, he is an obstetrician and gynecologist. And, when, during the cesarean section, the baby refuses to breathe, he is a neonatologist.

When a 5 year old comes in with a skull fracture after an accident, he is both neurologist and neurosurgeon. And later, when Bouba, an 18-year-old boy, comes in after being stabbed through the diaphragm for calling his cousin a donkey stealer, he is first a cardiothoracic surgeon and then a pulmonologist.

A 70-year-old man comes in with a huge prostate and the inability to urinate, and my husband becomes a urologist. But when a 6 month old comes in with severe anemia from malaria, he is a pediatrician. And then, when a 45 year old comes in with hypertension and irregular heartbeat, he is a cardiologist/internist.

If a 45-year-old woman comes in with advanced breast cancer, he is both surgeon and oncologist. Or, if the minister of health comes to the hospital to discuss how to prevent another meningitis epidemic, he is a specialist in preventive medicine. A 2 year old, who weighs only nine pounds, comes in, and my husband becomes a dietician. When our medication is running low, he is a pharmacist. And when a 20 year old comes in with renal failure and our lab tech is away at a meeting, he is a laboratory technician.

But not all the hats he wears are medical. When there are employee disputes, financial difficulties, fist fights between nurses and patients, theft of money and medications, committee meetings, difficulties with the police and army, and new nurses to hire, he is again the hospital director. (He is often also a psychologist/counselor in these situations.) When one of our maintenance men was having problems with his girlfriend, he gave advice and support and acted as surrogate father. When asked to preach, he is preacher (much outside his comfort zone).

It seems the tasks never end. When the metal grate covering the windows is sawed off by a thief and needs to be repaired, he is a welder. When the roof is blowing off in the high winds, he is a roofer. When we suspect that someone has been breaking into one of the houses on the compound, he is the "assistant" guard (armed with machete).

When the sink springs a leak, he is a plumber (even when it is fixed with an old bike inner tube). And just before a replacement doctor is due to show up at our house, and the toilet isn't working because the septic tank is full, and my husband's out there manually scooping out fifteen years worth of waste, what would you call that? I call him a saint.

At the end of the day, he comes home and is the spiritual leader of our home and the best father and husband anyone could dream of. Please pray for Greg and the many hats that he wears. It is a very difficult position that he holds, but God is supporting him moment by moment, day by day.

Audrey Shank, LLUSM class of 2001, is assistant professor in LLUSM department of family medicine. She and her husband, Gregory, LLUSM class of 1999, are serving at Hospital Adventiste de Koza in Cameroon.

January 10

And the King shall answer and say unto them, Verily I say unto you, Inasmuch as ye have done it unto one of the least of these my brethren, ye have done it unto me. Matthew 25:40, KJV

It's just another night at Shepherd's Hope,* where, over the course of two hours, more or less, three doctors will each see six-to-eight patients. Four nurses will assist these doctors, as will five office workers: the manager, receptionist, eligibility specialist, pharmacist, and interpreter. All are volunteers.

The visitors are waiting patiently behind closed exam room doors. Together, on this particular night, we saw twenty-five patients, but an additional twenty left, disappointed. They will probably return, just as we have some now who were turned away last week.

So here they are. My patients—eight of them in all: adults, ages 36 to 70; two men, six women—four of Hispanic heritage, two African Americans, two Caucasians. Of the three who speak no English, two are fluent in Spanish, one in French Creole.

Four of them have come primarily because they have run out of their medicines: prescription meds for elevated cholesterol, high blood pressure, and diabetes (one's blood sugar is 270 tonight). The one who needs thyroid replacement medication has been out of meds for three months, and her skin and hair are dry and brittle. Those are the easy ones . . . quick . . . pick up the medicine just down the hall or write a script. Goodbye. See you in two months.

Some take a bit more time. The 60-year-old grandmother who works every day in a laundry . . . lifting, pulling, pushing . . . has sustained a painful injury to her rib cage. Is a rib bruised or broken? She leaves with a bottle of ibuprofen for pain and an order for x-rays of her chest and ribs.

In the next room is a 36-year-old gentleman who is an eighteen-month sober alcoholic and recovered tuberculosis patient. He is referred to an ophthalmologist for his significantly blurred vision.

That leaves the bookends, the first and last patients I'll see this evening. Behind the first door is a 59-year-old Caucasian male, moderately obese, high blood pressure, elevated blood sugar, complaining of recurrent tightness in his upper chest and neck. Our nurse does an electrocardiogram (EKG). The test has abnormal results; and, despite his initial reluctance, he's off to the nearest emergency department for immediate assessment.

Behind the last door is a 38-year-old woman who's had diabetes most of her life. She works every day as a nursing assistant. But it is challenging to carry out her duties with her swollen foot. She removes her bandage to reveal a black and gangrenous large toe. She needs immediate hospitalization and surgery to save her foot. But she won't go now . . . she has a teenage child alone at home. She promises she'll go in tomorrow, when she can arrange for child care.

That's it. We're done. File the charts. Put away the equipment and supplies. Turn off the lights. Lock the door. It's just another night at the clinic . . . just another night at Shepherd's Hope.

---

*Shepherd's Hope, a faith-based organization in Orlando, Florida, provides free medical services for people who are uninsured.

Ted Hamilton, LLUSM class of 1973-A, is a family practitioner in Winter Park, Florida.

And the prayer offered in faith will make the sick person well; the Lord will raise him up. . . . Therefore confess your sins to each other and pray for each other so that you may be healed. James 5:15-16, NIV

One morning, while making postpartum rounds, I came across a young first-time mother who had tested positive for methamphetamine. Even though I was short on time and there was a long list of patients I had to round on, I felt I needed to talk to her about drugs. I sat down on a chair next to her bed.

Before I could bring up the subject, she told me that she had a confession to make. She said she did use drugs in the past, but now that she had a baby, she really wanted to quit. She had tried quitting before, but her friends always got her back into the habit. When asked if she attended church, she said she used to, and that she still believed in God. I told her that she would never be able to quit drugs on her own; that only God can help her stay away from drugs.

We talked about starting back to church, making a new set of friends, and staying away from her old friends who used drugs. Then I asked her if I could pray for her, and she said, "Yes." I prayed that the Lord would give her courage and strength to overcome this drug habit and that she would develop a relationship with Him. At the end of the visit, she thanked me profusely.

At her six weeks' postpartum visit, she was beaming with delight as she told me that she had started going back to church and that she was making new friends who were not on drugs. Our prayer was answered.

The Bible encourages us to pray for one another. How many times has the Lord directed to our practices patients who needed spiritual healing? And did we miss the opportunity to be an instrument of His to connect the patients with Him? You will find that, somehow, in spite of taking time to pray with your patients in the midst of a busy day, your day at the office will still end on time, and you will be blessed for it. Your world will be a better place because you took time to pray.

Caleb Liem, LLUSM class of 1970, is an obstetrician and gynecologist who resides with his wife, Doreen, in Marina, California.

January 12

Behold, the fear of the Lord, that is wisdom; and to depart from evil is understanding. Job 28:28, KJV

A story is told about the prime minister of France, who had become very ill and needed surgery. A specialist presided at his bedside, to whom the prime minister said, "Doctor, you will not treat me as you do those poor, miserable wretches at the hospital, will you?"

"Sir," the doctor said, fire kindling in his eyes, "every one of those miserable wretches, as you call them, is a prime minister in my eyes." This tale demonstrates how all of us must approach our fellow men.

The patient demands our time, skill, and very life. We must never forget or fail any person in need. We must not refuse to respond to any call from someone requiring help. This concept cannot be seen as an abstract rule or principle. George Bernard Shaw expressed this thought beautifully: "The worst sin towards our fellow creatures is not to hate them, but to be indifferent to them. That's the essence of inhumanity."

Being in the medical profession is a high and holy calling. The laboratory, the emergency room, and the operating room become as sacred as the pulpit—because God appears in each place.

The doctor should approach his work with a sense that it is holy ground. He must have a sacred reverence and concern for life, for the body, and for the physiologic and biochemical process of those patients in his care. He must associate himself and his work with the work of God.

Sometimes it becomes hard to perceive of some of the traditional clinical duties as being the work of God. Nevertheless, the surgeon's duty must ever be one of reverence and respect for the body. It becomes hard to see God in the frustrations of paperwork, the annoyances of routine, and the smells and fatigue of the operating room. Still, one must remember that "God's work" continues, even during mundane, monotonous, routine footwork, consisting of trudging along the hospital corridor, washing test tubes, taking histories, and doing physicals.

Drink of the delicious freedom of learning. Christ offers us complete hope: "If any of you lack wisdom, let him ask of God, that giveth to all men liberally, and upbraideth not; and it shall be given him" (James 1:5, KJV). Have you really tried the Lord?

Virchel E. Wood, LLUSM class of 1960, is professor in LLUSM department of orthopaedic surgery. He was LLUSM Alumni Association 1999 Honored Alumnus and its 2007 Alumnus of the Year, and he received the LLU Distinguished Service Award in 2004.

Bless the LORD, O my soul, and forget not all his benefits: Who forgiveth all thine iniquities; who healeth all thy diseases. Psalm 103:2-3, KJV

When I was a pediatric resident at White Memorial Medical Center in Los Angeles, California, in the early 1970s, I was on call at night for admissions to the hospital. One admission was a 3-year-old Hispanic boy who spoke no English and could not walk because of a tender, inflamed, and infected foot. I took the history from the parents and examined the child. It was a case of cellulitis that needed intravenous antibiotics.

After the evaluation, I started the intravenous therapy to administer the antibiotics. I thought no more of it as I went on to the other patients and duties of the night.

A few days later, all resident doctors had to go on teaching rounds on the ward. As I moved on to the next patient, I felt a tug on my leg. The patient I had seen a few nights earlier was pointing to his foot and was walking, a big smile on his face.

I will never forget that moment as it symbolizes why I enjoy pediatrics and, with God's healing and grace, the fast-healing of children.

Grant Masaoka, LLUSM class of 1969, is a pediatrician in Anaheim, California.

January 14

For I am not ashamed of the gospel of Christ: for it is the power of God unto salvation to every one that believeth; to the Jew first, and also to the Greek.
Romans 1:16, KJV

Fifty years ago, I had a few years of general practice and made house calls. I received a request to attend a gentleman at his home because he was unable to come to my office. I went to his home and knocked on the door. A family member directed me to his father who was in bed. I was informed that he had leukemia and was under the care of an oncologist. I noted a Bible at his bedside.

He was very pale but alert and answered questions normally. I gave him a prescription to manage his discomfort, and he requested another house call. During my second visit, the ill man presented to me a very searching question, after he announced that he was a Christian. But before his question, he gave a very unusual testimony.

He said, "Doctor, I was a drunk, abused my wife and family, and was miserable. I did not want to hear anything about religion. But God got hold of me. I read this Bible completely through on my knees. I found that it was what my family said it was: God's word. I gave my heart to Jesus."

He opened his Bible and I saw nearly every margin covered with writing and comments. Then he said, "Dr. Jackson, I don't know much about the church you attend, but can you say, with the apostle Paul, 'I am crucified with Christ, nevertheless I live, not I but Christ who lives in me'?"

I said, "Yes, I can. He is my Savior, my Lord."

The gentleman put forth his hand and said, "Brother Jackson." He died several weeks later.

Paul was unambiguous in stating "that if thou shalt confess with thy mouth the Lord Jesus, and shalt believe in thine heart that God hath raised him from the dead, thou shalt be saved" (Romans 10:9, KJV).

May we always have the holy boldness to proclaim to others our blessed Jesus and the gospel.

Paul W. Jackson, LLUSM class of 1953-B, is an otolaryngologist and plastic surgeon in Wallingford, Pennsylvania.

January 15

*But they that wait upon the L*ORD *shall renew their strength; they shall mount up with wings as eagles; they shall run, and not be weary; and they shall walk, and not faint. Isaiah 40:31, KJV*

Below is a poem entitled, "Remember Me," which I wrote for my father's memorial service. He passed away on January 15, 1997, at Loma Linda University Medical Center. My father was Elmer A. (Bill) Hankins Jr., LLUSM class of 1938. He was raised on the prairies of northwestern Colorado by his parents, Elmer and Colorado Pearl Hankins.

In 1934, after graduating from Colorado State University in Fort Collins, Colorado, my father hitchhiked out to California with $10 in his pocket to apply for admission to the College of Medical Evangelists. He was admitted on the spot, after an appeal to the admissions board. For fifty-one years, my father practiced as a therapeutic radiologist and general surgeon in Riverside, California.

This poem reflects in the American Indian way my father's connection with the Colorado prairies as a youth, and later his love for the ocean when he relocated to California. When I was a child, my father would see an eagle in the sky and say, "Billy, the eagle is a very special bird and must be respected." The eagle for many First Nations people is special, as it is thought to carry the prayers of the people upward to heaven.

My body is tired and worn out.
 I cannot stay any longer; there is no doubt.
Mother Earth will claim my bones and flesh,
 My spirit will now be at rest.
Do not be sad at my going away;
 Keep me in your thoughts every day.
Remember me in the song of the prairie wind.
 Of Colorado prairies, I am now kin.
Remember me when you see the Eagle in the sky,
 For now you know that I am free, do not cry.
Remember me when you hear the roar of ocean shores,
 That is me, in deep sleep with loud snores.
Remember me when sea birds glide over the ocean,
 That is my energy in perpetual motion.
For I am now a part of this native land
 Where for me and my ancestors it all began.
Grandfather above has called me home;
 In his care, I will never be alone.

This poem points out that, even though in death our flesh and bones will be claimed by Mother Earth, we are assured that Grandfather (God) will recall the breath of life for safekeeping until the resurrection.

E. A. (Billy) Hankins III, LLUSM class of 1964, is a dermatologist in Los Angeles, California. He received the LLU Distinguished General Service Award in 1990.

January 16

Be shepherds of God's flock that is under your care, serving as overseers—not because you must, but because you are willing, as God wants you to be; not greedy for money, but eager to serve; not lording it over those entrusted to you, but being examples to the flock. 1 Peter 5:2-3, NIV

A s physicians, we are asked to be leaders in our communities, a status that can give us power over others. Science defines power as a rate at which work is done; but it can be viewed as being forceful, having great influence, or control over a group of people.

Looking at Christ as a powerful leader, we see at the Last Supper how He used His power to show us what it means to be a servant leader. Chris Oberg, in a short homily, described it this way: "Wearing a towel around His waist and holding a bowl of water in His hands," He had the power to destroy and create with one word yet chose to serve in a capacity those closest to Him could not understand.

James Autry describes five principles of servant leadership:

(1) Be authentic, i.e., be who you are. Today's world teaches us to not allow the "real you" to show. This exposure can be perceived as a weakness. Authenticity comes from deep within us, where no walls or pretensions exist.

(2) Be vulnerable. Being authentic leaves you open to being vulnerable. Vulnerability requires you to be courageous, to be honest with your feelings, doubts, fears, and concerns. It also has a component of empathy—the ability to put yourself in another's situation, and understand that person's point of view.

(3) Be accepting. Acceptance is more than approval; it is not tolerance. Acceptance is a conduct, a behavior. The art of acceptance does not mean you take an individual's idea without critical analysis, discussion, or judgment. Disagreement is embraced as a process of work. Servant leaders do not see winners or losers; nor do they feel like a winner or a loser. Rather they see themselves as participants.

(4) Be present. To be present, the servant leader is not just being here or there in the physical sense, but rather is whole self open or available to others as your whole self. It is a difficult task to "be present," especially where "time is money" or patient turnover is important in a busy clinic.

(5) Be useful. Another way to look at this is to be a resource to those around you. As a manager, it is important to provide the resources people need to get their jobs done. Servant leadership in its heart is to serve others.

Leadership should not be about controlling people; it is not about being the boss. It is not about holding on to territory, and it is not concerned about pep talks. It is about caring about people, being available, building community at work; it is about letting go of ego and creating a place where people can do good, find their meaning, and grow, as Christ showed us. Power and position did not rule Him.

Lynda Daniel-Underwood, LLUSM class of 1991, is assistant professor in LLUSM department of emergency medicine. She is assistant dean for clinical site recruitment for LLUSM and is clerkship director for emergency medicine at LLUSM. She is married to Matthew Underwood, LLUSM class of 1992.

Trust in the LORD with all your heart, And lean not on your own understanding; In all your ways acknowledge Him, And He shall direct your paths. Proverbs 3:5-6, NKJV

As physicians, we are given an excellent, broad-based education and, when specializing, more focused training. As we leave internship or residency, we realize that we have been exposed to multiple mentors and have been able to glean what we consider to be the best methods and techniques from each. We may be convinced, because we are able to combine and adopt the best from each, that we may become better than any of them.

Confidence—as a result of one's education, training, and abilities—is essential. But we also need an attitude of humility and a dependence on God for direction in making decisions, for technical and surgical skills, and for compassionate relationships with patients and family. This dependence is crucial for the outcome that God desires to give in every encounter with patients and family.

God invites us to ask in His name for outcomes that are according to His will. In personal devotions, we may seek the Lord for these blessings. We may also pray with patients and families before surgical events, as well as in times of crisis and prior to decision-making.

Early in my practice, I was hesitant to ask patients if they would like me to personally pray with them prior to surgery. I then decided to give patients that option in a written statement on a card given to them with pre-operative instructions. If they want me to pray with them, they check "yes" on the card and hand it to the receptionist when checking in for surgery. With this method, there is no awkward discussion about prayer and no risk that the patient may say yes to just please the physician.

Using this card method, I've found about 80 percent of my patients ask for a personal prayer just before surgery. I pray for judgment, caring, and skill, as well as for healing without complication. It strengthens my faith to see so many people affirming their faith by asking for prayer.

The Lord has blessed me as He has blessed my patients as a result of these prayers. These prayers also initiate a spiritual connection with the patient. Many times patients will ask to also pray after I pray, and some reassure me later that they pray for me on an ongoing basis. The most touching example of this was the report of a mother of two pre-school girls on whom I operated for congenital cataracts. She said on one post-operative visit, "The girls pray for you every day." I know that I have been blessed beyond measure by prayers such as those from believing patients.

What a privilege we have as physicians to be instruments in God's hand to bring healing, comfort, or hope to His children, and to acknowledge that God is directing our paths as we put our trust in Him.

Howard V. Gimbel, LLUSM class of 1960, is professor in and chair of LLUSM department of ophthalmology. He received an MPH degree from LLU in 1978. He was an LLUSM Alumni Association 1997 Honored Alumnus. In 2003, he was LLU Alumnus of the Year. January 17 is his birthday.

January 18

Be strong and courageous. Do not be afraid or terrified because of them, for the LORD your God goes with you; he will never leave you nor forsake you.
Deuteronomy 31:6, NIV

While taking a continuing medical education course in Tempe, Arizona, over an extended weekend, I had found time to bask in the sun and the 84-degree temperature. When my flight home touched down in Pennsylvania at 12:15 a.m., the leather jacket I was wearing could not possibly replace the natural warmth of Arizona.

Sometimes, taking a break and leaving my medical practice is not worth it, for the chaos that follows seems to begin the hour I leave. It took me an entire week—working until midnight each night—to catch up on answering calls, addressing the results, filling out forms, and going through physician correspondence. I briskly walked to my car every night that week and fondly thought of Arizona, until the memories of brilliant sunlight dimmed and became a painful reminiscence.

It is my habit to leave my office at least sixty minutes prior to the opening of the Sabbath; so when I left the office that Friday, it felt strange to see the daylight. As I drove west towards my home, the sunlight became overwhelming. I was blinded unexpectedly—an experience made all the more terrifying because even my sunglasses could not help me.

That very sunlight in which I had basked less than a week ago now became my enemy. Less than one week ago that same sunlight had strengthened my relationship with God as I walked through the desert botanical garden and saw God in every cactus, bird, and flower. Within one short week, with little-to-no intervening sunlight, those same sunbeams had filled me with fear and intimidation.

I had lived that week in darkness, spiritually and physically. I had not spent much time on my knees, and my Bible was still sitting downstairs where I had unpacked it four days earlier. So, when I was exposed to the sunlight—spiritually and physically—as the Sabbath dawned in the brilliance of the setting sun, my mind turned to my walk with God. I was reminded that the more time I spend with the Son, the more natural my walk, talk, and actions will be. I will be unafraid to bask in the Son, for I will know Him as He is.

"The sun will be turned to darkness and the moon to blood before the coming of the great and glorious day of the Lord. And everyone who calls on the name of the Lord will be saved" (Acts 2:20-21, NIV). And, as Deuteronomy 31:6 says, we know He will never leave us. I trust you, Lord. I want to live in your glorious SUN/SON. Help me to do this daily so that I can live eternally with you.

Sharon Michael, LLUSM class of 1999, is a family practitioner in Williamsport, Pennsylvania.

If anyone does not know how to manage his own family, how can he take care of God's church? 1 Timothy 3:5, NIV

Every night before going to sleep, our older daughter, Lindsey, has me read stories from the Seventh-day Adventist children's magazine, *Our Little Friend*. We review her memory verse and pick one or two stories to read. Tanya, my wife, does the same with our younger child, Lauren, in the kids' room. Then we gather as a family and hold hands while Lindsey and Lauren lead the prayer. Recently, as I was tucking Lindsey in, she looked up at me and asked: "Daddy, how come Ompung (Grandpa and Grandma) have worship at their house and we don't?" I tried to emphasize to her that what we do every night IS worship.

"No, Daddy," she said, "I want the worship with singing like at Ompung's house."

"But we don't have a piano like the one at Ompung's," I responded.

At this point she raised her arms in frustration, exclaiming, "But you can play your guitar!" Right then I realized she truly wanted a full-blown family worship—the kind of worship my parents have always had.

Growing up, my parents made sure we had nightly family worship. Our Sabbath sundown worship was always a special one—the large-scale kind with singing, Bible study, reciting the entire fourth commandment, and prayer. Unfortunately, as I grew older and began to live independently, my spiritual life began to take a back seat. Prayers became sporadic and abbreviated, and worship only happened when I visited my parents. Although I promised myself to raise my own family differently, the habit I had developed seemed to carry over, to a certain degree, in my family life.

Every week my wife carefully plans our kids' menu, making sure they have balanced and nutritious meals. Processed foods and sugar are limited. We both are aware of the daily challenges we face in trying to provide proper nutrition. The competition is everywhere. We're surrounded by billboards with fast-food advertisements, see television commercials about junk food, and are enticed even on trips to our local grocery store. We have become diet conscious.

But that night, my 4-year-old daughter taught me a couple of other important lessons about "good health." First, there is the importance of a balanced spiritual diet. While my wife is doing a great job in making sure the family is fed balanced meals daily, I have been trying to curb our family's spiritual hunger with the equivalent of spiritual snacks and fast foods. Deep down, I believe we all long for the feast that's available, if we'll just stop running and pause long enough to partake.

Second, I have to reprioritize and put my family first. I meet monthly with several men in a Bible-study group. All of us hold a leadership position in Seventh-day Adventist institutions, ranging from senior pastor or senior executives to midlevel administrators. We discuss work, family, friends, our spiritual journeys, exercise, and goals. It's a good group; but I've been wondering lately, with all the competition for my time, if I've let my personal and family's spiritual needs come last.

As a member of the Loma Linda University family, I am committed to supporting our mission, "To make man whole." However, thanks to my daughter's insistence, I now realize my family's wholeness will have to come first.

Ron Siagian is director of LLUHS retail and services. January 19 is the day he and his wife, Tanya, had their first date.

January 20

Yet who knows whether you have come to the kingdom for such a time as this?
Esther 4:14, NKJV

I first met Adrian when he was 16 years old. He was fielding ground balls during baseball practice when one ball took a tricky bounce and hit him squarely over his right eyebrow. The damage was considerable, so he ended up in urgent care that afternoon in need of some skin repair.

While suturing up his laceration, I learned many things about this handsome, soft-spoken, and extremely well-mannered young man. Growing up, Adrian had avoided the drug and gang influences that had permeated and ensnared so many in his neighborhood. A good student and outstanding athlete, many Pac-10 schools had begun recruiting him. I also met his mother, Mary; and soon Adrian's entire family became patients of mine.

During his senior year in high school, Adrian survived a stabbing incident. He was with his girlfriend at a neighborhood party when gang members crashed it, and Adrian was the victim. Fortunately, the piercing had missed his vital organs. Through it all, Adrian was on track to graduate and continue his college education on a full baseball scholarship.

One Monday morning, my medical assistant pulled me aside and said, "I wanted to tell you: Adrian was driving home from work last night and was killed by a drunk driver. His mother is coming in to see you at 10:00 a.m."

I have had many difficult patient visits in my career, but none have ever been as difficult as my visit that morning with Mary. I didn't have many words to say, which was just as well. Mostly I listened, cried, and hugged a mother in her deepest moment of despair.

Just as Queen Esther was placed in her position for a purpose, as God's people, we are here on this earth for a similar purpose. A world filled with hatred, hopelessness, and death needs to know there is a greater love, a more perfect hope, and an everlasting life through a personal Savior. May we, as followers of Jesus, spread His love and truth to a world that so desperately needs Him.

Roger Batin, LLUSM class of 1993, is a family practitioner in Fontana, California. He and his wife, Lacy, have two daughters, Taryn and Bryn.

January 21

If any of you lacks wisdom, he should ask God, who gives generously to all without finding fault, and it will be given to him. James 1:5, NIV

My cat, Baby, was thirsty one day. There was nothing in the water dish. Instead of asking for a fresh serving, Baby remembered there was an unlimited and renewable supply of fresh water in the bathroom toilet. So he made his way there, perched precariously on the lid, and craned his neck to the fullest extent, barely reaching the surface of the water with his tongue. (My apologies to all readers who gross out easily.)

An instant later, a back paw slipped, and Baby plunged beneath the waves! This was not the outcome he had desired! He was a victim of the law of unintended consequences. Basically, the law works something like this: Whenever you act in a way that seems to be completely favorable to you and to others, you can count on negative outcomes that are rarely foreseeable at the time. This law is constantly at work in the realm of politics as well.

Allow me to give a political example of this law: During World War II, the Allies had their hands full, fighting Hitler's Germany. On the principle of "The enemy of my enemy is my friend," they decided to do business with the unsavory Josef Stalin, premier of the Soviet Union. They provided aid to Stalin in the form of food, weapons, intelligence, and technical assistance.

While the Soviet army was an absolutely essential part of the eventual victory over Hitler, this alliance of convenience strengthened the Soviet Union immeasurably and gave Stalin *de facto* control over more than half of Europe. The unintended consequence of this alliance was the Cold War between the Soviet Union and the United States. The ally in one conflict became the enemy in the next.

What the Bible calls sin is full of unintended consequences. It can look or feel right. A good-looking patient or secretary needs to consult with you about problems at home. An extra-large house or more luxurious car will meet your needs. An attractive opportunity will get your name in lights. To take best advantage of the opportunity, you let your boundaries slip just a little. It feels good. It feels right. But what Hollywood never tells you is that the sins of pride, lust, greed, and power always lead to unintended consequences.

In the healthcare field, it is right to fear unintended consequences. You try to make the correct diagnosis; you prescribe what experience tells you is the right medicine or the right test. You do your very best to get patient care right. Of course you do. And yet, sometimes things happen that you never expected and certainly did not intend. Whether our actions are sound or misguided, unintended consequences occur.

Unintended consequences remind me every day that I need a wisdom that is greater than my own, even when I am operating within my expertise. I need the Great Physician, the Wonderful Counselor, the Wisdom of God to be with me today and every day.

Jon Paulien is professor of religion in and dean of LLUSR. He is the author of 21 books and more than 200 articles, scholarly papers, and other publications. Born and raised in New York City, New York, he and his wife, Pamella, have three children.

January 22

Let your light so shine before men, that they may see your good works, and glorify your Father which is in heaven. Matthew 5:16, KJV

Some time ago, one of our students told me of her experience at the county hospital where a child was being treated for a gunshot wound. She said that all the physicians and nurses were rushing around trying to save the child's life as the family was standing by in shock and fear. The student felt she was of no use in caring for the child with so many others working on him, so she stepped over to the family to be with them. She invited them to a quiet corner and asked if she could pray for the family. "Yes," they responded.

But shortly after the prayer, the child lost his battle for life and died. The distraught family departed, and the unit resumed a more normal routine. A few days later, the student was surprised when the unit secretary said there were some people wanting to talk with her. After the student had tended to the needs of her patient, she left the room. She was met in the hallway by a couple she recognized as the parents of the child who had died from the gunshot wound.

The student told me that she was very surprised to see them again and wondered what they might want. The parents told her the reason for the visit was to say thank you, and that during their terrible ordeal, her prayer was the only thing that sustained them. They said they did not know how they would have survived without this expression of God's love.

How do we witness for Christ? I heard a story of a young man, who, when asked whether or not he was a Christian, replied, "You will need to be the judge of that." His reply caused me to contemplate the importance of our actions in life. It is not really the label we give ourselves, but the acts of life that speak of our character. We have the opportunity to reflect the love of God to others each day through what we say and do in our work and in our homes. And we can reflect this love much more fully in our conduct than in any sermon or lecture we might prepare and present. Our actions will show how close our relationship with God is.

The book of James expands on this thought by telling us that it is through our deeds that we show our faith; and, without these, our faith is dead. If our lives are connected closely with our faith, others will not need to ask if we are Christians because they will see our "good works" that glorify God.

Marilyn Herrmann has been dean of LLUSN since 2005. She received an MS degree in nursing from LLU in 1980 and a PhD degree in education from Claremont Graduate School (now Claremont Graduate University) in Claremont, California, in 1992. She and her husband, Cliff, have two children and four grandchildren.

When you pass through the waters, I will be with you; and when you pass through the rivers, they will not sweep over you. Isaiah 43:2, NIV

What must it have been like to live during the time when Jesus was on earth, as He performed miracles of healing? How exciting it would have been to witness these miracles firsthand! But, looking closely today, His hand of comfort and healing continues to be tangible and observable. On January 23, 2008, our grandson, Kanon Grey Williams, was born to our son and his wife, Shane Williams, LLUSM class of 2002; and Heidy, LLUSAHP class of 1999. Over the course of the next ten days, we witnessed an unmistakable display of God's grace, love, and a modern-day miracle of healing!

After our daughter-in-law had a cesarean section, performed because the baby's heartbeat was becoming dangerously low, she developed bleeding complications—which necessitated an emergency return to the operating room. Her bleeding was so horrific that more than sixty pints of blood (about five times the normal human volume) were transfused over a seemingly endless sixteen hours of surgery. Heidy approached the point of death on at least two occasions, as highly trained specialists were brought in from southern California to help her fight for her life.

As we raced to the hospital, we phoned friends and colleagues asking for prayer. Our minds churned with the unimaginable, the loss of Heidy—and then trying to imagine our son raising two little children without a mother. As people heard of Heidy's condition, prayer chains began to spread internationally! Urgent petitions on Heidy's behalf came from LLU administrators—kneeling for prayer around the Magan Hall conference table—and from the Loma Linda University Church board, whole classrooms of school children, families, and Bible study groups.

We learned that friends told friends about Heidy's condition, thus expanding the prayers around the world and across many faiths. Devout Muslims followed their faith tradition for special prayer for Heidy in Iran; and holy water was FedEx'd from a devout Catholic uncle of a friend on the east coast. The support that we received from these vast prayer petitions was immense. Our faith community surrounded us, providing amazing support and comfort in ways that we could not have anticipated.

On life support, Heidy was finally able to be moved to the intensive care unit; but soon it became evident that she was battling acute respiratory distress syndrome and possible brain damage. Her life hung precariously near death for the next several days. Suddenly, Heidy's condition improved so rapidly, to the physician's amazement, that she could be released to go home—a virtually unheard of recovery!

The gift of healing is appreciated to this day, as Heidy has made a complete recovery and, along with her husband, is joyfully taking care of her young family. We must never limit the power of Jesus to touch lives in the very way necessary to bring about His will.

Isaiah 43:2 reminds us that God does not promise lives free of difficulty, but He does promise that the difficulty will not overwhelm us because He gives us the strength to endure.

Rick Williams is vice chancellor for student affairs for LLU, and Linda Williams is director of student affairs for LLUSP. He holds a PhD degree.

January 24

The effectual fervent prayer of a righteous man availeth much. James 5:16, KJV

January 24, 2008, has special significance for me. One week earlier, my wife of fifty-two years was diagnosed with a possible malignancy. Urgent arrangements were made to complete the diagnostic work-up and schedule exploratory surgery.

As the oncology surgeon carefully outlined the prospects, prayers also became part of the program. These prayers were offered by a variety of friends and associates with diverse religious affiliations: Jewish, Seventh-day Adventist, Hindu, Buddhist, Islamic, Catholic. They all said that this woman was "too kind" to have anything bad happen to her.

The surgeon called us midmorning on January 24, while the surgery was still ongoing. He reported that the tumor was "benign." Since then, my wife has had a complete return to health.

We fervently believe in the power of prayer. We also bless the skills of the nurses, diagnosticians, surgeons, and anesthesiologists who participated in her care. Fervent prayers did indeed avail much.

Wolff M. Kirsch is professor in LLUSM department of neurosurgery and director of LLUSM Neurosurgery Center for Research, Teaching, and Education. He received an MD degree from Washington University School of Medicine in St. Louis, Missouri, in 1955.

January 25

Clothe yourselves with compassion, kindness, humility, gentleness and patience.
Colossians 3:12, NIV

O f the many stories of patients I encountered during my third-year clerkships, nothing stands out more to me than the experience I had in caring for Mr. P. He was a 57-year-old gentleman who had been diagnosed with metastatic malignant melanoma. I met him the first night on-call during my medicine rotation at the county hospital. The cancer had already spread to his brain.

Despite his poor prognosis, Mr. P was determined to undergo invasive surgery to remove the brain lesions causing his current symptoms. To everyone's surprise, he recovered rapidly and gained his strength back. Two months later, however, I received a call from his family informing me that he had passed away.

The responsibility of caring for Mr. P proved to be one of the most endearing and touching experiences I ever had with a patient. In spite of the trials and tribulations of his fluctuating glucose levels, the management of his insulin regimen with the escalating doses of Decadron, and his consults with multiple specialists, Mr. P remained calm and faithfully put his trust in our hands.

Each day, I learned more about him: his work as a janitor, his friends at church, his faith in God, and his will to live. He was a self-sufficient and determined person. He never complained and was always thankful for the services provided by the medical and nursing staff.

I was blessed to have had the opportunity to know Mr. P. The personal relationship I developed with him is something I would like to continue with other patients I meet as a doctor. There are many challenges physicians face on a daily basis. The joy and honor of serving others through God's will, however, makes this career life much more worthwhile in the end.

Priscilla Luke, LLUSM class of 2007—for which she was freshman-year senator for LLUSM senate—is a resident in ophthalmology at New York Medical College in New York City, New York. January 25 is the date of the passing away of her grandmother, Dorothy Aurawan Vassantachart.

January 26

For God so loved the world, that he gave his only begotten Son, that whosoever believeth in him should not perish, but have everlasting life. John 3:16, KJV

While teaching neuroanatomy and histology to freshmen medical students at LLU during the 1960s, I maintained my clinical skills by occasionally serving as an emergency physician. One time, while on duty at the San Gorgonio Pass Memorial Hospital in Banning, California, I saw a man running toward the hospital with a very limp, pale boy in his arms.

As he entered the emergency room huffing and puffing, he yelled: "Save my boy! Please save my boy! Whatever it costs, I'll pay it, but p-l-e-a-s-e, save my boy!" The nurse and I assisted in placing his unconscious son on the gurney, quickly assessing his son's condition. The man talked on: "A friend of mine likes to play chicken. When we meet on the road, he often steers his car toward mine to see who will chicken out first. I didn't notice him soon enough today to get out of his way, and we crashed head on! My son, sitting on the seat beside me, flew forward, striking his head on the windshield and his abdomen against the dashboard."

This was before the days of airbags, car seats for children, and mandatory seatbelts. I was concerned that the boy may have ruptured his spleen. As I inserted an intravenous line to obtain blood for tests—including type and cross-matching for transfusions—I requested that a general surgeon come immediately for definitive treatment. The patient's father continued talking as the nurse and I worked diligently to save his son. "If I had waited for the police to arrive, my son would have died. So I carried him across town, running all the way! It was about a mile from here," he exclaimed.

Fortunately, the surgeon arrived promptly and took the boy to surgery. He found the spleen intact but a large tear in the liver, with significant blood loss. The boy lived—thanks to a father who loved him enough to run a mile carrying him to the emergency room—with help from intravenous fluids, quick surgical intervention, blood transfusions, and tender loving care.

Lessons I learned that day: 1) Don't play chicken, because someone eventually is going to get hurt! Rules of the road should be obeyed! 2) Our loving heavenly Father loves each of us very much as His children. He says: "Save my boy! Save my girl! Whatever it costs, I will pay, just save my children!" And the cost was very much—the life of an innocent person. Jesus died, willing to shed His own blood to pay the supreme price for our salvation.

Everet W. Witzel, LLUSM class of 1962, also has an MHA degree and a PhD degree in anatomy, both from LLU. He and his wife, JoAn, live in Ridgecrest, California. January 26, 2009, is his 75th birthday.

In that day the deaf will hear. Isaiah 29:18, NIV

The human ear is an amazing instrument. Designed with the smallest bones in the body, each of the tiny drums, hammers, chambers, canals, and nerve pathways must all work in harmony to conduct sounds to our brains. This intricate hearing organ that our Creator has given us is vital to our everyday lives.

Unfortunately, our imperfect world can sometimes make this perfect system break down. While there are different levels of hearing loss, even mild deafness makes understanding speech difficult. As a result, hearing loss is a real disability, which can lead to social isolation, inactivity, or depression. It is estimated that as much as 15 percent of the population of the United States has some degree of hearing loss.

As an otolaryngologist, I have been able to treat many types of hearing loss, congenital or acquired. Although surgery and hearing aids can greatly improve the hearing of many individuals, hearing loss can be permanent in cases where there is damage to the hair cells in the cochlea. In cases of total or near total deafness in both ears, the cochlear implant is the only way to restore hearing. A cochlear implant is a surgically implanted electronic device that provides a sense of sound by stimulating what remains of the auditory nerve in a person who is profoundly deaf.

The first cochlear implant program in the Inland Empire was started in 1985 at Loma Linda University Medical Center. During one of my clinics, Desmond Doss, the Seventh-day Adventist World Word II hero and Medal of Honor recipient, came to discuss the possibility of receiving a cochlear implant. He had profound hearing loss and was, therefore, an excellent candidate for this surgery. I was pleased to perform Mr. Doss' surgery and was glad to experience how much his hearing improved afterwards. He said he was very happy to be able to listen to sermons in church again.

While technology has improved greatly in regard to hearing loss, the sound quality will never be the same as God intended. The sounds produced by a cochlear implant are not perfect, often described as an out-of-tune radio. Only our Creator can restore perfect hearing when we get to the New Heaven and New Earth; as noted in Isaiah 29:18, "the deaf will hear." Indeed, when Jesus was on the earth, He made the deaf hear, as stated in Matthew 11:5.

What about our spiritual hearing ability? Can we hear and understand what our heavenly Father wants us to hear today? We may have difficulty hearing Him, due to deafening worldly noises or blockages from sinful debris. Whether we have good physical hearing or not, "He who has an ear, let him hear what the Spirit says to the churches" (Revelations 2:29, NIV). Let us pay close attention as the Holy Spirit speaks to us today.

Timothy Jung, LLUSM class of 1974, is clinical professor in LLUSM department of otolaryngology: head and neck surgery. He also has a PhD degree in otolaryngology from University of Minnesota.

January 28

Now the body is not made up of one part but of many. If the foot should say, "Because I am not a hand, I do not belong to the body," it would not for that reason cease to be part of the body. And if the ear should say, "Because I am not an eye, I do not belong to the body," it would not for that reason cease to be part of the body. If the whole body were an eye, where would the sense of hearing be? If the whole body were an ear, where would the sense of smell be? But in fact God has arranged the parts in the body, every one of them, just as he wanted them to be. If they were all one part, where would the body be? As it is, there are many parts, but one body. 1 Corinthians 12:14-20, NIV

As I observed the eager faces of my classmates during orientation, I wondered: How will I survive medical school with all these types of people in my class? Some of my wonderful classmates graduated from Ivy League schools, others had been nurses, some had already earned graduate degrees, and many came from a family of physicians. I, on the other hand, was born to parents who were not married and had not even finished high school. Although they loved me dearly, they were limited in the things they could provide for me.

But there was one thing that my mother valued and for which she sacrificed much—my education. Although she had very limited education, she believed in the importance of good education and how it could positively change my life. When I graduated from sixth grade, my mother enrolled me at John Nevins Andrews School, a Seventh-day Adventist school in Takoma Park, Maryland.

In that school God turned my life around for the good, and I was encouraged to pursue academic excellence. I graduated from Takoma Academy, and was about to make family history. I was going to college! The Lord was still with me, and I not only attended college but graduated from college as well—the first to do so in my immediate and extended family.

Coming to medical school, I knew that there would be people from different backgrounds; but I did not realize the magnitude of the disparity. During the orientation, I was able to get a glimpse of where my classmates were coming from; and I started to feel as if I did not fit in. In my moments of distress, I was comforted by the words of 1 Corinthians 12:14-20.

God has given each of us different abilities and accomplishments outside of medical school, but everyone has to work hard to finish medical school. I may not be in the top 5 percent of my class, but I know that God has placed me in this university for a purpose. For this reason, I cannot look at my classmates and wish I were any of them.

I have learned a great deal about people, myself being one of them, within my first year as a medical student. My eyes have been opened to a greater world outside of myself—which will allow me to see things through the eyes of my patients, colleagues, and teachers. I thought that Loma Linda University's motto, "To make man whole," would only apply to the patients. But within this one year, God has worked in me to make me become more whole.

Brittany Brooks, LLUSM class of 2011, was born and reared in Takoma Park, Maryland, and graduated from Oakwood University in Huntsville, Alabama, with a degree in biology. She is a deferred mission appointee and is married to Jaysson, LLUSM class of 2011.

January 29

So God created man in his own image, in the image of God created he him; male and female created he them. **Genesis 1:27, KJV**

The following is from *The Set of the Sail*, the autobiography of Jacob Janzen:

"In the creation of man after His own image (Genesis 1:27), God endowed him with the power to think and to make conscious choices. Next to life, this is the most wonderful asset a man possesses. Normally, man has the liberty to choose, the chance for implementation of his divinely given prerogative.

"Very early in my life I cherished my liberty to choose, and I have always exercised it to the limit of my capacity and opportunity. I wanted to be free—free to think, and free to act. But not always was I accorded this God-given right. I happened to have been born in a land where independence of thought and action were first frowned upon, then progressively interdicted, curtailed, and eventually abolished by decree. No place remained for rugged individualists. Through local agencies, the State did the thinking for the masses and for individuals. It became a question of either submit or perish, unless one read the handwriting on the wall early enough for an escape—a final, irreversible escape.

"Foreseeing the evil day, I risked the latter, and came through alive. Not so other members of my family, one brother, four brothers-in-law, five nephews, and several women relatives.

"'Some ships sail east and some sail west,
But the selfsame wind doth blow.
'Tis the set of the sail and not the gale
That determines the way they go.'

"There may have been some minor deflections, or flutterings of the sail, but the main course was not altered, and with the Lord's hand on the rudder, shall not be changed until my life's barque finally runs into the safe haven of rest."

Throughout their married life, Drs. Jacob and Ernestine Janzen had daily morning and evening family worship. This activity consisted mostly of reading from the Bible, but it was also a chance to praise God for personal blessings. My father felt very fortunate that he was able to sponsor and send for numerous relatives, originally from Russia. A number of them lived with us, sometimes for years.

These were my parents. They were proud to be graduates of the College of Medical Evangelists, and they showed their gratitude by helping others and by serving as missionaries in Africa, Mexico, and India. They considered opportunity for mission service a gift.

Janesta Janzen, LLUSM class of 1962, is a specialist in emergency medicine in Pacific Palisades, California. She was LLUSM Alumni Association president from 1989 to 1990. Her father, Jacob Janzen, LLUSM class of 1931, was LLUSM Alumni Association president from 1958 to 1959 and was LLUSM Alumni Association 1981 Alumnus of the Year. Her mother, Ernestine Janzen, LLUSM class of 1946, was an LLUSM Alumni Association 1981 Honored Alumna.

January 30

But if we walk in the light as He is in the light, we have fellowship with one another, and the blood of Jesus Christ His Son cleanses us from all sin. 1 John 1:7, NKJV

Blood poured from her mouth, mostly bright red, with clots—gushing from her mouth, off the bed, onto the floor, almost to the door.

"Phyllis! What have you been drinking?"

"Vodka," came her reply, "about a liter a day."

Phyllis needed blood, at least six units, with fresh frozen plasma so her blood would clot. And the next step was the "scope." Where is the blood coming from? Was it an ulcer, a torn esophagus, or varices (those big varicose veins in the esophagus that come with advanced liver disease)? Sure enough, it proved to be three giant columns of varices, with one pouring out a jet of bright red liquid.

Phyllis recovered quickly after transfusions, but she was back three months later for more blood. Vodka? Yes, she picked some up on the way home from the hospital last time.

These being the days just before injection therapy and variceal banding, Phyllis got an end-to-side surgical shunt to take the pressure off the varices. Now, after a binge of drinking, instead of coming to the emergency department vomiting blood, she came in a coma—either combative or even unresponsive. She always woke up with treatment, but it was the same story every time: back to vodka within two days of leaving the hospital.

We talked. We remonstrated: "Phyllis, you can't keep drinking that stuff. It's killing you!"

"But I can't quit! It's the only way to feel good about myself . . . the only way I forget my worries. And my guilt."

"Phyllis, there is a better way. You still need blood. It's called the blood of Jesus Christ. That is the only real cure for guilt."

It took some time; but Phyllis accepted Jesus, let Him apply His blood, and she found freedom from guilt for the first time in her life. She even brought two of her friends to find the same freedom in Jesus.

Phyllis lived another six years after finding Jesus—long enough to raise her teenage son. She told me that those six years were the happiest and best years of her life, despite her end-stage liver disease. She allowed Jesus to apply His blood to her guilt every day and experienced the true peace that only Jesus can give.

Kenneth L. Kelln, LLUSM class of 1964, is adjunct assistant professor in LLUSM department of medicine, division of gastroenterology. He resides in Layton, Utah.

January 31

When he came down from the mountainside, large crowds followed him. A man with leprosy came and knelt before him and said, "Lord, if you are willing, you can make me clean." Jesus reached out his hand and touched the man. "I am willing," he said. "Be clean!" Immediately he was cured of his leprosy. Matthew 8:1-3, NIV

I reluctantly picked up the last chart at the end of a long, full clinic day and read, "Hanson's disease." The eponym filtered through my head for a moment, until I remembered the older, more emotional synonym: leprosy. I ran down the hall and burst through the door of the room, so I could catch my unusual patient before she left or turned out to be just another diabetes check-up. She sat comfortably in her flower-print dress, clutching her purse, like a hundred patients before her. Unlike them, she was a lightning bolt of history, jolting my tired brain out of its stifled perspective to see what all that paperwork was really about.

Leprosy conjures the images of biblical stories illustrated with felt figures of sick people cast out and judged while dressed like the mummified living. My patient was a tangible grounding of these previously inaccessible lessons. Two thousand years of history immediately overlapped, and I heard Christ's command to "Heal the sick, raise the dead, cleanse those who have leprosy" (Matthew 10:8, NIV). I heard it clearly within the fluorescent-lit halls of a community hospital and remembered the story of healing as my hands reached out to examine her hypopigmented patches.

Matthew 8:1-3 tells the story of Jesus healing a man with leprosy, and it reveals that Jesus listened to his patient. He took a moment to connect with this man in the midst of a long and busy day. My experience was different: working full days, I found myself spending less time communicating with my patients and more time gathering information and checking all the right boxes on a form. But this patient was too much of a reminder of the power of Jesus for me to simply check boxes; I was forced to see my pen in the shadow of Christ's extended, healing hand.

God placed this lady in my stack of paperwork to wake me up. I realized that I had become less willing to spend the energy to connect with my patients. As I filled out the medication refill form for the patient and sent her home to continue living a normal life, I knew that I must rely on Christ to truly connect and heal my patients. I had gotten lost in the machinery of healthcare, but this encounter with history reminded me that I am fulfilling a divine calling. A simple check up for Hanson's disease renewed a sense of the blessing and responsibility it is to do the Lord's work.

Maegen Clark, LLUSM class of 2009—for which she was freshman class president—grew up in the Inland Empire of California and completed her undergraduate studies at University of California, Los Angeles. She was married in January 2009 and is looking forward to being a family medicine resident.

February 1

I praise you because I am fearfully and wonderfully made; your works are wonderful, I know that full well. Psalm 139:14, TNIV

It was a magnificent sunset! The sun dipped into the ocean at a far-off spot called the horizon. The multicolored layers of lights stretching over the ocean created a panoply of splendor. Such artwork can only be splashed onto the canvas by a divine painter. It was a moment to savor. It wouldn't last long enough. Already night was trying to edge its way onto the canvas.

We stood transfixed, relishing the beauty. Our conversation was hushed. Our eyes were large. In our hearts, we yearned to imprint the scene on our memories so that we might call it up whenever life grew stale. What must it be to live in a place like this and have access to this splendor every twenty-four hours!

We turned to look up at the houses that lined the beach. I mused, "That must be some pretty pricey real estate. And what you pay for is the view." The house just above me had to be the most expensive one on the beach. Its windows were grand—giant picture windows staring out at the beach and the ocean beyond. "Imagine looking out those each evening," I thought, "at this splendid vista!"

And then I noticed something. A man was sitting in a large easy chair just inside one of the windows. I could see the back of his head. He sat watching a giant screen television. The screen was large enough that I could see the tennis match that had captured his attention. But there was something else. We noticed that every single chair in front of these grand picture windows was facing the television. Not a single chair faced the ocean.

Can you understand that? Or let me ask you about certain other scenes. Can you understand the man who stands in front of Michelangelo's "David" with his hat on? Can you understand the teenage girl who prances down the aisle of the Notre Dame Cathedral chewing gum? Can you understand the medical student who yawns his way through the observation of birth for the first time? Can you understand the physician who knows much about the detail and marvel of the human body and yet is not overwhelmed with gratitude?

It's hard for me to understand some of those. But I have my own picture windows where I sit facing the television. Occasionally, in my more lucid moments, I turn my chair toward the horizon and suddenly realize, "It's just so easy to grow accustomed to the sacred, to the splendor."

Maybe that's why the psalmist said, "I praise you because I am fearfully and wonderfully made; your works are wonderful, I know that full well" (Psalm 139:14, TNIV). Today would be a good time to turn your chair outward—toward the horizon—and praise God for the splendor of His handiwork.

Randy Roberts has been senior pastor at Loma Linda University Church of Seventh-day Adventists in Loma Linda, California, since 2000, and is also an adjunct associate professor in LLUSR. He received an MDiv degree from Andrews University in Berrien Springs, Michigan, in 1985; an MA degree in marriage and family therapy, from United States International University in San Diego, California, in 1991; and a DMin degree from Fuller Theological Seminary in Pasadena, California, in 1996. From 1987 to 1994, he served as a chaplain at LLUMC. He received the Outstanding Faculty Award from LLUSM class of 1994.

February 2

He who calls you is faithful, and he will do it. 1 Thessalonians 5:24, RSV

6:00 a.m.—I sit at my desk located in front of my north-facing window on the third floor of the faculty medical offices. I contemplate the day and wonder what will cause it to be different than anticipated. What successes will be achieved today? Will I encounter setbacks that will delay progress with various key initiatives? In the dark of the morning, I thank the Lord for the opportunity to serve at His institution.

6:48 a.m.—The sun begins to shine on the top of Mt. Baldy as the majestic colors of sunrise begin to blast against the rocks on the tip of the mountaintop. I am reminded of the omnipresence of our Creator and the light He promises in a world of darkness. Whether as administrators, as physicians, as staff, or as students, He so desires His people to serve others and work within His will. As the sun begins to rise in the east and shine brighter and brighter in a westward direction, I thank the Lord for the opportunity to serve at His institution.

6:55 a.m.—The sun has now lit up the whole mountainside to the west with brilliant colors and hues. The grandeur reminds me of God's awesome ability to heal. I pray a prayer for all the people within this institution who will commit their day to healing and teaching. I thank the Lord for the opportunity to serve at His institution.

7:13 a.m.—The sun has risen and Loma Linda University Medical Center is fully illumined. The cream color of Loma Linda University Medical Center and Children's Hospital glows bright yellow in the fresh light. My heart is full to overflowing. The Holy Spirit appears to be shining down on the building, granting a special blessing to those who are within. I ask the Lord to bless our patients with strength, encouragement, and hope. I pray for the many workers and students throughout the entire building who will soon fill the halls or be at their posts. I pray that each and every one of them will have discernment, energy, and compassion for those they serve. Before I begin the daily grind of my morning activities, I express one last word of thanks to the Lord for the opportunity to serve at His institution.

May the words of Paul bring you confidence as you place the trials of the day into His hands. It is my prayer for you that whatever your day brings, you can approach your day as a servant of the One and most powerful God who promises to be with you always. Say a word of thanks to the Lord for the opportunity to serve.

David Wren, LLUSPH class of 1988, received an MHA degree. He is associate dean for faculty affairs for LLUSM and is also chief executive officer of LLUHC.

February 3

Father, hallowed be your name. Your kingdom come. Give us each day our daily bread. And forgive us our sins, for we ourselves forgive everyone indebted to us. And do not bring us to the time of trial. Luke 11:2-4, NRSV

Prayer Before Starting Work

My Heavenly Father, as I enter this work place, I bring Your presence with me.
I speak Your peace, Your grace, Your mercy, and Your perfect order in this office.
I acknowledge Your power over all that will be spoken, thought, decided, and done within these walls.

Lord, I thank You for the gifts You have blessed me with.
I commit to using them responsibly in Your honor.
Give me a fresh supply of strength to do my job.
Anoint my projects, ideas, and energy, so that even my smallest accomplishment may bring You glory.

Lord, when I am confused, guide me.
When I am weary, energize me.
When I am burned out, infuse me with the light of the Holy Spirit.
May the work that I do and the way I do it bring faith, joy, and a smile to all that I come in contact with today.

And oh Lord, when I leave this place, give me traveling mercy.
Bless my family and home to be in order as I left it.
Lord, I thank you for everything You're doing and everything You're going to do.
In the name of Jesus I pray, with much love and thanksgiving . . .
Amen.

Author Unknown

Camilla J. Cobb, associate professor in LLUSM department of pathology and human anatomy, submitted this prayer. She received an MD degree from Meharry Medical College in Nashville, Tennessee, in 1977.

February 4

Don't let anyone look down on you because you are young, but set an example for the believers in speech, in life, in love, in faith and in purity. 1 Timothy 4:12, NIV

At a fundraising dinner of a school for learning-disabled children, the father of a student rose to speak. He said, "When not interfered with by outside influences, everything nature does is done with perfection. Yet my son, Shay, cannot learn and does not understand things as other children do. Where is the natural order of things in my son?" The audience was stilled by the query.

The father continued. "I believe that when a child like Shay comes into the world, an opportunity to realize true human nature presents itself, and it comes in this way: how other people treat that child." He then related an incident of walking with Shay past a park where boys, who knew Shay, were playing baseball. Shay asked his dad, "Do you think they'll let me play?"

Now Shay's father knew that most of the boys would not want someone like Shay on their team, but he also understood that if his son were allowed to play, it would give him a much-needed sense of belonging. So he approached a boy and asked if Shay could play. The boy looked around and said, "We're losing by six runs and the game is in the eighth inning. I guess he can be on our team, and we'll try to put him up to bat in the ninth."

In the bottom of the eighth, Shay's team scored a few runs but was still behind by three. In the bottom of the ninth, Shay's team scored again. With two outs and the bases loaded, the potential winning run was on base; Shay was to bat next. Should they let Shay bat and give away their chance to win the game? Surprisingly, Shay was given the bat.

Everyone knew that a hit was all but impossible because Shay didn't even know how to hold the bat. As Shay stepped to the plate, the pitcher moved in a few steps to lob the ball in softly. Shay swung clumsily at the first pitch and missed. The pitcher took a few more steps forward. As the pitch came in, Shay swung at the ball and hit a slow ground ball right back to the pitcher.

The pitcher snagged the ball and could easily have thrown it to first base. Shay would have been out and the game over. But, instead, the pitcher turned and threw the ball in a high arc to right field, far beyond the reach of the first baseman. Everyone started yelling, "Shay, run to first! Run to first!" He scampered down the baseline, startled and wide-eyed. Then everyone started yelling, "Run to second, run to second!" By the time Shay rounded first base, the right fielder had the ball. He could have thrown it to the second-baseman for the tag but intentionally threw the ball high over the third-baseman's head.

Shay ran toward second base, as the runners ahead of him headed toward home plate. Shay reached second base, a little confused. The opposing shortstop ran to him, turned him in the direction of third base, and shouted, "Run to third!" As Shay rounded third, both teams were screaming, "Shay, run home!" Shay ran home, stepped on the plate, and was cheered as a hero. "That day," concluded the father softly, "the boys from both teams helped bring a piece of true love and humanity into this world."

As a physician, my thought is that each of us has hundreds of opportunities every day to help realize the "natural order of things."

Irvin N. Kuhn, LLUSM class of 1955, is professor in LLUSM department of medicine, division of hematology and oncology. He was president of the Walter E. Macpherson Society from 1995 to 1996, and LLUSM Alumni Association president from 1990 to 1991. He was an LLUSM 2005 Honored Alumnus. The story came to him as an email from a friend.

February 5

And we know that all things work together for good to them that love God, to them who are called according to his purpose. Romans 8:28, KJV

One day, while working at the Pusan Sanitarium and Hospital in South Korea in the 1960s, the Pusan chief of police came to my office. He said he had received an anonymous letter stating that our cashier was embezzling money from the hospital and that the institution was a den of communism. He had found evidence that the first part of the letter was true and had already arrested the cashier.

Then he added that I must press charges against the cashier in order for them to keep him in jail. When I said that we did not want that type of publicity, he became angry. The next step, he added, was a full-scale investigation of the hospital.

I visited a representative of the United States embassy. After explaining the problem, he asked what type of hospital the sanitarium was. I replied that it was a Seventh-day Adventist mission hospital. He responded, "I know what you do and that you are not a center of communism. You see, I went to Lodi Academy [a Seventh-day Adventist high school in Lodi, California]!" After he contacted the national police headquarters in Seoul, South Korea, the local police left us alone.

A few days later, the assistant to the Pusan chief of police came to my office and informed me that his boss, the chief, was very ill. The chief had been ordered by the military government to host the Taiwan ambassador the next day, but he couldn't in his present state of health. Several local doctors treated him but he became more ill.

The assistant asked if I would please come and cure the chief—in one day. "Oh," I said, "I have never cured anybody. I know that God could cure him if He wanted, but I cannot cure him. I only treat people; God does the curing." A nurse and I went to the chief's home. He was very ill with severe sinusitis. I also told him that God could cure him, not I. We had prayer and I gave him antibiotics.

About a week later, the chief's assistant came back with a gift. He said his boss became well overnight and was able to perform his assignment the next day. After this incident we have never had any further trouble with the Pusan police.

Louis R. Erich, LLUSM class of 1955, is an obstetrician and gynecologist in Portland, Oregon.

February 6

He that dwelleth in the secret place of the most High shall abide under the shadow of the Almighty. I will say of the Lord, He is my refuge and my fortress: my God; in him will I trust. Surely he shall deliver thee from the snare of the fowler, and from the noisome pestilence. Psalm 91:1-3, KJV

In early January 2008, my wife was diagnosed with an incapacitating illness. This condition required four days of hospitalization. Upon her return home, she was extremely tired. Since she had very little energy, she spent most of her time in bed or in a recliner. After about two weeks, she was able to move around a bit.

About that same time, she began having slight swellings in both legs. At first, I (a physician with fifty-three years of experience in family practice) thought the swelling was due to ibuprofen. But with the passage of time, the swelling increased; and she gained eleven pounds. It appeared that there was some other, possibly more serious, cause for the swelling.

She had no shortness of breath or increased heart rate, so it seemed unlikely the problem was due to her heart. But the question was whether it might be a liver or kidney problem. On Sunday, February 3, I was able to reach her primary care doctor, who advised that she be seen that day in the emergency room (ER). The ER doctor ordered an electrocardiogram (EKG), chest x-ray, and appropriate lab work.

These tests revealed no evidence of heart, liver, or kidney problems. She was sent home on a diuretic (Lasix) and was advised to see a cardiologist no later than the end of the week. On Wednesday, February 6, the cardiologist saw and examined her, and looked at the chest x-ray, EKG, and lab work and sent her home to continue her regular medications and the Lasix.

The doctor also told her that she should have an echocardiogram in late April and to see him in early May. However, he was awake in the night, puzzling over her case. He finally concluded that she needed Doppler (ultrasound) studies of both lower extremities, and she had to get that work done as soon as possible.

Those studies, done on February 7, showed a large blood clot high in the large vein in the left upper thigh. It was determined that she needed immediate hospitalization and was started on blood thinners. Further tests showed that there had been no migration of the clot to any vital organs. One has to wonder if the clot wasn't present when she first started getting the swelling.

So here was a medical condition that I, the ER doctor, and initially the cardiologist missed. One reason we missed it is that it is rather rare for someone to have swelling in both legs when the clot is only in one leg. I could not recall seeing a case like this in all my years of practice. Clots of this nature have the potential to spread to vital organs with devastating consequences.

We are thankful for the work of our cardiologist and for the loving care of our Heavenly Father. Each of the promises in Psalm 91 means more to us now.

Donald E. Casebolt, LLUSM class of 1953-B, is a family practitioner and resides with his wife, Sunnie, in Farmington, New Mexico.

February 7

If you remain in me and my words remain in you, ask whatever you wish, and it will be given you. John 15:7, NIV

Throughout my years as a pulmonologist, I have become increasingly aware of the power that God brings when we are faced with the challenge of a critically ill patient. One of my most memorable examples of God's intervention occurred in a young woman with idiopathic laryngeal subglottic stenosis. This rare medical condition results in a circumferential web of fibrotic tissue that progressively narrows the airway just below the vocal cords.

We took this patient out of state to a world-renowned ears-nose-and-throat (ENT) surgeon, who had pioneered a surgical procedure to eliminate this airway structure. Postoperatively, an endotracheal tube was left in place overnight to help stabilize the site of the laryngeal-tracheal reconstruction.

About twenty-four hours after the endotracheal tube was removed, the patient developed inspiratory and expiratory stridor, indicative of edema at the surgical site. The attending physician and his resident were alerted of this development and ordered aerosolized epinephrine treatments, intravenous corticosteroid, and supplemental oxygen. In spite of these interventions, the stridor was worsening rapidly. The patient was using her accessory inspiratory muscles and was obviously fatiguing.

I anointed the patient with oil (according to James 5) and asked God to reverse the airway edema. It was obvious that reintubation was not feasible, since the airway was now severely narrowed from edema and there would be a high risk of tearing the surgical site where the trachea had been sutured to the larynx. Unless God worked a miracle, an emergency tracheotomy to prevent complete airway obstruction and death were imminent.

I hurried out to the nursing station and requested that the ENT surgeon be paged STAT. Upon returning to the patient's room several minutes later, I noticed a dramatic change in her status. She was now breathing comfortably, and the stridor had disappeared. In the forty years of helping to care for critically ill patients, I have never seen laryngeal edema clear so rapidly. From that point on, the patient steadily improved and was able to return to her home several days later.

God is the most important member of the healthcare team. Since that incident, I have started to regularly ask God for help with extremely sick patients. And I have seen many astonishing recoveries that would not have been expected from a scientific basis.

The Bible offers this assurance: "This is the confidence we have in approaching God: that if we ask anything according to his will, he hears us" (1 John 5:14, NIV). A relationship with God through the Holy Spirit brings the knowledge, wisdom, and discernment necessary to assure that our prayer is in accordance with God's will. It is this relationship that brings power to our prayers.

Incidentally, the patient described above is my oldest daughter. Her surgical reconstruction was in 2000. Our family is grateful to God that she continues to enjoy good health.

John E. Hodgkin, LLUSM class of 1964, is an internist specializing in critical care and pulmonary disease in St. Helena, California. February 7 is the anniversary of the answer to prayer, as described in the incident above.

February 8

Blessed are you when men hate you, when they exclude you and insult you and reject your name as evil, because of the Son of Man. Rejoice in that day and leap for joy, because great is your reward in heaven. For that is how their fathers treated the prophets. Luke 6:22-23, NIV

In the 1980s, I had an ear-nose-and-throat solo practice in the Maryland suburbs of Washington, D.C. It was during this time that Lynn Martell, then ministerial secretary for the Columbia Union Conference of Seventh-day Adventists, held evangelistic meetings at a public high school auditorium. Intending to help promote the event, I sent my paid-up, active patients a cover letter and a copy of the flyer for the meetings. I thought nothing of it, as several of my patients had sent me religious flyers announcing concerts and other events that they wanted to share with me.

Several weeks later, I received a letter from the Maryland Physician Licensing Board. They essentially advised me to cease and desist from ever doing something like this again—and they did not want to get another similar complaint. If they received further complaints, my license to practice medicine in Maryland could be in jeopardy. It seems the board had received a letter of complaint from one of my patients. That person did not appreciate receiving an evangelistic meeting invitation from my office.

Since then I have retired from private practice. I now work in a general practice setting in the same county. I so much appreciate being able to speak briefly and answer questions on spiritual topics as the opportunity presents itself. Recently, I was talking with a patient about good health practices and habits. I felt blessed to be able to share the pocket pamphlet, "What Happens When You Die?" This was given after the patient asked if I thought there was anything after this life. Praise the Lord for our blessed hope!

Over the years, I have learned that although not all may appreciate or approve of me sharing my faith, many do. And I know that I can rejoice in the Lord, who has a reward for each of us in heaven.

Rolf Nieman, LLUSM class of 1965, is an otolaryngologist in Silver Spring, Maryland.

February 9

Precious in the sight of the Lᴏʀᴅ is the death of His saints. Psalm 116:15, NKJV

On September 2, 1998, Swissair Flight 111 plunged into the ocean off the coast of Nova Scotia, Canada, killing all 229 people on board. My youngest son, Monte, age 19, was one of the fatalities. Before Monte left, our family gathered and prayed for his safety. Now I was forced to come to grips with my feelings toward God, His care, and His sovereignty. These issues were no longer just theological points to be discussed in some classroom.

I began to question God's goodness, faithfulness, and even His power. Does He really care? Do I like having Him in charge of things on this planet? Later on, a friend challenged me by asking if I would be more comfortable with God being in control or not in control. I wrestled over that and am happy to say that I can now affirm that I am glad He's sovereign.

We tend to feel that we have a right to pleasant circumstances, abundance, and long life. When that is not our reality, we often feel cheated or betrayed. But the life of Jesus reminds us that there is an intense war going on, with high stakes and casualties. And we are called to follow Christ in sacrificing for the sake of His kingdom.

They tried to kill Jesus four times, as recorded in the Gospel of John; but they couldn't touch Him. However, at His arrest, the purposes of the kingdom were so weighty that God's protection of His Son was removed. In that moment, the cost—the death of the Son of God—was dwarfed by the far-reaching purposes of God's eternal plan.

Just as with His Son, God assures His children that nothing can ever touch them with pain or loss unless it is dwarfed by the purposes of His kingdom. We are never the victim of random tragedy or just collateral damage. God has asked us to trust Him with this truth, even when we cannot believe our eyes or ears. No life experience or loss is ever wasted.

One day, I was grumping to my son, Darren, about where God was when Monte's plane became un-flyable and plunged into the ocean. Darren asked, "Dad, why are we here?" After listening to my lame answer, he suggested I was making it too complicated. Then he added: "We are here only for two reasons. The first is to make a decision to follow Jesus, and the second is to help others do the same. Your son, and my brother, took care of both. Everything else is just maintenance."

We don't complain because the Wright brothers only flew twelve seconds on their first flight. We celebrate that they flew. In only three short years of ministry, Jesus flew. Are we choosing to fly with Jesus with the time we have been given? Can we trust Him, as noted in Romans 8:18 (NIV), with the notion that "our present sufferings are not worth comparing with the glory that will be revealed in us"?

David L. Wilkins, LLUSM class of 1970, is associate clinical professor in LLUSM department of ophthalmology, and is a wellness consultant. He is the father of four and grandfather of six. February 9 is his birthday.

February 10

He that winneth souls is wise. Proverbs 11:30, KJV

On the resurrection morning, when you make morning rounds, how many of your patients will you see?

How does one turn a medical office into a real missionary outreach? Let me share how one College of Medical Evangelists graduate did it. February 10, 2009, would have been the 100th birthday of Marion C. Barnard, LLUSM class of 1944-A. He was my father, and he had a special gift for medical evangelism. During his long career, he brought hundreds of his patients to the Lord.

How? First, my dad made his faith the most important thing in his life. Many nights he would sit in his favorite chair, with his Bible and a Spirit of Prophecy book before him, as he prepared Bible studies for his patients. I never heard him utter an unkind or impatient word. He knelt by his bed each night, no matter the hour, to talk with his Lord.

Ministry of Healing was a book my dad especially enjoyed studying. He removed all literature from the clinic's waiting room that did not have a spiritual message. There was nothing wrong with travel and business magazines; but, he said: "I never heard of anyone finding their way to the Lord through them." As a result, a number of his patients read their way into the truth.

My dad hired employees who shared the College of Medical Evangelists vision. They watched for interests in the church and noted in red on patient charts any literature a patient asked to take home. Doctors in the group, all CME graduates, could easily see these red notations. Meanwhile, the nurses kept their list of interested patients; and when the time came for a new series of Bible studies, these former patients would be invited to our home.

Before surgery and on the day of discharge, my dad always prayed with his patients; and he always thanked the Lord for His help. One lady drove all the way from Alaska, passing many teaching hospitals on the way, to have her surgery done by a "praying doctor." She later donated a beautiful piece of property to the church for a summer camp. When a colleague complained that prayer gave Dr. Barnard an unfair advantage, the medical society decided that this colleague could pray, too, if he wanted to.

My dad opened his office on Sundays, and one colleague remarked that this must be good for business. With his famous smile, Dr. Barnard replied, "I think it is the day you close that makes the difference." He looked forward to the day when he could post a sign on his office door: "Closed, in compliance with the Sunday Law. Come join us for Bible studies."

My dad's greatest legacy to me comes when I sit in church and see there the members who trace their roots to his office. At the Annual Postgraduate Convention 2008, I was thrilled to see the emphasis on missions. At the dedication service, one mission appointee was a young man whose father had joined the church as a result of Dr. Barnard's witness. Now this son, too, is carrying the torch of missions—something my dad loved and often supported, both financially and personally. He took his vacations doing mission relief, but first and foremost, he was a missionary at home.

Jo Ellen Barnard, LLUSM class of 1966, is a surgeon in Bakersfield, California. Her father, Marion C. Barnard, was born on February 10.

February 11

Ye are the light of the world. A city that is set on a hill cannot be hid. Matthew 5:14, KJV

The chasm of centuries separating our era from the death and ministry of Jesus, the Great Physician, is bridged by men and women who, in their relationship to the universe, seek fellowship with the divine and who pattern their lives after Him whose purpose was to make men whole.

The College [of Medical Evangelists] cherishes its church relationship, and it encourages a respect for the creed and organizational Christianity; but it recognizes that a personal devotion to Christ transcends all loyalties. Medical evangelism is not a tool, a weapon, or a convenient device; it is the manifestation of God's implanted love in the heart of one who is competent to serve and who sees each patient as a needy child of God.

The Good Samaritan was touched by the deepest emotions known to the heart of man. His goal was not to transfer the religious allegiance of the suffering man from Jerusalem to Samaria. Indeed, he did not know that an account of his benevolence would be published in the world's greatest book and be read by millions. It was a labor of love.

The founding of CME was a labor of love. Its maintenance and support through the years have been sustained as a Christian act. Christian service is the goal of the graduates who best represent their alma mater....

CME can never tell its full story. Nevertheless, its mission is clear; its mandate is certain. The College will serve God and society if it continues to mobilize all its resources to make man whole.

William Frederick Norwood (1904-1988) was dean of LLUSM from 1945 to 1951. He also taught history of medicine at LLU. This devotional originally appeared in the February 1955 issue of the LLUSM Alumni Association Alumni Journal.

February 12

I have given them the glory that you gave me, that they may be one as we are one: I in them and you in me. John 17:22-23, NIV

I vividly recall a few moving experiences in a stateside, office-based practice:

Having a woman come in without an appointment, accompanied by her husband, just to tearfully hug and thank me for praying for her for fourteen years.

Seeing a young man, traveling through, who makes an appointment just to share that what I had said concerning health habits during a single visit ten years prior was not in vain. It eventually clicked; and exercise had begun, tobacco and alcohol were removed, diet was changed, and, "Oddly, I began attending church!"

Being a witness, on many occasions when men and women schedule appointments just to talk about spiritual concerns and topics.

Acknowledging patients who request that I pray for them.

Remembering the time, when giving a Sabbath church sermon away from home on why God is interested in health, that a person who didn't speak English claimed I spoke in an "international language"; he joyfully stated he understood clearly every word.

Watching the joy on a mother's face after hearing council given to her preteen/teen daughters during routine medical visits about the importance of avoiding licit and illicit drugs and out-of-wedlock sexual encounters.

Receiving patients who come early to appointments, saying they need the peace my office brings.

Sharing with foster children their first Bibles.

Meeting with a middle-aged woman who stops by the office just to say thanks for taking the time to talk to her about her friend nine years ago: "She took your advice and is now alive and active because of you."

Hearing with humility, a woman say that when her family members leave my office, they feel they have counseled with Jesus Christ.

Moving experiences, yes. As I painfully know myself, I marvel and rejoice that they can see Christ in me. His name be praised!

This LLUSM graduate is a family practitioner, who wished to remain anonymous.

February 13

Cast your bread upon the waters, for after many days you will find it again.
Ecclesiastes 11:1, NIV

Showing others God, we find Him through them. In blessing others, we are blessed. Is the universe stingy? Is God stingy? If we give to others, do we have less in the end? Should we be careful and take account of our stock before we give? We cannot give what we do not have. In the end, we do get more because of giving.

In 1964, after I had graduated from medical school and had some surgical training, I wanted to carry out my plan to go work for God. So, when the General Conference of Seventh-day Adventists called and said surgeons are needed in our African hospitals, I was ready to go. "Where?" They said, "Well, we need a surgeon right now in Benghazi, Libya." This was when Libya was an impoverished country—before the oil. I took off to perform as a surgeon-evangelist.

Living in a little penthouse on top of the hospital in downtown Benghazi, I knew the surgeries were mine; the anesthesia was ether. Now, if you are a real general surgeon, nothing is as much fun as actually operating on everything that comes through the door—heads, chests, bellies, bones, genitourinary, obstetrics and gynecology.

We had many excellent nurses, most who spoke Arabic; so I learned medical Arabic quickly. One of the nurses, a recent graduate of the American University of Beirut (Lebanon) was the beautiful Odette, with whom, in time, I fell in love. We were married in her country two years later.

One interesting incident occurred when President Kennedy was killed. Those were the days when everyone had transistor radios, including the Bedouins, and all tuned to Radio Cairo. Even they had heard about our president being killed. Near this time, I was seeing patients in the clinic when a middle-aged lady came in. I couldn't understand what her medical problem was. She was rambling on about "Americanee."

It turned out she had heard about President Kennedy's death on the radio; and, as some of her tribe had been treated at the hospital, she knew there was an American doctor at the Seventh-day Adventist hospital. This woman had undertaken to walk forty kilometers to find me and tell me how sorry she and her people were that my president had been killed. I was so amazed.

I gave her a huge, Western hug and thanked her for this wonderfully sweet thought. She then turned and walked away. I saw my other patients, and only later did the significance of that generous, spontaneous act sink in. Even today, in my mind's eye, I can still see the wonderful Bedouin lady with the bare feet and tired, lined face.

Our Christian hospital took care of the people in Western Libya and was deeply loved by that large community. The staff members and I had many invitations to visit homes and villages and always had opportunities to speak for God and our mission with the Libyan people.

These are just some of the innumerable happy experiences with these wonderful people that I came to love and with whom I had so much fun. Our mission expressed to everyone what a warm and wonderful mutual God we love, in both our personal and international community.

Rob Johnson, LLUSM class of 1961, was associate director for healthcare at the General Conference of Seventh-day Adventists Health Ministries Department. He is an orthopaedic surgeon in Corona, California.

February 14

Praise the LORD! How joyful are those who fear the LORD and delight in obeying his commands. Their children will be successful everywhere; an entire generation of godly people will be blessed. They themselves will be wealthy, and their good deeds will last forever. . . . They share freely and give generously to those in need. Their good deeds will be remembered forever. Psalm 112:1-3, 9, NLT

A homeless man stood at the end of the freeway off-ramp, holding up the usual cardboard sign with big black letters: "Homeless, Hungry and Desperate." What caught my eye was the small, poorly printed words below: "Jesus loves *me* this I know." The light turned green and I was obliged to maneuver into the traffic. But I was intrigued—the typical sign most of us have seen reads: "Jesus loves *you.*"

I pulled into a fast-food parking lot on the other side of the overpass and walked back to the old, bedraggled man. At first, he was stunned to see me—dressed as I was in shirt and tie, wearing a Loma Linda University badge and a pager on my belt. "Why" I asked, "do you have 'Jesus loves *me* this I know' on your cardboard sign?"

The man, who I guessed to be in his 60s, broadly grinned and began to sing in a deep baritone voice:

> Jesus loves *me* this I know
> For the Bible tells me so.
> Little ones to Him belong
> They are weak, but He is strong.

I held back the tears, remembering my mother singing the same song to me as a kid growing up in Central Africa. I had not heard it since. As we chatted, he unfolded his story. As a youth pastor in the South, he had "taken a couple of bad turns in the road." He got divorced, lost his family, friends, automobile, and the respect of his community.

I took a $10 bill out of my wallet and asked if this would be used for "booze" or food. "No booze, sir. I have not had a drink in twenty-four years. It will be used for two days' worth of junk food." I believed him! Any bedraggled chap who could sing so beautifully at the side of an exit ramp was, in my books, a genuine stranger in need. I was reminded of Dr. John Townsend's view that we must learn to be more accepting of people—whether or not we agree with them or approve of them.

As you read this story today, remember that we have but this *one* day. Yesterday is gone; tomorrow looms ahead. May *this day* be used for good—good thoughts, good words, and good deeds.

John E. Lewis is professor in LLUSM department of pathology and human anatomy. He received a PhD degree in microbiology and immunology from LLU in 1969. He was LLUSM Teacher of the Year in 1997 and LLU Alumnus of the Year in 1999. He lives with his wife, Jan, in Redlands, California. February 14 is his birthday.

February 15

The secret things belong to the LORD our God, but those things which are revealed belong to us and to our children forever. Deuteronomy 29:29, NKJV

While the World Watched, A Star Flew By! It had been several months since my Navy physician friend and I had performed an ultrasound exam on my daughter-in-law, Clarissa, a patriotic and hard-working Army wife. Also in that darkened Bremerton naval hospital exam room was my son, Army Warrant Officer Gregory Thomsen.

He seemed to be exuding a matter-of-fact fearlessness that belied that he was soon to go on a mission, far away from us all, including the active unborn baby there with us. He would shortly, again, return to fly his Black Hawk helicopter in the dangerous night battle skies of Iraq. Both Clarissa and Greg requested that no one reveal the sex of their unborn baby. They wanted it to be a surprise. But I knew, from the ultrasound, and squelched the urge to shout out, "You have a girl—a beautiful, healthy active little girl!"

Some time later, at our home in Silverdale, Washington, in the early morning of February 15, 2005, I awaited news of this very special delivery. I had learned the patience of early morning labors, having delivered more than 4,000 babies in my thirty-one years of Army service. This time the labor had been long and difficult; but Clarissa had the coaching of her mother, Amy, on one side and my wife, Tina, on the other.

For my part, all I had to do was wait and pray, not only for those who labored at the maternity unit of the Community Hospital of the Monterey (California) Peninsula, but for Greg, whose powerful Black Hawk, along with nine others, gave comfort to ground troops in the dangerous battlefields near Taji Airbase north of Baghdad, Iraq. Greg had called his mother at the hospital just before his latest mission lifted off but lost contact as he stared into the greenish haze of his night vision goggles. He, too, must wait for news.

And then, in Iraq, it happened! A brilliant "star" flung across the dark sky, across the path of the heavily armed Black Hawks. Always alert for missiles, for rocket-propelled grenades, or for heavy machine gun tracers, each pilot was startled to alertness. But nothing followed. It must have been a shooting star of some type. Somehow, it gave a degree of comfort to Greg. A few minutes later, safely back on the sprawling pad at Taji, each pilot recorded the unusual "shooting star," including its time. They all agreed; it had crossed them at 4:21 a.m., February 16, 2005, Iraqi time.

About five hours after his last phone call, Greg called to find out if he had a baby. "Yes," Tina assured him, "you have a healthy, alert, beautiful, baby girl; and Clarissa was a real trooper." At that moment, Crystal Sierra was making her first attempts to breastfeed. Greg was eager to find out when she was born. Tina replied, "5:21 p.m." (Pacific Standard Time), exactly the moment when he saw the shooting star. What an awesome coincidence! It was something we would all remember with special meaning.

Russel J. Thomsen, LLUSM class of 1968, is an obstetrician and gynecologist in Silverdale, Washington.

February 16

When thou passest through the waters, I will be with thee; and through the rivers, they shall not overflow thee: when thou walkest through the fire, thou shalt not be burned; neither shall the flame kindle upon thee. Isaiah 43:2, KJV

It was 12:30 a.m. I was exhausted. My first day on cardiology call had been difficult. Suddenly a nurse insisted that I was needed in the emergency department (ED). The resident had been missing all day, leaving me to do all the charting. Frustrated, I told the nurse that the resident, not the intern (me) did the cardiology consults in the ED. She didn't back down. I seethed all the way to the ED, thinking I had had all I could take.

The ED was a zoo, and none of the secretaries had paged me. Frustrated, I turned to leave. As I walked out, I peeked in the cardiac room. They were coding an infant. "Why are they coding that baby? He's dead." Suddenly, I noticed something familiar: a blue sleeper similar to the one I'd packed for my brother to dress my son in. "No, it couldn't be."

I tried to work my way around the code team, attempting to sneak peeks at the center of attention. I pelted the code team with questions, trying to figure out how the baby got to the cardiac room. No one answered me. I finally made it to the head. The face was unrecognizable with all the tubes, tape, and flying hands. "What's the baby's name?" I asked. "I don't know," snapped a doctor. "Would you shut up or leave the room? You're disrupting the code." "I, I think it's my baby," I stammered. The code came to a halt. All eyes stared at me in absolute horror. The code quickly resumed. Someone said, "We don't know anything about the baby, except that a sheriff and paramedic responded to a blue baby call." Then my brother arrived. When I saw his tear-stained face, the truth hit. It took everything just to stay standing.

What could have gone wrong? I grappled with a million random thoughts. A doctor sat down to discuss the code. The information streamed in and out as my mind wrestled with the facts. "What do you want to do?" he asked. After some consideration I blurted, "Stop the code!" The doctor agreed and left. The code team left. I touched my son. He was cold, hard, and waxen. I recoiled. Babies were supposed to be warm, soft, and cuddly. I sat there thinking. I prayed. I asked God for a miracle. Silence. I asked God to raise Michael back to life. The audible single word "no" was clearly heard. I looked around the room. No one else was present. "Okay," I thought. "Just promise me that someday You'll explain why." Suddenly a sense of peace and calm came over me.

I learned a lot about being a person and a physician that night. As I've reflected over the years on the experience, I have come to be grateful for the personal growth, the lessons learned and the insights gained. The spiritual quest I embarked upon led me to a real and vital relationship with God. While life is unpredictable and painful, it is also enjoyable and real. I discovered that God is a faithful Friend and solid anchor in an unsafe world.

I am grateful that I learned as a 27-year-old what my priorities should be. I understood as never before that patients are whole beings with spiritual, mental, emotional, social, and physical needs; and I have tried to be a more compassionate and caring physician. I also learned to cherish my three sons and their unique and special gifts. And lastly, I discovered that crises do not make us; they reveal us. The revelation of Michael's death (from sudden infant death syndrome or SIDS) caused me to take a long honest look at my life and begin to make changes. It is a journey of personal growth I continue this day.

Delbe Thomas Meelhuysen, LLUSM class of 1987, is an internist in Joshua, Texas. This devotional originally appeared in the May 19, 2006, issue of Medical Economics. *February 16 was the birthday of her son, Michael.*

February 17

He shall cover thee with his feathers, and under his wings shalt thou trust; his truth shall be thy shield and buckler. Psalm 91:4, KJV

In the late 1950s, we lived at a country crossroad near the village of Cupids in Newfoundland, Canada. One day, February 16, 1959, the forecast was for a severe snowstorm and very high winds starting that evening. I saw patients all afternoon in my in-home medical office. When the last patient left, I still had a call to make in a village about five miles away. It was already snowing and the wind had started to blow, but it seemed reasonably safe to make just one house call. Soon, however, the storm intensified greatly.

My wife called the patient's home to tell me to stay there overnight. Fortunately (as we learned later), I had already left, having been asked to see another patient in a different house—and then a third. Later, driving home was extremely difficult. The wind-driven snow made visibility very poor. Snowdrifts filled most of the left lane and in some places covered the entire road. Once I got stuck but was able to back out and get around the drift. When I arrived home, my wife, Verna, and I thanked God for His care.

We had two sons, the younger one less than two years old. During the night, he awoke and cried. I heard him and immediately smelled smoke. Running downstairs, I found a small fire on the floor under our oil burning "space heater." Grabbing a small container of water from the kitchen, I easily doused the fire.

Moments later, as the storm raged outside and Verna and I stood thanking God and holding on to each other, the lights went out! When we contemplated what our situation would have been had we awakened five minutes later, when the lights and the electric water pump would have been out, our gratitude to God was multiplied. (And what if I had not been home?)

This storm proved to be the worst blizzard ever to hit Newfoundland, with winds as high as 125 miles per hour and snowdrifts up to twenty-one feet deep in parts of St. John's, Newfoundland. If the fire had made much headway, we would not have been able to get downstairs. Our only escape would have been through a window that opened above a slanted roof over the veranda. Dropping to the snow banks below, in night attire, with two small children, and fighting our way through the storm to the neighbor's house would have been difficult, if not impossible.

As we stood there, Verna could only think of the wonderful words of the hymn—
  "Under His wings I am safely abiding;
  Though the night deepens and tempests are wild . . ."
Fifty years have passed, and every time we hear that hymn we remember that night; and whenever we remember that night, we have always thought of that hymn.

Ellen G. White wrote the following words, which I also ponder upon in connection with this experience: "As I saw the great care which God has every moment for those who love and fear Him, I was inspired with confidence and trust in God, and felt reproved for my lack of faith" (*Testimonies for the Church*, vol. 1, p. 347).

Arthur A. Moores, LLUSM class of 1953-B, resides in Paradise, California.

"Which of these three, do you think, was a neighbor to the man who fell into the hands of the robbers?" He said, "The one who showed him mercy." Jesus said to him, "Go and do likewise." Luke 10:36-37, NRSV

My relationship with my father was ruptured when, at 17 years of age, I was baptized into the Seventh-day Adventist Church. He was totally opposed and vehemently exclaimed, "You are no longer my son. You have no place in this home!" So, with deepest agony of soul, I ran away one dark, wintry day.

With church support, I was later transported to what is now Andrews University in Berrien Springs, Michigan, to begin studying in preparation for the ministry. Upon arrival I felt fatherless, motherless, and brotherless—certain I would have no friends but would remain an anonymous and isolated person. How wrong I was!

Before I left for Andrews University, my minister referred me to Mark 10:29-30. In that text, Jesus promises that those who have to leave father and mother, brothers and sisters, for His sake and the gospel's, will receive not only the promise of eternal life, but an abundance of family in this world. So true! Church members became like parents, supplying so many of my needs; and caring college friends became brothers and sisters. I was surrounded by an incredible love.

Little did I surmise then, but that very love would later turn my father's heart to God, my church, and to me (as Malachi 4:5 promises). It happened several years later. While on a visit to his homeland of Croatia, my father had a massive heart attack. A Seventh-day Adventist physician gave him a shot in the heart, which kept him alive until he reached the hospital. Her sister was also a Seventh-day Adventist physician, who worked in that very hospital, along with a Seventh-day Adventist nurse. They began visiting my father.

Living right next door to the hospital were the parents of a Croatian student couple who were in my class at Andrews University, where I was teaching. These parents visited my father every day, even though they were complete strangers. They brought him food he could not eat and drink that he could only sip.

These loving Seventh-day Adventists touched his pain-wracked body. They lifted him up and laid him down, turned him this way and that, to ease his suffering. And they talked to him of the love of God and invited him to accept Christ into his heart. He did. Soon after my arrival, my father told me, "If they make people behave like this, then I want to be a part of this people and be baptized."

One day, as I was standing at his bedside, my father, who had once told me I was no longer his son, now looked at me intently and affirmed, "You are my son!" I believe that when he said that, God was bending over him saying, *"And you are my son!"*

What made the difference and brought my father to a deep conversion experience? It was not doctrine, but God's love operating through people. We are God's language, His hands and feet. The word of His love becomes flesh in us.

Ivan T. Blazen is professor of biblical interpretation and theology in LLUSR. After graduate studies at Union Theological Seminary in New York City, New York; University of Heidelberg in Germany; and Drew University in Madison, New Jersey, he received a PhD degree from Princeton Theological Seminary in Princeton, New Jersey, in 1979. He has authored journal articles, book chapters, and books. He has three daughters and five grandchildren.

February 19

In everything give thanks; for this is God's will for you in Christ Jesus.
1 Thessalonians 5:18, NASB

There was no doubt what her diagnosis was. The echocardiographic images clearly demonstrated a very hypertrophied right ventricle with a large ventricular septal defect. The findings at catheterization confirmed severe obstruction of blood flow to her lungs, oxygen saturation of 68 percent in the aorta, and a hematocrit of 66 percent. The operation, called repair of tetralogy of Fallot, was scheduled for the next morning.

I glanced over her history and physical: "29-year-old lady, Spanish speaking only . . ." and co-signed the consult. I intended to use my limited Spanish vocabulary to explain the operation and its complications. My busy schedule would not allow for the long wait to get an interpreter. I hurried into room 4705 and introduced myself to Mrs. Ramirez. I assured her we would take good care of her and was about to have a prayer with her when she uttered a long sentence in Spanish. I could understand only the first word, "doctor," and the last, "mi hijo." Then I sat by her bed and called for an interpreter.

Mrs. Ramirez was not afraid of dying, nor was she concerned about the risks of surgery. She had experienced much adversity—the latest just a month ago. For the first time in her life, she left her town in Mexico to come to California to say goodbye to her husband, a migrant worker who was killed accidentally.

Throughout her adult life, she was told that having a full-term pregnancy was not only an impossibility, but also that she would be risking her own life. She had challenged the odds and was blessed with a healthy baby, who was now 7 years old and all she had! She was led to believe that her congenital heart disease was incurable; and, therefore, she learned to "live" with its limitations: constant fatigue and shortness of breath. Her cyanotic and fainting spells had become so frequent that she found herself doing more squatting and less walking. Hence, her question to me that day was, "Doctor, will I be able to walk with my son?" There was not a dry eye in the room as all present experienced the depth of love behind that simple question!

Two weeks later, Mrs. Ramirez came for her first postoperative check-up. She was exceedingly grateful and most excited that she had the energy to walk with her son without having to squat or feel short of breath. And, pointing to her now warm and pink fingers, she said her son was no longer afraid to hold her previously cold and purple clubbed hands. "Gracias a Dios" were my last words to her, as she walked out of the office.

Yes, "thank you," God, for the blessing you sent my way through Mrs. Ramirez. Help me slow down, lest I miss out on such a wonderful experience with my next patient. And "thank you," Mrs. Ramirez, for the valuable lessons you taught me in perseverance, love, courage, and faith. I no longer take for granted the walks my family enjoys on Sunday mornings. Moreover, I feel especially blessed when my 7-year-old son holds my hand.

Anees J. Razzouk, LLUSM class of 1982, is professor in and chair of LLUSM department of cardiovascular and thoracic surgery. He and his wife, Teresa Thompson, LLUSM class of 1990, reside in Redlands, California.

Fools think their own way is right, but the wise listen to advice. Proverbs 12:15, NRSV

I am a fortunate individual. I have taught for more than thirty-five years at the same institution, a place where spiritual guidance and value are constantly sought, and where those values are incorporated into all levels of its educational programs.

I was raised in a "disadvantaged" home. My father was a clerk in a drugstore and my mother was a maid in a rest home. We never owned a home. My parents bought their first new automobile when I was 28 years old. We were poor in material things but rich in family, work ethics, and Christian values. My parents sacrificed so that I could get a Christian education at the local Seventh-day Adventist academy, where I worked as a janitor to help finance my schooling. An unknown benefactor who had faith in me matched what I made as a janitor. Thank you!

The academy faculty was long-suffering. They should have dismissed me for numerous "infractions" that I'm too embarrassed to admit! They dealt with me in a loving "go and sin no more" manner and never mentioned my delinquencies to my parents. I'm indebted to them for the education I received that went far beyond "reading, writing, and arithmetic." These teachers were true Christian educators, whose personal concern will never be forgotten.

This foundational experience carried me through my undergraduate and graduate years. My bachelor's and master's degrees were earned at San Diego (California) State University. I experienced culture shock going from an academy graduating class of thirty-five to a state university, where undergraduate general education class enrollments numbered in the low hundreds. But I was successful; I learned how to compete. I was the first in my family to get a college education.

While completing my master's degree in zoology, I was hired by the University of San Diego, where for four years I taught general biology to seminary students; as well as embryology, histology, and anatomy in the College for Men. But it became obvious to me during that period that I needed a stronger foundation in the anatomical sciences.

I was accepted to the Loma Linda University PhD degree program in anatomy the day I interviewed in 1969! I was fortunate to be taught again by Christian educators—Harold Shryock, LLUSM class of 1934; Herbert Henken, LLUSM class of 1946; Dan Mitchell, LLUSM class of 1947; Guy Hunt, LLUSM class of 1942; Walter Roberts, LLUSM class of 1939; Robert Schultz, LLUSM class of 1946; and others. I was mentored through my research project by Arthur Dalgleish.

The same devotion to Christian education that I received in the academy embraced me again at Loma Linda. I owe whatever success I have today to hardworking, loving Christian parents, a devoted Christian Seventh-day Adventist academy, and an LLU graduate faculty who instilled in me the need for including Christ in my decision making . . . Thank you; I have no complaints!

P. B. Nava is professor in LLUSM department of pathology and human anatomy, and is head of the division of anatomy. He received a PhD degree in anatomy from LLU in 1973. He is course director for anatomy and embryology at LLUSM. In 2003, he was LLU Alumnus of the Year. February 20 is his birthday.

February 21

Peace I leave with you; my peace I give you. I do not give to you as the world gives. Do not let your hearts be troubled and do not be afraid. John 14:27, NIV

He was a large, tough looking middle-aged man. He had a braided ponytail coming out from under his bandana; and he was still wearing his sunglasses, despite the fact that we were in the emergency department. I was sure he had a "Born to Kill" tattoo hidden somewhere under his leather jacket. The chart simply said that he had come in to be evaluated for an abscess on his arm.

As a medical student, I was in the room to obtain a more thorough history of what was going on and to evaluate his abscess. After answering a few of my questions, he began, hesitantly at first, to tell me his story. In the not-too-distant past, he had been diagnosed and treated for cancer. Over time, things seemed to return to normal; and he felt as though he had his life back. But now, more recently, he was starting to feel sick again. He feared that the abscess growing on his arm was a sign that his immune system was failing.

Looking down, he took his sunglasses off. With stress in his voice and fear in his eyes, he looked directly at me and said he was afraid the cancer was back. This was a very scared man. I empathized with him and told him we would order some tests. Still, I felt like there was something more I could do right then. I felt that maybe I should offer to pray with him, but that just seemed crazy.

Stereotypically, he looked nothing like the kind of man who would want me to pray with him; in fact, he looked like the kind of man who would break me in half for even mentioning it! Still, sort of sheepishly, I asked him if he would like me to pray. With great enthusiasm and energy, he said, "Would you, please?!" I was shocked.

We bowed our heads and I asked that God bring him peace, comfort, and understanding in the tough times that might be ahead of him. When we were done, he had tears streaming down his face. He thanked me, saying no one had ever prayed with him at a hospital before. I could immediately see in his eyes that much of the fear had lifted. I know that it may not always be appropriate to pray with patients. But this instance reminded me that there are times when it may be the best thing we can do for them.

Allen Patee, LLUSM class of 2010, is from Devore, California, and received a BS degree in emergency medical care from LLU. He and his wife, Mercedes, LLUSM class of 2005, want to do mission work following his residency.

February 22

When they call on me, I will answer; I will be with them in trouble. I will rescue and honor them. Psalm 91:15, NLT

I was an intern, and I was in trouble. I had fallen in love. Although I was an adult, I didn't want to disappoint my parents, who had a different view of this man. They said we would not be compatible—there were too many differences between our cultures and backgrounds. I was confused and agonized over what to do. I had a hard time concentrating on my work. I prayed, cried, and prayed some more. In my turmoil, God heard me and answered me through my patient.

At that time, I was on the oncology part of the program and had a patient with metastatic breast cancer. I no longer remember her full name or the details of her case. Her words, however, still ring in my ears. As I walked into her room one sunny afternoon, she advised, "Follow your heart." Just like that, out of the blue. I was taken aback. Did my anguish show that much? Had she read my mind? No, she was not talking about me.

She then recounted her past: her lost love, how she never married, and how lonely she was. She was in love once, but her father did not approve of the match. As I left her room, she instructed me again to "follow your heart." She was discharged, and I never saw her again. Little did she know how much she would change my life.

After that conversation, I felt my burden lifted and my head freed of cobwebs. Yes, there were many differences between my loved one and me, but there were also many similarities. I followed my patient's recommendation and decided to marry this man. Now came the hard part—telling my parents how I felt. In spite of their initial reservations, they came to support us. We stepped into a new multicultural world and visited places I did not know existed. I changed. I became a richer person.

This happened twenty-three years ago. I learned three valuable lessons from this experience. The first lesson is that I cried to God and He heard me. Since then, I have called on God over and over, and He has always answered me. At times, the answers were not easy to follow. The second lesson is that God spoke through my patient. God uses all sorts of avenues and individuals—even patients. God can communicate through me, even me. What a tremendous responsibility! The third lesson is this: This patient touched me because she shared her heart and soul with me. Am I willing to share, willing to be vulnerable? Can I humble myself so God can work through me?

Euly Langga-Sharifi, LLUSM class of 1985, is assistant professor in LLUSM department of medicine. She was born in the Philippines and reared in Los Angeles, California. Her husband, Mozafar Sharifi, was born in Iran. February 22 is his birthday.

February 23

And now these three remain: faith, hope and love. But the greatest of these is love. 1 Corinthians 13:13, NIV

One especially busy day, I was taking care of several intensive care-unit patients and a number of floor patients. Then, on top of those duties, I got an admission, even before we were done rounding. I felt overwhelmed with the work. And, I was bitter that I seemed to be working much harder than some of the other members on our team.

Next, it came time for "Love Rounds," our spiritual discussion with Wil Alexander, PhD, Whole Person Care leader. My first thought was, "I don't have time for this!" Then, as we sought to reach out to a patient spiritually, I was reached. Following are my reflections.

"Though I speak with cultural sensitivity and can communicate very effectively, but have not love, I am become as sounding brass, or a tinkling cymbal. And though I have the gift of healing and though I understand all the art and science of medicine and though I have the resources to help all of my patients, but have not love, I am nothing. Though I devote all of my time and though I give my body up to sleepless nights on call, but have not love, it profits me nothing."

"Love suffers long and is kind. It does not envy a man who is more knowledgeable or skillful. It does not seek prestige, but is humble. Love does not behave rudely even to hospital staff, does not seek to only cover its tail, is not easily provoked by noncompliance, thinks no evil even toward managed care. It does not rejoice in iniquity, but rejoices in the truth; bears all things, believes all things, hopes all things, endures all things, even charting."

"Love never fails: but whether there be medicines, they shall fail; whether there be studies and evidence, they will change; whether there be knowledge, it shall vanish away. For we know in part, and we practice in part. But when that which is perfect is come, then that which is in part shall be done away."

"When I was a child, I spake as a child, I understood as a child, I thought as a child: but when I became a man, I put away childish things. For now we see the creation marred by sin through a microscope and with x-rays, but then we shall see the Creator. Now I know in part; but then shall I know even as also I am known. And now abides faith, hope, love, these three; but the greatest of these is love."

J. Seth Lukens, LLUSM class of 2007, is a resident in family medicine rural track at LLUMC and Hanford Family Practice Residency Program in Hanford, California.

If anyone desires to come after Me, let him deny himself, and take up his cross, and follow Me. For whoever desires to save his life will lose it, but whoever loses his life for My sake will find it. For what profit is it to a man if he gains the whole world, and loses his own soul? Or what will a man give in exchange for his soul? Matthew 16:24-26, NKJV

On February 24, 1997, L.W., a 47-year-old woman, came to see me at the Better Living Clinic because she had been suffering from chronic and persistent abdominal pain without relief for six months. In March, I performed an esophagogastroduodenoscopy (EGD), which revealed a gastric ulcer 15 mm in diameter. I recommended that she discontinue the NSAID (a nonsteroidal anti-inflammatory drug) she was taking for osteoarthritis (OA, a form of degenerative disease) for pain control.

I started L.W. on Biaxin and amoxicillin for helicobacter pylori eradication, along with treatment for her gastric ulcer. The repeat EGD, after three months of this intense treatment for the ulcer and the infection, revealed a complete, beautiful healing of the ulcer. She was grateful, even though she had no health insurance and could not pay for the treatment.

About five years later, in January of 2003, L.W. came to see me again. She was suffering from recurrent abdominal pain. I performed another EGD, which revealed six gastric ulcers 10-to-15 mm in diameter. She was placed on Protonix. To my utter surprise and joy, she made rapid progress and recovery from the gastric ulcers, with complete resolution of her abdominal pain. And, once again, I treated her free of charge—with joy in my heart for her complete recovery twice!

With overflowing gratitude, she told everyone who would listen—relatives and neighbors, even those on the street—about her experience. To my big surprise, so many were impressed by her personal experience that they came to see me for consultation for a variety of illnesses. As I witnessed all these patients, who came as a result of L.W.'s powerful testimony, I came to an important realization and logical conclusion.

I treated L.W. for an illness, with her best interest in mind. With joy and a smile, I took good care of her medical problem when she needed it most, even though I knew from the very start I would not be paid. But it was L.W. who sent and referred many patients with good health insurance benefits to see me at the Better Living Clinic. She taught me some interesting but illogical mathematics:

$1+1 = 2$ (regular mathematics)

$1+0 \geq 10$ (God's mathematics, mathematics of service)

I realized there was something profound by looking at these two sets of mathematics. My heart was deeply touched, and I lowered my head in recognition of this "new found" math. It is truly a paradox! You lose, but you also gain! I was reminded of the words spoken by Jesus recorded in Matthew 16:24-26, and I was deeply touched.

To sum up, there is a BIG DIFFERENCE between regular mathematics and God's mathematics. This fact really dawned on me during this experience and has never left me. I was deeply humbled by this realization: YOU LOSE SOME, BUT YOU GAIN MORE!

Yoshinobu Namihira, LLUSM class of 1980-B, is a gastroenterologist in Vicksburg, Mississippi.

February 25

This righteousness from God comes through faith in Jesus Christ to all who believe. There is no difference, for all have sinned and fall short of the glory of God. Romans 3:22-23, NIV

I recently cared for two women, who shared a hospital room. They were admitted for observation while completing a bowel prep in order to have a colonoscopy. Both women had gastrointestinal issues, and both were very prone to dehydration. They were similar in age—mid 30s—though dissimilar in all other ways.

The first was an angry, manipulative woman, with a history of many surgeries for gastric ulcers. I'll call her Ms. Bitter. She was chronically addicted to narcotics and abused the medical staff when not given the meds she wanted. The second was a sweet, kind woman who, one year prior, had been in a car accident and lost her sight and the use of her legs. This happened barely one year after she and her husband were married. I'll call her Ms. Gentle. She always had a smile on her face, always asked how I was doing, and never complained.

One morning, Gentle asked me, "Dr. Wrighton, what do you look like?" I described my features, and she giggled and said, "Thank you. You sound cute." This was just five minutes after Bitter had yelled at me to leave her room because I had explained she was ready to go home (which meant no more narcotics).

The comparison was striking! I was outraged with Bitter. How could she be like that? And my heart broke for Gentle. How could she be so sweet with no hint of bitterness? I wanted to say to Bitter, "Look at Gentle, what she has been through. You see her complaining?"

But then it occurred to me that Gentle was gentle because she knew the love of Christ. And Bitter was bitter because she knew of no such love. And it made me wonder who I'd be without Jesus, my Lord, and His wonderful salvation. I might be Bitter—holding on to regret, longing for something to fill me, angry at the world. I sometimes am bitter, even WITH the knowledge of His great love.

It is easy to get frustrated with difficult patients, especially after long hours of work and being tired. But these two women reminded me that my only obligation is to love my brothers and sisters—out of the overflowing of the love that Christ has shown me. And by doing that, maybe Bitter's heart would be melted, and she would need a new name—maybe Thankfulness or Mercy or Grace.

I thank God for all that He has done, even for a sinner like me.

Lindsay Wrighton, LLUSM class of 2007—for which she was freshman class co-pastor and senior class pastor—is a general surgery resident at LLUMC. From Groveland, California, she received a BS degree in biopsychology from University of California, Santa Barbara. She plans on being a missionary surgeon.

February 26

I am the LORD, there is no other . . . I will strengthen you though you have not known me. Isaiah 45:5, NEB

When I awoke that morning, something was wrong—I could not lift my head from the pillow! It was February 28, my thirteenth birthday. Before leaving on a business trip before daylight, my parents had left birthday gifts on the foot of my bed. With difficulty, I tried once again to sit up and reach for a coveted tennis racket I could see there on the bed. But once again I found it was impossible to sit up. Besides, my head throbbed and I felt nauseated.

I decided to just lie patiently until Mrs. Cochran came to my bedroom to wake me up. Only a week before, our family had made a sad move—from our beloved country home on a three-acre fruit ranch to the nearby city where my grandmother lived. She had become a recent invalid from a broken hip. Mrs. Cochran, a practical nurse, was her attendant.

Soon I was under Mrs. Cochran's care, but I did not improve. She became increasingly alarmed as the day wore on and night fell. Of course, there were no cell phones in those days to hasten my parents' return. It was nearly midnight when I roused to hear my mother's concerned voice: "Even though it's midnight, we must phone Dr. Cunningham and ask if he will make the ten-mile trip into the city because we are not acquainted with a doctor here!"

After our faithful doctor, who had seen our family through many medical crises, arrived and examined me, I detected a concerned look on his face as he said: "Fever, no stiff neck, she hasn't passed urine all day . . . I need a urine specimen, however small!" He soon left with a meager specimen.

Very early the next morning, Dr. Cunningham returned with the grim diagnosis: acute nephritis. He then described the treatment to be administered: "Every two hours, you must cover her with frequently changed hot, moist blankets, to make her sweat. Poisons must be eliminated from her body through the skin, since her kidneys aren't working! Have her drink plenty of water."

How I hated those hot applications! I began to notice a most disagreeable odor in the room—an odor that I would not identify until many years later as an intern at the White Memorial Hospital (now White Memorial Medical Center) in Los Angeles, California. Uremic fetor! Evidently this was the right therapy. Within two days, I began to improve with no other treatment. After two weeks, and a tonsillectomy, I returned to my new school and junior high classes. My favorite subject became anatomy and physiology.

This entire episode was my introduction to medicine; and, from that time on, I determined to become a doctor. This incident proved to be but the first unrecognized Providence that, in time, made me realize that God had a plan for my life.

Ethel Read Nelson, LLUSM class of 1948, was an LLUSM Alumni Association 1978 Honored Alumna. She and her husband, Roger, LLUSM class of 1945, reside in Dunlap, Tennessee.

February 27

Each of us was given grace according to the measure of Christ's gift.
Ephesians 4:7, NRSV

When I went through college, I had almost nothing in the way of outside financial resources. I worked up to twenty hours a week at three different on-campus jobs while taking a full chemistry-major load; this money went directly to pay my tuition. Spending money, what there was of it, consisted of a relatively small portion of the money that I had earned the summer previously, with the remainder also going toward tuition payments. As a result, I found it necessary to be extremely frugal at all times.

One thing that I desperately wanted was a pair of contact lenses. The glasses that I constantly wore were thick, old-fashioned, and awkward. And they certainly didn't enhance my self-confidence or social life! Although obtaining contact lenses seemed an impossible dream, I started saving for them. I budgeted a small amount of "spending money" each week, but would also try to save out a small amount—maybe $1 or $5— that I'd put in an envelope labeled "Contact Lens Fund." Unfortunately, that fund didn't grow very quickly, so I had no expectations of achieving my goal anytime soon.

Birthdays in our part of the dorm were frequently celebrated with a birthday cake or cupcakes, often prepared by the roommate. So, I wasn't surprised when I was called to the lounge area on some rather lame pretext on February 27, my birthday. What I discovered when I started opening the envelopes and cards, however, absolutely blew me away: My roommate and suitemates had organized a campaign to get perhaps 20 people each to contribute something—$5, $10, $20—to my contact lens fund!

Not only had they collected enough to buy the lenses, but they had also contributed enough to pay for the eye exam and had even made the appointment! The effect on me was immeasurable. I had no idea that so many people cared about this very personal goal of mine. Or that my roommate and suitemates were willing to take time away from their own work and studies to organize the process.

I have no idea if any of these people even remember this incident, but I will never forget the surprise or the grace I experienced through my friends that day. Sometimes, I think, surprise may be one of the most amazing things about grace; when you have no expectation or sense of entitlement to something good, the good things that do happen have the capacity to amaze, to awe, and to change the way you see the world.

May we all be willing to serve as conduits of God's surprising, amazing grace.

Penelope Duerksen-Hughes is professor in LLUSM department of basic sciences, is vice chair of the division of biochemistry, and is assistant dean for graduate academic and student affairs for LLUSM. She has a PhD degree in biochemistry from Emory University in Atlanta, Georgia.

February 28

He hath made every thing beautiful in his time. Ecclesiastes 3:11, KJV

Early one March afternoon during my first year of medical school, I stood wearing my formaldehyde-scented lab coat in the clinical laboratory at LLUMC, staring at a petri dish and trying desperately to look clinical. "Well," said the lab tech blandly to me, "there's your answer." I glanced briefly at his face, trying to read it for some indication of the meaning of those swirling white speckles in the dish. I had no idea what they meant. "Um," I stuttered. "Congratulations," he looked up and grinned. I gulped. I nodded. I grinned back. I was going to be a dad! I needed to call my wife, whose nonlatex-agglutinated hormone excretions I had been staring at.

The weeks that followed were eventful, tumultuous, and overwhelming. Shelley quit her job, determined to be an at-home mom. I, on the other hand, scrambled. Crazy thoughts filled my head. What do I do? Find a job? Quit medical school? Take out more loans? This baby idea changed everything. I was desperate. My parents had no resources to share. I had no idea what to do. So, I prayed. I applied for a job as a research assistant, working in the perinatal research department under Dwight Smith. I worked hard, and my employers were incredibly understanding of my scheduling concerns.

And on November 15, 1981, my beautiful daughter was born—at home. We had no money. We lived well below the poverty level. We moved three times. But somehow we scraped by, between Shelley's childcare business at home and my research salary. Over the next three years, I worked whenever I could. My bosses were gracious. They gave me a raise.

Near the end of my medical school days, Larry Longo, LLUSM class of 1954, sat down with me to talk about my plans. He asked how I was doing. I voiced to him my appreciation for the opportunity to work, the flexibility of my hours, and the opportunity to publish. I don't know if I expressed clearly enough how much of a difference this had made for me, to hold on to and complete my dream of becoming a physician and to provide for my young family. Dr. Longo discretely asked me during that interview if I needed any financial help. I didn't want to lie to him; so I explained that we were a little short on our tuition, but that we were doing all right with living expenses. A couple of weeks later, I received a call from the financial office. An anonymous donor had paid the remaining $3,000 on my expenses. I would be able to graduate!

I look back over those years to the present, and I marvel at how this kindness changed not only my future, but also the future of my children and the next generation. I'm not sure how to say thank you, but allow me to try. To Larry Longo and the perinatal crew: I say thank you with the accomplishment of three finished publications. To the anonymous donor: I say thank you by passing your kindness on to others—with three years of service in Malawi; eight short-term mission trips; and twenty-one years dedicated to caring for the poor, the underserved, the uninsured.

And finally, I thank my Maker for the chance to see history repeat itself, in watching my beautiful daughter—born not according to our sense of timing but according to Your plan—a graduate of LLUSM, class of 2008. Oh, and in 2008, our daughter Allison gave birth to her first-born son, my first grandchild, at LLUMC.

Barry J. Bacon, LLUSM class of 1984, is a family practitioner in Colville, Washington. February 28 is the day his first grandson, Aidan Avery Jenks, was born.

March 1

He hath shewed thee, O man, what is good; and what doth the LORD require of thee, but to do justly, and to love mercy, and to walk humbly with thy God?
Micah 6:8, KJV

Wherever you may be, command your spirits to keep watch and ward over this humble place. By prayer, in tears, and with sacrifice it was brought to the birth. Soon the silent artillery of time will have laid us low, and it will be for you to bear aloft and onward those standards soon to fall from our hands.

Humbly do we beseech Thee, O Thou Great God in the Highest Heavens, that when the strings of the harps of our lives shall be muted; when these wards and walls shall know our walk and way and hear our voices no more forever; that in humility we may have in this place, so taught you, our children not only in the science, but in the spirituals of medicine, that thousands of afflicted ones who will enter in within these portals shall say as was said of our blest Lord and Saviour in the long ago: "Surely he hath borne our griefs, and carried our sorrows" (Isaiah 53:4, KJV). "Himself took our infirmities, and bare our sicknesses" (Matthew 8:17, KJV).

In this hard hour when a welter of war and woe mantels this old earth like a death shroud, when hatreds and the vilest passions of men and women are flooding the land, it is for you to be clothed with divine ideals of the healing art. Never allow commercialism and materialism to find an abiding place in your souls.

When such glorious transformations have taken place, then it will be true of the men and women who go forth into the world from this place that "a man shall be"—to the patients committed to his care—"as a hiding place from the wind, and a covert from the tempest; as rivers of waters in a dry place, as the shadow of a great rock in a weary land" (Isaiah 32:2, KJV).

In all things let Christian modesty adorn your lives, bearing in mind the words of an old French *abbé*: "He who would build a church to God and not to fame,
Must never mark the marble with his name."

Percy T. Magan (1867-1947) was LLUSM dean from 1916 to 1928 and was president of CME from 1928 to 1942. This devotional originally appeared in the 1941 March of CME.

March 2

So that they should seek the Lord, in the hope that they might grope for Him and find Him, though He is not far from each one of us. Acts 17:27, NKJV

"We can never thank you enough for taking such wonderful care of Ashlee. You did more than care for her and treat her illnesses. You bonded with her and with us. We can never thank you enough for all you've done. God will bless you with crowns of gold and peace in your hearts."

Ashlee's mother continued on, saying she believed that Ashlee was given another year of life so that circumstances would play out, allowing Ashlee and her twin sons to move from back East and come in contact with us at LLUMC. Sobering, yet an exhilarating thought! God put Ashlee amongst us to prepare her and her family for Ashlee's death at age 19 years.

Ashlee had mediastinal fibrosis from histoplasmosis–a devastating condition. Without good treatment, the disease progressively squeezes the vital blood vessels with bands of scar tissue caused by a fungal infection. A pulmonary vein had been stented back East, but Ashlee came to us dying.

On February 27, I was at her bedside doing routine hospital rounds. She was sedated, on a ventilator, and did not appear to be aware of her surroundings. For some strange reason, I felt compelled to say something to her about God. I initially resisted the urge, for Ashlee, even when lucid, had not given any indication of an interest in spiritual things. Indeed, quite a few elements of her behavior in her short life had been anything but spiritual. The words that eventually came out as I prepared to leave her bedside were, "G-God is with you." I stumbled over the words and it sounded like a dumb thing to say; but the words were already out. Ashlee just lay there, showing no sign that she had heard me.

Two days later, on March 1, Ashlee's mother asked to speak to me. She said that, at a time when Ashlee was less sedated, she had written a note to her mother—Ashlee was unable to speak–that she couldn't fight any more, had made her peace with God, and wanted her medical treatment withdrawn. She asked her mother to take care of her twin boys. Then she wrote, "God is with me."

I could hardly believe my ears! Almost the exact words I had said to an apparently unconscious Ashlee two days before. But she must have been listening and had taken my stumbling words as the signal that God accepted her and that it was okay to give up the struggle and turn herself over to God's care and keeping.

After verifying that this was indeed Ashlee's request and that her family supported her in this request, we made her comfortable with medications and removed her from life support. As her life ebbed away on March 2, she had a calm, trusting expression on her face—confident that God was with her.

David Bland is associate professor in LLUSM department of medicine. He received his medical degree from University of New South Wales in Sydney, Australia. He is a specialist in pulmonary disease critical care. March 2 is the date Ashlee passed away.

March 3

As newborn babes, desire the sincere milk of the word, that ye may grow. 1 Peter 2:2, KJV

Derived from the Latin word *miraculum,* meaning "something wonderful," miracles have been described as divine intervention by a supernatural being in the universe (God) by which the ordinary course of nature is overruled, suspended, or modified.

The Old Testament shows a number of ways miracles are said to occur. God created matter out of nothingness. God breathed life into inanimate matter. God, through Moses, parted the Red Sea to permit the Israelites to flee bondage. And in the New Testament, we learn that Jesus fed the multitudes with a few loaves of bread and three fishes, restored sight to the blind, cured the scourge of leprosy, and restored life to Lazarus.

According to the philosopher David Hume, a miracle is "a transgression of a law of nature by a particular volition of the Deity, or by the interposition of some invisible agent." In an era of "evidence-based medicine," how do we physicians come to an understanding of miracles or those unexplainable remissions of disease? Or explain survival, beyond a consensus of experienced physicians, that a patient's recovery defies the odds and expectations of modern medicine?

Let me give an example of a recent case. A one-pound, one-ounce premature infant was referred to LLUMC neonatal intensive care unit (NICU) with a perforated bowel, on assisted ventilation, and with systemic fungal sepsis. The infant was deemed too critically ill to undergo surgery. Her health issues were many. The infant's tiny veins would only permit intermittent infusions of antimicrobials, and the baby's lungs were so immature that assisted ventilation was required. This ventilation would be very slowly weaned as the lungs grew.

This infant was deemed so critical that two conferences were held with the parents, indicating to them that the infant's chances of survival were slim; the child was very likely to die. A death summary was being started in the medical record.

But after weeks of meticulous care by the nursing staff, respiratory therapists, and the neonatology staff—and with prayer by the parents and those caring for this tiny baby—this infant overcame her illness and was discharged from the NICU on March 3, 2008.

Is this infant a "miracle" granted by God for a special baby undoubtedly with a divine mission; or was it simply an unexplainable event, a lucky patient, an outcome not understood within the usual rules of "evidence-based medicine"? Was this infant's survival merely a statistically unlikely but beneficial event? Should this outcome be regarded as "wonderful" because she "beat the odds," or was her survival a miracle? Is our dedication to scientific evidence so focused that we might miss the opportunity to witness divine interventions?

Of those who care for tiny infants, many believe that miracles are still occurring. Of course, only God knows; but to many in the NICU, this infant represents what most of us believe is a "miracle," or a wonderful event. For these times, we thank God and can better understand what the miracles in the New Testament are telling us about God's love for us all.

Thurman Merritt is professor in LLUSM department of pediatrics. He received his MD degree from University of Kansas in 1972. March 3 is the date a very special patient was discharged, and is also the birthday of Travis, one of Thurman's sons.

For he shall give his angels charge over thee, to keep thee in all thy ways. Psalm 91:11, KJV

An icy rain was falling that dark winter morning as I hurried along a deserted sidewalk, with my coat drawn up around my ears, on my way to morning rounds at Massachusetts General Hospital (MGH) in Boston. I was startled from my thoughts by a voice from behind me that asked, "Would you like to share my umbrella?" I turned to see a tall woman, whom I didn't recognize, walking up behind me. We started chatting about the dreadful weather, which she said had her dreaming of southern California. I said I, too, loved southern California from the days when I'd attended medical school at Loma Linda University. What happened next, if a little hard to believe, is true.

The woman gave an exclamation of surprise and said that she had been head nurse of Loma Linda University Medical Center surgical intensive care unit for many years—including 1984, when I rotated there as a medical student! As we waited to cross the street outside the entrance to MGH, I reflected on the astonishingly low probability of the encounter I was experiencing that winter morning in Boston. I thought about how it was based on a nurse's inclination to help a stranger in need of shelter from the rain. Then, just as with stories about angels, she was gone. I haven't seen her since. This story leads me to one of my favorite comparisons, which is between nurses and guardian angels.

There are many references in the Bible regarding the various roles of angels. The book of Daniel includes a number of ideas about angels, according to *Encyclopedia Mythica*, including the existence of named angels and guardian angels. It also includes the idea that all the nations of the world have their own angelic prince and that there is a hierarchical arrangement of angels. Guardian, or tutelary, angels act as ministering spirits, protectors, and intercessors for their subjects. A guardian angel is assigned to each human when the soul enters the body.

In my experience working at medical centers across the country, it seems to me that nurses share many of the characteristics of guardian angels. Patients have a nurse assigned to them from the moment they enter the hospital. Personal and physical interactions occur between nurse and patient many times during each shift; and for this reason, patients tend to open up emotionally to their nurse.

Wil Alexander, PhD, professor of clinical ministry and theology at Loma Linda University, told us to "touch your patients"—shake their hand as you greet them, put your hand on their shoulder when you encourage them. Words are no substitute for human touch, he said. Nurses touch patients at some of the most vulnerable times in their lives. Nurses intercede on behalf of their patient in innumerable ways, all for the healing of their patient.

The woman I met on a winter walk to morning rounds served to confirm my belief that those special people who choose nursing as their life's work are akin to guardian angels.

John W. Henson, LLUSM class of 1984, is a neurologist in Cambridge, Massachusetts. March 4 is the day he received his acceptance letter from LLUSM.

March 5

In all their distress he too was distressed, and the angel of his presence saved them. In his love and mercy he redeemed them; he lifted them up and carried them all the days of old. Isaiah 63:9, NIV

It was on a mission trip to a remote Nepalese village in the foothills of the Himalayans that I got to see my angel. On my return trip home, I climbed onto an overloaded jeep that would take me back to civilization. We traveled on roads that had been scratched along the cliffs of the magnificent mountains. Four hours later, we reached the first real town. Only six more hours to go and I'd be at the airport. But, to my alarm, this first town was on a general strike! Rather than the banner-waving crowds or piles of burning tires seen at some strikes, the whole town was quiet.

When Nepalese wish to protest the government, they call a strike and shut down the town—including shops, businesses, and transportation. It could last a day or a week, and I had to get to the next town before my plane left. Moreover, I had to cover my emergency room shift as soon as I got home; so I *couldn't* miss my plane. My cries for sympathy landed on deaf ears. Was there anyone willing to break the strike? Even being the big person that I am, my powers of intimidation didn't outweigh the fear of what might happen to someone who breaks the rules of a strike.

The sun was setting. My plane was leaving the next morning. Even if I were to get any form of transportation, no one would travel at night for fear of the Maoist rebels. Things looked pretty dismal. I started to walk down the road, dragging my two seventy-pound Samsonite suitcases (I had a lot of souvenirs!).

"You're not going to make it home," my mind kept saying. That's when a gentleman walked out of the rice paddy. Speaking perfect English, he asked, "Why are you carrying your bags?" I tried to explain my plight. "You will never make it to Katmandu," he said. It was a fact I didn't need to be reminded of. "I'm a pharmacist from India," he said, and added, "You will be sick."

"No, I don't feel sick," was my reply.

He took out a yellow piece of paper and wrote in both Nepalese and English: "Refer to the hospital for needful watchfulness." He signed it, but I couldn't read his signature.

A car drove up, but I wasn't sure where it came from. I got in—with the yellow paper. On our journey, we were stopped at twenty-one military check posts, each manned by a dozen youthful soldiers pointing their machine guns directly at me. With trepidation, I would hand them the yellow note. They would read it and, without a word, wave us on.

I did make it home on time. In my distress God helped me. I know I saw my angel. I still have the yellow paper with his signature to prove it!

Mark Harding, LLUSM class of 1990, is a specialist in emergency medicine in Kalispell, Montana.

64

With long life I will satisfy him, and show him my salvation. Psalm 91:16, RSV

The Doctor's Psalm

He that by familiar custom feels perfectly at home in private consultation with the Divine Chief of Staff shall live and practice under the protective influence of the Ultimate Authority.

The experienced say that this secret consultation with the Lord of all physicians is a refuge for calm thinking about unsolved problems and a fortified position from which to attack them. They say that their Chief never has failed this trust.

Surely He shall deliver thee from the snare of folly and from nauseating pretentiousness.

He shall cover thy fears with faith, and under His watchful wings shalt thou entrust thy doubtful diagnoses, but His standard of truth and straight thinking shall be thy therapeutic shield and buckler.

Thou shalt not be afraid for the lonely terror of emergencies by night, nor for the arrows of arrogant criticism that fly by day;

Nor for the psychoneurotic who fondly walks in his own darkness, nor for the malignant destroyers that waste life in its noonday.

A thousand shall fall into bad habits at thy side, and ten thousand into mediocrity at thy right hand, but self indulgence and indolent decay shall not come nigh thee.

Only with thine eyes shalt thou behold and see the extinction of the expedient and the consternation of the careless.

Because thou has made the Lord, which is our refuge from wrangling and resentment, even the Most High, the master of thy habitation, there shall no evil estrangement nor bitterness befall thy household or office, neither shall any plague of impurity come nigh thy dwelling. For He shall give His angels charge over thee, to keep thee in all thy daily ways from bed to bedside and back again.

They shall bear thee up with their hands at that delicately adjusted altitude between self condemnation and self confidence, so that thou fracture neither thy foot against discouragement nor thy skull against presumption.

Thou shalt tread down the lion of lust and the adder of avarice; even the young lion of loose language and the dragon of deceit shalt thou trample under foot.

The "Chief" Speaks for Himself

"Because he hath constantly preferred My consultation, therefore will I deliver him. I will take him into permanent association because he hath used My Name so well.

"He shall call upon Me, and I will answer him, and we will face trouble together, until trouble is no more.

"Then will I honor him with admission to an eternal postgraduate course in which he shall satisfy his desire to learn what he always wanted to know—how lives are really saved."

Albert F. Brown, LLUSM class of 1933, is emeritus associate professor in LLUSM department of pathology and human anatomy. He resides in Loma Linda, California. From 1961 to 1962, he was LLUSM Alumni Association president; and in 1981, he was named an LLUSM Alumni Association Honored Alumnus. This devotional originally appeared in the LLUSM Alumni Association Alumni Journal, vol. 32, no. 8, in 1961, and has been the most requested document ever published in the Alumni Journal. March 6, 2009, is his 102nd birthday.

March 7

Then shall ye call upon me, and ye shall go and pray unto me, and I will hearken unto you. Jeremiah 29:12, KJV

The knock on the examination room door was resolute. "Dr. Oliver, may I speak with you?"—the voice on the other side was unmistakably insistent. Once in the hall, the person knocking told me, "It's Dr. Hansen on the phone." I stepped into my office to take the call. With some trepidation, I lifted the receiver to my ear.

I was the junior partner in a busy practice that included 20 obstetrician and gynecology physicians, who were spread over four offices. Jim Hansen was one of the senior physicians who worked at the office farthest from mine. During private conversations at our monthly staff meetings, we shared our mutual faith; and I had been grateful to know that there was another Christian believer among my new colleagues. But why was he calling me in the middle of the day?

"Jim, what's going on?" I began. "Dan, I'm in real trouble here. I need you to pray. I don't know what else to do. We've been in the operating room for four hours. It was just a simple laparoscopic procedure, but we got into some bleeding. I called in backup surgeons. We've given her four units of blood—more is on the way. We've tried everything. Dan, I don't know what else to do. I had to take a break for a minute, and all I can think of is to ask you to pray."

"Jim, let's do that right now," I said. I had experienced miraculous answers to prayer, and I am absolutely certain that there is no problem God could not and would not solve. Thrilled at the privilege of laying this case before the Lord, I poured out my heart in urgent supplication on behalf of Dr. Hansen and his patient. When I concluded, Jim sounded somewhat heartened as he said, "Thanks, Dan. I guess I better go back to the operating room now. Keep praying."

But I never had the chance to continue my prayers. After we hung up, I headed back to my patient in the exam room. As I reached for the doorknob, the office phone rang and my nurse whispered, "It's Dr. Hansen again."

"Jim—" I managed to say before being interrupted. "Dan, you won't believe it!" The voice on the other side was ecstatic. "I went back into the operating room, and I heard one of the surgeons announce—'I think that's it!' The bleeding had just stopped. He said he didn't know what he had done, but it worked. I just had to call and tell you, even though I have no idea what just happened."

"Jim," I remonstrated, "you know what happened; God has just answered our prayers! C'mon, we've got to thank Him now." And our voices rose in joyful gratitude to the Great Physician—our God who is alive, who hears and answers our prayers, and who stopped the bleeding in the patient.

Daniel Oliver, LLUSM class of 1983, is an obstetrician and gynecologist in Napa, California.

March 8

Blessed are the poor in spirit, For theirs is the kingdom of heaven. Blessed are those who mourn, For they shall be comforted. Blessed are the meek, For they shall inherit the earth. Matthew 5:3-5, NKJV

I could cut the tension in the air with a #11 Bard blade as we entered Mary's room that day. With my team of medical students and intensive care medicine residents, I was about to reveal Mary's prognosis to her family. She had been working in her garden and cooking for her family a couple of weeks ago. And now, she was in a coma on a mechanical ventilator following a massive stroke.

Despite years of critical care specialization, one is never entirely ready for this type of discussion. My medical residents and students have heard me give this "talk" before. It would take a few minutes to deliver the message, and we would be on our way to the next patient. I began in my usual confident tone of voice. I discussed the pathophysiology of the stroke, the scientific basis for the artificial support to maintain her physiologic functions, and, finally, her prognosis: *poor, very poor.*

All eyes were focused in my direction. There was silence. Nothing but the occasional whimpering and the rustling of bodies here and there could be felt. By the family's reaction, I surmised that most of them already suspected this to be Mary's outcome. They were subdued, but all eyes were still on me. I was confused. I thought my part was done, but they appeared to be begging for more. Mary was dying from an irreversible condition that neither the neurosurgeon nor I could do anything about, and that was that . . . but I discovered my job was not yet complete.

Mary, the family's matriarch, was dying, and they were at a loss. The family was in need of emotional and spiritual care, and I was missing the cue. Many of them had not been seen or heard from for many years. I sensed that many of them didn't like each other very much. Mary would have been happy and proud of their presence. By her own example, she worked hard to raise a family that loved God with all their heart, and it was finally paying off.

In that crucial moment, I looked at each of them and recognized my task. I realized that Mary was no longer my focus. Mary would pass away, and I could not change that; and so I began to remind the family of God's everlasting love and that Mary's broken physical being was not how we should remember her. Instead, we should remember the loving wife, mother, grandmother, sister, niece, cousin, and wonderful friend; and recall all the lives she had touched.

I reached out to hold the hands of the two people standing closest to me, and I prayed: "Oh, God, send Your angel to guide and comfort this family today. Help us remember Your profound and unconditional love for each one of us. Keep Mary in Your care until Your Second Coming, and, please, may Your will be done. Amen."

There was a deep sigh in the room. Instead of the tension and arguments among the members that began the day, all of them started to embrace one another with a sense of deep love that no words can describe. In that instant, I realized that my job at Loma Linda University Medical Center was not only that of an intensivist. I could and should be a "spiritual consultant" as well. As I watched the transformation in that family, I was humbled and at the same time elated by what God helped me do for Mary's family that day.

Takkin Lo, LLUSM class of 1986, is assistant professor in LLUSM department of medicine, division of pulmonary medicine. He also has an MPH degree. He was LLUSM Alumni Association president from 2004 to 2005.

March 9

The earnest prayer of a righteous person has great power and produces wonderful results. James 5:16, NLT

Tyler walked into the office, looking tired, pale and frightened—very different from the handsome, tanned, 28-year-old landscaper I had met once at a department party. He complained of a dry cough that had begun just a week ago, but he seemed unable to shake it; and now he felt exhausted and short of breath. He denied having any fever, chills, or flu-like body aches.

After asking a few more questions about his symptoms, I moved quickly to the exam since he was clearly in respiratory distress. Other than a few scattered crackles, there was a paucity of lung findings, which surprised me. So, I sent him to get a chest x-ray, with instructions that he return to my office with the x-ray results.

A greater surprise was still to come. When he returned with the yellow film jacket, I removed the radiograph and put it on the view box. As I looked at the almost bilateral "white-out," I tried to suppress a gasp, and, instead, spoke in a matter-of-fact tone: "Tyler, you have pneumonia, and I'm going to make arrangements for you to be admitted now. I'll also call your partner, Jason, and let him know what room you're in." No matter how calm my demeanor was, I knew that Tyler probably read his own fears in my eyes.

Seeing the x-ray, I knew immediately that this was pneumocystis pneumonia (PCP) because the symptoms were so out of proportion to the x-ray. Even though Tyler and Jason had been monogamous partners for almost five years, the specter of AIDS had finally struck. During my residency at LLUMC in the early 1980s, I heard for the first time about the HTLV-III, later identified and simplified to HIV. Now a few years later, treatments were available; but mortality was still high.

Back in Tyler's room, his intravenous Bactrim was begun, and he was breathing much more comfortably with oxygen. Although his HIV test was not back, Jason (a physician himself), Tyler's mother, Tyler, and I—without saying a word—all knew the diagnosis as we stood around his bed.

It was late and I needed to get home to my family. What could I say to give them hope? Should I offer to pray with them? Finally, after giving him a hug, I settled on something simple: "Sleep well, Tyler; I'll be praying for you. Good night." Then I walked out the door.

As I started walking down the hall, Jason ran after me. "Are you not telling me something? Is Tyler about to die?" He was clearly agitated.

"No, why do you ask?" I was puzzled.

"Because you said you would be praying for him and I thought that meant he needs last rites."

I reassured him that I pray for patients who are ill or afraid or sad, not just the dying ones. Jason and Tyler, nonchurch goers, misinterpreted my gesture and were frightened. It was a lesson learned that I have never forgotten—every encounter with a patient is cross-cultural, and even a well-meaning spiritual phrase can be taken out of context.

Rebekah Wang-Cheng, LLUSM class of 1978-B, is an internist in Kettering, Ohio. She was an LLUSM Alumni Association 2003 Honored Alumna.

March 10

I waited patiently for the LORD; he turned to me and heard my cry. Psalm 40:1, NIV

He lay in his bed. He could not move, and he became steadily more "paralyzed" and stoic. The aging African-American choir director was admitted to the Jerry L. Pettis Memorial Veterans Affairs Medical Center for his progressive paralysis and an urgent stroke work up. I was a junior medical student at the time and was assigned to his case. All the testing we performed, the endless imaging and other work, showed minimal abnormalities. We could find no reason for his paralysis, except, quite likely, somatization.

After several days in the hospital, I began to uncover his story from his wife. He had not spoken to our medical team in a few days now. His wife relayed the fact that he had multiple stressful triggers, and was possibly beginning to be tired of not only directing the choir, but playing the piano and organ for the group as well. She was confident, however, that he loved his choir and his church.

One day, as he was lying motionless in bed, just staring up, I had an idea. At the time, there was a popular movie out called *The Preacher's Wife*. The soundtrack had some wonderful gospel tunes. I brought the CD and a CD player to his bedside one day after rounds. I told him I wanted to play him a song or two. He didn't look at me or acknowledge my words, the same reaction as every other day. I put the headphones on his head and proceeded to play him a song. The soloist began the beautiful melody in a clear tone with the piano:

"I love the Lord,
He heard my cry
and pitied every groan.
Long as I live, and troubles rise
I'll hasten to His throne,
I'll hasten to His throne."

For the first time, his eyes no longer stared; they closed. And with the next verse, and the full gospel choir backing the soloist, the same words continued again. Then it started. The tears began to roll down his face, and he began to cry. This was the first "break" we'd had with this gentleman since he had arrived in the hospital a few days before. His wife began to cry also, and so did I. It was at that moment, I believe, that the healing began. He had not responded to anything before, after all the medical team had said and done. That song spoke to him in a way that we could not. The words of an understanding and compassionate God in a song were what had made the difference for him. I'll never forget that moment.

Traci Williams, LLUSM class of 1997, is assistant professor in LLUSM department of pediatrics.

March 11

Christ shall give thee light. Ephesians 5:14, KJV

Brilliant afternoon sun bored down from vividly blue Tibetan sky; and bronzed, ripe barley fields spread below us. Six miles distant, encircled by towering Himalayan peaks, lay the dusty city of Lhasa. Our China Project training team had just emerged from a tour of the 600-year-old Drepung Monastery, the largest of three monasteries near Lhasa. Multistoried stone-block walls leaned into the mountainside. This enormous building once housed 10,000 lamas; but now only a few hundred lived there.

Ambling slowly along the dark hallways on several levels, we peered into prayer halls and libraries and gazed at salt-dried embalmed remains of Dalai Lamas encased in richly decorated upright coffins. Pungent aromas wafted from incense burners and the ever-burning bowls of yak butter. Passing monks turned prayer wheels. We were overwhelmed by the firm grip the worship of dead lamas had on their minds and hearts of many of God's children.

Disturbing our minds were weighty questions. "How can the Good News of a living Savior ever penetrate the centuries-old layers of tradition that so effectively obscure the eternal truth of salvation by faith in Jesus Christ?" "How can we, as health education trainers-of-trainers, break through the seemingly impenetrable cultural barriers?" Open espousal of Christianity is restricted here.

Subdued and a little downcast at the apparent human impossibility of even a little success in such an effort, we slowly followed our Tibet Health Education Institute hosts out into the eye-squinting, high-altitude sunshine.

Suddenly, at a landing, an unusual sight arrested our attention. In the middle of the square stood a small tripod of thin branches bound together at the top with cords. Hanging from the apex was a tin teakettle, which would hold about four cups of water. Wispy steam floated from the spout. But under the kettle was no fire. Like Moses before the burning bush, we ventured closer to see how a teapot could be apparently boiling with no obvious source of fire beneath it.

Puzzled wonderment gave way shortly to delightful appreciation for the ingenuity of the teapot's owner. Behind us, against the wall, sat a thin old man—cross-legged and scantily clad—holding a concave mirror about one foot in diameter. Carefully adjusting its angle and attitude to the westerly sun, he reflected the solar heat and light to the side of his teakettle, thus keeping his water hot.

Instantly there came to mind Jesus' instruction to "let your light so shine" (Matthew 5:16, KJV)—not to "make your light shine." And tumbling through my memory were Ellen G. White's various commentaries explaining that our minds, our lives, must be positioned in the right attitude to the Light of the World, our Lord Jesus Christ, in order for us to perfectly reflect His warmth and His light of love and truth.

At the conclusion of another training workshop we conducted in the northwest city of Urumqi, our host earnestly declared to the audience: "These people are Christians. They come with a love-heart to China. We should be more like Christians!" As the Bible says: "Let your light so shine before men, that they may see your good works, and glorify your Father which is in heaven" (Matthew 5:16, KJV).

Hervey Gimbel, LLUSM class of 1955, is a specialist in preventive medicine in Centralia, Washington. He also has an MPH degree. He was an LLUSM Alumni Association 2005 Honored Alumnus.

March 12

The thief comes only to steal and kill and destroy; I have come that they may have life, and have it to the full. John 10:10, NIV

The policeman demanded to see the identity card of a lady on the streets of Tsuen Wan in Hong Kong. She hurriedly pulled out of her pocket two cards and handed them to him.

"What are you giving me two cards for?" he asked. He recognized one as being the proper card, but the other was strange to him.

"Oh," she said, "One is my passport for Hong Kong, and the other is my passport to heaven." She went on to describe how she had recently obtained the other card, her baptismal certificate. She went further and told him that he should be sure and get a passport to heaven as well.

This incident was the witness of one of the enthusiastic converts in the newly organized sanitarium church. Along with fifteen others, she had followed her Lord in baptism soon after the church was created. The "right arm" of the message was relatively late in coming to Hong Kong, but it was making its influence felt.

The hospital considered itself very fortunate to have a business manager, Pastor Tan, who was also an ordained minister. During his leadership, he conducted evangelistic efforts and guided the missionary activities of the church. These new members included patients and hospital workers. The evangelistic effort—entitled "The Abundant Life"—integrated Pastor Tan's Bible lectures with presentations given by the hospital doctors so that the series was presented as the total life of a Christian—including the physical, mental, and spiritual spheres. This approach appealed to the audience so much that the attendance increased night after night.

It is worth considering the concept of spreading the gospel, as described by Ellen G. White. She named Jesus as the Head of the Church, the gospel ministry as the body, and the medical ministry as the right arm. How true and applicable that description appears in this story.

Roger Heald, LLUSM class of 1949, is an internist and resides with his wife, Jean, in Fort Myers, Florida. He also has an MPH degree from LLU. He served as a medical missionary and administrator in the Far Eastern Division of the Seventh-day Adventist Church.

March 13

You were not redeemed with perishable things like silver or gold from your futile way of life inherited from your forefathers, but with precious blood, as of a lamb unblemished and spotless, the blood of Christ. 1 Peter 1:18-19, NASB

One late night around 10:00 p.m. in Alumni Hall on the LLU campus, I was studying microscope slides of human tissue. On a walk to my locker, I accidentally dropped the box; and all the glass fixtures fell to the floor in a dramatic crash—scattering shattered glass and tissue all around me! I stood there alone in the dim school hallway thinking, "I have broken something extremely valuable, and I don't know what to do."

Then another thought hit me in the gut. "How much will this cost me?" How expensive are human cross-sections of heart and kidney? How much would it cost to replace a piece of human eye or stomach? I didn't know. I took the broken glass slides to the person I borrowed them from and said quite plainly, "I'm sorry. I broke these. I don't know what to do but to give them back to you. Do you know how much this will cost me?"

This is the bad news of life. It is the precedent of the gospel. Our lives are these glass fixtures of dead tissue broken on the floor—shattered all around us. We have broken something very valuable; we have broken it and we can't fix it. Even if we could mold the glass back together, could we afford the cost of new livers and eyes to make new fixtures? Never.

What's worse is that this human tissue called life didn't ever belong to us . . . we have broken something on loan. And we have to bring it back to the Owner and say, "I'm sorry. I broke this. My life is in this bag of broken glass. I'm giving it back to You. Will You take it?"

And Jesus said, "Yes. But do you know how much this will cost Me?"

Dear God, thank you for dying for me. Amen.

Jennifer Jung, LLUSM class of 2010, was born in the Philippines and grew up in Santa Rosa, California. March 13 is the date this incident occurred.

March 14

He that keepeth Israel shall neither slumber nor sleep. Psalm 121:4, KJV

It was an unusually calm mid-morning journey on the freeway from Loma Linda University to Ontario International Airport in Ontario, California. I was going there to meet an old friend; we were to rendezvous at the baggage carousel. We had been medical school classmates (at that time, barely out of our teens) and roommates. We were also interns at Los Angeles County-USC Medical Center in Los Angeles, California. During the eight years that she served as a missionary doctor in India, we remained friends through frequent correspondence.

I didn't want to keep her waiting. Having arrived early at the airport, I turned off to a resting spot at a local mall. While waiting, I have to admit I "nodded off" a bit; but thankfully while I was sleeping, God was not.

I heard friendly male voices and observed three men garbed in white work clothes, followed by a small white truck. Spontaneously, I had a strong urge to check out my ignition. When I did, the battery was dead! Hastily, I exited the auto and rushed a few steps to the passing gentlemen and sought their help.

Obligingly, they quickly swarmed around my car. They had the appropriate working cables, and their resuscitation efforts were successful. To my relief, I made our meeting at the airport on time. While this may appear to be an insignificant event, to me it was a miracle from God that demonstrated He is always watching. Thank you, Father! Thanks, thanks, heavenly protectors!

Jean Marie Hoag, LLUSM class of 1941, is a child psychiatrist. March 14 was the birthday of her late husband, Elvin W. Hoag, LLUSM class of 1947.

March 15

Whatsoever ye shall ask in prayer, believing, ye shall receive. Matthew 21:22, KJV

Suddenly, it stopped! That lancing pain piercing my chest with every respiration had finally stopped. I was only eleven years old, but up to this time I had been praying to die. I was lying in a hospital bed on Long Island, New York, and it was during Thanksgiving vacation; we were away from our Takoma Park, Maryland, home.

The year was 1931 before the use of antibiotics. X-rays had revealed that one lung, and all but one-fourth of my other lung, was filled with consolidation of lobar pneumonia. The physicians had just told my parents they could do no more. At this news, an immediate wire was sent to the Seventh-day Adventist Church headquarters, stating my problem and requesting prayer.

And then my pain stopped. Later, it was found that their hour of prayer coincided exactly with my instantaneous health. I had been healed by the power of prayer! It was then that I decided to devote my life to medicine.

Ever since that time, I have seen God's guiding hand and have realized that, "Ask and ye shall receive," actually means, "Ask and you'll get My attention, but what you receive will be My will—do with it what you can."

Phyllis L. Presley, LLUSM class of 1945, is a family practitioner in Alhambra, California.

March 16

He will call upon Me, and I will answer him; I will be with him in trouble; I will rescue him and honor him. Psalm 91:15, NASB

On March 13, 2007, I left Iraq after a six month uneventful deployment as a senior physician at a medical clinic near Tikrit. In Iraq, I was given a book about Psalm 91, and its application to life. I found my faith challenged to really believe. I met many soldiers who frequently faced danger and death, but I was never in danger; so how could this chapter be relevant to me? After a stopover in Kuwait and a long uneventful flight, we arrived at Fort Dix in New Hanover, New Jersey, early in the morning. I was looking forward to being home the afternoon of March 16.

We then found that no tickets had been purchased for the continuing flights home. Some would get to fly immediately, and the rest would have to wait until a single flight was available for all who were going to one location. This was awful news!

I called the travel agency and found flights available the same afternoon. My reservations were made; and as my orders were being sent by fax, I left on a bus for the airport. As I attempted to check in, however, I found the reservation had been made but not paid. No problem. My government credit card would work. Oh no! It was expired!

At the USO in the airport, using free phones and computer access—and after sending faxes three times and pictures of my orders three times—I finally had tickets to Dallas, Texas. I had missed three reservations, and this was the last flight to Texas. I called my wife, Nancy, and asked her to drive the three hours to Dallas to pick me up. I wouldn't be coming into Killeen.

I had only a half hour to get to the gate for a flight to Dallas. The security lines were very long, but I was sent to the front of the line. As I gave my ticket to board, a second clerk grabbed the ticket and told me to step aside. What now?! Good news—my seat now was first class! At that point, the tears came. It was a great flight, and Nancy met me at the bottom of the escalator. I was HOME! We drove to Killeen, and we were in our house at 12:30 a.m. on March 17.

In my trouble, He had completely fulfilled Psalm 91:15. He had rescued me. In fact, Psalm 91 applies in all situations to those who abide in the shelter of the Most High. May we not take any situation into our own hands but abide in Him.

Clifford D. Friesen, LLUSM class of 1969, is a pediatrician specializing in allergy and immunology. He resides in Killeen, Texas. March 16 is the date this incident occurred.

March 17

Let the same mind be in you that was in Christ Jesus. Philippians 2:5, NRSV

Recently in my reading, I came across the idea that we *are* the decisions that we have made. And again, I *am* what I do. There seems to be much truth in both of these statements; however, is there more to it?

Scriptures and other references remind us constantly that our Christian objective is to become more like Christ each day. Our lives are the only Bible some people will ever read. Romans 8:29 tells us we are to be "conformed to the image of His Son." Further, 2 Corinthians 3:18 (RSV) suggests that we "are being changed into his likeness" by the "Lord who is the Spirit."

How does this work? Many Bible texts are helpful in this regard; however, Romans 12:2 (NRSV) to me is a key thought: "Be transformed by the renewing of your minds, so that you may discern what is the will of God—what is good and acceptable and perfect." Along these lines, I saw on the Internet (original source unknown) an interesting sequence that goes like this:

Watch your thoughts: they often become words.
Watch your words: they often become actions.
Watch your actions: they often lead to habits.
Watch your habits: they make your character.
Watch your character: it becomes your destiny.

Ellen G. White in *Christ's Object Lessons*, page 332, notes that the only thing that we can take to heaven is our character.

How do we gain this transformation? It is through Jesus (and His Spirit). "And the peace of God, which surpasses all understanding, will guard your hearts and minds in Christ Jesus. Finally, beloved, whatever is true, whatever is honorable, whatever is just, whatever is pure, whatever is pleasing, whatever is commendable, if there is any excellence and if there is anything worthy of praise, think about these things" (Philippians 4:7-8, NRSV). "The one who began a good work among you will bring it to completion by the day of Jesus Christ" (Philippians 1:6, NRSV).

Ralph J. Thompson Jr., LLUSM class of 1951, is emeritus professor in LLUSM department of surgery. He was LLUSM Alumni Association 2005 Alumnus of the Year. He also received the LLUSM Distinguished Service Award in 1993 and the LLU Distinguished Humanitarian Award in 1996.

I have told you this so that my joy may be in you and that your joy may be complete. John 15:11, NIV

S omeone has said, "Smell and enjoy the rose in the vase, rather than looking at the dust on the table."

It is frightening to realize that it was nearly thirty-seven years ago, after completing a nephrology fellowship in Dallas, Texas, that I, with my family, returned to LLU to join the teaching and practicing faculty at the School of Medicine. Little did I imagine that the next nearly four decades would bring me immeasurable fulfillment— many more roses!

Being born and brought up in New York state, I was "expected" to return east and not follow in the footsteps of so many medical graduates of LLUSM, who elect to remain in the land of sunshine and "milk and honey." In retrospect, God had other plans for my life than the beckoning eastern shores. Thus, eight years postgraduation, I found myself caring for patients and interfacing with some of the most beautiful people in the world . . . the medical students of LLU!

Words cannot capture the joy and excitement I have experienced mentoring students (now literally in the hundreds) over the decades. A new, bright, fresh, and eager crop appears year after year, representing students from all walks of life. Some even have different religious persuasions than mine; but most are Christian, seeking not only to learn the typical "nuts and bolts" of becoming a physician, but also wanting to become a "to make a man whole" physician in society (a unique breed).

I have flashbacks of seeing sixty-to-eighty medical students, wall to wall (folding chairs, couches, on the floor), in our living room, worshipping on a Friday evening . . . voices accompanied by guitars in praise worship, personal sharing, the opening of the Word, and collectively praying. I have flashbacks of students I have encountered as part of the mentor-mentee program on campus. In this program, on a voluntary basis, a faculty member is paired up with a freshman medical student.

Other "outside the classroom" experiences have been many—such as traveling one-on-one with a medical student to a mission hospital in Trinidad and experiencing mission life together, or traveling to a war-torn area, or visiting an impoverished family in Afghanistan with a previous mentee. What memories!

Let me return to my initial, hopefully provocative, statement. In our personal lives, in churches, in businesses, in politics, in institutions, there is, if we are honest, some unattractive "dust on the table." We humans, even would-be saints, can become fixated on the "dust on the table" and fail to see, appreciate, or smell and enjoy, the rose in the vase. From my vantage point as a faculty member of some thirty-seven years at LLUSM, I see not just one rose to enjoy and smell, but a large bouquet!

I invite you this morning to pray for LLUSM—its administration, faculty, alumni, and students. To the leadership of LLUSM, I say, "Be strong and do not give up, for your work will be rewarded" (2 Chronicles 15:7, NIV). To that I would add, "Lord, may I refuse to dwell on the negative and reveal the positive aspects of life."

Bob Soderblom, LLUSM class of 1963, is associate professor in LLUSM department of medicine, division of nephrology. He was LLUSM Alumni Association president from 2001 to 2002 and was an LLUSM Alumni Association 1998 Honored Alumnus. In 2006, he was LLUSM Teacher of the Year.

March 19

Thy kingdom come. Thy will be done in earth, as it is in heaven. Give us this day our daily bread. And forgive us our debts, as we forgive our debtors. And lead us not into temptation, but deliver us from evil: For thine is the kingdom, and the power, and the glory, for ever. Amen. Matthew 6:10-13, KJV

On National Match Day, my daughter, Anna, LLUSM class of 2008, and her classmates were learning—after much exploration, traveling, and interviewing—where they had been matched for training programs. A computer had determined the outcomes—based on the matches between the students who had ranked their residency programs in order of priority and the training program that had done the same. For Anna, many questions arose during this process. "Where is God in this decision making?" "Which field fits me best?" "How will this choice affect the important people in my life?" "How will it affect my spiritual life?"

In addition, at age 20-something, there is often little practical spiritual experience with the role God is willing to play in our decision making. Thus the struggle with other questions: "Will God see to it I get my first choice? I really think it's the best." "I can't think of anything more perfect." "What if I'm making the wrong choice. Will God somehow stop me or change my mind?"

In 1978, I had similar worries during the matching process. I was/am married to Fred—a classmate who was also matching, thus complicating matters. We matched for our internship year, but not for our subsequent residencies. Fred had chosen internal medicine while I looked forward to a career in obstetrics/gynecology (ob/gyn).

During our internships, my husband, who had never tried to influence me, came to me asking that I not reapply for ob/gyn. He felt it would be difficult for me to combine that particular subspecialty with family, and it was with family in mind that he was choosing radiology rather than a surgical subspecialty. Family was important; yet his words stung my "liberated," independent heart.

Was God redirecting me? I had placed my life in His hands and prayed for His direction all along the way. I didn't hate what I was doing, and, frankly, had to admit that lifestyle was more of an issue than I had realized. Could I fulfill God's plan doing internal medicine? Did God intervene because I had asked Him to lead? Was He giving me some perspective (wisdom) that I hadn't had in 1978? Yes, ALL of that was true.

Now, years later, I am satisfied with the balance I've managed between my practice as an internist and my family. I have been able to share God's love with my patients in so many ways. In order to tweak my life and follow God's leading, it was necessary to make choices along the way—choices that became easier because I understood that God works in many ways to lead those who trust Him. He has been with me as I made good and bad choices, and He has brought joy and emotional/spiritual growth from them. I am reminded of the words of Plato: "O ye gods, grant us what is good whether we pray for it or not, but keep evil from us even though we pray for it."

Consult God daily. Do your homework. Replace worry and doubt with faith. Place your life plans in God's capable hands—AND RELAX. God can handle the stress.

Polly Cinquemani Dengel, LLUSM class of 1978-B, is an internist and lives with her husband, Fred, LLUSM class of 1978-B, in Avon, Ohio. March 19 is National Match Day in 2009.

Thy word is a lamp unto my feet, and a light unto my path. Psalm 119:105, KJV

If the Christian physician is to be properly implemented for his sacred calling, he must have a mature devotional life. By that I mean he must know how to meditate and pray. The small child "says prayers"; the adolescent prays mainly for things; and the adult prays for insight, divine guidance, and the Christian spirit.

Many a person never gets beyond the adolescent stage in his prayer life—and some not far beyond the infant stage. Such a devotional life will never be adequate for the adult professional person, any more than the clothing worn in the teens would fit the mature figure.

This matter of prayer and devotion involves a mature concept of God. One does not come by accident to an adequate understanding of God. It takes thought and prayer and spiritual insight to come to know a heavenly Father, personal yet spiritual, transcendent yet immanent, "in him we live, and move, and have our being" (Acts 17:28, KJV). The Christian medical student [and physician] must grow in prayer, in spiritual thinking, in worship. This can be done only by the practice of these virtues, by a personal acquaintance with Christ, and by a growing familiarity with the Bible and the best devotional literature.

The second essential of religious training I would suggest is a proper understanding of the Bible. By this I do not mean that the student will become a finished biblical scholar. The most learned theologian realizes that the Bible is a "boundless, shoreless sea." The person engaged in medical ministry must have a proper appreciation of the Bible and must know how to use the inspired Book. It must be to him more than a collection of proof texts. It must be illumination—"a lamp unto his feet and a light unto his path." He must know how to analyze a paragraph, chapter, or book of the Bible and how to avoid incorrect interpretations of its message.

Henry Ward Beecher said: "God's word is a vast forest; and as a man can build, out of timber that is growing in the forest, a hut, or a common mansion, or a palatial residence, so out of the word of God man can build a poor theology, or a rich theology, or a glorious one, according as he is skilled in his selections."

The medical student [and physician] must learn how to find God's message from the Bible for the discouraged, the sick, the dying—and for himself. He must know how to find moral values in the Book and how to apply them to living. He must understand the redemptive message of Christ, he must make it his own, and he must be able to mediate it to others. Such a grasp of the Bible can no more be achieved without thought, study, and training than can anatomy or pathology.

Norval F. Pease (1910-1995) was a Seventh-day Adventist educator, theologian, speaker, and author. This devotional was taken from comments made by him on a panel discussing "Relationship of Medicine to Religion" in March 1949. This devotional originally appeared in the April 1949 issue of the LLUSM Alumni Association Alumni Journal.

March 21

And the prayer of faith will save the sick, and the Lord will raise him up. And if he has committed sins, he will be forgiven. James 5:15, NKJV

I t was my last weekend on trauma call at Riverside County Regional Medical Center in Moreno Valley, California. At 11:00 p.m. on Friday night, the hospital operator announced that a level "A" trauma was en route to the emergency room. The medical student, resident, and I arrived just as a young man, splattered with blood, was wheeled in while paramedics were giving him oxygen. They said his heart had stopped two minutes before arrival. He had two large stab wounds in his left chest.

External massage was begun, and intravenous fluids and blood were given on the way to the operating room. His left chest was opened. Blood was coming from a hole in the pericardium, which was opened further to relieve the tamponade. There was a large hole in his heart, on which I was able to place two fingers and temporarily control bleeding in order to allow resuscitation. The laceration was then closed; and he was taken to the intensive care unit—very cold, with fixed and dilated pupils that signified brain hypoxia.

Many prayers were offered that Sabbath. He was returned to the operating room Sabbath afternoon to evacuate clots from his chest, and from that point he made a rapid recovery. After having received forty units of blood during his ordeal, he was discharged one week later with normal brain and cardiac function. After his recovery, he told me that while in the ambulance, as he felt his life slipping away, he offered a simple prayer to God to save him. All the human effort only aided the Lord in allowing Jerry to live. This was truly a great miracle, but a greater miracle occurred when Jerry gave his heart to Jesus.

Dr. Alexis Carrel, known as the father of modern vascular surgery, made the following statement: "Prayer is as real a force as terrestrial gravity. As a physician, I have seen men, after all other therapy has failed, lifted out of disease and melancholy by the serene effort of prayer. It is the only power in the world that seems to overcome the so-called laws of nature. Occasions in which prayer has dramatically done this have been termed miracles. But a quieter miracle takes place hourly in the hearts of men and women who have discovered that prayer supplies them with a steady flow of sustaining power in their daily lives." To this I say, "Amen."

God has a role for each of us to play in patient care. God directed many individuals, including the forty anonymous people who donated blood, to help Jerry survive. We are all part of the body of Christ in giving love and care to all of God's children. As we do this, we will fulfill the Loma Linda University motto: "To make man whole."

Clifton Reeves, LLUSM class of 1960, is professor in LLUSM department of surgery. He was president of the Walter E. Macpherson Society from 1989 to 1990, and LLUSM Alumni Association president from 1983 to 1984. He was an LLUSM Alumni Association 1985 Honored Alumnus, and was named LLU Alumnus of the Year in 2000.

Don't shuffle along, eyes to the ground, absorbed with things right in front of you. Look up, and be alert to what is going on around Christ—that's where the action is. Colossians 3:1-2, MSG

I was running late for an early-morning meeting at Loma Linda University. After carefully crossing Anderson Street, I took out my note pad and began to jot down a couple of ideas. Having traveled the route from my office to Loma Linda University Medical Center many times, I knew every bump and crack from memory. Squinting above my glasses, I checked my position—directly ahead was LLUMC. In several yards, I would take a right just east of the Schuman Pavilion. Once again I looked down at my paper.

In the distance ahead of me, I heard an unfamiliar, yet rhythmic sound—clunk . . . scrape . . . scrape; clunk . . . scrape . . . scrape. As I continued on, the rhythmic sound grew more pronounced. Glancing up, I saw the source—an elderly lady, withered from years of service, clutching a walker. She would raise the walker, thrust it forward a few inches, and let it fall to the sidewalk—clunk . . . her two feet slowly followed—scrape . . . scrape. On occasion she would pause, as if to take a breath. Then the process would begin again—clunk . . . scrape . . . scrape.

Trimming my gait slightly to the right, I again turned my thoughts to the meeting. And the rhythmic sounds continued—clunk . . . scrape . . . scrape; clunk . . . scrape . . . scrape. But then there was silence. Looking up again, I could make out her frail features: her bony, quivering hands and fingers were twisted around the walker handles.

Even though her face was wrinkled, her cheeks pale, her shoulders stooped, and her legs bowed, there was a riveting determination in her eyes, set below thick eyebrows, which grabbed my attention. The countenance about her channeled face gave me pause. As I strode past her, she gave me a snaggle-toothed grin and, with a chirpy voice, spoke to me.

"'Tis a beautiful day!"

I hadn't noticed. Was it a beautiful day? I stopped dead in my tracks and took in my surroundings. Birds in nearby trees were singing their morning tune. In the distance, a dog was barking. On the nearby lawn, a toddler, squealing with delight, was trying to outrun his dad. Taking a deep breath while tucking the notes back in my pocket, I looked up. The azure sky was clear. The scent of orange blossoms was heavy in the morning air. Overhead a red-tailed hawk was soaring, riding the gentle morning breeze. To my right, the undulating flight of an acorn woodpecker as it glided over the parking lot caught my eye. Yes, spring was in the air. IT WAS A BEAUTIFUL DAY!

As I neared my destination, I thought of the words of the psalmist—"This is the day the Lord has made; let us rejoice and be glad in it" (Psalm 118:24, NIV).

Dennis E. Park has been executive director of LLUSM Alumni Association since 1993. He has an MA degree in management and finance from University of Redlands in Redlands, California. On March 22, 1970, he began his working career at LLU Foundation as a cost controller.

March 23

Therefore do not worry about tomorrow, for tomorrow will worry about itself. Each day has enough trouble of its own. Matthew 6:34, NIV

Growing up on an island in the southern part of the Philippines, at the center of the Equatorial Convergence Zone, I was definitely exposed to all sorts of rain and typhoons. I remember once when the roof on our first house, made from leaves of the Nipa palm, was blown away by a strong gust of wind. I was so scared that my mom told me to hide under our little dining table as the strong surge of rain came rushing in. We ended up sleeping at my cousin's house, where we watched helplessly as the typhoon whipped our little Nipa house furiously.

It could rain for days in my hometown, Catarman. I remember being very bored inside our house during these times. All I could do was look outside the window in dismay as the rain hammered everything in its path.

But no matter how long the rain cast its gloom over our island, it would always end somehow. And after the rain, the sunshine would surely appear. We would see butterflies proudly flapping their wings, as all the flowers bloomed once again. Life would go on.

Rain in our lives will surely cast its gloom sometimes, but that's the best time to retreat and take shelter within God's loving arms. He will stay with you until the sun rises once again; and, like the butterflies, we can proudly spread our wings and face the world. There is no need to fear what tomorrow might bring because flowers are always plentiful around God's garden called LIFE.

JD Sevilla is web and graphic manager for LLUSM. He served in the United States Navy.

March 24

Surely our griefs He Himself bore, And our sorrows He carried. Isaiah 53:4, NASB

It had been the worst of days, weeks, actually, for that matter; residents on vacation or out sick, 24-hour call every other day, the clinics overflowing, the emergency room drowning, and our patience running dry. A county hospital, known in its heydey as a tuberculosis sanitarium, was now a center for the training of diverse medical specialties. Here, many shared the macabre with the mundane under sallow fluorescent lights that highlighted the patched-upon-patched plaster walls and history-laden linoleum.

This particular day was playing out like chapters from *Williams Obstetrics* or *Novak's Gynecology*: preterm labor, pelvic inflammatory disease, incomplete miscarriage, and on and on. As the on-call third-year obstetrics/gynecology resident, I turned the pages of my day quickly—speed reading from one near disaster to the next.

The coolness of the recovery room greeted me as I helped wheel a patient into the room. The anticipation of some "down time" vanished, however, with the stern appearance of the medical records supervisor. Her presence yet again reminded me of my infamy—I led all departments for the most incomplete charts! The supervisor advised me of my impending suspension, if some fifty-five waiting charts were not completed that same day, or I would soon have another summons from my department chief, "El Jefe."

Preparing to respond with injured dignity and grace, I did nothing more than burst into tears and run sobbing from the room, finding solace under a desk in the dark doctors' dictation room. My woe was complete. Past remarks made by other department chiefs, who weren't as yet enchanted with me (or women in medicine, for that matter) played in my head.

Sitting there on the dark floor, I felt that I had utterly failed and brought not only disgrace to my department but also to my gender as well. And then, into my misery walked El Jefe, calling, "Where is my resident?" His thick Spanish accent made the summons all the more soothing and endearing. El Jefe, a man who carried himself with quiet dignity, treated his patients with great empathy, and with his gargantuan guffaw filled an aging hospital corridor with hilarity. A true Renaissance man, he not only excelled at medicine but also read and wrote in several languages—digesting art, cinema, and the antiquities.

It was this revered great man, having received an update from the shocked supervisor, who found me sobbing on the floor. He brought me to my feet, dusted me off, and announced that he would take my house calls that evening. I was to go home, get some sleep, and see medical records in the morning. He would take my place until my delinquency was corrected. As gratitude flooded my soul, resolve stiffed my spine, and self-doubt fluttered away. I knew then that I was going to make it. Someone believed in me!

Over the years, I have met many a gifted doctor, accused of brilliance and/or great skill. But none have garnered a fraction of the regard I have for this man. He taught by example, expecting no more from us than from himself. Many other doctors and nurses today share my regard of him for seeing them through the years of training. I will never forget our revered El Jefe, Wilbert Gonzalez-Angulo, LLUSM class of 1967.

There is Another who has taken our "call," who has taken our shame of delinquency. No matter how unworthy, whatever the duty, He has stood in our place so that we might prosper and have a lighted path on which to walk.

Ruth Koch, LLUSM class of 1980-B, resides in Riverside, California. March 24 is her birthday.

March 25

Instruct those who are rich in this present world not to be conceited or to fix their hope on the uncertainty of riches, but on God, who richly supplies us with all things to enjoy. 1 Timothy 6:17, NASB

D are I admit to a birth with the proverbial silver spoon in my mouth? As the middle child in the family, I felt loved and cared for in every way, even to the nurturing of my Christian faith. My mind swims with a rich heritage of memories: John Harvey Kellogg, MD, dressed in a white suit, bicycling down the streets of Battle Creek, Michigan; my baptism in the very church where Ellen G. White preached; Uncle Arthur Maxwell telling character-changing stories to the young ones during Seventh-day Adventist Autumn Council; marching to music during Saturday night socials in the Battle Creek Sanitarium—later to be turned into the Percy Jones General Hospital during World War II.

Medically trained relatives on both Mom and Dad's sides of the family left little uncertainty as to my career choice. College days sped by with close associations monitored by faculty families whose own youth became my companions. Soon I progressed to Loma Linda University for further training, further blessings, and Christian friendship and mentoring—even to romance and marriage.

Clinical training intensified as we tackled medical specialization. My mind floods with appreciation as I recall the clinicians willing to share their expertise with the yet "green" medical students. And too soon our senior year arrived, and with it a blur of life choices—where to apply for further training, where to locate in the real world, and what plans did God have in mind for this team of almost physicians?

And then, without apparent warning, the "bomb" was dropped on me—the come-uppance. I was faced with a dreadful assignment of SIX EXTRA case studies, all to be completed pronto—or no graduation, no promotion. How could this happen to a conscientious, accurate, studious, meticulous, very apprehensive young person? I was mortified! Why me? The attending physician on my service perceived my attitude as "less than becoming" for that of a Loma Linda University School of Medicine graduate.

I could NOT believe it. I had sailed through my young life as the "fair-haired child," only now to be classified as a failure—for this is how I perceived the onerous assignment. I spent hours seriously applying all of my newly acquired skills and submitted those case studies after much prayer and fasting. I was not to be charged as high-minded!

In the process, I learned to depend upon my Heavenly Parent for wisdom and a new attitude of courage and stamina. Yes, this passage is so true: "As many as I love, I rebuke and chasten" (Revelation 3:19, KJV). Equally true is 1 Timothy 6:17—I was supplied "with all things to enjoy."

Shirley O. Thiel, LLUSM class of 1953-A, resides in Fairfield, Washington. She practiced for more than forty years with her late husband, Francis A. Thiel, LLUSM class of 1953-A. She is the mother of four and the grandmother of seven.

March 26

For he shall give his angels charge over thee, to keep thee in all thy ways. They shall bear thee up in their hands, lest thou dash thy foot against a stone. Psalm 91:11-12, KJV

Today is my birthday. I am glad and grateful to be alive. It could easily have been otherwise.

Decades ago, my two now-adult children were preschoolers, asleep in the back of the station wagon I was driving. I don't recall our destination. I do remember that it was a warm, sunny afternoon. My wife dozed in the front passenger seat. To facilitate their rest, the radio and 8-track cartridge player were silent.

I have nearly fallen asleep at the wheel a number of times during my years of driving. Usually I have some warning, a prodrome—in which event I put down the window, turn on the radio, or pull off the road. If another driver is with me, we switch places.

This particular day, for some unknown reason, the transition between wakefulness and sleep was rapid and imperceptible. One moment I was awake. The next I was not. This had never happened before, nor has it since.

I was awakened by the blaring of a car horn. I looked toward the sound of the horn and saw a man motioning me toward the side of the road. I slowed to a stop on the shoulder. He got out of his car and came over to me, obviously angry.

"Why were you tailgating me?!" he demanded in a loud voice.

"What do you mean?" I asked.

"You were right on my bumper," he said. "You couldn't have been more than a few feet from me, for quite awhile."

"I'm sorry," I mumbled. I couldn't bring myself to tell him I had fallen asleep at the wheel.

Only partially mollified, he stomped off—leaving me to shiver in the cold sweat that, despite the day's heat, had enveloped me.

I have pondered this incident a number of times since that day, and wondered why my family and I were saved from accident, or worse. Years before, in college, a classmate, driving home with several other young men, fell asleep while driving and struck a tree, killing all four occupants. I am not convinced that I, or my family, deserved to live more than they.

No less a thinker than Albert Einstein opined that there are two ways of viewing life. One is to believe that there are no miracles. Another is to believe that everything is a miracle.

Miracles have been wrought in my life.

Sam Chen, LLUSM class of 1965, is a diagnostic radiologist in La Crescenta, California. March 26 is his birthday.

March 27

God is faithful; he will not let you be tempted beyond what you can bear. But when you are tempted, he will also provide a way out so that you can stand up under it. 1 Corinthians 10:13, NIV

I am grateful and privileged that, over the years, I have had the opportunity to work with many amazing patients at Loma Linda University Medical Center. Sadly, by the time I see them, most of the patients I treat are at a most challenging time of life. This circumstance is especially true for relatively young patients, who have their expectant future lives completely altered when they are diagnosed with a catastrophic disease such as cancer.

Unlike surgery or pediatrics, oncology is a practice where a complete cure is rare. Even in an era of rapid progress for cancer therapy, the miracle of medicine is not usually the answer for most of my patients. As you can imagine, I am in a medical discipline where the doctor doesn't always have the solution; yet everyday I witness amazing strength and faith in my patients.

These patients have already struggled to try to accept their dreadful diagnosis of "cancer," and they hope that I can cure them. But, instead, I must tell them that treatment is not at all easy or even likely to be successful. What's more, I must tell them that if the treatment is not successful, then death is the consequence.

As I prepare treatment plans for my patients, I realize, invariably, that I can only provide limited solutions and comfort for them. How can I ever truly comfort my desperate patients? In contrast to my expectation of looking for a sense of hopelessness in their eyes when I inform them of bad news, many have no fear or worry on their faces. "That is truly amazing," I contemplate in my heart. And yet, the answer is soon forthcoming; they lack fear because of their faith in our God.

It is easy to praise our God when things are going well in our life, and a church gathering can be like a weekend party. This is not the scenario in the cancer wards. Yet, God's words are powerful; and they are tested again and again without failure under such circumstances.

Just like one dear psychiatrist friend used to tell me, antidepressants cannot cure depression. They may protect you from "falling down" too much, but they will not bring happiness and joy. Only God brings true peace and happiness and rebuilds our souls.

I am fortunate to work with many of my patients who are "bearing" cancer. Their strength, a reflection of the grace that comes from our Father, carries me and brings hope to my personal life. I tell my patients, "You are my teachers," and, "Thank you for allowing me to work with you!"

CS Chen is professor in LLUSM department of medicine and is head of the division of hematology and oncology. He received a PhD degree in mole oncology from University of Minnesota in 1992 and a medical degree from China Medical College in Taichung, Taiwan, in 1985. March 27 is the birthday of his wife, Linda.

March 28

I will answer them before they even call to me. While they are still talking about their needs, I will go ahead and answer their prayers! Isaiah 65:24, NLT

The end of March 1978 was a time of increasing frustration and desperation because I could not find my red data booklet with the written expenses for the previous year. I needed it to fill out the income tax return due April 15.

We had moved to Auburn, California, a few months earlier to be involved with the beginning of the live-in NEWSTART® Health Education program at Weimar Institute. Things were topsy-turvy as we lived out of boxes.

Over the previous weeks I had searched off and on for the booklet without success. April first, I turned into Mr. Anxious. At lunch I asked my wife, Irma, to kneel with me and pray that I might find the booklet. Just as we were kneeling down, the phone rang. The lady caller wanted a home consultation about a nutritious diet for her daughter who was recuperating from a serious car accident. I told her I would stop at their place on the way home from work at the office of Zane Kime, LLUSM class of 1966, who was teaching me to treat the chronic degenerative diseases with God's natural remedies. Irma and I then prayed.

I picked up my doctor's bag from under the bathroom sink and went to the office. After the house call, back in the car, I opened the bag wide to put the stethoscope back in, and there at the bottom of the bag was my red data booklet! I had put it there at Christmas time when I had taken the bag on our ski trip.

God knew I would not have looked in that doctor's bag until our next trip to the mountains the following Christmas time, if then. He was working through the call of the lady before we prayed. God delights to answer prayer. What an awesome God to give us the desire of our heart, even in trivial matters. I know there is a God who cares and delights to show Himself strong. He is the Omnipotent, Omniscient, and Omnipresent Lord God Jehovah! Praise be to Jesus our Lord and Savior! We have found God's word in Isaiah 65:24 to be true.

George Chen, LLUSM class of 1964, is an ophthalmologist in Lodi, California.

March 29

And Jesus went about all Galilee, teaching in their synagogues, preaching the gospel of the kingdom, and healing all manner of sickness and all manner of disease among the people. Matthew 4:23, KJV

About 10:00 a.m. one morning, a truck stopped in front of Mindanao Sanitarium and Hospital in the Philippines, and an 18-year-old boy was carried in on a door, used as a make-shift stretcher. The upper end of his right femur was sticking out of his pants and pointing upward.

He had fallen out of a mango tree, under which a water buffalo was tied. The upper end of the broken femur gouged deeply into the mud where the buffalo had stood. To attend to him were Mrs. Peter Donton, the anesthetist, Dr. Arturo Lasta, and me. Fortunately, the men who brought him in had not attempted to put the protruding bone back in place.

After cutting off his clothes, Dr. Lasta and I began to clean the bone and remove the mud from the marrow cavity. We cleaned and cleaned and cleaned. We did not use any antiseptic, only saline and cotton applicators. He then received the anesthetic, as we put the bone back in the flesh.

We covered the bone over with a little muscle, so it would not be exposed to air, and made the wound a bit wider. We did not suture the wound, but put him in a Balkan frame in traction. We followed the course with x-rays and after two weeks Dr. Lasta did a wound closure. The Lord blessed the treatment.

Six weeks later, he walked out of the hospital on his own, without crutches! Once more, we experienced the Lord's healing and blessing.

Willis G. Dick, LLUSM class of 1941, is a retired family practitioner and surgeon who resides in Bakersfield, California. He was an LLUSM Alumni Association 1971 Honored Alumnus. He spent twenty years as a missionary in Southeast Asia.

March 30

For surely I know the plans I have for you, says the LORD, plans for your welfare and not for harm, to give you a future with hope. Jeremiah 29:11, NRSV

Just as my junior year of medical school at Loma Linda University was drawing to a close, I suddenly realized that I had absolutely no clue as to what I was going to do with the rest of my life! I began to reflect over my previous rotations and weighed my options about what field would be a good fit for me. As I thought about the pros and cons of each one, I panicked; I realized I didn't really want any of those!

Fortunately, I had scheduled myself for a two-week elective in anesthesiology and decided to put off worrying until after I had finished that. I was planning to go back home and relax. Once at home, I decided to go to church before I started my rotation. But I couldn't get thoughts about my future prospects out of my head.

While chatting with my friends before the service started, I was introduced to a gentleman who had just started attending church there. He and I began talking about medicine, and I learned that he was an anesthesiologist who had worked in the United States Air Force for many years. He asked general questions about where I was going to school and if I had picked a specialty. When I told him LLU and that I hadn't decided, he smiled politely and wished me luck.

The pastor asked us to focus on things in our lives that were bothering us and to pray. As I bowed my head, I felt a gentle tap on my shoulder. I turned around to see the doctor handing me a piece of paper. He then whispered, "I felt impressed to write these words to you." As he returned to his seat, I looked at the words he had written on what appeared to be a postcard. I read:

> "Gird up the loins of your mind
> Gird up the loins of your heart my Daughter . . .
> Fear not, for I AM with you
> To show myself strong on your behalf
> Because your heart is loyal to ME, says the Lord Jesus."

I smiled as I read his kind words. As I turned the postcard over, my jaw almost hit the floor in disbelief! Chills ran up and down my spine. It was a Nathan Greene painting, like the ones so familiar to me in the waiting area in Loma Linda University Medical Center. What was even more eerie was that the painting pictured was the same one my Mom cherished. Since I was a child, and whenever she saw this particular painting, it reminded us both of how God had a special plan for my life.

I was completely overcome. Here I had been worrying about what I was going to do with my life, when God already had it all figured out. How? Look at the sequence: I almost didn't schedule my elective in Colorado, almost didn't go to church, unexpectedly met a stranger who felt impressed to write significant words on a postcard he just happened to have with him. All we have to do is ask and listen. God knew from day one that I was supposed to be an anesthesiologist; it just took a postcard and a stranger for me to realize that He had it all under control and that all I had to do was follow!

Kellie Stivers, LLUSM class of 2009, is from Colorado and graduated from Union College in Lincoln, Nebraska, with a degree in biology. This incident occurred on March 30.

March 31

Cast all your anxiety on him because he cares for you. 1 Peter 5:7, NIV

I have been caring for Mary for multiple problems, including overweight and high blood pressure. I would like to report that she has lost the excess weight, exercises daily, and eats a Mediterranean diet, but this is not true! Not surprising, the absence of lifestyle change has not helped her blood pressure either. Recently she agreed to begin pharmacologic therapy for her hypertension. Despite this effort, her office blood pressure was unaffected.

Mary takes her blood pressure at home and at her last visit reported: "In the morning my blood pressure is good, about 118 over 70; but after work, it is much higher—165 over 98." "I gather you are relaxed in the morning and that work is stressful and demanding; am I right?" I asked. She agreed.

"Why don't you tell me about your work day?" She has many conflicting demands. Although she works rapidly and is efficient, people continue to want more. Despite her best efforts, she cannot meet all the expectations and please each person who wants her to quickly finish a personal project first. This troubles her. "I try so hard to do better; I just can't," she admitted.

"Tell me, Mary, if you were phenomenally efficient, did everything just right, and were totally on top of everything, would the impossible demands continue?" "Yes!" she responded with surprise.

"I hear you saying that regardless of what you do, nothing will be quite adequate. It seems to me that your work situation is out of your control, right?" With a sheepish smile, she agreed.

"Is there anyone who is pleased with you, Mary?" Smiling broadly, she pointed up and said, "God is pleased with me!" I readily agreed as, during the next two minutes, we each shared a little of God's goodness. "Mary, why don't you change who you work for?" She looked puzzled. I smiled: "Since God is so good and He loves you so much, why don't you take Him as your boss?" She was thinking.

"Instead of trying to please people in such an impossible situation, be a good steward and do your best, not trying to please any human. Instead, submit to God. You know that God is with you; so frequently consult with Him about what He wants you to do next. As you do your work, see Him smiling at you and cheering you on." She answered with a broad smile, "I can do that."

To my question, "Would it help you if I prayed for you before I leave?" she responded, "Always!"

Harvey Elder, LLUSM class of 1957, is professor in LLUSM department of medicine, division of infectious diseases. He was an LLUSM Alumni Association 2007 Honored Alumnus.

Jesus said, "Have the people sit down." There was plenty of grass in that place, and the men sat down, about five thousand of them. Jesus then took the loaves, gave thanks, and distributed to those who were seated as much as they wanted. He did the same with the fish. When they had all had enough to eat, he said to his disciples, "Gather the pieces that are left over. Let nothing be wasted." So they gathered them and filled twelve baskets with the pieces of the five barley loaves left over by those who had eaten. John 6:10-13, NIV

I was peacefully sleeping on the blanketed army cot when, suddenly, several men's voices urgently called my name as they threw open the flap of the canvas tent. Putting on my scrubs as I hastily left the tent, I learned that someone "stole the water" and that I needed to "come quick." The handful of men who, thankfully, guarded the area led me through the light-filled darkness of the medical compound of Stenkovich II, one of the largest refugee camps in Macedonia during the Kosovo war. My wife, Ayme, and I volunteered to work with the refugees during this humanitarian tragedy.

Rushing through the compound, I had no clue about the meaning of the broken English phrase "the water is gone." I asked myself, "Is it possible to steal water? Water comes from a faucet linked to pipes linked to a huge tank . . . so how is it possible to steal it?"

As I was concluding that there must be a break in one of the main lines, we reached the top of a hill. What greeted us was a large, wet flat area with an open-ended pipe leading down the slope. Recognizing that the dripping pipe had previously been hooked up to something, the phrases being uttered began to make more sense. I learned that a 5,000 gallon plastic bladder that used to reside at that very spot had nefariously vanished into the night. What I hesitated to confirm was that this was the main water supply for one-fourth of the 12,000 refugees.

The questions abounded in my brain. "Who steals a 5,000 gallon bladder? How do you steal a huge bladder, and where do you hide it? What do you do with the water while you're stealing it?" And the most intriguing question, "What do you do with it after you've stolen it? . . . eBay? Try to sell it in the local classifieds?" These questions unfortunately do not dig a well that 3,000 people will need shortly after the approaching sunrise.

While these questions kept distracting me, I knew I had to come up with a solution. I felt this gnawing desire to find the answer, to take care of the refugees, to be the hero. I learned that night that the desire to be the helper-hero is very hard for professionals to suppress.

But after much painful (but useless) solo thinking, I was able to put my thoughts together with camp management so that an auxiliary line was arranged and tapped into a main line from another sector of the camp. It was so simple, but my desire to control the situation clouded my more collaborative nature. I was reminded that God is in control—a very difficult lesson to remember when I was the highly educated head of the medical compound.

The other corollary lesson I learned again that night was that God provides. Since I was not in control, how could I have provided water for 3,000? If He can provide lunch for 5,000, He certainly could provide water. My role is not to control or provide but to believe, listen, and act.

Eric Frykman, LLUSM class of 1996—for which he was senior class president—is assistant clinical professor in LLUSM department of preventive medicine.

April 2

No one can come to me unless the Father who sent me draws him, and I will raise him up at the last day. It is written in the Prophets: "They will all be taught by God." Everyone who listens to the Father and learns from him comes to me. No one has seen the Father except the one who is from God; only he has seen the Father. I tell you the truth, he who believes has everlasting life. John 6:44-47, NIV

He lay crumpled in a bed in his house, a boy the size of a 14-year-old adolescent in a 20-year-old body. The nurses had told the intensivist that he was unwilling to live. That doctor called me, a psychiatrist, to consult the case. The boy's history was rather sad. Jesse (not his real name) had suffered from cystic fibrosis; and his lungs had required surgery at Stanford University in Palo Alto, California, by a renowned specialist. But after the surgery, he gained thirty pounds and started to grow into adolescence.

He got interested in cars with his older brother, who suffered from a milder form of cystic fibrosis. What was amazing was that he started getting involved in demolition derby racing. His eyes lit up as he recounted his exploits and how he repaired the cars to keep going. Jesse identified with their broken frames and steel determination.

But something happened, whereupon he lost his will. He was off the transplant list because of his father. Jesse had always been close to him; but two years earlier, he had held back his father's dog with a choke chain as it tried to attack his cat. The father struck Jesse in the face, as he shouted, "You're choking my dog!" Jesse moved out after that. Stanford sent the yearly update to transplant-list patients, but his dad never forwarded it.

So, Jesse was off the list. He had to move in with his brother because of his declining health. The race car keys hung on the wall. "I would like Dad to act like he cared. I would like him to always be there like he was in the past," he lamented. I knew I could have spent hours in this area of loss, but I was there to assess his lethality and treatment options. But I lingered. I said a silent prayer for God to impress upon me what I should pursue.

I asked Jesse about his fears and his hopes. What about his dreams? His racing? What happens after one dies? Did he think he could heal his hurt with Dad? I talked an hour on these thoughts and on something else—about Jesus and how He loved him. I spoke of the hope that is out there, and how Jesus wants us to be close to the Father. In the end, I asked if he would be willing for me to have a prayer with him. He agreed.

I left the room praying that this message might take hold like the adhesive Bondo to his damaged heart. Would he ever leave that bed to participate in another race? The next morning I arrived at my office to see flowers on my desk. It was a message of thanks from the intensivist. He wrote, "Jesse wants to be on the transplant list, and he wants to know Jesus. Thank you so much."

Thomas J. Andrews, LLUSM class of 1978-B, is a psychiatrist in Palo Cedro, California.

And it shall come to pass, that before they call, I will answer; and while they are yet speaking, I will hear. Isaiah 65:24, KJV

In 1973, the United States Agency for International Development (USAID) announced that the Tanzanian government in East Africa was beginning a large national effort to improve its rural health services. The agency had committed to supporting the government's maternal and child health (MCH) program. This effort included a plan to build eighteen MCH schools in which to train 2,500 MCH aides, plus assistance to the MCH program in developing policy and new infrastructure for the entire nation. The query came: Would Loma Linda University be interested in providing the technical assistance for this large and complex multimillion dollar project? The initial answer was "yes." However, the bureaucratic wheels ground slowly; and with no word from USAID, Loma Linda put the project on a back burner.

Then, suddenly, after months of silence, USAID announced in April 1974 that they were ready to entertain a proposal bid from LLU. I was on staff at LLU and decided that Richard Hart—at the time doing Johns Hopkins University research at Kilimanjaro Christian Medical Center in Moshi, Tanzania, for his Doctor of Public Health degree—would be an excellent field director. The competitive bid was due in twelve days. Previous conversations with Hart had found him reluctant to accept an academic position at LLU. In the absence of any telephone contact, how could I communicate this complex project to Hart in such a way, using a cable format, as to receive an immediate (and hopefully positive) response from him?

I was sitting in my office in Nichol Hall, contemplating how to word a cable to Hart, when the mail arrived. It included a letter posted two weeks previously from Hart. In it, Hart had answered every question I was thinking to transmit to him, including his willingness to be the first field project director of the MCH project! I bowed my head, eyes full of tears. God had answered my request before the request had even been made.

Working night and day, my staff and I completed the contract proposal and submitted it by the deadline. It won out against the proposals of two other universities, and Loma Linda began a significant relationship with Tanzania that was also a great blessing to LLU and its international programs.

Just how did this communication miracle occur? The USAID health director had traveled from Dar es Salaam, the capital of Tanzania, up to Moshi two weeks earlier. He found Hart on a Friday afternoon changing the oil on his old VW Combi. This man, whom Hart had never seen before, started out by saying: "Both Johns Hopkins and Loma Linda University are submitting proposals for our MCH contract. Both are nominating you to be the physician-in-charge."

Astonished, Hart had to hear more. After the director explained all the details of the project and the appointment, Hart decided he would accept only under the Loma Linda banner, and immediately wrote to me. The really incredible part of the incident turned out to be the fact that Loma Linda, at that time, had not decided to enter the ring, and Johns Hopkins never applied. Misinformation had worked a miracle in communication.

P. William (Bill) Dysinger, LLUSM class of 1955, is emeritus adjunct professor in LLUSM department of preventive medicine and is also emeritus associate dean of LLUSPH. He resides in Williamsport, Tennessee. April 3 is the birthday of Richard Hart, LLUSM class of 1970.

April 4

O LORD, do not stay far away! You are my strength; come quickly to my aid!
Psalm 22:19, NLT

I guess it's fair to say that I've been beset by doubt for much of my adult life. The rigors of a science education in biology and medicine have not always lessened that tendency. In the past couple of years, however, I had experiences where maybe God was trying to tell me something.

One such experience was on a rafting trip on the south fork of the Trinity River, located a few hours from my home in northern California. It was a two-day trip in April 2006. We'd had rain almost nonstop the previous month; and the river was very swollen—5,000 cubic feet per second at the put-in at Hyampom, and no doubt at least twice that amount at the take-out point twenty-seven miles downstream.

The first day went well enough. There were three rafts—one with six guides, and two with the paying customers—plus a guide at the stern. There were multiple class 5 rapids and several sites where we had to portage to avoid class 6 hazards. The second day we floated for a half hour before we came to a large class 5, with a couple hundred yards of churning whitewater, plus a four-to-five foot drop right in the middle of the stream.

We scouted for a while, but then the guide's raft went first and successfully negotiated the treacherous stretch and set up as a rescue boat for the rest of us. The second raft also made it without trouble and moored on the opposite bank. Then it was my boat's turn. We did fine until we came to the drop, but we didn't have enough momentum to carry us through the hole. We stalled, with the front end remorselessly levitated; and we all went into the maelstrom.

As I went into the water, my helmet immediately popped off, due to a faulty snap. I was tumbled in the hole for what was probably no more than half a minute, although it seemed much longer. My buddies were all soon rescued, but I eddied out about 200 yards downriver, after finally being flushed out of the hole.

My wife, who had serious misgivings about this enterprise from the start, was staying with her sister in the San Francisco Bay Area. When we arrived back at our cars and again had cellular reception, I called to let her know I was okay. The first thing she wanted to know, of course, was if any of us had fallen into the river. Well, yes, I said somewhat reluctantly. She then told me how she had this overpowering feeling that day that I was in trouble and needed help around midday. She wondered when we had had our problem.

I'm not sure if her premonition was precisely at the exact time I was in harm's way. But I definitely was comforted to know I had a praying wife who was on the line with God about the time I needed Him!

Geoff Rice, LLUSM class of 1981, is an ophthalmologist in Ukiah, California.

I no longer call you servants, because a servant does not know his master's business. Instead, I have called you friends, for everything that I learned from my Father I have made known to you. You did not choose me, but I chose you and appointed you to go and bear fruit—fruit that will last. Then the Father will give you whatever you ask in my name. John 15:15-16, NIV

It was Friday evening, the sun was setting, and all was not well. My hands were deep in an inert atmosphere box fitted with rubber gloves, which allowed me to manipulate the contents of the box without exposing them to the ambient atmosphere. This particular box contained extremely reactive and explosive compounds, and I had accidentally shattered the barrier separating the inert atmosphere inside the box from the reactive atmosphere outside. My index finger was temporarily serving the role of cork. If this hole didn't get plugged fast, an inferno would ensue! In desperation, I tried one stopgap solution after another.

As the only Seventh-day Adventist this research group had ever seen, I was a curiosity. My mental status became even more frenzied as the realization struck that this was not a good precedent to set for religious observance after the careful negotiations that had been necessary to extricate myself from Sabbath duties. My frenzy seemed at its height when my friend H.T. arrived.

"Better stand clear of Paul," H.T. cautioned the crowd. "It's Sabbath, he's still here, and I can't vouch for God's aim with lightning!" My anxiety began blending with irritation, an explosive mixture of frenzied emotion. Suddenly, the philosophical member of the group, Andre, approached, put his arm around me and spoke. "Don't worry," began Andre with supreme confidence, "if God exists, He must be the King of Mitigating Circumstances; and what you have here qualifies. Relax and fix it."

The anxiety and irritation subsided. Two minutes later, the hole was plugged, the problem was solved, and congratulations were expressed. H.T. sent me on my way, promising to clean things up; after all, it was my Sabbath.

Although the church sermon that week has faded from memory, Andre's words have not. Nor has the recollection of an unusual request from my sometimes acerbic friend, H.T. It happened a few years ago. The phone rang; it was H.T. His wife had just delivered their firstborn after sustaining massive complications. Baby and mother were both in the intensive care unit, the baby with sepsis. "Can you think good thoughts for me?" asked H.T. I gave him assurance that he had my prayers.

"Thanks. I wanted prayer but didn't ask because my bargaining position with the Almighty can't be very good," was all H.T. said. I prayed fervently. The baby is now a star student and an athlete in high school. H.T.'s wife is well. They are a happy family living in the Midwest.

In human affairs, mitigating circumstances are common. The historical and biblical narratives are full of them. We see them in the hospital daily. I don't understand why sometimes the babies get well, while other times the ending is bitter. The Master's business often seems unclear, but one fact comforts: The King of Mitigating Circumstances calls all of us His friends; after all, He chooses us.

Paul Herrmann, LLUSM class of 2000—for which he was senior class president—also has a PhD degree and is associate professor in LLUSM department of pathology and human anatomy.

April 6

I can do all things through Christ who strengthens me. Philippians 4:13, NKJV

To be a doctor like my father, Merrill Dart, LLUSM 1932, was my ambition as I was growing up. I worked in his office in the summers, in his eye, ear, nose, and throat practice. He took me to watch an autopsy when I was 14 years old and to see a baby delivered when I was 15 years old.

At Union College in Lincoln, Nebraska, I took pre-med. I worked in the chemistry stockroom in the college's science building. It was there I met a brilliant, dashing, teasing pre-med student, who was known to say, "I will never marry a woman doctor." Four years later, when he was a sophomore medical student and I was a freshman medical student, we were married. That was only the beginning of my story.

It was uncommon for women to apply to medical school in the early 1950s. I would hear, "Why do you want to take a man's place in medical school? You know you won't practice long. You will get married, have children, and drop out." But Walter Clark, dean of admissions for LLUSM, was encouraging and supportive of women entering medicine.

My class of medicine began in 1954 with five women and ninety-one men. There was a closeness and camaraderie in my class that remains today. After receiving my MD degree, I worked as a school physician for the Los Angeles City (California) School System. My boss was Dr. Harriett Bulpit Randall, whose name is carried on Randall Visitors Center at LLU. During these early years, I conducted well-baby clinics, then family-planning clinics, and also chaired the board of the first daycare center at Loma Linda University Church of Seventh-day Adventists.

Fifteen years after earning my medical degree, with three children—ages 5 to 12—in the home and a promise from my husband to help run the household, I took a residency in obstetrics and gynecology. The children learned to wash clothes, change beds, buy groceries, cook, and get the Christmas cards out! I came home sleep deprived, was gone every third night, left daily at 6:30 a.m.; and I wanted to QUIT. "What was I doing leaving my family day and night? But to quit could jeopardize future women with children being accepted into this residency," I said to myself.

I did not quit. Philippians 4:13 was my encouragement. At the end of my residency, I was invited to join the obstetrics and gynecology faculty at Loma Linda University Medical Center; I became the first woman in that group. Now, thirty years later, fifteen women are in that department. The medical school classes now have nearly 50 percent women.

To join that obstetrics and gynecology group was a joyful day for me. Christ had strengthened me then, and continues to do so to this day.

Marilyn Joyce Dart Herber, LLUSM class of 1958, is retired from LLUSM department of gynecology and obstetrics. She was LLUSM Alumni Association president from 1999 to 2000 and was an LLUSM Alumni Association 1997 Honored Alumna. She and her husband, Raymond, LLUSM class of 1957, received the LLU Distinguished Humanitarian Award in 1995. April 6 is her birthday.

The eye is the lamp of the body. If your eyes are good, your whole body will be full of light. Matthew 6:22, NIV

"You better not let go of me or I'm gonna hit her!" The person he was talking to was me—the guy trying, for all he was worth, not to let go. The person he was going to hit was my ophthalmology attending. The person speaking was a 35-year-old, 6'5", 230-pound veteran soldier. This was how my ophthalmology rotation began at the beginning of my third year as a medical student.

The large man in the examining chair had reluctantly come into the clinic for an eye exam because of persistent pain and pressure in his eyes. Unfortunately, he had a severe phobia of anything touching his eyes. To the man's horror, a tonometry test was required to measure his intraocular pressure. Even though drops are administered to numb the eyes, a probe must make direct contact on the cornea to accurately measure the pressure.

As the probe moved closer to the patient's eye, he began to tremble uncontrollably and to grip the armrest of the chair so hard I thought it would buckle under his power. It was at this moment the patient volunteered for me to come behind the chair and hold him, before he knocked out my attending.

As my hands attempted to grip the man's bulging biceps, I remember not only being concerned for my attending's safety but also thinking to myself that probably the fastest way to fail a rotation was to allow your attending to be hurled across the room by your patient! I prayed for strength from above and kept holding. After what seemed like an unbearable amount of time, my attending calmly and professionally finished the exam. We all breathed a sigh of relief.

Although we may not harbor the same intense protectiveness for our eyes as the patient in the story, we all place incredible value on them. In fact, most of us would probably rank our orbits just below the vital organs as necessary for life. God surely knew what He was doing when He gave us the wondrous gift of sight. Yet, perhaps God intended our eyes to have a purpose that goes deeper than mere sight. Maybe our eyes provide a gateway of communication into our hearts.

Have you ever looked into another's eyes and seemed to know what they were feeling or thinking? What do you see when you look into your patient's eyes? More importantly, what do our patients see when they peer into ours? Do they observe eyes that are impatient, frustrated, bored, annoyed, wandering, or apathetic? Or do our eyes reflect the light, empathy, compassion, love, trust, and acceptance of our God? Our eyes communicate much about who we are without our ever saying a word. In fact, sometimes, it is only our eyes that speak for us when words are inadequate.

What do we want our patients to see when they look into our eyes? Imagine how we will feel when at last we can look into our Creator's eyes.

Kevin Schultz, LLUSM class of 2009—for which he was sophomore class president—attended Walla Walla University in College Place, Washington, for his undergraduate studies. April 7 is the birthday of his grandmother, Dori Siemsen.

April 8

Grace and truth came by Jesus Christ. No man hath seen God at any time; the only begotten Son, which is in the bosom of the Father, he hath declared him.
John 1:17-18, KJV

You may have heard of an ugly woman who had the false impression that she was very beautiful. Not having the advantage of possessing a mirror in which she could see her reflection, she was persistent in her smug conceit. One day, so the story goes, a trader visited this isolated spot. Among other things, he left a large looking glass. The deceived woman is said to have taken a look at herself, and then, in anger, she smashed the mirror. She was sure the trouble was with the glass and not with herself.

Are you willing to take an honest look at yourself and admit the truth of what you see? Most people lack sufficient courage to do this. The most heroic task before you is that of facing the truth about yourself. If you are honest, you will take leave of conceit and give yourself to the spirit of humility.

What is man? This question has engaged the best minds of all generations. It is the primal question of philosophy and religion. To receive the true answer to this question is the prerequisite of all genuine Christian living.

Many answers are given, and have been given, to the question of dealing with the nature of man. Scientists will attempt an understanding of man on a purely scientific basis. Philosophers seek to understand man largely from the viewpoint of human reason. The moralist seeks to know man on the basis of man's moral and ethical capacity. The sociologist assumes to understand man from the viewpoint of the environment and culture in which he lives. The psychologist reflects a picture of man on the basis of behavior he can observe.

If we are to have an authoritative answer to the question of understanding ourselves, we must transcend mere human reason and speculation to something more definite. If human reason, unaided by the Divine, is made the center, we are likely to be led into a great deal of confusion.

Man can be fully understood only from the viewpoint of God. If God is left out of our reckoning, we shall err miserably in understanding ourselves.

Arthur L. Bietz (1913-2001) was professor of applied Christianity at LLU. He was also senior pastor of the White Memorial Seventh-day Adventist Church in Los Angeles, California. This devotional originally appeared in the April 1951 issue of the LLUSM Alumni Association Alumni Journal.

The Lord sustains them on their sickbed; in their illness you heal all their infirmities. Psalm 41:3, NRSV

I'm a patient on the fourth floor of Loma Linda University Medical Center. I'm just waking up after having my kidney removed. My mind is blurred from the anesthesia. Through my clouded mind, I hear the continuous daytime dull roar of activity at the nursing station. Phones ring. Conversations continue. Occasional laughter filters to my ears. I vaguely remember wishing I could go out and join in the conversations. I try to move, but the pain is too great; so I just lie back down and close my eyes.

Sometime later a voice asks, "Mr. Weismeyer, are you awake?" I think, "My first nonfamily visitor." "Yes, I'm awake," I say. Then the response, "Hello. I'm one of the chaplains here at the Medical Center. I just want to let you know that if there is anything that we can assist you with, please call." Then the chaplain leaves, never to be seen again.

Hours pass. Blood pressure is taken, intravenous lines are changed, blood is drawn—all necessary "evils" of a hospital stay. But my thoughts keep returning to the central issue of why I am in the hospital. Did they get all my cancer? Will I be okay?

Early the next morning, I awaken to a slight rustle. "Good morning. I'm sorry to disturb you. I'm the housekeeper. How are you doing this morning? You'll do fine. I'll see you tomorrow. God bless you."

Next, my physician comes in. He looks like a knight in his white coat. He, through God's help, saved my life, didn't he? He says, "Good morning, Mr. Weismeyer. How are you doing?" "Fine," I say. "Everything is looking good," he adds. "The surgery went well. We should receive the pathology report later in the week. Then we'll know where we are going." I feel a little better. Everything went well surgically. But did they get all the cancer? Hopefully, I will know for sure in a few days.

At 6:00 a.m. a couple of days later, I am awakened by an energetic voice. It was my medical student physician. "Good morning, Mr. Weismeyer. We got your pathology report back. The tumor was a very aggressive type of cancer. Your physician will give you more details when he comes to see you later in the morning." Then he leaves.

I am terror-stricken. Yes, it is cancer. And it is a very aggressive type. I won't see my physician until he comes in on his rounds. Ten o'clock seems like an eternity. But a little more than an hour later, I have a visit from an angel. My angel is in the form of the housekeeper. She comes in and in her cheerful voice says, "Good morning. How are you today?" I say something like, "I'm so scared. They say I have an aggressive cancer. Will I die?"

My angel, in housekeeper's clothes, says, "God will take care of you. Let me pray with you." This blessed woman then takes my hand and says a simple heartfelt prayer to God to "give me strength and courage." She then continues about her business. But before she leaves, she says, "I will continue praying for you." Immediately, I feel better. I know everything is going to be all right. And it was.

To this day, I don't know the name of "my" housekeeper—the one who ministered to me during my darkest hour. I can't even remember her face, except I do know it was the face of an angel. I know someday I will meet her again, where I can properly thank her for her compassion and lifesaving prayers.

Richard Weismeyer is director of LLU Public Relations. He began his career at LLU in 1960 while still in high school. He received an MA degree in English from La Sierra University in Riverside, California. April 9 is the day he had his surgery.

April 10

But he was wounded for our transgressions, he was bruised for our iniquities: the chastisement of our peace was upon him; and with his stripes we are healed. Isaiah 53:5, KJV

The first time I saw a severely beaten man was Monday morning, January 11, 1974. I was a 27-year-old, recently qualified physician on my first posting in Lesotho. After the Basutoland Congress Party was denied its electoral victory by Chief Leabua Jonathan, groups of party faithful mounted an ill-fated uprising. On Sunday evening, January 10, they intended to capture local police stations and use the weapons there to overthrow the existing government.

The man brought from the police station at Mapoteng, Lesotho, had been beaten without mercy. His black back was more darkly blackened by long, juicy bruises; and purple black edema welts covered almost every part of his arms and trunk. His face was swollen and his eyes were hard to see. I am not sure how he made it alive to Maluti Adventist Hospital, or how he lived for the few hours until the Police Mobile Unit (a paramilitary strike force used by the government to quell dissent) showed up and he was forcefully taken away. I later learned he was shot—his body added to a pile of other bodies in the attacked police station.

I had not seen a worse beaten body until 2004, when I saw *The Passion of the Christ* at our local movie theater. It was a late showing on a workday night. The film's novelty had long passed. In fact, our family was the only one in the theater—just three of us watching. The face of the actor Christ is marred with a huge periocular ecchymosis, making this Christ look unlike any crucifix you have ever seen. He peers out from under a huge deforming swelling. It is very upsetting and has turned many away from the film.

Why did Justice permit the Beloved Son to endure this punishment? Because Jesus was, in fact, guilty. He chose to become an accomplice to evil and evildoers by what I like to call "the high crime of Mercy."

Cain kills Abel, and God does nothing; or worse than nothing—He protects Cain from retaliation. Joseph Stalin murders millions under the reign of secular atheism; but God does nothing, and Uncle Joe dies quietly in his sleep. Adolph Hitler seeks to exterminate the chosen race; and on his last day, he has a quiet supper with his mistress and then dies a painless, self-induced death. Sinners rarely experience God's Justice; most of us only taste His Mercy.

And the One who extends that Mercy—that gift of life—takes responsibility on Himself for the result of giving life to bad people—like Hitler and Stalin and you and me. God, we cry, You could have stopped sin way back there at the gates of Eden! Yes, God replies, guilty as charged. So pour it on Him, beat Him four times more than was permitted by law, whip Him harshly, bruise Him deeply, and crown Him with thorns.

Indeed, we do worship a God guilty of the High Crime of Mercy. It is "the chastisement of our peace" that is upon Him.

John B. (Jack) Hoehn, LLUSM class of 1971, is a family practitioner in Walla Walla, Washington. April 10 is Good Friday in 2009.

April 11

Jesus said, "Let the little children come to me, and do not hinder them, for the kingdom of heaven belongs to such as these." Matthew 19:14, NIV

It was time for morning rounds on the pediatrics ward at Riverside General Hospital in Riverside, California. I was a third-year medical student, very eager to impress others with my ability to confidently present the history and physical exam of a 2-year-old boy our team had admitted overnight for dehydration and gastroenteritis. I was told our new attending physician was John Mace, LLUSM class of 1964, the chair of the pediatrics department; so I wanted to do an especially good job in my presentation.

I had memorized the entire script and was ready to quickly recite it: the history of the present illness, the birth history, the milestones, the immunizations, the family history, the vital signs, the weight loss both in grams and as a percentage drop from the previous visit in the clinic, the key findings on the physical exam, the random chemistry profile from the night before, the morning electrolytes, the differential diagnosis, the assessment, the plan, the urine output in ml/kg/hour overnight, and on and on.

Our group of white-coats went from room to room, seeing each patient, finally arriving at my small patient's room. It was a big group: the attending, the senior resident, the two interns, the four medical students, the charge nurse, and the social worker. We walked in and all surrounded the tall bed with the vertical metal bars. To me, it looked like a small portable jail cell.

As we approached, the little boy grabbed the bars and stood up; he looked around and promptly started to cry. He was obviously scared and was probably wondering what was going to happen next. Not quite knowing what to do, I launched into my prepared presentation. I was barely into my first sentence ("This 2-year-old Caucasian male child . . .") when Dr. Mace looked at me and said, "Please stop." He then opened the tall bed rail guards, took the little boy in his arms, smiled, and told him, "You'll be all right." He then turned to me and said, "Now, doctor, tell me why this little guy is here."

Countless morning clinical rounds have come and gone since that day, all filled with new patients, the discussion of various clinical details, the possible etiologies, the relative value of different decisions. I have forgotten much, if not all, of the rounding minutiae. But I will never forget the impact that morning had on my decision to become a pediatrician, who would treat patients, not diseases.

Ricardo Peverini, LLUSM class of 1984, is a specialist in neonatal and perinatal medicine and is associate professor in LLUSM department of pediatrics. He is associate dean for clinical faculty for LLUSM.

April 12

I will instruct thee and teach thee in the way which thou shalt go: I will guide thee with mine eye. Psalm 32:8, KJV

Early on the morning of April 9, 1940, I was awakened by a student shouting down the hall at Onsrud Mission School, a boarding junior college in Norway. The cry was that Germany had attacked our country at several locations along its coastline. That news changed the future for all of us. The principal announced that as many of us as were able should go home Friday, the twelfth, because he would not assume responsibility for more than one hundred students in the event of an air attack.

My parents had arranged for a place to which they could evacuate in case of war; and although I was familiar with the area, I had forgotten the name of the farm. I decided to ride my bicycle the fifty miles to Harestua, a little community approximately thirty miles north of Oslo, Norway.

I did not know the name of the farm to which I was going. However, because I had colporteured—traveled around selling books—the summer before, I was neither afraid of meeting people nor worried about my trip. The next morning found me on my knees praying to God, reminding Him of my past and asking for His protection on the ride.

After about three-to-four hours on the bike, I came to a long hill. No one had passed me in either direction, and the atmosphere felt lonely, almost spooky. When I came around a bend, I was surprised to see the road filled with cars packed so close together that I could not pass. I had to take my bike off the road, wade through a foot of snow, and climb over a barbed wire fence onto the railroad tracks.

Fortunately, I did not have to worry about oncoming trains. I saw that a couple of hundred feet in front of me the rail bridge had been blown up. After getting back on the road again and passing a detachment of Norwegian soldiers, I realized for certain that we were at war and that action was expected any time.

After traveling for a while alongside a little lake, I eventually came to a fork in the road. I sat down by a large fir tree, resting and thinking and trying to decide: right or left? right or left? It was then that I heard the gasps and steps of a man running down the road toward me. He shouted to me: "I have to borrow your bike. I have to report to the captain down there that someone is speaking German up in the hills!"

I let him borrow my bike, knowing he would have to come back. This was the only road in the area, and he would not be permitted to pass by the detachment of soldiers I had passed earlier. He was back again in ten minutes, and I decided to go with him.

We finally arrived at a farm with two houses and a barn. As we entered the house that was straight ahead of us, he said, "This is where I live." He added, as he pointed to a door farther down the hall, "There is someone living over there." Why, I wondered, did he say that? I knocked on the door he had indicated and was surprised by who opened it: my mother and my two sisters!

The Lord had led me to the very place for which I was searching. Just when I needed guidance, he sent a man to me under the guise of someone who had something important to report to an officer. And that man even told me which door to check. Praise the Lord for His goodness and mercy! He did not let me down.

Svein R. Nilsen, LLUSM class of 1962, is a family practitioner in Loma Linda, California. He was reunited with his family on April 12, 1940.

April 13

From everyone who has been given much, much will be demanded; and from the one who has been entrusted with much, much more will be asked. Luke 12:48, NIV

Being a physician is more than just a job: It is a way of life. It is humbling when one realizes the incredible privilege it is to be a physician. People allow us to enter their most private places—emotionally, spiritually, and physically. Along the way, we often take that trust for granted.

Eva came to me last year seeking my advice and treatment for weight loss. When she started talking, it was easy to see that the system of medicine had not treated her well. Years before, while complaining of intractable back pain, she was given a prescription for Methadone. When that medication didn't suffice, she was given Oxy IR. Of course, with the depression that ensued, she was put on Effexor XR. One day, she went to the doctor complaining of burning in her feet. She was quickly treated with Neurontin. She then started to become fatigued and was treated with Welbutrin SR. Her story is an example of the life of a patient in this day and age, when medicines are made for any type of ailment.

On subsequent visits, we began to share experiences from our lives. One particular visit stands out in my mind. On this day she began to cry, frustrated with her life and the decisions she had made. She had sacrificed decades of her life to a man who was unfaithful and, as a result, she felt that she was a nobody. I quickly reminded her of her three children—who she had often reared on her own—and how they loved and respected her. I reminded her of their successful careers and how blessed they were to maintain their connections with God after all this time.

I assured her that I would immediately give up all that I have and all that I am for the security of knowing that my children would grow up to be like hers. We both had tears as we prayed. That day, Eva became a new person. It wasn't her treatments or her medicines (which we had mostly taken away) that changed her: It was the power of God. I was blessed that God had given me the opportunity to make a difference in her life.

With the great power that is ours to change a patient's life—for good or for bad—also comes great responsibility. We must always remember that God gave us the talent to become doctors and bless others. Our experiences and our choices will mold us into the physicians and characters that we will become. May God give us the humility and the wisdom not only to be great physicians, but to be great Christians as we fulfill His great commission.

Andrew Oswari, LLUSM class of 1997, is a family practitioner but currently practices mostly integrative medicine. He and his wife, Jane, and their children, Caleb and Abigail, live in Mount Laurel, New Jersey.

April 14

For it is God which worketh in you both to will and to do of his good pleasure.
Philippians 2:13, KJV

Dennis was a pleasant 72-year-old patient who always showed up at my clinic with a racing form in his pocket. He liked to bet on the horses and had quite a checkered past. He had led a rough life as a hobo, riding around the nation in empty train cars. He had been an alcoholic and had the bulbous nose to prove it. He was living on Social Security, now, just finishing out his days.

He came to my evening clinic one night; nothing really new—just the usual maintenance problems associated with hypertension, diabetes, and obesity aggravated by the typical American diet. As I was examining him and reviewing his records, I felt the strong impression that I should share a copy of *Steps to Christ* with Dennis. I kept a box of them in my office to give away at opportune times.

I didn't think this was an opportune time. I did not consider Dennis to be a person who would be receptive to *Steps to Christ*. If the material I was going to share with him didn't have to do with secular themes, such as horse racing, I was certain that Dennis would not be interested. But I continued to feel an urging to give him the book, and my feelings grew stronger and stronger. It got to the point that I was practically arguing with the Holy Spirit in my head.

Finally, I had either to give in or renounce my Christianity. I asked Dennis to excuse me for a moment, walked to my office, and picked up a copy of *Steps to Christ*. I breathed a little prayer and walked back to Dennis, handing him the book.

He took it from me and looked at it. It had a portrayal of Christ's likeness and the title in block letters across the front. He looked up at me, smiled, and said, "Thanks. I'll read this!" I was shocked. His response was totally unexpected. You could have knocked me over with a feather right then!

After that experience, I have learned to lean less on my own understanding and more on God's.

Karl Sandberg, LLUSM class of 1974, is a primary care practitioner in Ola, Arkansas.

I will pour out my Spirit on all people. Your sons and daughters will prophesy, your old men will dream dreams, your young men will see visions. Joel 2:28, NIV

"I have seen your God before," said the young Buddhist girl. She repeated, "I have seen your God!"

"How is it that you have been so blessed to have seen my God?" I asked.

Then she told me how my God had chosen to reveal Himself to a young girl whose only knowledge of other gods was of fearful, harsh, and exacting supernatural beings.

"I was sleeping one night when I had the most dreadful dream. Two demons were chasing me. I was running for my life. They were getting closer and about to catch me. All of a sudden, there in front of me was a deep drop-off. I could either stop and let the evil spirits catch me and kill me, or I could jump into space, not knowing where I would land. I chose to jump. All of a sudden, a giant hand out of nowhere caught me in midair.

"I landed with such weightlessness, like landing on pillows. I looked up at the arm of this giant hand. Over the arm was draped a robe. As I looked up into the face of this being, I saw the most kind and loving face. It was a face I had never seen before. It had long hair and a beard. This being then spoke to me: 'Go ye therefore and spread my word.' He repeated it twice and then I woke up."

The young girl went on with her story. "Several weeks later, as I was walking past a Christian book store, I was impressed to look inside. On the wall was a picture of the same person I saw in my dream. I had to go in and see who it was. It was your God! Now I know your God is a loving God."

This young girl's father had just undergone surgery in our hospital. After his release, she sent us a letter thanking the hospital, doctors, and nurses for caring so well for her father. "I know your God is a God of love because of what I saw in my dream and by how the doctors and nurses took such good care of my father while he was in your hospital. I don't know if I will ever become a Christian, but I know your God is a loving God."

We never know how or when God may speak to other people. To some, God may choose to reveal Himself through our lives and actions. To others, He may choose to show Himself through a dream. God has many ways of revealing Himself, but the most common way is through our daily actions, words, and example. Are we revealing a God of love to the world around us?

Kenneth Rose, LLUSM class of 1988, is a surgeon in Buchanan, Michigan. April 15 is his birthday.

April 16

But He said, "The things which are impossible with men are possible with God."
Luke 18:27, NKJV

A miracle occurred at the Okinawa Adventist Medical Center in Okinawa, Japan. On February 16, 1993, the *Magleby Maersk*, a Danish merchant ship, was streaming between Okinawa and Taiwan when its captain suddenly became severely ill. He was rushed to our "American" hospital in Okinawa, where he arrived in shock, delirious, and with severe abdominal pain. His pulse was barely palpable; blood pressure registered 60/0. Tests revealed significant problems, including fluid in the abdominal cavity and a 5 cm tear in the lower bowel. His condition appeared to be caused by fecal spillage, foul discharge, and severe infection.

The captain was rushed into surgery, where the bowel was repaired and the abdominal cavity was copiously irrigated and closed. But postoperatively, the patient developed additional complications—including a spiking fever and low blood pressure—despite the large amounts of intravenous fluid replacement.

Within a day or two, his condition worsened. He had multiple organ failures. His blood platelet count dropped to 14,000/μl (normal: 120,000-350,000/μl). He also developed adult respiratory distress syndrome. Chest x-rays revealed the rapid spread of splotches on his lungs. Even on 100 percent oxygen administration, his blood-oxygen saturation was low. (A patient with his combination of symptoms presents less than a 50-50 chance of living.) Several times his heart stopped; he had to be resuscitated.

Men's extremity is God's opportunity. I called our hospital staff together, and we had a solemn season of prayer for Captain Henrick Solmer. We pleaded with God for His divine intervention. Our Great Physician heard our prayers and took over the case. The patient's condition began to improve. His platelet count rose. His blood-oxygen saturation improved. He regained some consciousness and his fever began to subside. Day by day, he got better. Truly God was performing a miracle before our eyes! His wife, who had flown in, and the ship owner's wife who accompanied her, both rejoiced.

As Captain Solmer began to improve, I had several opportunities to talk to him about God and His miraculous healing power. The captain mentioned that when he was young, his grandfather had read to him from the Bible; but for the past twenty-five years, he had not given much thought to things spiritual. As he learned of the miracle God had performed in saving him from death, he resolved to know God better.

The doctors, nurses, and the entire staff of the hospital showered Captain Solmer with tender, loving care and followed his progress with deep interest. When it was time for his discharge, a farewell party was given on his behalf with speeches, good food, and gifts. And, as he departed down the hospital stairs, there were many hugs and tears of joy. It was a marvel to see what God had wrought. Here was a man brought to our hospital near death, and that glorious morning he was walking out on his own!

After a month or two of recuperation at his home in Denmark, he was once again on the high seas, captaining the world's largest sailing vessel, a completely computerized ship. Then, a year later, we had the privilege of meeting him again on my annual leave, when his ship docked at Long Beach, California. We rejoiced to see him looking so robust—a testimony to God's miraculous power to save!

James S. Miyashiro, LLUSM class of 1961, also has an MPH degree. He is a general surgeon, who worked for more than twenty-five years in the mission field. He resides in Honolulu, Hawaii.

April 17

*Trust in the L*ORD *with all your heart and lean not on your own understanding; in all your ways acknowledge him, and he will make your paths straight.*
Proverbs 3:5-6, NIV

It was getting late, and I was anxious to get home. There had already been a flight delay, and from what I could tell, the pilot had taken off to the west. East was towards home, and after takeoff I kept waiting for a quick turn toward my home airport. Like any type-A surgeon, I knew where I was going and thought I knew how to get there. Two, three, maybe four minutes went by, and we still hadn't turned. What was this pilot thinking? I wanted to get back home!

Then I peered out my window in all directions. Behind us I saw the lights of Denver, Colorado. We were headed east, in the right direction. If the pilot had gone in the direction I had thought was correct, we would have been way off course. Face it, I only had a small airplane-window view of my surroundings, but I thought I had things figured out. The pilot not only had a better view, but he also had all of the latest technology showing him where to go.

How much is that like the way I try to guide my life from an airplane window-sized view of life? Jesus, of course, has the full view of the present, past, and future. He understands many things about which I do not have a clue, but I still think I know better. Jesus, in contrast to our pilot, will turn the controls over to me at my request. But, oh, what a mess I make in getting off course when I take control. As Proverbs 3:5-6 says, "Trust in the Lord . . . He will make your paths straight"—straight toward home, even when it feels like you are going the wrong direction.

DuWayne A. Carlson, LLUSM class of 1989, is an orthopaedic surgeon in Lincoln, Nebraska.

April 18

Those who love me, I will deliver; I will protect those who know my name. When they call to me, I will answer them; I will be with them in trouble, I will rescue them and honor them. With long life I will satisfy them, and show them my salvation. Psalm 91:14-16, NRSV

The border customs people seemed to be disturbed by something in my passport and later also in Vern's. We awakened our translators to find out what the problem was. At first it was not exactly clear, but soon we got the picture: We had only a single-entry visa, and this was the second time that we were coming into the Ukraine.

Unfortunately, we were out in the middle of nowhere on May Day, 1995—a day when no government officials, except customs, were working; and these officers were pulling us off the train. They had our passports, and we were not going anywhere. One of our translators, Oxana, slammed the train compartment door shut and said, "Let's pray"—and pray we did! The soldiers waited for us to get our things together, a process they had thought we were doing when we shut the compartment door to pray. Soon we were out and off to the interrogation quarters. Our train pulled away without us, leaving us with an odd, sinking feeling inside.

The captain of the border guard had been rousted out of his bed and was not happy. I likened his attitude to that of Pilate's nearly 2,000 years before. His verdict was to send us back to Moscow. We had no visa indicating that we had ever been in Russia, and the Russians would never let us back in to get a visa at the embassy. And even if we could get back, that visa process could take weeks. We were not going anywhere. Worst of all, no one was friendly or seemed to care about us at all.

Many prayers were offered, because we needed to get back. Finally, in desperation, Oxana told the officials: "These Americans are to catch a plane back to America; and if you cause them to miss that flight, you may well have to pay for a ticket for them to go home." Immediately, there was action. The Holy Spirit had given her the key to unlock our problem. They looked at my airline ticket, and saw the departure date; within a few minutes they had decided to let us go. They did not, however, return our passports.

Another train was coming in an hour, but no one directed us about what to do. Then another miracle happened as a young soldier stepped out of a group of about a dozen that were there. Although nobody had said anything to him, he came over and talked to Oxana. Without another word, he got our passports, took us to have our tickets validated in an out-of-the-way place that was hard to find, and then escorted us to the train and searched, from one end to the other, until we had seats together. We all thanked him for this kindness and offered to pay him, but he refused. He wished us good fortune and was gone. You will never convince any of us four that we hadn't seen a miracle before our eyes.

We were the first ones to come through the checkpoint, and we knew that we had at least fifteen more Americans in our group who would have trouble. We thanked God for our deliverance and asked Him to be with those who would follow us. Each of our group, except one, was stopped. But because the Lord had used us as pathfinders, none of them were taken off the train; all were allowed to proceed to Kiev. Some barely caught the plane, but by God's grace we all made it.

Leo Herber, LLUSM class of 1956, is a family practitioner in Scottsdale, Arizona.

Jesus answered him: "Very truly, I tell you, no one can see the kingdom of God without being born from above. Nicodemus said to Him: "How can anyone be born after having grown old? Can one enter a second time into the mother's womb and be born?" Jesus answered, "Very truly, I tell you, no one can enter the kingdom of God without being born of water and Spirit." John 3:3-5, NRSV

I was born in Korea in 1949, four years after the independence of Korea from thirty-five years of Japanese occupation. In 1950—when I was a little over a year old—the Korean War broke out and my father was killed. My mother was just 20 years old.

When I finished elementary school, my grandfather told me and my uncle—who was two years my elder—that we were going to learn how to be good farmers. I loved the idea because that meant I would not have to go to school anymore. We lived on an island, which allowed us many opportunities for fishing and swimming. Most of all, I did not want to leave my lovely mother. She was my all.

Soon a scholarship offer from Jeil (First) Junior High School in Mokpo, a faraway city in Korea, came to my teachers. They visited my grandfather continuously, until he finally said, "Yes, Kilsan may go to school." It proved to be a big sacrifice for my family to further my education; but all my uncles and aunts, plus many relatives, helped. For me to go to school meant my Uncle Hawon had to give up his chance to study.

My mother and grandparents saved every penny to send me to school. Later, when I moved to Seoul, South Korea, to attend Seoul National University, Uncle Hawon came to Seoul to support me. Again, it was an all-out struggle for my family. When I finished studying pharmaceutical manufacturing, I was offered a job at a large pharmaceutical company. I began to make good money.

Spiritually, however, I was slowly dying. I was deeply depressed because I could not find God. Ever since I was 15 years old, I had been searching for God. I felt totally hopeless when I had thoughts that someday I would die. But when I looked at the beautiful flowers, trees, blue oceans, skies, and stars at night, I knew that there was a Creator God. I wanted to meet Him.

Since I worked at a new product-development department at the company, I needed to speak English well. God led me to the Seventh-day Adventist language center. There I met very peculiar people who went to church on Saturdays and would not eat certain foods because "the Bible says so." My English teacher, Pat, asked me to attend weekend evangelistic meetings. When I heard that Jesus was coming again, I was shocked! I thought Jesus had died on the cross. I never knew He was resurrected and had conquered death. (It was at the English language school that I first heard about Loma Linda University and decided to go there for medical school.)

When I heard about the love of God and the beauty of heaven, I felt I was too sinful to get there and to meet God. However, after many months of prayers, I finally learned that I could be born again through the grace of the risen Savior, as described by Jesus in John 3:3-5. I decided to be baptized and did so on April 19, 2005. All my questions in life were answered; and for the first time in my life, lasting peace and joy came to me.

Kilsan Koh, LLUSM class of 1983, is a surgeon in Indio, California.

April 20

"See, I will send my messenger, who will prepare the way before me. Then suddenly the Lord you are seeking will come to his temple; the messenger of the covenant, whom you desire, will come," says the LORD Almighty. Malachi 3:1, NIV

Before the mid-1950s, it was very difficult for any graduate of the College of Medical Evangelists to become a board-certified ophthalmologist. The ophthalmology residency at the White Memorial Hospital (now White Memorial Medical Center) in Los Angeles, California, started in the early 1940s as a two-year program, but board tests were given on Saturdays only. Obviously, this schedule made it very difficult for conscientious Seventh-day Adventists, as requests to be examined on other days were always denied.

But God used an unlikely person, namely the late Dr. George Kambara, a Japanese-American doctor, to correct the problem. He earned his BA and MD degrees from Stanford University in Palo Alto, California. However, his professional life was interrupted during World War II, when all Japanese people living on the west coast were interred in relocation camps. Dr. Kambara was sent to Tule Lake, California.

While he accepted his fate dutifully, his professors at the Stanford University School of Medicine petitioned the authorities at the camp, requesting that Dr. Kambara be allowed to finish his specialty training. Recommendations from his previous mentors made it possible for him to complete his ear-nose-throat training at the University of Tennessee and his ophthalmology residency at the University of Wisconsin.

Dr. Kambara's goal was to serve the Japanese people in East Los Angeles. What he soon found was that in Los Angeles hospitals, Japanese physicians could admit patients only under another (non-Japanese) physician's service. However, the White Memorial Hospital accepted his application and had no restrictions. Thus began his association with the White Memorial Hospital and the College of Medical Evangelists.

At the White Memorial, he was faithful in attendance for forty-one years. He was not a Seventh-day Adventist Christian, but he acquired a comprehensive knowledge of the standards of the institution.

Because it was very difficult for Seventh-day Adventist ophthalmology residents to take the board examinations due to Sabbath observance, Dr. Kambara became determined to help change the test day. His professional achievements and his personal associations with members of the American Board of Ophthalmology helped to influence the change in policy. After several requests, Seventh-day Adventist ophthalmology residents were granted variances to take board examinations on days other than Saturdays.

The majority of the ophthalmologists who have since graduated from Loma Linda University owe a great debt of gratitude to an outstanding ophthalmologist and teacher, Dr. George Kambara. Even now, the yearly Kambara Lectureship, which he endowed, is a constant reminder of his tremendous gifts to Loma Linda University. God surely works in mysterious and wonderful ways!

Ernest Zane, LLUSM class of 1956, is associate professor in and vice chair of LLUSM department of ophthalmology.

April 21

And walk in love, as Christ also has loved us. Ephesians 5:2, NKJV

She had waited today—not so much for service at the county hospital, but rather to seek answers. She was one person among so many who were passing though the halls of the surgery clinic on this day, a day not otherwise unlike any other. Once again, there were more patients than time to effectively attend to their needs. But somehow she stood out, if only briefly. And, in doing so, I would remember her far beyond the few more months she would live.

I was one member of a parade of students and residents she courageously or graciously allowed to examine the festering red rash on her exposed skin. By the time I first saw her, she already knew that this was worse than even she had feared. Or did she?

This was our education. We students were told that there was no treatment that would have any significant impact on her survival, which would be a few months at best. Then we were hustled on quickly to attend to other patients, without any time to reflect on the case we had just seen and experienced.

Later, as I rushed down the hall, I noticed that the door to the room where she had been was ajar. In a fleeting glance, I saw her inside—now alone and fully gowned, cradling in her arms her right breast that would kill her. In that moment, I became aware of her humanness, and, in turn, that of countless patients who would follow her.

Brett Robinson, LLUSM class of 1989, is a family practitioner in Salem, Oregon.

April 22

My God, my God, why hast thou forsaken me? Matthew 27:46, KJV; Father, into thy hands I commend my spirit. Luke 23:46, KJV; It is finished. John 19:30, KJV

As we removed the covering to begin learning, something seemed strange. We were in anatomy lab, and something made me uncomfortable. While attempting to understand this feeling, someone covered the face of the silent being on the table—the face of one who would show us so much. For some mystical reason, that action made everything okay. But why?

Why did a piece of cloth make a difference? Was I afraid to be reminded that this "study" is a human? Was I afraid to realize that this face represents a heart that loved, and hurt? Was I afraid to see, in those eyes, those who have gone before, or would I even see myself? Death will be as much a part of my existence as was my birth, but I don't like being reminded. I have experienced sufficient loss to know it's hard. When considering my death, I fear for those who will love me on that day. I fear it will lack meaning.

Back in anatomy lab again, I was led to look at the face once more. As fear conjured up an uneasy feeling, God whispered, "I can use death as much as I can use life." Suddenly, before me were beings who, in death, will touch as many people—if not more—as they did in life, because through their gift they have become teachers. They are part of the knowledge that will make me a healer. Thus, the number of lives that they can touch through their students is almost limitless.

Yes, death can be used just as much as life. Still, it's difficult to entirely grasp this. This silent teacher before me never knew his students. He couldn't see the fruition of his gift, yet he made that sacrifice. In some beautiful way, his gift carries on the significance of his life. But did he understand that there was meaning beyond a darkness he couldn't see past?

Jesus cried, "Father, why hast thou forsaken me?" In the face of death, His humanity feared the unknown. Yet He somehow knew that His death would reverberate throughout history. So He entered separation from His Father with His humanity, unable to see the other side. And salvation becomes ours, because His unselfish choice made His death as great a part of His existence as did His life.

Later in lab for my final assignment, I realize I'm being taught more than I thought—more than muscles, nerves, and vessels, more than the fact that God uses death. I perceive, perhaps most significantly, a glimpse into the heart of God in Christ. How? Because before me is an example of one who entered the unknown unselfishly, hopeful of a significance he would someday see. Thus, if we listen to their silence, we will hear the calling to use our knowledge to touch lives, to live fearlessly and selflessly through gain or loss.

Truly, the significance of the lives of these silent teachers didn't end with their final breath. And as hard as it may be for my mind to comprehend, this much is evident: God can use death as beautifully as He can use life.

Nathan Dario Brinckhaus, LLUSM class of 2011—for which he is sophomore class secretary/ treasurer—was reared in Humboldt County in northern California. April 22 was the date of the anatomy memorial service in 2008.

They will see his face. Revelation 22:4, NIV

When I was in my early elementary school years, my family lived in Mayaguez, Puerto Rico, where my father was the general surgeon at Bella Vista Hospital. While my father enjoyed the challenges of diverse types of surgery, he obtained the most joy from reconstructing the features of children with cleft palates. I can remember seeing frightening 35 mm slides of these poor kids before the operation—and then seeing the "after" pictures, with the amazing smiles of both the children and their parents. The delight my father took in transforming their faces made life more meaningful for him.

In many places around the world, parents still respond to the stigma of a disfiguring cleft palate by hiding their children away from society. By the time these children become adolescents, they have acquired the habit of hiding their faces from their peers.

Since the Fall of Adam and Eve in the Garden of Eden, the damaging effects of sin have caused humankind to avoid the society of God—to hide our disfigured hearts from the One whose compassion is boundless and who loves us with an everlasting love. When we read John 1:14 (NKJV), however, we are reminded that God's loving disposition toward us moved Him to action that would eradicate this estrangement: "The Word became flesh and dwelt among us." More than two thousand years ago, people living in Palestine were able to once more commune with God face to face. This brief moment in history provided a preview of the glorious future of the redeemed, described in 1 Corinthians 13:12 (NIV): "We shall see [Him] face to face."

Our Master Surgeon, Jesus Christ, extends to us His grace gift—the opportunity to have our disfigured hearts and sinful natures transformed. Our delight will know no bounds when we one day stand fully reconstructed in the presence of the One who gave all "to make man whole." And when we get to heaven, we will know the greatest joy of all: "We will see His face."

Dwight Evans, LLUSM class of 1973-B, is associate professor in LLUSM department of medicine and is assistant dean for veteran affairs for LLUSM.

April 24

For promotion cometh neither from the east, nor from the west, nor from the south. But God is the judge: he putteth down one, and setteth up another. Psalm 75:6-7, KJV

While attending Loma Linda University School of Medicine, I was very active on and off campus. With my active schedule, I did not spend much time on my own schoolwork and that inattention led to academic trouble. I suffered from what I perceived back then to be the shame of having to repeat coursework and delay my graduation date by one year. God comforted me during this time. I even gave public testimonies during this season of trial. But I asked God why He would allow this to happen when I was trying so hard to serve Him.

During that year of repeated coursework, I met my future husband. We dated while he was in Texas and I was in California. Had I been in my clinical rotations year, I would not have been able to travel as much as I did and explore where our relationship would lead. This extra year also provided a much-needed break. With this year of "rest," I really took the time to learn pathophysiology—which has helped me gain the respect of my colleagues in medicine, both then and now. More importantly, I continued to grow closer to God through reading Scripture and serving others.

When it finally seemed that I was over the hump and graduation was around the corner, I was struck with further disappointment: I could not pass the United States Medical Licensing Examination Step 2. I was unable to allocate sufficient study time because of personal issues; and now my graduation date would be postponed again, this time for two more months. I knew that God caused all things to work together for the good of those who love Him, but I just could not understand what good could come out of this.

I had to drop out of the match and participate in the scramble in order to ensure that I would get into a residency program after graduation. On scramble day, one of my advisors strongly felt that I had a better chance of getting into a residency program that was less competitive than a psychiatry program. But I had prayed about it and felt God led me to psychiatry. Through His guidance, I was accepted into a psychiatry residency program.

God has shown me that only He is in control. God chose to bless me in spite of my setbacks. The Bible says in 1 Corinthians 1:27 (NIV), "But God chose the foolish things of the world to shame the wise." I am now in a specialty that I love very much and am happily married and feel I am right where God wants me to be.

Dorcas Adepoju-Olajide, LLUSM class of 2006, is a resident in psychiatry at University of Kansas and lives in Wichita, Kansas.

April 25

Come over into Macedonia, and help us. Acts 16:9, KJV

I was born in 1924, the third of three children of devout Seventh-day Adventist parents. In 1939, my parents and I moved from Mississippi to Collegedale, Tennessee, where my siblings were already enrolled at Southern Junior College (now Southern Adventist University).

I was drafted into military service in 1943; but, through a remarkable series of providential events, I was able to complete my pre-med requirements and enrolled in the College of Medical Evangelists on December 30, 1944. My roommate at Loma Linda was Louis Ludington, LLUSM class of 1949, a fellow Southern Junior College graduate and son of missionaries to Burma. He married Aileen Butka, LLUSM class of 1948. She became an anesthesiologist, while Louis became a general thoracic surgeon.

Following radiology training in Memphis, Tennessee, I began practice in east Tennessee, at Knoxville General Hospital in Knoxville, Tennessee. After a few months, I was invited in 1953 to join the staff at Blount Memorial Hospital in Maryville, Tennessee. Also in 1953, I married a bona fide Kentucky "hillbilly" student nurse named Dusty. In 1954, we moved to an old farm. As I had been reared on a farm, I could not bear the thought of living in town.

Early in 1961, we received a call to join the medical staff of Bangkok Sanitarium and Hospital, which was founded by Ralph Waddel, LLUSM class of 1936. Overseas slots for radiologists were and are quite rare. Responding to the call was somewhat complicated; but one thought kept recurring forcefully in my mind: "If you refuse this call you will regret it the rest of your life." As I recounted the cornucopia of blessings God had given me, I could not refuse Him.

In July 1961, after attending to the myriad details of the move, we flew out of Los Angeles to Tokyo, Japan, for a brief stopover. That intermission led to our first encounter with Irvin Kuhn, LLUSM class of 1955, and his wife, Doreen; and with George Tolhurst, LLUSM class of 1948, my fellow college student. Then it was on to Taipei, Taiwan, for a weekend with another classmate, Roger Heald, LLUSM class of 1949, and his wife. Finally we arrived in Bangkok—truly one of the great cities of the world by any measure! I suffered some degree of homesickness, but my wife Dusty loved it from day one.

The Bangkok Sanitarium and Hospital had a cosmopolitan and congenial medical staff. The radiology department equipment was acceptable and quite up to the standards of that day. We did both diagnosis and therapy. The exams were interesting and not greatly different from those in the United States.

I continued in my practice until 1997. As I approach my 84th birthday, I look back over my life with its joys and sorrows; and I marvel at the forbearance and love that God has for each one of us. To say the least, I have not one regret that we went to Bangkok. One of the lasting impressions that I brought home was an immense sense of awe as I recount Loma Linda University graduates who have given a lifetime of devoted service overseas and, like Paul, heard the call to come over and help.

John Bowen, LLUSM class of 1949, is a radiologist in Louisville, Tennessee. He and his wife have two children and two grandchildren.

April 26

Then from heaven, your dwelling place, hear their prayer and their plea, and uphold their cause. 1 Kings 8:49, NIV

F. B. Meyer said, "The greatest tragedy of life is not unanswered prayer, but unoffered prayer." As a medical student, I learned that even talking about prayer can be therapeutic.

"Mr. Jones" was an elderly and simple male with prostate cancer. His treatments had failed, and the cancer had spread throughout his body—even to the point of multiple, visible masses throughout his spine. We admitted him to the hospital to try to control his severe pain.

Mr. Jones' wife, Mrs. Jones, was in denial.

In conversations, she couldn't—or wouldn't—recognize the gravity of her husband's illness. Her comments included contradictory statements such as, "There ain't nothin' wrong with him," and "Y'all better figure out how to fix him." Somehow, she managed to simultaneously imply that he was faking it, and that we were incompetent in failing to fix whatever was wrong with him.

As the situation progressed, and he required more and more medication for his pain, it became clear that Mr. Jones was facing his last few days on earth. After hours of medical consultation, after attempts to educate Mrs. Jones on her husband's prognosis, and after multiple unproductive family conferences, we became concerned that he would pass away without her recognition of what was happening.

At that point, I met quietly with Mrs. Jones. I told her, "I would like to pray with you, for your husband. What would you like me to pray for?"

She burst into tears.

Sobbing at first, she eventually caught her breath. I wasn't sure what was happening, so I waited. After a while, she finally said, "Pray that he don't suffer. Jus' pray that he don't hurt."

So we did.

Tait Stevens, LLUSM class of 2000—for which he was alumni association representative—is assistant professor in LLUSM department of pathology and human anatomy.

April 27

And the Word was made flesh and dwelt among us, (and we beheld his glory, the glory as of the only begotten of the Father,) full of grace and truth. John 1:14, KJV

The neonatal intensive care unit (NICU) identification badge chafed against my wrist as I fumbled through page after page of organic chemistry reactions for my final exam. Just for a moment, I let my mind wander over what had happened during the last several hours. At 34 weeks, 5 days, my wife had unexpectedly gone into preterm labor while wheeling her cart through a grocery store. Two hours after arriving at the hospital, our first-born son was delivered. I cut the cord at one minute till midnight, and he was taken by the NICU team and assessed.

Over the next several hours, the neonatologist invited me to follow him as he cared for my son. We sat together looking at chest radiographs and talking about babies, medicine, and life. As he assured me that everything would be fine, a window began to open on the world of medicine. Here was a physician, until now a perfect stranger, up in the middle of the night, taking care of my child. In the quiet, while most of the city slept, he charted orders, gently examined, thought, and perhaps even prayed for direction in the care of my precious treasure.

Glancing up at the five-pound miracle, sleeping peacefully amidst a jumble of wires, I noticed the monitor overhead; it assured me that he was fine. I marveled at his tiny, but perfectly proportioned fingers, at his nose and little ears. I rose and stood over him. I longed for him to be free. I wanted to hold him without rearranging wires. I ached for him to know his value and how much he was loved. I prayed that I would have strength to be a wise father.

I bent down and, like thousands of subsequent times, kissed his little cheek. I felt vulnerable as a new parent. How could I help him to experience the joy of life? What could I do to protect my son from the dangers of this world, and from disappointment, pain, and grief? And how could I gently lead him to understand the love of God. I thought of God, who, as a Father, sent His Son as a helpless babe, surrendering Him to a life of misunderstanding and rejection mixed with joy, as He gave us the opportunity to experience wholeness.

I could not have asked for a more appropriate climax to the years of schooling I'd undertaken in preparation for medical school. As I spent the next three days in and out of the NICU at all hours of the day and night—mingling with doctors and nurses, lactation specialists and janitorial staff, or seeing parents suffering at the sight of their three-pound little ones, while others were rejoicing at the news of imminent discharge after months of treatment—all these proved a confirmation for me to continue in the path to which God has called me. In the great cosmic battle to make man whole, God gave Himself, His whole self, though small and helpless, for our redemption.

Mark Warren, LLUSM class of 2010, grew up in Colorado. He and his wife live with their two sons in Colton, California. April 27 is the birthday of his first son, Asher Skye, older brother to Micah Henley.

April 28

Do nothing out of selfish ambition or vain conceit, but in humility consider others better than yourselves. Philippians 2:3, NIV

Here is an open letter dedicated to all who have donated their bodies to Loma Linda University's Bodies for Science Program.

Dear Friend:

Although we never met, we spoke over the telephone many times. You told me about your career, your family, and your beloved spouse. You spoke proudly of your children and their accomplishments. I learned even more about you once I looked over your application to our body-donor program, as well as the various letters you sent in over the years. For your medical history, you listed among your ailments a broken arm, a hip replacement, skin cancer, and "love sick at age 14." A big smile came across my face as I read that last one.

I remember the day you died. I received the call that afternoon. I proceeded with all of the arrangements, just as we had planned; and your body was brought here that evening. Now you lie on a table in our anatomy lab. But you are not alone. Our labs are filled every year with people just like you that have made the same decision, the same sacrifice.

Some say that death has no meaning, but I am sure you would take issue with that. I think of the families that I see in the hospital visiting their sick parent, child, or friend; and about the doctors taking care of them. These doctors possess the knowledge to take care of the sick and injured, thanks to people like you.

I thank you for your gift, this decision you made to donate your body to science. In this world, it is often hard to think that one person could really make a difference for so many. Thanks to you, I see the world differently; for you have done what so many think is impossible. Your decision has had an impact on me that will last the rest of my life.

Words cannot express the gratitude that I have for what you have done. Thank you for training the orthopaedist who will one day take care of my broken bones. Thank you for training the cardiologist who will one day take care of my weakened heart. Thank you for training the obstetrician who will one day deliver my grandchildren.

I thank God for your humanity, your humility, and your sacrifice—your special gift to me and to all of mankind. With your death, you have given the gift of life. I look forward to that day in the New Kingdom when we will finally meet face to face.

Respectfully yours,
Darrell Petersen

Darrell Petersen is instructor in LLUSM department of pathology and human anatomy. He is also director of anatomical services for LLUSM. April 28 is the date in 2009 for the annual anatomy memorial service.

April 29

Heaviness in the heart of man maketh it stoop: but a good word maketh it glad.
Proverbs 12:25, KJV

I was feeling a bit sentimental. I had decided to move my practice north to a neighboring county. Closing down one practice as I was establishing the other, I was going to a colleague's office once a week to finish residual follow-up care of patients. This was the very last day of my work there, and she was the last patient.

Marge was a lady in her mid-80s. She was cleanly dressed with neatly groomed, short gray hair. "Doctor, this is the last day that I can see you. My son is coming tomorrow to take me to his home in Buffalo, New York." I thought to myself, cold Buffalo instead of San Diego at her age? Why would she want to move in that direction?

She reminisced about her younger days as an opera singer. Her husband would always sit in the front row, and in her mind she was singing for him. Then I thought, more than the warmth of the weather, she needs warmth in her heart surrounded by the care of her kinfolks.

Abruptly, she stopped and asked me, "Doctor, do you remember what you said to me when you first saw me?" I couldn't remember. She said, "'You will walk again.'"

Sure, an elderly lady breaks her hip, and I do what I am supposed to do as an orthopaedic surgeon: fix the hip and get her to walk. Routine practice. Nothing special.

"Doctor, after I fell and broke my hip, helplessly lying on a gurney, I thought, 'This is it for my life.' After all, since I lost my husband, I had lost my sense of life. But your first words brought me hope. It changed my outlook. I felt the will to live surging in me with an assurance that I could live normally again."

From time to time, I think about Marge. I wonder whether she moved to Buffalo safely and found comfort in her son's care for the remainder of her life. But as I become more conscious of myself, I wonder what I might have said today to another Marge and what effect it may have had on her this time. Was I an agent of hope? Or have I condemned myself to be simply a deliverer of facts?

Andrew Kim, LLUSM class of 1979-B, is an orthopaedic surgeon. He and his wife, Young, reside in Temecula, California. They have two sons and two daughters.

119

April 30

And the God of all grace, who called you to his eternal glory in Christ, after you have suffered a little while, will himself restore you and make you strong, firm and steadfast. 1 Peter 5:10, NIV

It was 2:00 a.m., and my pager was going off again, as it did so often in those days. I rolled over in bed and groped in the darkness for the intrusive device. Sure enough, the display read the dreaded number of Loma Linda University Medical Center emergency department. "Hey, are you on call for facial trauma?" the emergency room attending asked. I was. "I've got this drunk here who fell down and split his forehead open. I need you to come in and sew him up."

I grumbled all the way to the hospital. I was exhausted. Why couldn't these drunks hurt themselves in the daytime? When I arrived in the emergency room, I was directed to the trauma bay where my patient was waiting. I heard his slurred yelling before I even saw him. I drew back the curtain and was met with the overpowering stench of blood, vomit, and alcohol. My patient looked to be in his 50s, very poorly kept, his face covered in blood and grime.

I hastily introduced myself and collected what I needed. I explained what I was going to do and began to clean the man's wounds. He wasn't cooperative. He cursed, thrashed, and let loose a continuous stream of verbal abuse. I began to get frustrated. Couldn't he hold still for even a minute? I began to inject the local anesthetic too quickly (which stings considerably). I wasn't there to make him comfortable, I reasoned.

His obscenities now came out at a considerable volume, and I had to practically chase him all over the gurney to numb his forehead. Eventually, however, I succeeded and he fell into quietness. The sutures began to go in, closing the 10 cm-long gash over his left eye. In my mind, however, I continued to despise him. Why was I out of bed in the middle of the night to take care of a foul-smelling, uncooperative bum who wouldn't appreciate the care I was providing and almost certainly had no insurance?

My patient stirred and briefly opened his eyes, but remained quiet. Suddenly, in a low but steady voice, he said to no one in particular, "The grace of God is all I've got left." I nearly dropped my instruments. Had he really just said that? After a minute of silence, he spoke about how alcohol had cost him his job, his family, his self-respect. I listened in silence, ashamed of the thoughts I'd had moments earlier. His voice faded and he fell asleep again. I quietly finished my work and left.

I've given considerable thought to what my patient said that night. Careers, loved ones, prestige, and position can be taken from us much faster than we'd care to think about. Thank God that the one thing we really need cannot be removed—His grace.

Christopher Church, LLUSM class of 1996, is associate professor in LLUSM department of otolaryngology: head and neck surgery. He is a specialist in rhinology.

I am sure that nothing can separate us from God's love—not life or death, not angels or spirits, not the present or the future, and not powers above or powers below. Nothing in all creation can separate us from God's love for us in Christ Jesus our Lord! Romans 8:38-39, CEV

I am waiting for news about my 81-year-old father, who is struggling for his life on the ninth floor above me. During my quiet prayer vigil, I stare at Romans 8:38-39 on a large poster hanging on the wall in the LLUMC chapel. I have spent hours in the hospital every day for the past two weeks, checking on his progress and giving him love and courage. He has spent a total of six months out of the past twenty months at LLUMC with four unrelated diagnoses. However, today was the first day that he did not respond to my voice and touch.

The demands of his twenty-month-illness "roller coaster" have left us with very little "down time" to regroup. I see the strain on all those around me: my mother, my husband, my extended family, and friends and colleagues at work. I am sure they see it in me, as I try to keep up each day with the multiple demands of work, teaching, research, and life in general—working it all in between visits to Dad's bedside. Physicians are trained to help our patients' families deal with life-threatening illness; but we have our turn to experience these lessons of grief, too.

Jesus also stood beside His father's deathbed, when He was still a youth or a young man. He must have felt a deep bond with Joseph, His earthly father who loved and sheltered Mary from ridicule, protected Jesus heroically from Herod's massacre plot, sheltered Him for years in Egypt, and taught Jesus a trade with his rough carpenter's hands.

And while the healing power of heaven resided in Jesus' nervous system, He stood beside Joseph and helplessly watched him take his last breath. Turning toward Jesus, Mary's tear-stained face was no doubt filled with pleading, as if to say, "Son, isn't there anything You can do?" Years later, when He raised others from the dead, don't you think He remembered the day He watched Joseph's life slip away and held His weeping mother?

How do you say thank you and goodbye to the one who gave you his DNA, was your perpetual cheerleader and faithful example throughout your life? No one else can fill the void left by a good father. My Creator knows firsthand the weight of my heavy heart and hears my aching prayer ascending from the quiet, dark chapel. He promises me no one can take my father away eternally. Nothing can eternally separate me from God or those who love God. I sit here and read John's Revelation about a New Heaven and a New Earth, where Dad will be free from pain, no tears will sting his cheeks, and death will never threaten him again.

I can imagine meeting Joseph in heaven and introducing him to my father. And Jesus and I will exchange a brief assuring glance that He understands exactly how helpless I felt while standing beside Dad's intensive care bed. I can hold on until then.

Linda Hyder Ferry, LLUSM class of 1979-B, is associate professor in LLUSM department of preventive medicine and assistant professor in LLUSM department of family medicine. She also has an MPH degree. She and her husband, David, LLUSM class of 1976-A, reside in Yucaipa, California. May 1 is her birthday.

May 2

Let us come before His presence with thanksgiving; Let us shout joyfully to Him with psalms. Psalm 95:2, NKJV

The melanoma had metastasized. He suspected it deep down, as I examined the lump in his breast; and I knew it from the biopsy result I had yet to reveal. The disease had recurred once on his upper arm, and the 88-year-old gentleman recognized that his prognosis was now worse. I listened as a surgeon had a compassionate discussion with him about the biopsy, new lung metastases, and treatment options.

After their discussion, his demeanor was suppressed; and our little clinic room had an understandably sad atmosphere. Earlier, in my interview with him, he had told me, "My Christ took all my bad habits." He then elaborated that his personal relationship with his Savior Jesus had enabled him to quit smoking and drinking, and that Christ had been a source of power in his life.

As I share that faith with him, we reintroduced ourselves as brother and sister in Christ; and we established an even deeper rapport. Now, as he sat in his wheelchair deep in thought, I asked him if he would like to pray. He took my hand, bowed his head, and addressed our God with reverence and thanksgiving, pouring out his heart in a mixture of English and Hebrew. I lost count of how many times he said, emphatically, "Thank you, Lord!"

A few weeks later, I visited him again in his hospital room. He had been unable to undergo the procedure to remove the lump because of other developing medical problems. But he was full of joy as he recited Scriptures that encouraged him, confident that God's grace had saved him through faith. He knew that his Savior had given His life for him and was now living and mighty. He believed that all things were working together for his good and was looking forward to the place Jesus prepared for him in heaven.

Further, he instructed me to "always come into the presence of the Lord with a song of thanksgiving on your lips! No matter what the circumstances." He continued to advise that "if something bad happens, say, 'Thank you, Lord!'" I listened in wonder as he lived his powerful faith.

We enjoyed portions of the Bible together, including Psalm 103:1-2, 13-17, 22 (NKJV): "Bless the LORD, O my soul; And all that is within me, bless His holy name! Bless the LORD, O my soul, And forget not all His benefits: . . . As a father pities his children, So the LORD pities those who fear Him. For He knows our frame; He remembers that we are dust. As for man, his days are like grass; As a flower of the field, so he flourishes. For the wind passes over it, and it is gone . . . But the mercy of the LORD is from everlasting to everlasting On those who fear Him . . . Bless the LORD, O my soul!"

We prayed together again and he offered many thanks. I was inspired by this man whose God gave him such incredible inner power, despite a failing body. His faith challenged me to live my life "with a song of thanksgiving on my lips," no matter what the circumstances.

Elisa Joy LaBenne, LLUSM class of 2010, is from Colorado Springs, Colorado. Her husband, Jason, is in the United States Coast Guard. May 2 is the date she encountered joy when she first met the patient in this devotional.

May 3

You therefore must endure hardship as a good soldier of Jesus Christ. 2 Timothy 2:3, NKJV

Gus Hoehn and Erwin Crawford, my brother, were roommates and classmates in Loma Linda University School of Medicine, class of 1945. They continued to be close friends, although they saw each other only a few times during the next thirty years. This is their story.

After his internship, Gus and his family went to Africa as medical missionaries. Gus developed polio in 1948 and was flown back to Los Angeles, California. He spent several months in a so-called "iron lung." He chose to specialize in the treatment of skin diseases, as he was confined to a wheelchair for the rest of his life.

Erwin took four years of postgraduate study in the field of obstetrics and gynecology. He spent six months training under the famous Dr. George Papanicalou, the developer of the now familiar "Pap smear." Within a few years, Erwin became chief of the obstetrics and gynecology sections of two large Toronto, Canada, hospitals.

In addition to their love of medicine, Erwin and Gus shared a strong love for God and spiritual things. For part of his "giving back," Gus collected samples of medicine from his medical friends and sent them to his former hospital in Africa. In time, Erwin gave up his clinical practice and became medical secretary of the Seventh-day Adventist Church, a position that connected him to a larger network of hospitals and clinics throughout the world than any other Protestant denomination.

Erwin felt that God had called him to integrate the spiritual and medical activities of the Seventh-day Adventist Church. When he developed cancer of the colon in 1973, he expected a complete recovery so he could continue his work. When the cancer recurred in 1976, he wondered if God had let him down at this important stage in his career. He tolerated the nausea, vomiting, and diarrhea associated with the chemotherapy. But he could not accept the thought that his vital work might be cut short by cancer.

Dermatologists take care of skin diseases but not colon cancer. However, on one day in May 1976, when Gus visited Erwin in the hospital, he gave Erwin a treatment that changed his life. By this time, Erwin was thin, weak, and depressed. His liver was full of cancer, and he was slightly jaundiced. He intimated to Gus that God seemed to be letting him down.

Gus said, "Well, you know, Erwin, we sing that old hymn 'Onward Christian Soldiers.' If you're in the front line of God's army, you're most likely to get hit."

The idea appealed to Erwin. He looked at Gus sitting in his wheelchair and said, "Well, Gus, I guess you would know."

Erwin lived less than a week. However, his attitude was completely changed. He was a man with a purpose, a soldier who had been wounded in the front line. Gus lived twenty more years. When his post-polio syndrome made it more difficult for him to breathe, he refused to use a ventilator. Gus died peacefully, knowing that he, too, had served God on the front line.

Raymond B. Crawford, LLUSM class of 1949, is emeritus professor in LLUSM department of medicine. He is an internist in Seal Rock, Oregon. He was an LLUSM Alumni Association 1986 Honored Alumnus.

May 4

● can't help remembering

1 white t-shirt stretched over ripe, rounded stomach
   she rests her hand under it
   unconsciously supporting, as she talks
   about onesies and blankets and bibs
   code words for protection and care and so much hope
   "coming this spring"

   but i can't help remembering, earlier that morning—

   white sheet pulled up over bony shoulders
   his wrinkled hand hangs lifelessly off the side of the bed
   with his wedding band still encircling his ring finger
   reminiscent of love and commitment and so much hope
   rest now. nearby a bouquet, with cruel irony
   "get well soon"

   heartbreakingly strong contrast.

   so strange—and acutely, intricately sweet
   the moments we pull together to make a life.
   never-ending transience;
   that sometimes asks to be eaten whole,
   mouthful so large it can barely be chewed. happy gluttony.
   but other days asks too much—and all that i've seen
   only makes me feel older.

   i want to tell them all, with care—

   wherever you are, little man, for tonight
   tucked snugly into a crib or a hospital bed
   or somewhere in between
   i wish you courage to face your transitions:
   to shape them into something beautiful, with acceptance
   and so much hope

Kristin Schmid, LLUSM class of 2008, is completing her internship in internal medicine in San Francisco, California, in preparation for her ophthalmology residency in Detroit, Michigan.

May 5

I will rejoice because of the LORD; I will be happy because of the God who delivers me. The sovereign LORD is my source of strength. He gives me the agility of a deer; he enables me to negotiate the rugged terrain. Habakkuk 3:18-19, NET

I never thought I would become a doctor's wife. But in the two years I've been the wife of a man studying to be a doctor, I've had the chance to examine what this role means now and what it could mean for a lifetime. Yes, being married to a medical student is hard. Yes, he keeps long hours studying. And yes, it's hard when he's on-call and he doesn't have cell phone service in the hospital.

But I remind myself that all marriages have their challenges; many occupations require long hours (i.e., business owners, lawyers, and accountants in April). Throughout history, people have survived without cell phones.

During our relatively short married life, I have found ways to endure the times he's gone. The most important thing I can do for both of us is to pray. Prayer is a lifeline of comfort and strength, even when the cell phone doesn't work. I can pray for him no matter where he is, what he's doing, or who he's helping.

Even though I cannot be there to encourage him throughout the day, our God is there by his side. And our God is with me, too, as I drive to work, interact with people, and come back home to a happy dog and a pile of dirty dishes. Our relationship gets its strength from each of us individually looking up to our Creator and then looking to each other. I don't know how we would survive without prayer sustaining us daily.

As the wife of a future doctor, I see my growing responsibility to my community. My involvement in various organizations can be a vehicle for giving back to the world by aiding needy families, helping with projects at LLUCH, tutoring students, or bringing food to lonely elderly people in town. It doesn't take much time to make a difference, in someone else's life as well as my own.

When I first moved to Loma Linda, it was hard to find a job and make new friends. It took some time to establish a social network; but now I have my own friend niche, and I reach out to others who are new to the area and likely lonely. I often call a friend with whom I can exercise, I've joined a Bible study, and I frequently have a girls' night out or even a girls' weekend. All of these options are better than sitting on a couch alone, waiting for my husband to come home.

Hands down, one of the most important things I've learned is to be there for my husband when he has time to watch a movie or when he wants to get some ice cream. I will always have more free time than he will; so when he is free, I try to be open as well.

Sometimes mundane activities can waste the precious time we have together. I try to prioritize my day, clearing my schedule as best I can when my man wants to play tennis or take the dog to the park. Adults need laughter as much as kids do. Besides, making fun memories is much better than doing the dishes any day!

Louisa M. Kellar is the wife of Jesse Kellar, LLUSM class of 2010. Both are from the state of Washington and graduated from Walla Walla University in College Place, Washington. She is currently vice president of the Junior Medical Auxiliary of the LLUSM Alumni Association. May 5 is his birthday.

May 6

I am come that they might have life, and that they might have it more abundantly. John 10:10, KJV

Abraham Lincoln once said, "And in the end, it's not the years in your life that count. It's the life in your years."

His curiosity and ebullience died just a few days before his heart stopped. On tough days, I put on the camel hair sport coat he left me and feel a little stronger.

Charles Richmond Tourtellotte—"Dr. T" or "Charlie," depending on the context—28, boarded in internal medicine; and after returning from service in Korea, he joined the medical staff at Riverside (California) General Hospital in 1955. A slim 5' 10", he moved with athletic grace. A perpetual smile eventually etched his face. He was soon elected president of the medical staff and appointed chair of the department of medicine. Doctors with sick family members sought him out for care, and it didn't have to be oncology.

Only his *vita* heralded past accomplishments. Born in 1927, he graduated summa cum laude from Dartmouth College in Hanover, New Hampshire, one month after his eighteenth birthday; and completed the four-year medical school curriculum in three years, Alpha Omega Alpha. In 2004, Loma Linda internal medicine residents gave him the "Faculty of the Year" award.

In 1997, Dr. T celebrated his 70th birthday and retired from private oncology practice in Riverside. He plunged into building oncology services at the county hospital. He grew the service from a half-day-a-week clinic to a five-day-a-week outpatient oncology service. Over the next eight years, he quadrupled patient volume and provided round-the-clock telephone consultation. To his dying patients, he might say, "John, you're not going to make it." Then he stood by, making sure of the details of care.

A perpetual insomniac, he filled his nighttime hours with reading—and daytime breaks describing progress in the human genome project. Whether consilience, string theory, supersymmetry, the golden ratio, new discoveries in medicine—he shared his insights and gave away his well-marked books.

In 2001, Dr. T learned that he had a serious illness. Expert physicians directed his care—and Dr. T took infusions alongside his own patients for a number of months. The disease progressed relentlessly. In May 2005, Dr. T came to my office and handed me an envelope. "Keep this and don't try to resurrect me," he instructed. It was his living will.

Not till the last Thursday of his life in 2005 did he observe, "*Something strange has happened in the last few days. I don't want to read. I don't even want to listen to good music . . .*" That was the day I cried. The passion that had become habit had finally succumbed. A few days later, Dr. T took his last breath.

Joy in discovery, doing the job right, a funny limerick, a patient who says, "You helped me, Doc"—these are the things that bring back memories of a smile, and of a man who came and did God's work at the county hospital.

Douglas Hegstad, LLUSM class of 1980-A, is associate professor in and chair of LLUSM department of medicine. In 1998, he was LLUSM Teacher of the Year.

Trust in the LORD with all thine heart; and lean not unto thine own understanding. In all thy ways acknowledge him, and he shall direct thy paths. Proverbs 3:5-6, KJV

I faced some hard decisions in 1944 when I graduated from medical school. I wanted to pursue internal medicine and had been encouraged by Loma Linda to apply for their nine-month residency program. During the draft in World War II, if one were appointed as a resident, he was assured that the military service would not take him for that period. So all of us wanted to get a residency appointment.

In those days, class rank was a major factor in influencing the selection of residents; I received word that the department at Loma Linda had approved my class rank. Therefore, I thought I was safe choosing internal medicine. When the department chair talked to me specifically at my wedding, I believed military service for me would at least be delayed.

Then I learned I had not been accepted into internal medicine; I realized that I would probably receive a notice from the army instead and I was very disappointed. Not long after, I did receive orders to report in uniform to North Carolina.

I talked with my commanding officer there, a Jewish physician, and told him I was a Seventh-day Adventist. He assured me that he would "be able to work things out." When our outfit went to out staging area, I asked to be excused from a lecture that was scheduled on Sabbath. This same colonel refused and countered with a direct order and warning that if I did not go, he would immediately start court-martial proceedings! However, I did not attend the lecture.

For many weeks following this event, I expected to be summoned regarding my stand; nothing ever happened. Some thirty-five years later, the chaplain in my outfit took a trip to California and looked up my wife and me. He then told me what took place that Saturday. He said the colonel had explained to him what he planned to do. The chaplain responded by telling the colonel that if he did start proceedings, he, as chaplain, would have to stand with me, because, as he understood it, I was within my rights. Thankfully, the colonel dropped the whole matter.

The chaplain and I went on to become very close friends. One night he wanted to talk further about religion, and asked for some literature; I had my wife send a few Bible studies. These he carefully studied; and after a few weeks, he told me he wanted to become a Seventh-day Adventist! We both felt it wise for him to tell our commanding officer. The colonel commented that Dr. Hadley "had not been a problem;" so he did not foresee any reason why the chaplain could not follow his conviction.

Shortly after this occurrence, we received orders that our evacuation hospital was to go to the Pacific. Morale was low aboard the troopship, as many casualties were expected if an attack on Japan occurred. About four days later, the captain of the ship announced that the war was over and we would be going to Boston! I shall never forget the feeling of relief and thankfulness as I watched the troopship take a 90-degree turn to the north. Again, it built confidence in the realization that God certainly does have a plan for each of us.

G. Gordon Hadley, LLUSM class of 1944-B, is professor in LLUSM department of pathology and human anatomy. In addition to serving as dean of LLUSM from 1977 to 1986, he has also served in Afghanistan, China, and India. He was named LLUSM Alumni Association 1985 Alumnus of the Year, was the 1989 recipient of the LLU Distinguished Service Award, and was named 1996 LLU Alumnus of the Year.

May 8

Before they call I will answer; while they are still speaking I will hear. Isaiah 65:24, NIV

During World War II, no personal automobiles were made for several years. On Victory in Europe Day, May 8, 1945, I was a sophomore at Loma Linda University. In anticipation of the end of World War II, I ordered a new Ford, with probable delivery in March or April of 1946. But the car was a year late, cost $1,500, and had no heater; so I added a very inadequate heater for my Colorado internship. I was driving it in Beach, North Dakota, when the following incident took place.

My brother, Ed, had ordered a new car in 1946. He had assured us by letter that he could handle the finances. He had been teaching church school in the Oregon area but now was working in the woods to put food on the table for his growing family, which included identical 2-year-old twin boys.

Money was not flush. I had gotten through medical school with small loans, help from an excellent working wife, and an internship of $100 per month, plus a $20 meal ticket. I was seeing patients on October 22, 1948, when a strong impression came to me to send Ed $100. I ignored the impulse but couldn't ignore the almost audible command to do it before the second mail pick-up of the day. (Two mails left Beach, North Dakota, daily.) With patients waiting, I called my good wife. She mailed the check.

This is a quote from my brother's letter, October 26, 1948: "We received your letter and check tonight, and you'll never know how much it is appreciated. The new car came to more than I was prepared for, and I had to take $100 less for my old car. I had to give a check for the down payment without having enough money in the bank. I figured on borrowing $100 from somebody, but didn't know who or how, and I had so much difficulty getting the deal sewed up, I lost a whole day's work, instead of a half day, and I knew the boss would be plenty sore about my not working in the p.m."

Edna, Ed's wife, also wrote us on October 27, 1948: "I feel rather at a loss to know just what to say. It surely seems to us the Lord set about to answer our prayers before we voiced them. At the time you mailed the check, we didn't realize our extreme needs. This is the first day for months that I haven't gone to the post office during the afternoon, but I had unexpected visitors. Ed arrived home around 6:30. The children had eaten, and Ed joined us for worship. We had special prayer for guidance in our financial situation, and Ed went to the post office. Unless you have had a similar experience, you just don't know how we felt when we opened the letter and the check fell out."

This turn of events impressed my wife, Elaine, and me so much that we have kept both letters and the cancelled check. The Lord knows us well enough to make things work in spite of our trying to ignore Him.

Omer Drury, LLUSM class of 1948, is a family practitioner in Troy, Idaho.

And you also are witnesses. John 15:27, RSV

"There's spirituality, if you want it" was one of the reasons mentioned in the "Top 10 Reasons Why General Surgery Is a Great Career" by Richard C. Thirlby in the May 2007 issue of *Archives of Surgery*. I believe this same view can be applied to everyone who interacts with patients. Patients bring themselves to us in their most desperate, hardest times, and in their most joyful times. This connection I find to be a privilege. Everyday you are allowed to bring God to your patients, and your patients, in return, are able to bring God to you.

The following poem, attributed to Teresa of Avila, echoes this thought:

> "Christ has no body now on earth but yours, no feet but yours, no hands but yours.
> Yours are the eyes through which the compassion of Christ is to look out on a hurting world.
> Yours are the feet with which he is to go about doing good.
> Yours are the hands with which he is to bless all now."

One of the most grateful people I have ever seen was a stroke victim, who, after weeks of not being able to move his arm, was able to move it slightly. These are the people who teach me gratitude. Most people would have considered his range of motion to be unacceptably low, but he found that slight movement to be thrilling!

God brings Himself to us in patients such as this. And God allows us to be Him to those who need Him most. So if we want it, everyday we have a chance to live out the gospel and be reminded of how amazing and alive God is in this world.

Sarah Killian, LLUSM class of 2011, is from Garden Grove, California, and received a degree in biomedical engineering from University of California, Irvine.

May 10

Direct your children onto the right path, and when they are older, they will not leave it. Proverbs 22:6, NLT

Mrs. J was a teacher. She and her husband, a successful businessman, worked hard and loved what they did. When Mrs. J became pregnant, they were excited and made plans for a long and happy life with children.

When their "Matt" was born, the doctors immediately recognized that he had a congenital problem that would include mental retardation, blindness, and lack of motor skills. This was not what they had expected.

Mr. J told his wife they would have no more children, and that they would spend their resources taking care of this one. The doctors advised against it—telling them to put "Matt" in a state institution since he would not likely amount to anything, and that they would not be able to handle his care at home.

Mrs. J quit her job as a teacher and stayed home, taking on the challenge of caring for this child. Over the years, she patiently and persistently taught him, over and over, the things normal kids would pick up naturally. She taught him how to eat, how to dress himself, and how to talk to people. She taught him how to read (a little) and how to carry on a conversation. She taught him the importance of caring for himself and the importance of having a job. Then, when "Matt" began losing his eyesight, she taught him how to get along with that problem as well.

Mr. J died, having provided for his family in such a way that Mrs. J could continue staying home and caring for her now-adult son. She continued to teach him. She taught him how to keep a bank account, how to write checks, and how to catch the bus. She taught him how to find a job, and he was hired by Goodwill Industries.

By the time they both became my patients, Mrs. J was well into her 80s and "Matt" was in his late 30s. It was obvious that Mrs. J had also taught him how to talk to his doctor. He easily asked questions and could understand the answers, as long as they were in simple terms. We had an immediate rapport. Mrs. J never came to his office visits, believing that he needed to learn how to do this on his own.

Now, in her mid 90s, Mrs. J comes in whenever "Matt" gets worried about her. She is in an assisted living facility and "Matt" visits her often. They have somehow traded places, with "Matt" calling my office whenever he thinks his mom might be ill. It is always the same: he calls and tells us what is ailing her and says he thinks she should come in, and don't we think so, too? Of course my staff always obliges him, and she comes in.

Recently, she has been telling me she thinks she really should die soon, because no one would choose to be alive "at this age."

"You know," she says, "I worry about 'Matt,' but I think he will do fine when I'm gone. I've taught him as much as I can. In fact, I wish he would loosen up a bit and just leave me alone! I can't cough without him telling me to go to the doctor." I hug her and reassure her that she has done a wonderful job raising her son and that I think he will do just fine. He has a mom, and she gave him everything she could. He was her best work.

Like Mrs. J, God, our Heavenly Father, patiently works with us and trains us in the way we should go. Through His guidance, we can learn how to show others to follow Him and do their best work here on earth.

Rima Bishara, LLUSM class of 1986, is a mother of two and an internist in Waco, Texas. May 10 is Mother's Day in 2009.

Take therefore no thought for the morrow: for the morrow shall take thought for the things of itself. Sufficient unto the day is the evil thereof. Matthew 6:34, KJV

That dauntless apostle of equanimity, Sir William Osler, once warned a group of medical students: "An anticipatory attitude of mind, a perpetual forecasting, disturbs the even tenor of his way and leads to disaster. Years ago a sentence in one of Carlyle's essays made a lasting impression on me—'Our duty is not to see what lies dimly at a distance, but to do what lies clearly at hand.' I have long maintained that the best motto for a student is 'Take no thought for morrow.' Let the day's work suffice; live for it, regardless of what the future has in store, believing that the tomorrow should take thought for the things of itself . . . nor is there any risk that such an attitude may breed carelessness. On the contrary, the absorption in the duty of the hour is in itself the best guarantee of ultimate success."

An attempt to anticipate the future is, of course, a logical defense against society's allowing its technology to drive ahead of its ethics—a circumstance fraught with present and future danger. . . .

What we need not experience, however, is the shaking of the basic moral foundations by these future developments. Our collective wisdom may be strained to the limits as we try to apply established principles to the business of keeping ethically abreast of a burgeoning technology, but this we may know: God is not taken by surprise.

It is on this ground that Sir William Osler's statement (and that of Jesus) seems presently relevant. As the great philosopher Leibnitz once put it, "*Le present est gros de l'avenir*"—The present is big (pregnant) with the future. It is our present skill at applying our God-given moral verities that guarantees the future.

What next? Who can say for sure? Will we be able to handle the future when it comes? Probably, providing we attend with intelligent persistence to the problems we face today.

Jack W. Provonsha (1920-2004), LLUSM class of 1953-A, was emeritus professor of philosophy of religion and Christian ethics in LLUSR; as well as an ordained Seventh-day Adventist minister. He received an MA degree from Harvard University in Cambridge, Massachusetts; and a PhD degree from Claremont Graduate University in Claremont, California. From 1964 to 1965, he served as LLUSM Alumni Association president and was named Alumnus of the Year by this organization in 1978. In 1988, he received the LLU Distinguished Service Award. This devotional originally appeared in the May-June 1989 issue of the LLUSM Alumni Association Alumni Journal.

May 12

The angel of the LORD encamps all around those who fear Him, And delivers them. Psalm 34:7, NKJV

The sun was setting over Manila Bay as Hedrick, Elmar, Severino, and Severino's little son walked to the car. They were about to take a fifty-kilometer drive from Manila to Philippine Union College (now Adventist University of the Philippines) in Silang, Cavite, Philippines. As they approached the car, Elmar, a visiting faculty from Loma Linda University School of Medicine, asked if he could drive Hedrick's car. "Certainly," Hedrick replied, as he handed over the car keys.

They drove for the first forty kilometers on the newly opened South Superhighway. Alas, the smooth asphalt ribbon did not go all the way to Silang. They had to take the Balibago Road, flanked on both sides by tall sugar cane fields, for the last ten kilometers. Balibago was notorious for its potholes. There were large potholes and small potholes, shallow potholes and deep potholes. At that time, the area was also known for lawlessness and carjacking.

In the tropics, the sun sets very quickly, so it was dark by the time the little group got to Balibago Road. Suddenly a loud bang shattered the dark stillness! The car shook violently. They heard an unwelcome sound, bump, bump, bumpity bump. Elmar and Hedrick looked at each other knowingly. Pulling to the side of the road, the two men got out to inspect the damage. The impact was so forceful that the wheel was dented and the tire was flat. Just then, a large vehicle, which looked like an army van, pulled up beside them. Three men dressed in army fatigues got out of the van. They looked like soldiers.

"What is the problem?" they wanted to know.

"We have a flat tire, and we don't have a jack," Hedrick responded.

"Do you have a flashlight?" Unfortunately, he did not have a flashlight in his car, either.

"You should never drive out here without a flashlight." One of the soldiers admonished sternly.

"We will help you," the soldiers said, as they unscrewed the tire bolts. Two soldiers lifted the car up, while the other slipped off the flat tire, inserted the spare tire, and bolted it on.

Gratefully, Hedrick, Elmar, and Severino thanked the soldiers and got back into their car. As Elmar started the engine, they looked across to say one last goodbye to their benefactors. Amazed, they stared at the empty road. The army van was not there! They had not heard the engine start, nor did it pass them on the narrow road. It had not backed up, nor could it have penetrated the thick sugar cane fields on either side of the road. Where had the truck gone, they wondered.

From the back seat came the small voice of Severino's little boy. "They must have been angels," he mused. Were they really angels? Perhaps. Or could they have been soldiers sent by angels for protection on that dark and lonely stretch of the Balibago Road?

Lenoa Edwards has been assistant dean for admissions for LLUSM since 2001. She has an MPH degree. She was born in Nicaragua and was a missionary in the Philippines.

Trust in the LORD with all your heart, And lean not on your own understanding; In all your ways acknowledge Him, And He shall direct your paths. Proverbs 3:5-6, NKJV

Throughout my career as a medical student, I wrote the inscription, "God's thoughts, my hands," at the top of every test I took. This statement was never truer than at the end of my second year of medical school.

My only brother and his wife were expecting their first child at the end of May 2002. I jokingly told them that they were not allowed to have the baby on either May 13 or 14 because those were the two days just prior to my most difficult final exam. This exam had the capability of significantly altering one's medical career, as advancement to third year was dependant upon a passing grade on this test.

As God so wisely planned it, my niece entered this world on May 13 at 7:40 p.m. Without a second thought after learning of her arrival, I scooped up my study materials, said goodbye to my friends, and drove to meet my new niece, Mia Grace, an hour away. Her parents beamed as I entered the room, and they introduced me to her for the first time. She was a bundle of perfection and innocence, an irresistible little person from the start.

I attempted to study the next day in the hospital cafeteria, as I intermittently held her and looked at God's finery in human form. Late that evening, I returned to Loma Linda to cram in some last-minute studying before the final exam, as well as to get some rest. The next morning, I arrived with my classmates to take the feared exam and penned my favorite inscription on to the top of the page with more fervor than ever before.

Three-and-a-half hours later, God had delivered me through the exam. And then, with trepidation, I waited for the score. Later that week, when I eagerly snatched the score out of my mailbox, God's graciousness was evident as I discovered that He had delivered me through the exam with flying colors and a passing grade.

This event in my life taught me a great deal about trust and priorities. Nothing in life is more important than the people God has given to you to love. My memories of Mia in her first hours of life and our bond are irreplaceable gifts, as is the lesson I learned in letting God take control of my life. "Trust God with all you heart. . . ."

Jennifer (DeKraker) Barker, LLUSM class of 2004—for which she was freshman class president and sophomore-year president for the SM senate—is chief resident for the Indiana University combined residency in emergency medicine and pediatrics. In 2004, she received the Leonard Marmor Award.

May 14

Beloved, I wish above all things that thou mayest prosper and be in health, even as thy soul prospereth. 3 John 2, KJV

During my graduation ceremony in May 2004, a provocative statement was made that has stayed with me throughout my general surgery residency. "Patients remember most about their surgeon what they observe while they are awake," remarked Dr. Roger Hadley, dean of Loma Linda University School of Medicine. Patients remember how well you treated them before and after surgery. Jesus gave us the ultimate example of "bedside manner" and the power of a touch.

When Jesus healed people, He would often touch them—even if they were considered untouchable due to leprosy. A simple touch on the shoulder or holding a patient's hand tells patients that you care about how they feel. Touch is an inaudible transmission of caring. Doesn't God touch our lives, even when we are sometimes untouchable? Doesn't He bless us when we don't deserve to be blessed?

None who came to Jesus went away without any help. In body, mind, and soul, individuals were made whole. As physicians, these opportunities to make persons whole are available to us. God says: "I the Lord have called thee in righteousness, and will hold thine hand, and will keep thee, and give thee for a covenant of the people, for a light of the Gentiles; To open the blind eyes, to bring out the prisoners from the prison, and them that sit in darkness out of the prison house" (Isaiah 42:6-7, KJV).

People may be imprisoned in the darkness of sin, depression, abuse, or addictions; or have sorrow, despair, or poor health. And the Lord is calling us to release these prisoners in His name. Beginning with a simple touch, we can transmit the Savior's love and alleviate their pain.

During my surgery residency, I have had many opportunities to use the skills I acquired at Loma Linda University to share my faith with others. Some people want to pray before surgery to help ease their anxiety and fears. Some people want prayer for their loved ones who will be going through surgery. There are times I have the opportunity to give God glory when there has been a miraculous save on a trauma patient and the family members are tearfully thankful.

We are His hands—to touch those around us, to communicate His healing power and love to those whom society has deemed untouchable but for whose salvation Jesus died. "And, behold, there came a leper and worshipped him, saying, Lord, if thou wilt, thou canst make me clean. And Jesus put forth his hand, and touched him, saying, I will; be thou clean. And immediately his leprosy was cleansed" (Matthew 8:2-3, KJV).

Naeem Newman, LLUSM class of 2004—for which he was freshman class senator for the LLUSM senate—is chief resident in general surgery at Washington Hospital Center in Washington, D.C. He and his wife, Mytonia, have two daughters, Rhiane and Mya. May 14 is his birthday.

Do not neglect to do good and to be generous, for God is pleased with such sacrifices. Hebrews 13:16, ISV

Just a few months after I began my work at Loma Linda University School of Medicine, I received an envelope from an elderly man living in a small town in Oregon. The envelope contained a check for $2,000 for the department of ophthalmology and a carefully typed note. It said:

"I would like to give you an explanation of why I am sending this donation. About 35 years ago I had an accident that severed my tear duct completely in half. Gordon Wheeler, LLUSM class of 1964, was a good friend and sent me to Loma Linda where the fine doctors sewed my tear duct back together.

I had a wife and three children and no health insurance and was struggling to make ends meet. The hospital and doctors did not charge me. I am sorry it has taken so long to pay something back. Enclosed is a check for $2,000 that may help someone in the same predicament that I was. I thank the hospital and doctors for taking care of me. My tear duct has worked perfectly!"

The letter is touching and poignantly illustrates the effect of a competent, caring, Christian physician. I think it is awe inspiring to consider the incredible legacy of the more than 9,500 physicians trained at Loma Linda University School of Medicine over the past 100 years. Take a moment and reflect on the lives these doctors have touched in the course of their own lives and careers.

Every day, Loma Linda University School of Medicine administration prays for guidance as they continue to train physicians "to continue the healing and teaching ministry of Jesus Christ, 'To make man whole.'"

Over the next 100 years, may we never lose sight of this noble mission.

Treva Webster is assistant dean for development for LLUSM. She has an MBA degree and is a registered nurse.

May 16

A soft answer turns away wrath, But a harsh word stirs up anger. . . . A wholesome tongue is a tree of life, But perverseness in it breaks the spirit.
Proverbs 15:1, 4, NKJV

Even a doctor's most difficult patient can be his most effective teacher. Little did I know just what kind of lesson I was in for when Mrs. S walked into my clinic. She was a 70-year-old female, who was scheduled to see me for a follow-up visit from the emergency room. She had an unfortunate diagnosis of maxillary sinus cancer, which had metastasized to her lungs. A review of her records revealed that she had been in and out of the emergency room several times in the past few weeks for various reasons—a red flag to any medical provider.

As I watched the medical assistant take her vitals, I saw a frail and emaciated elderly lady. Noticeably, she was a very devout Catholic, for she would repeatedly express that she was praying for a miracle and kiss the cross that hung around her neck. She was accompanied by her son, who was her primary caregiver, and, ironically, was serving time doing community service to pay for a petty crime.

As if my first impressions needed further elaboration, the patient presented what seemed to be an infinite list of complaints, including dissatisfaction with her previous doctor. This twenty-minute "routine visit" was turning into an emotional nightmare! By God's grace, I had enough patience to address her multiple medical concerns during that appointment and many subsequent ones over the next several weeks.

The time finally came for Mrs. S' final admission to the hospital. I had the opportunity to meet and talk with her family, to speak words of comfort as they prepared for her inevitable death. Later that night, Mrs. S took her last breath—in peace and surrounded by loved ones. And life for me went on as usual.

Then, one Sabbath, he walked into church. It was Mrs. S' son . . . at camp meeting! After greeting him and discovering that he was a fellow Seventh-day Adventist and the only one in his family, I realized the test that God had started at that dreaded first visit. Who knows what would have happened to my faith, or his, if I had spoken to and treated his mother and family any differently than I did.

Whose ears will your words fall upon today? Make it a prayer for God to use your words to turn away wrath and to give life.

Michael Mercado, LLUSM class of 2004—for which he was junior-year senator for the LLUSM senate and senior-year co-pastor—is a lieutenant in the United States Navy and is currently stationed at the United States Naval Hospital in Guam and deployed in Afghanistan. He received the Wil Alexander Whole-Person Care Award in 2004. He and his wife, Gemma Miranda-Mercado, LLUSM class of 2004, were married on May 16, and they have two children.

Prove all things; hold fast that which is good. 1 Thessalonians 5:21, KJV

The honest scientist who is looking for truth will be expected to make his investigations as carefully and as thoroughly as possible, and accurately to record his findings. Further, it will be expected of him that he make his conclusions strictly upon the evidence which has been made available. Also, it will be expected of him that, if the evidence requires a change from his previous concepts, he must be willing to make that change.

Certainly, one of the attitudes of a mature person, relative to religion, is that its doctrines must withstand critical investigation and experimentation. As a matter of fact, the Scripture advises this method as being essential to spiritual growth. Similarly, as well-proved evidence becomes available, one must be willing to make transitions in his thinking and in his living, in accord with the added knowledge which he has obtained.

If one has a sincere desire and makes an honest effort to find spiritual truth, to find God, to find security and salvation, he will be well satisfied with his findings and not be disappointed. . . .

If you are to perform your work well, you must do your best to be honest, hard-working, and conscientious scientists. You must make every effort to maintain the discriminating and critical thinking of a scientist. . . .

The world needs what I believe you are qualified to give. I ask you to give it.

Walter E. Macpherson (1899-1996), LLUSM class of 1924, was dean of LLUSM from 1955 to 1962. He was LLUSM Alumni Association president from 1931 to 1932 and from 1938 to 1939, and was LLUSM Alumni Association 1948 Alumnus of the Year. This devotional, a portion of a commencement address to the LLUSM class of 1951, originally appeared in the July 1951 issue of the LLUSM Alumni Association Alumni Journal.

May 18

Blessed be the LORD, for he has heard the sound of my pleadings. The LORD is my strength and my shield; in him my heart trusts; so I am helped, and my heart exults, and with my song I give thanks to him. Psalm 28:6-7, NRSV

Let me introduce to you Asato Tsuji, who was born in Bofu, Yamaguchi Prefecture, Japan, on February 5, 1996. Around her second birthday, she was diagnosed with cardiomyopathy—which, by age 4, had become what is termed *end-stage*. She was transported from Osaka University to Loma Linda University Children's Hospital for possible heart transplantation. "So," you're saying to yourself, "nothing unusual about that. Where's the shock? Where's the awe?"

Shortly after arrival, Asato was placed on the waiting list for a donor organ. She was initially cared for as an outpatient, but she quickly decompensated. She required hospital admission and intravenous drug support. She was advanced to highest priority on the waiting list.

Then, one day, suddenly and without warning, her heart arrested. Ventricular tachycardia! She was immediately given lidocaine, which chemically shocked her heart back into a normal rhythm. Her heart began to squeeze again. Several more tense days went by. Then cardiac arrest episodes became more frequent, something called "malignant" ventricular tachycardia. Discouraged, the pediatric cardiologists declared that Asato could die at any moment. Clearly, her life was in its final day.

On that very day (June 20, 2000), we got word of a donor, a 20-month-old drowning victim in Hershey, Pennsylvania. But how were we going to cross the country, recover the donor heart, and return to do the transplant on Asato, when she might easily die within the next hour or two? Here comes the awe!

Before leaving for Hershey, and to ensure that Asato would still be alive when we got back, we took her to operating room number 13. There we put her to sleep, opened her chest, and connected her to a heart-lung machine. Her body was cooled to a temperature of 20° C. We left her there in room 13, essentially hibernating, while a few of us drove to the airport, boarded a Learjet, and flew east. In concert with other organ recovery teams, we removed the donor heart and returned to Loma Linda. The "new" heart was used to replace Asato's own "kill-her" heart. It was a perfect fit.

After more than sixteen hours in the operating room, attached to a heart-lung machine for circulatory support, Asato's recovery was unremarkable. Her new heart performed flawlessly. I'm reminded of her story because I just received a photo of Asato on the occasion of her graduation into middle school. She is now 12 years old, and she is living well with her American heart. What are the odds?

However you and I might characterize it—Providence, divine oversight, miracle, or just plain awe—Asato is a miracle personified, one that radiates not only in our own hearts and minds but widely throughout Japan as well. She's a living, loving example of our daily walk with God.

Enjoy your walk today.

Leonard L. Bailey, LLUSM class of 1969, is distinguished professor in LLUSM department of surgery, division of cardiothoracic surgery. He was LLUSM Alumni Association 1986 Alumnus of the Year and was LLU Alumnus of the Year in 1987. May 18 is the birthday of his wife, Nancy.

May 19

Let all things be done decently and in order. 1 Corinthians 14:40, NKJV

My husband, Scott, and I were flying home after celebrating our wedding anniversary. Unexpectedly, over the public address system of the plane, Scott heard the words, "Is there a doctor on board?" Those six words terrify me, as I have heard horror stories about doctors, while in the air and with limited resources, trying to help sick people.

An elderly gentleman, directly across the aisle from Scott, had fainted and was slumped in his seat. Scott, elbowing me over and over, trying to wake me up, said, "Shouldn't you do something?" Finally, my sleepy mind cleared and my eyes focused in the dark cabin. "I'm a new intern!" I muttered. "Surely there must be someone else who can help!"

But the "patient" was in such close proximity to me that I couldn't just ignore him in good conscience. I stood up and said, "I am a doctor." Those words made me sound more competent than I was feeling; and, in retrospect, I am sure they made me sound more competent than I was!

The "patient" did not respond to a shake of his shoulder and a loud "How are you?" So, I instructed the surrounding passengers to vacate their seats and proceeded to lay him flat. He appeared to be breathing and, before I could do anything else, an automatic external defibrillator (AED) was shoved into my hands. It seemed like a good idea, so I fumbled with the packaging, the patches, the wires, and the machine.

Eventually, it was all hooked up. "Turn the AED on," I said in a loud voice. However, before the cabin attendant could do anything, I detected a nervous, tremulous voice that carried throughout the plane. I heard, "But I don't want to be shocked." During the ruckus of organizing the AED, I hadn't realized my "patient" had awakened and was watching the proceedings with horror!

As I think back on that incident, I am sure I was very confidence-inspiring as I ripped open the AED, threw packaging around the cabin, and almost defibrillated a man who was awake and talking! I sat down in defeat and wondered why I hadn't remembered to check his pulse (as in "airway, breathing, then circulation") before I even considered defibrillating. Thankfully an older doctor emerged from the back of the plane and I could see the relieved look in everyone's eyes.

Yes, we should "let all things be done decently and in order." But in life, it is easy to get the order of things mixed up (i.e., work, school, God, family, entertainment, etc.). Whenever I remember that eventful plane ride, I once again become determined to let all things in my life be done "decently and in order."

Mindi Guptill, LLUSM class of 2006, is a resident in emergency medicine at LLUMC. In 2006, she received the Society of Emergency Medicine Award. She is also a deferred mission appointee. She and her husband, Scott, were married on May 19.

May 20

And heal the sick there, and say to them, "The kingdom of God has come near to you." Luke 10:9, NKJV

Graduation has always been an important milestone in medical education, and that is true for Loma Linda University as well. The landscape here on this campus has changed, but the importance continues.

Many alumni remember commencement activities in the old Loma Linda Bowl on the hill. The bowl was a bit too small, but, situated as it was near the hospital and among the great eucalyptus trees, it made a meaningful place to hold graduations.

Then there were the services at the Pasadena (California) Civic Auditorium, at the Redlands (California) Bowl, and now on the mall in front of the School of Medicine building at Loma Linda University. While there have been many venues, the significance of the ceremony has always been there for the graduates and their families.

Each graduation launched the new physicians into a changing and often unknown future. During World War II, nearly all the members of the class received their military officer's commission during the graduation ceremony, and then they were soon off to the armed services.

In the earlier years, most graduates became interns and then general practitioners. Gradually, the internship has faded into the first year of a specialty residency, and the demands on the young physicians have changed.

The reasons for entering the profession of medicine are changing, also. For some graduating seniors here at LLU, there is a rapidly growing interest in international health; these men and women have a desire to serve abroad.

Our alumni have seen many changes in medicine over the years, too. Not only have they been part of these changes, but they have also been instrumental in implementing some of them.

Our Loma Linda University graduates are well trained. And we are confident they can also manage as the face of medicine evolves. But even with all of these challenges, one constant remains; I urge each of you to model your professional lives after the Great Physician.

Thomas J. Zirkle (1936-2008), was an LLUSM graduate, class of 1962. He was assistant dean for continuing medical education for LLUSM and was associate professor in LLUSM department of plastic surgery. He was LLUSM Alumni Association president from 2006 to 2007. Thomas posthumously received the LLUSM Distinguished Service Award in 2008 and was also the LLU Alumnus of the Year in 2008. This devotional was adapted from an article he wrote for the July-September 2006 issue of the LLUSM Alumni Association Alumni Journal.

For the LORD giveth wisdom; out of his mouth cometh knowledge and understanding. Proverbs 2:6, KJV

An important message, one that I have followed for more than fifty years, is this: *first, seek the wisdom of God.* God has provided us all with a formula for success that has the power to support each one of us in our endeavors throughout our careers and our entire lives.

God's wisdom is freely available; all we need to do is ask for it, pay attention to it, and use it. We can tap into God's wisdom through our daily prayer and through reading the Bible, which is laced with insights that help us apply the knowledge we learn in school and in life.

One of the great kings of antiquity, Solomon, son of King David of Israel, provides us with the premier example of obtaining and utilizing God's wisdom. For example, in 1 Kings 3:12 (KJV), we learn about King Solomon's gift of wisdom: "I have given thee a wise and an understanding heart; so that there was none like thee before thee, neither after thee shall any arise like unto thee."

This "wise and understanding heart" was the great gift that God gave to the greatest of Israel's kings. This blessing led King Solomon to become the world's leading king, as evidenced by the many other world leaders who recognized his exceptional competence in leading Israel, and who came to him for guidance with their own leadership problems.

Solomon never forgot or underestimated the value of this great gift. Later in life he wrote about it, as in Proverbs 2:6. And again, in Proverbs 3:21 (KJV), we find, "My son, let not them depart from thine eyes: keep sound wisdom and discretion." Pearls like this are found all though Proverbs—indeed, all through the Bible—and as you ponder these verses and continue reading these discussions of wisdom, you will find that four valuable issues become very clear.

The first of these is the simple requirement to *ask God for His wisdom.* This requirement is so simple that we can easily overlook it, but it should become a daily model or motto for guiding our entire life. Second, we can then expect that our *knowledge* will increase beyond that which we usually receive from our studies and from life's experiences. Third, we can expect an increase in our *understanding* of the knowledge we obtain. Fourth, we will also experience increased *discretionary* capabilities; that is, we will know how to best utilize this knowledge and how best to apply it in our lives.

Build into your daily practice a simple prayer seeking God's wisdom. Don't worry about the words you use, just ask. Then, begin observing increased knowledge as you study; greater understanding of the knowledge you are obtaining; and a deeper, more mature discretionary ability to apply that knowledge and understanding in your work with patients and your profession. Again, begin your day with prayer to *first, seek the wisdom of God.*

James M. Slater, LLUSM class of 1963, is professor in and immediate past chair of LLUSM department of radiation medicine. He was LLUSM Alumni Association 1995 Alumnus of the Year, and in 1994 was LLU Alumnus of the Year. This devotional is excerpted from a commencement address for LLUSM presented on May 25, 2008.

May 22

"I was in prison, and you came to Me." Then the righteous will answer Him, "Lord, when did we see You hungry, and feed You, or thirsty, and give You something to drink? And when did we see You a stranger, and invite You in, or naked, and clothe You? When did we see You sick, or in prison, and come to You?" The King will answer and say to them, "Truly I say to you, to the extent that you did it to one of these brothers of Mine, even the least of them, you did it to Me." Matthew 25:36-40, NASB

There are many types of prisons. Most do not have steel bars. Which of your patients is in prison?

In a special county program, I provided psychiatric care directly in homes, back yards, and on the street. "Alice" lived in a drug infested, overcrowded room-and-board home. She was only 19 years old but had seen more than most 50 year olds. Abandoned by her father in infancy, abused by a series of stepfathers, her emotional foundation was unstable, her moods unpredictable and intense. She often sought solace in sex and methamphetamine.

She had been trying to get off drugs and to make her relationship with her latest boyfriend work. But this day she was clearly wound high on speed. Irritable, loud, crying, shouting inflammatory remarks, she was about to start a fight at her home when I arrived. Dehydrated and having not eaten in a long while, she was willing to come with me to a nearby Del Taco, where I bought her food and soft drinks (as allowed in this program). She ate ravenously and gradually calmed down.

I mostly listened at first. She told me that her boyfriend had just dumped her, and her mother never wanted to speak to her again. We spoke of her pain, of drug treatment, and of God; we spoke of how much progress she had been making. More than anything else, I wanted her to see that I (and God) valued her and believed in her—even on speed. I never saw her again. She vanished with a boyfriend, and we couldn't track her down. Alice lived in many prisons.

Which of your patients is in prison? The one trapped in an abusive relationship? In addiction? In the false comfort of promiscuity? In psychosomatic pain? In anxiety? In self-affirming rationalizations? In a victim mindset?

Are you willing to come to them there? Notice that Jesus doesn't say, "I was in prison, and you freed Me." Many remain in prison. Even with a way out, some choose to stay—for now. We have to believe that it is just "for now."

What do you say to someone in prison—especially a prison they helped build? First, simply acknowledge their pain. Then, offer the gift most precious to prisoners: hope. Hope can be offered even in a harried clinic schedule. Hope is only real if you yourself believe they can be released from their prison. Believe in these patients, even when they have stopped believing in themselves. Believe in these patients even when it feels like you have to use denial to do so. If they will let you, tell them about the Source of all hope.

It starts by being willing to come to them in their prison, to sit within those confining walls. That must happen even when they have built the walls themselves, even when they are "the least of them" in deservedness. And then whisper words of hope, over and over.

George Christison is professor in LLUSM department of psychiatry. He received his MD degree from University of California, San Diego, in 1982. In 2002, he was LLUSM Teacher of the Year.

May 23

And I am praying that you will put into action the generosity that comes from your faith as you understand and experience all the good things we have in Christ. Philemon 6, NLT

"Thank you for your interest in Loma Linda University School of Medicine. I have enjoyed our conversation. Before the interview is completed, do you have any questions for me?"

"Yes, thank you. What is so special about Loma Linda, Dr. Killeen? You, your father, brothers, wife, daughter, and now your son have all attended Loma Linda University School of Medicine. You have been a faculty member for over twenty-five years. Surely there is a reason why your entire family attended Loma Linda, and why you have stayed here for so long."

"Uh, I guess it's because we feel comfortable here."

This conversation occurred during medical student applicant interviews. Applicant interviews are one of the high points of the academic year. There is nothing like the amazing personal stories of those bright-eyed, altruistic students.

And, as indicated in the above conversation, I always give the applicants an opportunity to ask me some questions at the end of the interview. This inquiry helps me to gauge their true interests and insights. But, this spontaneous personal response to why my family feels "comfortable" at Loma Linda was thought provoking.

One of my earliest memories is of my maternal grandfather, Joseph Bishop. Joe was an orphan from Czechoslovakia, who had been adopted by a Seventh-day Adventist family named Bishop. He worked his way through Pacific Union College in Angwin, California, as a lumberjack. He had been accepted to the Loma Linda University School of Medicine, but he declined, due to financial constraints.

Joe eventually built a flourishing chain of health food stores in San Diego, California. At the end of a long day, he would deliver orders to his handicapped customers. I loved to ride with him in his 1950 Studebaker as he made his rounds. He was rarely paid for his deliveries, but I could see from the look on his face how much satisfaction he received from the simple respect and compassion he showed his customers.

When my father was accepted to Loma Linda University School of Medicine, he also was prepared to decline, due to his poor finances. However, my generous grandfather agreed to loan my father the amount needed for tuition. On graduation day, my father received a congratulatory card from my grandfather. Inside was a note stating, "Consider the loan paid in full!"

The example of my grandfather became the role model for my family. Hard work, compassion, generosity, honesty, faith in our Lord, and service to mankind were all imprinted into our thought processes early in our lives. We were all taught by example.

"To make man whole," the motto of Loma Linda University, is really much more. As I thought more about why my family is "comfortable" at Loma Linda, I realized it is because the motto and our family goals are the same. Compassion, service, generosity, faith, and teaching are part of all of us here. Loma Linda does not just make "man" whole; Loma Linda makes "ME" whole.

J. David Killeen, LLUSM class of 1975, is professor in LLUSM department of cardiovascular and thoracic surgery. He and his wife, Jeanne, LLUSM class of 1973-B, live in Redlands, California.

May 24

"For I know the plans I have for you," declares the LORD, "plans to prosper you and not to harm you, plans to give you hope and a future." Jeremiah 29:11, NIV

At the beginning of my senior year at La Sierra University in Riverside, California, I nervously filled out my application to medical school. The year before, I had left Jamaica, hoping to one day go to medical school at LLU. Months went by and I didn't hear from LLU. In the meantime, many of my classmates were getting invitations to interviews, even acceptance letters. By February, my faith began to dwindle, but I continued to pray and trust in God. About that time, God had blessed me with a scholarship. At La Sierra's awards banquet, I saw Dr. Roger Hadley, the dean of LLUSM. Perfect, I thought to myself. His hearing many good things being said about me would cause him to go back to LLU, meet with the admissions committee, and convince them that I was a good candidate. Later that night, I introduced myself to Dr. Hadley—letting him know that I had applied and was awaiting a response.

I went home that Saturday night with a glimmer of hope. The next day I opened my mailbox to find a letter from the School of Medicine. I thought it must be a rejection letter, considering it was mailed days ago, and knowing Dr. Hadley had not had a chance to meet with the committee to tell them of my good qualities. I became sad and tossed it aside, refusing to spoil my morning with bad news. Then a still, small voice whispered, "For I know the plans I have for you . . . plans to give you hope and a future." Upon opening the letter, I realized that it was not a rejection letter but an invitation to an interview! Long before I tried to impress Dr. Hadley, God had already spoken to the admissions committee. A week after my interview at LLU, I was accepted.

Now that I was accepted, it was time to think about paying for medical school. Being an international student, it was difficult to get student loans. My mom, being a single mother and a student herself—certainly could not afford to pay for my tuition. In addition, when I first came to the United States, I was told that LLU does not offer scholarships to international students. But I trusted God. Some weeks later, I received an unexpected letter from LLU. It stated that the scholarship committee, to which I never applied, had met and decided to award me a scholarship. By the time I finished medical school, that scholarship amount doubled. God is truly an awesome God!

On May 24, 2009, not only will I be celebrating my 24th birthday, but I will also be completing a major phase of this journey: I graduate from medical school. Today I receive my diploma, my reward from God for trusting in Him. But even though I have now become a doctor, the journey doesn't end here. Now it is time for me to give back to God, through the practice of medicine, to further the healing and teaching ministry of Christ.

Sherieka Wright, LLUSM class of 2009, was born in St. Thomas, Jamaica.

144

May 25

At least there is hope for a tree: If it is cut down, it will sprout again, and its new shoots will not fail. Job 14:7, NIV

Four years of medical school have left me with many lasting impressions. The most outstanding of these is that the practice of medicine is all about extremes and holding onto hope. Frequently throughout my education at Loma Linda University, I saw multiple examples of statistical impossibilities that reinforced this conclusion. The following two experiences are striking examples of just how extreme life can get in the world of medicine.

One night on call in my third year of medical school, I was on my obstetrics and gynecology (ob/gyn) clinical rotation and met a 30-year-old woman who was thirty weeks pregnant with quadruplets. She had been on a fertility drug because, despite multiple attempts, she was unable to get pregnant. Traditionally, the occurrence of quadruplets is one in 512,000 pregnancies—though this incidence may be higher now because of the increased use of fertility drugs and reproductive techniques. That night, I had the privilege of assisting my ob/gyn residents and attending physician with a cesarean section to deliver all four babies. While the mother did have a few complications after birth, she and all the babies eventually went home together. The Bible readily acknowledges the excitement that comes from having a baby. John 16:21 (NIV) says that once "her baby is born she forgets the anguish because of her joy that a child is born into the world."

The following day in clinic, I went from witnessing a joyous extreme to a heartbreaking one. I met a young lady about 25 years of age, who had delivered a still-born baby a couple of weeks earlier. She had a condition called antiphospholipid antibody syndrome, which is known for causing recurrent spontaneous abortions. She cried tears of despair as she explained to me how she had gone through multiple miscarriages in the past.

I have reflected on these experiences multiple times, and I have now come to the realization that these two women, who went through extremes of childbearing, had one thing in common at some point in their individual lives: hope. For the woman who delivered quadruplets, there was a hope that was fulfilled when she finally became pregnant. For the woman with recurrent miscarriages, there was the yet unfulfilled hope to still be fulfilled of finally having a successful pregnancy.

If you are not holding onto hope when you are going through the extreme situations you face in your life, you will find your life much more difficult. Regardless of the outcomes of the extreme situations we have gone through or will go through, Jesus has a promise: "He will wipe every tear from their eyes. There will be no more death or mourning or crying or pain, for the old order of things has passed away" (Revelation 21:4, NIV). Jesus went to the most extremes imaginable when He died for us because He has hope that we will follow Him to the extremes in service for Him.

Ryan Maybrook, LLUSM class of 2008, is a resident in surgery at University of Colorado in Denver. May 25 was the date of his graduation from medical school.

May 26

Let your light so shine before men, that they may see your good works, and glorify your Father which is in heaven. Matthew 5:16, KJV

Paris Souval, son of a U.S. diplomatic corps officer, had begun to study medicine in France. However, his draft board ordered him to return to the U.S. to serve in the military. Enlisting for four years in the U.S. Air Force, he was classified as a lab technician and assigned to a hospital lab at Burderop Park in southwest England.

On May 26, 1953, a young Seventh-day Adventist pathologist (and LLUSM graduate), drafted out of his residency, arrived from the U.S. to take charge of the lab. The lab personnel recognized that this officer was different; he did not smoke, drink, or use foul language. He maintained his composure when things went wrong. Those personal attributes, along with practical leadership, astonished the personnel, especially Paris.

The pathologist sent Paris to a U.S. Air Force lab in London for three months of training. There, the pathologist in charge was another Seventh-day Adventist, James Schooley, LLUSM class of 1949. The pathologists were friends. Paris admired Dr. Schooley and determined to find out more about Seventh-day Adventism.

Back on base, Paris began asking questions and always received a biblical answer. These answers amazed Paris, who thought only priests could have such biblical knowledge.

Six months later, the pathologist and Paris went to a London meeting featuring noted speaker George Vandeman. He preached a powerful message that moved Paris to think deeply about his own life. That was a week before the Burderop pathologist returned to the U.S., in August 1954. He told Paris, "We'll see you in California, and I'll take you to Loma Linda to see about becoming a medical student." Paris only laughed.

When Paris attended his second Vandeman service in London, an appeal was made for a commitment to Christ. Paris mentally struggled, but finally decided to walk down the aisle. After the meeting, Paris met Vandeman, who prayed with him personally. That prayer removed all doubts left in Paris' mind about the truths he had just heard.

Shortly after, in December 1954, Paris arrived in California. The next day, he and the pathologist went to Loma Linda to see about medical school. Paris returned to England.

An acceptance to Loma Linda came to Paris in March 1955. But what could he do with two years still to serve? Paris remembered a regulation, providing for a discharge to anyone who had completed two years and had been accepted to an approved medical school. So off went a letter to Loma Linda. When it arrived, the secretary quickly sent back an acceptance. It reached Paris the day of the deadline! The Lord "came through"; and on August 25, 1955, he arrived in Loma Linda to start school.

This remarkable series of events convinced Paris that the Lord wanted him at Loma Linda; and after studying with the campus chaplain, he was baptized into the Seventh-day Adventist Church on November 5, 1955. Subsequently, his sister and mother also became Seventh-day Adventists. His father, though never baptized, recognized the truth that Paris lived out before him.

Paris Souval, LLUSM class of 1960, set up a successful practice in Georgia, where his influence was prominent in his daily contact with patients and in his church where he ministered in many capacities. Surely, Paris would agree: "I'd rather SEE a sermon than hear one, any day."

Herbert I. Harder, LLUSM class of 1951, is an anatomic and clinical pathologist in Glendale, California. He was LLUSM Alumni Association president from 1985 to 1986.

Let your conversation be always full of grace, seasoned with salt, so that you may know how to answer everyone. Colossians 4:6, NIV

As a first-year medical student, I continue to discover the staggering complexity of the world for which I am being prepared. Every concept I learn seems riddled with layers of intricacy that never fail to confound my desire to understand. During my first weeks on the wards, I was consistently struck by the innumerable subtleties that colored every patient-doctor interaction—events that would happen even before being muddled by the science itself, even before the translation into layman's terms, even before the translation between languages! Everything I witnessed seemed to be entangled in a flurry of co-factors that always left me wondering if I would ever see a simple solution again.

The vision I had for myself as a Christian physician only added to the burden created by my chosen profession's romance with complexity. Finding a basis for interacting with people about my faith had never been easy, but now it seemed absurdly complicated. How could I find a way to allow my faith to shine through in the midst of a barrage of distraction? Would I even find an ethical way to offer patients the chance to see what Christ had done for me?

My chance came one Friday afternoon in a whole-person care practicum during an exercise to learn how to address patients' spiritual needs in the midst of illness. The exercise consisted of asking patients a few simple questions regarding their experiences and allowing conversations to run their course. When I entered the room of the patient I was to interview, I found David—a tough-looking, 30-something-year-old man from Los Angeles, California, who had undergone major surgery. After introducing myself and chatting lightly, I inquired if I could ask him a few questions about his spirituality.

He agreed, and I quickly learned that his experience with God had been very limited and poignantly ugly. The only man David knew who had converted to Christianity had ceased to be his friend. Not only that, but that same man's wife had left him for their new pastor. I asked David how these two experiences with Christianity had affected the way he saw God. He pondered momentarily before answering, "Man, you guys are doctors and you care about God?" I was struck by the simplicity and the depth of what had impressed him: not that I had imparted any theological truth or compelling testimony but simply that God mattered to me at all.

David showed me the simple answer to the question I had thought so profoundly complicated. By allowing God to factor into our interaction, I demonstrated that God matters to me, and that talking about Him is part of being healed completely. While my experience with David didn't lead to his conversion or even an outward expression of openness toward God, I was left with the meaningful impression that if we, as clinicians and caregivers, can find a way for our interactions to include open-ended conversations about God, then we open the door to the deepest facet of patients' well-being as we offer them the opportunity to see Him as their healer.

Nathan Blue, LLUSM class of 2011, is from Palm Desert, California. May 27 is the date of his wedding engagement to his wife, Cheri, who is completing a degree in speech pathology at LLU.

May 28

For I hold you by your right hand—I, the LORD your God. And I say to you, "Don't be afraid. I am here to help you." Isaiah 41:13, NLT

A s I reviewed the computed tomography (CT) scan before entering the exam room, I felt certain that Michele had a cancerous tumor in her right kidney. It was around 5 cm in size and quite suspicious looking. "Will I have to remove the entire kidney . . . or can I surgically remove the tumor from the kidney?" I asked myself. "Can this be done laparoscopically so that she will have less pain and a quicker recovery?"

Michele was a young mother of two children and a devout Christian wife. As I described the radiographic findings, I could sense her anxiety over the almost certain diagnosis of cancer. At the conclusion of her consultation, I recommended that she have surgery to remove the tumor from the kidney (partial nephrectomy). I also recommended that this surgery be done via an open approach or large incision. We talked about performing this laparoscopically, but I discouraged this course, because of the size and location of the tumor. Her surgery date was then set.

Driving to the hospital the morning of Michele's surgery, I asked God to guide my mind and hands as I operated that day. I also asked Him, "Am I doing the right thing for Michele?" Within minutes of my prayers, I was moved to change my surgical plans. Excited and confident that God was there changing the plans for me, I explained to Michele that I thought I could perform the surgery laparoscopically. She agreed, and we then proceeded to the operating room.

The surgery was at first very straightforward. The tumor was located and the kidney was prepped for the resection without much effort. However, as I began incising around the tumor I ran into unexpected difficulty. The tumor was larger than anticipated and tissues began to bleed excessively. I was concerned that I wouldn't be able to do a proper resection. I said to God, "Why is this so difficult? I thought You wanted me to do this laparoscopically? Please help me!" I wish I could say that from then on the surgery went smoothly, but actually the difficulties continued. I was able to complete the tumor resection satisfactorily, however, and the bleeding stopped. Michele recovered quickly and went home from the hospital in two days.

One week later she returned to my office for the pathology report. Amazingly, the tumor was benign! As I read the report, everything suddenly became clear. God knew the tumor was benign and that's why He wanted me to spare Michele the pain and recovery of a surgery that involved a large incision. Tears of relief welled up in her eyes as she listened to the report. The story doesn't end there.

Almost one year later, I was the one in need of help. A personal relationship had abruptly ended, and I was really struggling. On one of my darkest days, I randomly received an email from Michele. She said, ". . . for some reason, I was compelled to write to you and tell you that God is with you and has big plans for you." I was instantly better. The sheer randomness and timing of her message pointed me right back to God. How was it that Michele knew how much I was hurting at that moment?

Isn't God an awesome God! As physicians, He will bring us patients whom He wants us to help, and He will bring patients into our lives who can help us also.

Jeffrey Yoshida, LLUSM class of 1996, is a urologist in Huntington Beach, California. May 28 is Michele's birthday.

Then said the Lord to him, Put off thy shoes from thy feet: for the place where thou standest is holy ground. Acts 7:33, KJV

We were ready to start our surgery rotation; it would be our first experience in the sacred environs of the sterile field. After months of internal medicine, the shift to surgery was anticipated as one of the most exciting rotations, full of drama and emergency, real "life and death" cases. Bright and early in the operating room (OR) circulating area, seven eager, third-year medical students clustered around a pair of porcelain scrub sinks with the head OR nurse.

Since the time of Louis Pasteur, students have been instructed in the methods of sterile procedure. Before entry to the sacred OR—we had to prove we were clean, perfect without blemish or bacteria. We were scrubbing nails, elbows, and hands with the strong antiseptic cleanser and washing in the scrub sink, avoiding contact with any source of possible contamination. We then were shown how to gown and glove, alone or assisted. Not until the almighty scrub tech pronounced us ready were we allowed to come near to the operating table.

Professional eyes of the surgeon carefully scrutinized us over the rim of his mask. We knew we were clean because we had washed in the sink and now wore the robe of surgical righteousness. With confidence, we could approach the operating field.

Is this how we should prepare for heaven? Could our good works and careful sterile procedure ever make us acceptable in the eyes of an angry, arbitrary God? If so, then why the Cross?

While studying the experience of Moses at the burning bush, I was struck by a new perspective. He was asked to remove his shoes, to make himself more presentable on the Holy Ground. Is this the best perspective? Was God afraid that Moses' unclean shoes would soil His Holiness? What about Moses' dirty feet? Perhaps he needed a celestial scrub tech to make sure he washed his feet with proper sterile procedure, so as not to contaminate the sacred field.

Or is it something else? What is between you and your God? God asked Moses to come to Him with less. God wanted to be closer to Moses. He was not in any way concerned that Moses' sinfulness would harm Him. To the contrary, perhaps God wanted to be so close to Moses that His righteousness itself would infuse Moses. Being near our Friend changes us. God's Holiness was transforming to Moses, and God did not want anything in-between.

Examine your life. Is God, your Friend, asking you to remove something that separates you from Him? He longs to make you holy. Come stand on the Holy Ground with your shoes off.

Jon Edwin Lloyd Ermshar, LLUSM class of 1988, is a family practitioner in Grants Pass, Oregon. May 29 is his birthday and his date of graduation from medical school.

May 30

Let me understand the teaching of your precepts; then I will meditate on your wonders. Psalm 119:27, NIV

As I ran down the stairs from my general medicine clinic, a surgeon stopped me and asked if I would see one of his patients that afternoon in consultation. "So sorry," I replied, "but I'm on my way over to the hospital to teach physical diagnosis, and my med students are waiting for me. Perhaps one of my colleagues?"

"You take time away from clinic to teach?" he exclaimed. "What a shame! Clinic is so much more important than teaching!" I just grinned and started down again, tossing over my shoulder at him, "Oh, I don't think so!"

It's impossible for me to explain the incredible satisfaction I receive from teaching the next generation of physicians. Whether it's showing him the intricacies of an ophthalmoscope, changing her grip on an otoscope, or repositioning his fingers over a thyroid, teaching clinical skills to freshmen is, quite simply, a kick. He'll grin when an optic disc pops into focus, she'll squeal when she sees a tympanic membrane, his eyes will light up when he finally feels a thyroid gland—I wouldn't trade these moments for any clinical prestige.

At the end of the year, the freshmen come back to the physical diagnosis lab for their clinical skills exam. Yesterday, I had the honor of proctoring two women. They had been practicing all morning and were still so very nervous. They asked me to pray with them; and as we bowed our heads together, I asked for the gift of confidence on their behalf. Then they each nailed every skill I asked them to demonstrate: blood pressure, eye-ear-nose exams, percussion, auscultation, jugular venous pressure ("up, down, down!"), abdominal palpation, reflexes. When they finished, I whooped—then we all laughed and hugged each other in celebration of their passing the last test of their freshman year. Joy!

The students come back as sophomores and again as juniors to demonstrate their clinical skills. Each year they get more competent and more efficient—you can see them becoming doctors before your very eyes! Last week I watched one of our juniors examine a standardized patient with grace and poise. Just two years before, I had taught her how to percuss for the first time. Now, as I witnessed her expertly flow through the abdominal exam, the beauty in her touch moved me to tears, and I realized she had developed the hands of a healer. And when we debriefed after her exam, the look of incredulous joy that came over her face when I told her I thought she was faculty material and that I'd like to help mentor her over the next decade: priceless.

Teaching isn't about the money, trust me. It is sometimes boring, or it is sometimes hard when you have to fail a student. But still, the moments of awe are far more frequent.

It occurred to me this week that the Master Physician takes more joy in the growth of young healers—people dedicated to becoming His hands in the world—than I was even capable of imagining.

Debra Stottlemyer, LLUSM class of 1986, is assistant professor in LLUSM department of medicine.

May 31

But as for me, I am like a green olive tree in the house of God; I trust in the lovingkindness of God forever and ever. I will give You thanks forever, because You have done it, And I will wait on Your name, for it is good, in the presence of Your godly ones. Psalm 52:8-9, NASB

The cherry crop was full. The best in years! Trees were hanging with beautiful, ripe, delicious cherries. The crew of twelve pickers was scheduled to arrive at 6:00 a.m., according to their boss. Two hundred boxes of prime cherries were contracted for shipment on the next day, Friday. Thursday dawned bright and clear.

At the appointed hour, the picker boss and one picker arrived. "I can't get pickers—everybody is busy," he stated. This shock was compounded when the phone rang and the cherry contractor's voice said, "Sorry for the bad news, but the cherry wholesale market is flooded. I can't move your cherries since everyone has them in abundance!"

The price had dropped below what we could pay the pickers to pick them—had pickers and a buyer been available. Frustration, disappointment, and major concern replaced optimism in one day as the disaster unfolded.

We had thanked God for answering our prayers for a good crop which He had sent. Because the profits from cherries and berries on our U-pick farm go to some charitable project such as Maranatha Volunteers International or Gospel Outreach, we couldn't understand our dilemma. We prayed that God would manage "His" crop somehow.

The next day the phone rang incessantly! People were anxious to come to our ranch. They informed us that they had learned about our ranch in *Sunset Magazine*'s June 2007 issue. We hurriedly obtained a magazine copy. There, listed first, was our American River Cherry Company, with a picture of our Utah Giant cherries, under a heading: "Things to do in June in Northern California." The response was truly miraculous! More than 200 families arrived on Sunday to pick cherries and berries. They came from Nevada, Sacramento, and San Francisco over the next few weeks as the crop ripened; and they picked it completely.

Trusting God for problem solving in business and personal life is a way to enjoy His grace and enjoy life. Let Him lead when things are good and He will bless and provide what is best when things get tough. Ask Him, as your Friend and perfect Substitute, to come into your mind to reflect the mind of Christ in all you do today . . . and every day.

Reginald Rice Sr., LLUSM class of 1963, is a family practitioner and lives with his wife, Shirley, in Placerville, California. May 31, 2007, is the date this incident occurred.

June 1

I am going to send an angel in front of you, to guard you on the way and to bring you to the place that I have prepared. Exodus 23:20, NRSV

During times of stress or illness, patients often ask me if there is a God and if He is truly involved in our lives. I respond by telling them this story about my father. When I was growing up, my father worked as a literature evangelist. He went door to door selling books like *Uncle Arthur's Bedtime Stories*, *My Bible Friends*, and *My Bible Stories*. Through this ministry, he brought many people to Jesus. However, this job was not without risk. He was often assigned to high-crime areas where people were robbed or assaulted.

Preparing for one of those assignments soon after our regular family worship—during which he asked God for His protection—He left our house. He went to his assigned area, knocking from door to door and speaking to those who were willing to listen. As evening drew near and he was preparing to return home, a woman from one of the houses stopped him. My father will never forget what she said. Coming up to him, she asked: "Those two men who were with you, where are they?"

My father was initially confused and asked, "What do you mean?"

The lady then told him that all day long, while my father was going from door to door, two big men dressed in white had accompanied him, one on each side. My father was amazed! He offered a prayer of thanksgiving to God, for His protection.

Our omnipresent God wants to be involved in every aspect of our lives. There is no doubt about it.

Danilyn Angeles is assistant professor in LLUSM department of basic sciences, division of physiology. She is course director for physiology at LLUSM. She has a PhD degree in physiology from LLU and an MS degree in nursing from University of California, Los Angeles.

June 2

Therefore I tell you, do not worry about your life, what you will eat or drink; or about your body, what you will wear. Is not life more important than food, and the body more important than clothes? Look at the birds of the air; they do not sow or reap or store away in barns, and yet your heavenly Father feeds them. Are you not much more valuable than they? Who of you by worrying can add a single hour to his life? Matthew 6:25-27, NIV

The first time I saw the flashing pixel that represented the heartbeat of my child, it made my own heart skip with joy. However, nothing could have prepared me for what came next. The obstetrician shifted the ultrasound view, and a second small bump, with its own flashing pixel, came into view. At that point something entirely different happened to my heart . . . and to my knees!

After years of deliberation, my wife and I had finally decided that the freshman year of medical school was as good a time as any to have a child. But twins? Predictions of academic failure and financial demise came quickly to mind. Of course, we made up our minds to plow ahead, no matter what the challenge.

In retrospect, I do not believe that I will ever face a more challenging time than those three years. The first challenge was to get the children out of the neonatal intensive care unit. The strongest evidence of God's hand in my life, thus far, was my rejection by my own state's medical school, and my acceptance at Loma Linda University. While the rejection stung at the time, the quality of care that my children received while at Loma Linda University Children's Hospital was world-class.

Academically, there is no greater deterrent to studying than two adorable toddlers begging for your attention. Harder still were the clinical rotations. Once, during a particularly busy general surgery rotation, I found myself sitting at a table with the dean of student affairs discussing the implications of dropping out of medical school. At that point, I had just gone an entire week without once seeing my children awake.

However, a potent mixture of prayer, resolution, and late-night studying did the trick and helped me turn the corner. At our graduation awards ceremony, I was honored to receive the Chancellor's Award. Honestly, I would love to take credit for this achievement. But, I know that this gift comes first from God and also from my family who supported me. In the end, however, this all pales in comparison with the ultimate gift from God: my two healthy, vibrant children.

While medical school is now a fond memory, and residency and beginning my children's education are the prime concerns, I only need to look back to those years to remind me of how God's hand guides and provides for us. At times it may be difficult to understand why we face hardships. Sometimes, when the challenges seem unfair or insurmountable, we may not understand. One needs only to read Jesus' words in His sermon on the mountainside. If God cares for the birds of the air and the lilies of the field, how much more then does He care for and watch over us?

Jeremy Deisch, LLUSM class of 2006, is a resident in anatomic and clinical pathology at University of Texas, Southwestern Medical Center in Dallas, Texas. In 2006, he received the LLU Chancellor's Award. June 2 is the birthday of his twin sons, Jacob and Joseph.

June 3

Before they call I will answer; while they are still speaking I will hear. Isaiah 65:24, NIV

I was a junior medical student on obstetrics rotation at Riverside General Hospital in Riverside, California. Obstetrics was my first clinical rotation, and, of course, I was feeling scared and inexperienced. I remember praying before I left my apartment that afternoon, asking God to give me wisdom and to be with me while I was on call. It was a busy night, and the family practice resident from Riverside and I did not get much sleep.

The two of us headed back to the bunk beds provided for residents on the floor. We had just crawled into bed and were heading off to dreamland when the resident's beeper went off again. There were two ladies to be seen in the emergency room. Both the resident and I moaned and rolled out of our bunks.

We scurried to the emergency room. The resident said, "You take one room and I'll take the other, so we can get back to bed more quickly." I took the chart and walked in. She was a single Hispanic lady in labor. She didn't speak any English. I spoke some Spanish. I figured out she was having labor pains and was expecting twins.

I examined her and felt something soft and pulsatile in her open cervix. I hadn't been on obstetrics rotation too long, but I knew what I was feeling was not the baby's head. I quickly exited the room and got the resident, who came and examined her and then quickly called the obstetrics resident. She confirmed prolapsed cord.

Then the excitement started! The woman was placed in a knee/chest position to keep pressure off the cord. I was ordered to hold my hand against the cervix and not allow the cord to prolapse further. We were rushed to the operating room. The surgeons performed the emergency cesarean section; and two healthy, screaming boys were delivered to the hands of the staff of the neonatal intensive care unit.

Later, as I lay back on my bunk exhausted, I breathed a prayer of thanks. "Thank you, God, for being with me tonight and giving life to two baby boys."

Rhonda Ringer, LLUSM class of 1984, is a family practitioner in Orlando, Florida. She is married with two stepsons and two daughters. June 3 was her graduation date from medical school.

When I consider thy heavens, the work of thy fingers, the moon, and the stars, which thou has ordained; What is man, that thou art mindful of him? Psalm 8:3-4, KJV

Compare a man with space, endless space. Suppose we take our man and place him here, on a square foot of ground. Then we travel away two or three miles, and he fades from sight, unless our eyes are extra good. We go on a hundred miles, and the whole hill upon which he stands fades from view. Suppose we leave the earth and go as far as the moon. A million horizons have appeared and vanished since we began our journey into space.

From the moon, lakes, rivers, mountains, all fade away, and we see a disk of light somewhat larger than the moon looks to us from Earth. This disc is covered with fantastic shadows, which mark the continents, and with spaces, where the oceans keep up their eternal surge. Where is our man in all those vast distances, amid those lights and shadows?

Suppose we ascend from the moon and go as far as the sun. The earth is now a tiny globe, and the moon a speck above it. We go on farther, toward the center of our galaxy. One after another the planets move toward each other, until at last they disappear into the embrace of the sun. Where, in the midst of that tiny speck of light far away, is the man whom we left behind us?

But farther still we travel to other island galaxies. The sun, with all the millions of other suns in this system, coalesce into a dim blob of light in the far heavens. Where, in the midst of all the grandeur of these suns and stars and systems, is the human mote that we left behind us? Compared with the universe, what is man? He is nothing. . . .

Suppose we measure man by spiritual law. . . . He is helpless, for "the wages of sin is death" (Romans 6:23, KJV). "Whatsoever a man soweth, that shall he also reap" (Galatians 6:7, KJV). The eyes of spiritual law are never shut; they never wink at the wrong. Custom, expediency, etiquette—all these things are local; they depend upon the time and the place. But right is always right; wrong is always wrong. . . .

"Behold, what manner of love!" (1 John 3:1, KJV). When we see that, we shall see how much men are worth. All who give their lives to bless humanity, both physically and spiritually, need to look through the right end of the telescope; they need to know the worth of a man. We can know it only when we behold the Man, when we look into the face of Christ.

H.M.S. Richards Sr. (1894-1985) was founder of the Seventh-day Adventist radio broadcast, the Voice of Prophecy. This devotional is a portion of a commencement sermon for CME on June 10, 1950. The complete text originally appeared in the July 1950 issue of the LLUSM Alumni Association Alumni Journal.

June 5

This is real love—not that we loved God, but that he loved us and sent his Son as a sacrifice to take away our sins. 1 John 4:10, NLT

It was past midnight; and as a third-year medical student on a relatively quiet call for internal medicine, I was tiptoeing through the wards toward my sleeping quarters. But I noticed Mr. Aster (not his real name) wasn't asleep. My 94-year-old patient, who had refused his celestial discharge by stubbornly and successfully fighting a fulminant peritonitis, was awake, staring out his moonlit window.

Devoid of his family, and also devoid of his left arm midhumerus and his right leg below the knee, Mr. Aster was someone I had inherited with some trepidation on my first day on service. Now, we were both leaving: he to a nursing home, and I to another rotation.

Over the past month, I had always been the first person to see him every morning, bellowing a forced, cheery "Good MORNING, Mr. Aster!" in his one good ear. I'd shake him awake so I could poke, prod, and otherwise plunder his slumber for the sake of a progress note. Nonetheless, his good humor, after being so rudely awakened, had gradually won me over.

Mr. Aster then interrupted me with a wave of his stump and told me how much my coming in each morning "to see an old man when no one else cares" meant to him. It culminated in the most touching and heart-warming compliment I had ever received from a stranger. At the time, it seemed to secure my entire professional choice and even my existence. I had been validated, my *raison d'etre* confirmed.

That morning, after rounds, I was paged to assist with an electrocardiogram (EKG) on a new admission. The patient was an 84-year-old demented man, punted from his nursing home for gastrointestinal distress. Considering his already chronic diarrhea, "out of control behavior" was the reason between the lines. With his worsening agitation and suspected cardiac history, a baseline EKG was indicated.

The patient was neither cooperative nor compliant; and, as we attempted to place the leads, much verbal handholding and explaining were necessary. Speaking in soothing tones while taping a lead in place on his shoulder, I attempted once again to provide the rationale for disturbing his peace. After ignoring the nth repetition of why this was necessary, the patient smeared his bilious excretions on my hand, stabbed his finger at me, and literally spat, "You know, you're not too helpful." With his contempt punctuated by two types of body fluid, I ceased trying to be helpful and endured the rest of the process required in procuring an essentially normal EKG.

Later, driving home, I contemplated the events of my latest thirty-six-hour shift. On one hand, my self-esteem had been lifted to unseen heights by a single compliment; on the other hand, it had been rudely plummeted earthward by a single condemnation. Well, at least the universe was balanced.

We find solace in our patients' accolades, gathering these tributes to bolster a sense of worth in the face of a withering social support network. All too often, this "comfort" is an unfortunate adverse effect of our chosen occupation. Indeed, if we have not yet learned that our self-worth must not rest on the shoulders of our patients, then it is my sincere prayer that the times we are found to be not too helpful are outweighed by the times we are loved. More importantly, may we all realize that the only One who gives worth to any of us at all, loves us unconditionally.

Ron Foo, LLUSM class of 1998, is assistant clinical professor in LLUSM department of psychiatry.

June 6

I will praise you, O LORD, with all my heart; I will tell of all your wonders.
Psalm 9:1, NIV

On this particular day, I was one of the first students in my group of eight to arrive in the lab. On the table was a clear plastic container filled with a solution of 10 percent formaldehyde. The container sat on a tray—a tray like one might find in a cafeteria.

I slipped the tray out from underneath and carefully opened the container. The smell was strong; the liquid looked a little brownish. I reached in, my gloves on, and pulled out a human brain—well, half of a human brain. It had already been cut down the middle—a clean cut separating the left and the right brain.

That day's lab required examination of only one hemisphere. Already arbitrarily choosing one side, I placed my half-brain onto the tray and went to the sink specifically set aside to rinse off the formaldehyde solution. Standing in line, I looked around. It was a weird scene: students waiting in line, all holding cafeteria trays that carried a human brain.

After finding and identifying all the structures on our checklist, it was time for us to leave the lab. The brain slices were returned to their smelly solution. Most of our nostrils burned. Some people's eyes were teary.

Neuroscience lab was a little strange that day. Gross examination wasn't that bad. I'd seen plenty of brains in pictures. It was the slicing that I felt weird about. It cut so easily. Almost like a kiwi, without the skin. Or maybe like JELL-O, the kind with fruit inside.

But, I think the best example, if you're familiar with it, would be tofu—the hard kind—not the soft tofu used for soup. It's actually how neurosurgeon Katrina Firlik described the consistency of the brain in her book.

A classmate commented that it's so strange to watch a human brain getting sliced. We are, after all, cutting up an actual person's brain. At one time, the cells in this brain fired off electrical impulses. It commanded muscle groups and regulated complex functions. It held someone's memories. In our hands, we held an absolutely incredible organ.

As a first year student, it is so easy to get caught up in the fast pace and the mountain of information we need to memorize; it can be exhausting. And it's during those times that it is easy to neglect our personal walk with God.

But occasionally I experience moments like these—moments in which I stand in awe. I am amazed at what I am holding or touching or seeing. There are moments when I realize that I have the privilege of examining and learning from the human body—the crowning jewel of God's Creation—as few others ever do. And it is in these moments that I am mentally refreshed; but more importantly, I am reminded of how mighty, magnificent, and wonderful is the God we serve.

Jeffrey Wonoprabowo, LLUSM class of 2011, was born in southern California and is a graduate of Glendale Adventist Academy in Glendale, California, and of Walla Walla College (now Walla Walla University) in College Place, Washington. June 6 is his birthday.

June 7

Deeply moved, Jesus touched their eyes. They had their sight back that very instant, and joined the procession. Matthew 20:34, MSG

My nose burned. I could feel my airway contracting as I breathed in the odor of his unwashed body. I stayed at the foot of his bed—my eyes straying toward the door, my lungs straining for a breath of fresh air. My eyes widened as I watched her walk to the head of his bed and greet him with a smile. She then leaned down so her gaze met his; and clasping his grimy hands in her own, she asked, "Mr. J, what can I do for you today?"

She did not seem to notice that there were layers, it seemed, of dirt under his untrimmed finger nails, or that his oral cavity had not seen a toothbrush for some length of time. I observed as his suspicious demeanor changed when he realized her interest in him was genuine. He relaxed a little and began recounting tales of how he managed to survive on the streets of Los Angeles, California, by stealing beer, staying in hospitals, and sleeping in bushes.

Dr. K listened nonjudgmentally, and she did this over and over again as we visited patient after patient. I watched eyes, faded by the ravages of dementia, brighten to the warmth they received. I saw the vacant gazes of those broken by life's tragedies briefly livened by the spark of kindness shown to them.

A passage in the Bible, Matthew 20, flashed through my mind, as I mulled over the events of the day. I pictured Jesus, making His way through the throngs, when He heard the shouts of two blind men. He was deeply moved with compassion at their condition. They were worthless in the eyes of the crowd, but He saw the infinite worth of their souls. He stopped and He touched them—healing the two men, both body and soul.

I wondered what kind of a difference I could make, if I were to see people the way Jesus did. So I tried it as I traveled the road of internship. The 85-year-old female with a history of dementia and noncompliance became Ms. Judy H, a homemaker, who lost her husband of fifty-five years and was living by herself for the first time. The drug addict, with altered mental status, became Mr. Billy E, who had been studying engineering in college at one point, but dropped out after the sudden, tragic death of his father.

I began to realize how often I had unwittingly judged people, seeing only the diseases of body and mind, but never looking beyond to see their souls. Through her actions, Dr. K taught me how to just accept the human being before me. She did not perform miracles, but, quietly day by day, added a touch of humanity to her practice of medicine. I saw Jesus in that hospital that day. I hope and pray that as we make our way through our clinics and hospitals that what moves the heart of God moves our hearts, too, and that our patients will see Jesus walking their way.

Pamela D'Souza, LLUSM class of 2007, is a resident in ophthalmology at University of Missouri, Columbia. June 7 is her birthday.

My God shall supply all your need according to his riches in glory by Christ Jesus. Philippians 4:19, KJV

The graduation of the forty-sixth class of College of Medical Evangelists School of Medicine at the Redlands Bowl in Redlands, California, on June 8, 1958, seemed a complete success. The graduates felt as if they had climbed the mountain and reached its summit. Everyone left the Redlands Bowl happy. Well, not quite everyone. Geneva, the wife of Arthur Christensen, LLUSM class of 1923, had traveled 70 miles from Glendale, California, so she could personally congratulate one doctoral graduate and honor him with a gift. She had befriended him in 1945, when he was a teenager.

Alas! She couldn't find him in the crowd and returned home disappointed but not discouraged. She eventually contacted the new doctor and apologized for having missed him. Could he visit her soon? Of course, he'd be pleased to come see her. She had provided work for him during his last two years at Glendale Union Academy in Glendale, California. She had found a variety of household and gardening chores for him to do, even though she had her own housekeeper and gardener. Once, she had him scrub the outside stairs of an apartment she owned.

Geneva was this student's favorite employer, especially since she voluntarily paid 25 percent more than any of his other after-school employers. So the student was thankful that this kind lady had sought his services. Geneva had learned of his need for work from another CME doctor's wife. And, in turn, that doctor's wife had learned from her husband, Dr. H. G. Westphal, of this student's willingness to do household chores.

As is usual for word-of-mouth recommendations, Dr. Westphal heard about this student during a routine pharmaceutical detail visit with a pharmaceutical representative, who had recommended the student's services to Dr. Westphal. This "detail man" liked the way the student mowed his lawn and vacuumed his rugs.

And now this student had graduated; so Geneva requested that he visit her because she had a gift for him. About a week after his graduation, he was pleased to visit her and, after the usual greetings, was presented with an envelope. It contained a paper he had seen before, his promissory note to Geneva for $500.

During a time of need, Geneva had loaned him $500 for tuition in his sophomore year of medical school. Each of the next two years, she offered more funds, but these were not needed. When the student looked at the paper, he saw Geneva had written "cancelled" on the note. What a gift! An unnecessary kindness!

And does not "cancelled" on this promissory note given me prefigure "forgiveness" on my divine note? That "note" demonstrated my need then; and "cancelled" demonstrates, for all time, the goodness of God as bestowed by one of His children. At least that is what a now nearly 80-year-old doctor believes. For in his medical theology, Paul was not referring to streets of gold and gates of pearl as constituting the riches of God. Rather, God's "riches in glory by Christ Jesus" are the kind acts that His children render to those in need.

George L. Vannix, LLUSM class of 1958, is a family practitioner in Somis, California. June 8 is the day this incident occurred.

June 9

But when the king came in to see the guests, he noticed a man there who was not wearing wedding clothes. "Friend," he asked, "how did you get in here without wedding clothes?" The man was speechless. Matthew 22:11-12, NIV

It was during my first days as a junior medical student. John E. Peterson, LLUSM class of 1939, chief of medicine for LLUMC, was making daily rounds with the residents, interns, and medical students. There was a definite pecking order in these rounds, with the senior resident close to Dr. Peterson's side and taking notes, followed by a cascade of more minor members of the team.

Interestingly, a kind of medial pomp was also evident. The chief asked a question and answers were quickly supplied. There would be impatience by the senior resident if an intern or student had to consult the chart to retrieve the results of a lab test or x-ray. If we came upon a patient and the differential diagnosis list provided by a student was pitifully small, Dr. Peterson took charge. He would quickly cite an incredibly long list of conditions that might manifest exactly the same way, in regard to the patient lying before us.

In one room, our crowd caught the patient emerging from the bathroom. She was wrapped in a hospital gown and stood there in her bare feet while her case was discussed. Dr. Peterson addressed her directly and asked if she had any problems with which he could help. She quickly pointed to her right foot and indicated a problem with one of her toes.

Dr. Peterson immediately dropped to his knees on the floor, put on his glasses, and took her foot in his hands. The residents and students dropped back to make room. He made a detailed examination of her foot and toes and asked further questions regarding her symptoms. This minor concern had been ignored by the students and residents as being not really relevant to her primary problem. But it had Dr. Peterson's attention.

Something immediately clicked in my mind. While major medical problems must be addressed during a hospital stay, even the smallest issues should be investigated and documented. Seeing Dr. Peterson on his knees, holding the patient's foot, reminded me of Jesus washing the disciples' feet. This great professor of medicine was focused on the patient, not the crowd around him.

I determined, at that very moment, to always humble myself before my patients and to show the greatest concern for their every need, no matter how large or how small. I wanted to be like John Peterson and Jesus.

Elvin Adams, LLUSM class of 1967, is an internist specializing in HIV disease. He and his wife, Marie, reside in Burleson, Texas. June 9 is their wedding anniversary.

June 10

But seek first the kingdom of God and His righteousness, and all these things shall be added to you. Matthew 6:33, NKJV

Graduates, you join an ancient fraternity. Its alumni have scaled the heights of Olympus, Sinai, and Calvary. You are living links in a healing chain from every age. Your touch combines your own efforts with the experience of all who have preceded you. Your motivations will carry the meaning of what you do.

The heavenly kingdom is won by small decisions, continued patiently and persistently over time. How do we "seek the Kingdom of Heaven" in our work? First, we need to remember that one of the most profound revolutions in religious thinking is the Sabbath. Its spiritual good goes beyond the ritual. It is the ultimate statement that the world does not own us, but that we are made for rest and holiness, as much as we are for career and ambition.

Second, don't sacrifice your family on the altar of career. Don't let the ladder to success devalue your role as a parent, nurturer, and teacher of your own children. A Yiddish song written in 1887 about a man who worked in a New York sweatshop could be just as true today:

I have a son, a little son, a boy completely fine.
Whenever I see him, it seems to me that all the world is mine.
But, seldom do I see my child awake and bright,
I only see him when he sleeps, I'm only home at night.

Third, don't judge yourself by what you do but by the meaning you bring to it. Meaning does not lie in work. It is in what you bring to your work. For instance, I once thought the title "Dr." would do something for me. It did—it improved my seat at a restaurant. I thought this is great! Then a waiter tapped me on the shoulder and said, "Another diner has had a heart attack, could you help?" I had to tell him I wasn't that kind of doctor.

But your title is important when caring for people. The title is important when you are serving people. Your title is important if you have, in fact, been transformed by its acquisition. If you have, you will use it very carefully. If you have been transformed, you will "seek first the Kingdom of Heaven" and *not worry* about what is added to you.

Take the best of those who provided for you and give it to your children. Remember the best of those who have taught you their skills and their ways and reflect it in your face and in your manner, as you treat your patients.

Make your best a habit. Resist the belief that, because of some outside force, you can only do less than your best. Do not give away your dream that you can be helpful to people, that you can make a difference, and that you have healing, divine healing, in your hands.

Jerry Davis (1938-2006) served as a chaplain at LLUMC beginning in 1970 and headed the chaplaincy department at LLUMC from 1978 to 2002. He had an RelD degree. This devotional, submitted by his wife, Sylvia Clark Davis, who was director of admissions and recruitment for LLUSD, is excerpted from a baccalaureate sermon for LLUSM and LLUSD. June 10 was her husband's birthday.

June 11

He will cover you with his feathers, and under his wings you will find refuge; his faithfulness will be your shield and rampart. You will not fear the terror of night, nor the arrow that flies by day, nor the pestilence that stalks in the darkness, nor the plague that destroys at midday. A thousand may fall at your side, ten thousand at your right hand, but it will not come near you. Psalm 91:4-7, NIV

I am writing these thoughts in June 2008, almost thirty-one years after I began working at LLUMC as a pediatric neurologist. I was the ninth member of the pediatric faculty that now numbers 100 physicians. At that time, there were four residents, and now there are approximately ninety. We also have LLUCH, and great plans are underway for building a new children's hospital and clinic building.

I have given much of myself to Loma Linda University and Medical Center in the care of patients, and in teaching, research, writing, interaction with colleagues, and working with a wonderful group of individuals. Those relationships include my secretary, Ann Elliott, with me for close to thirty years; and my nurse, Cindy Kronbeck, with me for nearly twenty years. I have also been blessed to work with outstanding colleagues as well as supurb clinicians—including Sarah Roddy, LLUSM class of 1980-B; Stanford Shu, LLUSM class of 1992; Chalmer McClure, LLUSM class of 1992; Doctors David Michelson, Debra Demos, and Mary Silvia.

In addition I have been blessed to have had as chair, for more than twenty-five years, John Mace, LLUSM class of 1964, who guided our department to its current status as one of the premier children's hospitals in California. Since receiving the leadership baton, Richard Chinnock, LLUSM class of 1982, has done an exemplary job as chair; and Ricardo Peverini, LLUSM class of 1984, has also contributed to the solidity and growth of our department.

There are literally hundreds of little stories that I can recall about patients. However, the one that remains in my mind—and the one I most frequently tell patients—occurred fifteen years ago, when I was asked to see a 4-year-old child with leukemia and facial nerve palsy. After I had finished examining him, we talked a little bit (how much can one say to a 4-year-old?). Then, he looked at me and said, "I got the disease, but the disease doesn't got me." This was an extraordinary insight and a great philosophy, and something that I found incredible for such a young child to articulate. That incident reminds me of a book by Fred Epstein—world-famous pediatric neurosurgeon—entitled, *If I Get to Five: What Children Can Teach Us.* Fred suffered a severe head injury from a bicycle fall; he was in a vegetative state and then slowly recovered, using these lessons.

The main lesson, of course, is that we all need to be adaptable, and flexible, and to have courage and character. What I like about Loma Linda is that it has provided an environment in which to practice outstanding clinical medicine and to provide excellent patient care—and to do so in a caring and collegial environment.

I never truly understood why I decided to come here and to stay here; but next to marrying my wife, Eileen, it has been the best decision of my life.

Stephen Ashwal is distinguished professor in LLUSM departments of pediatrics and of neurology. He received his MD degree from New York University in New York City, New York, in 1970. In 2006, he received the LLUMC Physician Professional Recognition Award.

The LORD will always lead you. He will satisfy your needs in dry lands and give strength to your bones. You will be like a garden that has much water, like a spring that never runs dry. Isaiah 58:11, NCV

To give a realistic portrayal of God's leading in my life, I would be amiss if I didn't share God's leading in the lives of my parents. My father's family lived in Ukraine. Through studying the Scriptures and the Holy Spirit's leading, they discovered they were worshipping on the wrong day. Not knowing about Seventh-day Adventists, they called themselves "Soobotnyekee," which meant "Sabbath keepers," and were persecuted for their beliefs. At 15 years of age, my father left Ukraine for Canada.

My mother and her family also came from Ukraine, and they were Mennonites. They, too, were persecuted; and they settled in Saskatchewan, Canada. A couple of miles from them lived two Farnsworth brothers, who were instrumental in establishing a new Seventh-day Adventist church, which my mother's family joined.

It was my father who encouraged me in my early teens to become a physician. Several years later, I was accepted to the College of Medical Evangelists and started school there in 1941. As freshmen students, we had barely settled in when the December 7, 1941, Japanese attack on Pearl Harbor took place. This resulted in drastic changes at Loma Linda!

Financing my medical education was not easy. My parents could send no more than $100 a month, and this was money they had to borrow. Also, that amount was all the government of Canada would permit to leave the country per month during war. During the four weeks of vacation after my freshman year, I worked at the Hollywood Presbyterian Medical Center in Los Angeles, California, as a surgical orderly. My pay was $100.

A year later, during the next four-week break, the Lord led me to canvass, or sell Christian books. I canvassed in Brawley, located in California's Imperial Valley, for two weeks and then delivered books for two weeks. The Lord blessed me exceedingly. I earned enough money to cover my tuition for the third and fourth years. I graduated debt-free and thank God for His leading.

One more example of God's leading in my life came after I graduated from medical school. My two classmates, Irwin Horsley and Gustave Hoehn, and I did our internship in British Columbia, Canada. During our internship, the time came when we were to write examinations to obtain the right to practice medicine in Canada. One of the exams was on the Sabbath. All three of us CME grads chose not to write the exam. We were hoping that we would be able to write the exam six months later on another day.

Near the end of my internship, I made an appointment with the registrar of the College of Physicians and Surgeons of British Columbia to see how I could be accommodated. I did not have a license to practice medicine. He informed me that a doctor was needed in the northern part of Vancouver Island. It was an industrial and family practice, serving an area with a pulp mill, sawmill, and whaling station. Here, again, I praise God for His leading. I was given verbal permission to go—nothing on paper—and license to practice. God undoubtedly rewarded my faithfulness in not writing the examination on Sabbath. Throughout my life, these incidents remind me of how God has led.

Reuben Matiko, LLUSM class of 1945, was an LLUSM Alumni Association 1993 Honored Alumnus. He and his wife, Frances, reside in Victoria, British Columbia, Canada.

June 13

And that to thee, O Lord, belongs steadfast love. For thou dost requite a man according to his work. Psalm 62:12, RSV

To be glad because life gives us moments to fill with work and with kindness, and opportunities to express appreciation of earth's mysteries and beauties;

to be not forgetful of our origin—our homes, our school, our church and the friends who have been responsible for our success;

to give deference to our colleagues, courtesy to our helpers, heartfelt sympathy to those across whose lives is flung the veil of sorrow;

to fear nothing but our own hesitation at difficulties and to loathe nothing but dishonesty and cowardice;

to gain the respect of our teachers, the confidence of our patients, the approbation of our fellowmen;

to retain our poise in the face of victory or defeat;

to remove the ill that grieves and place the balm of healing in its stead;

to be ashamed to die until we have achieved some triumph for humanity, whether it be an improved therapy, a perfect experiment, or a rescued life;

to guard the cradle, protect the workmart, hover tenderly near our human trusts even to the portals of the tomb;

to be ever mindful that today, lived in service for the Great Physician, makes "every yesterday a dream of happiness and every tomorrow a vision of hope"—these are the little waymarks in our footpath of service.

Joseph Mossberger (1908-1996), LLUSM class of 1939, wrote this devotional for the June 1-15, 1950, issue of the LLU The Medical Evangelist.

June 14

And that he died for all, that they which live should not henceforth live unto themselves, but unto him which died for them, and rose again. 2 Corinthians 5:15, KJV

I lost my best friend, Hersha King, because of a car accident during our first year of medical school. Being a very shy person, I am not good at making new friends. However, now I have many friends in the class because of Hersha.

One day in my religion class, the instructor pointed at each student and then asked the other classmates to tell something they knew about that person. Only a few students knew me; so I was worried what would happen when my turn came. Fortunately, Hersha was in the class; and she introduced me to the others. She was one of my few close friends; so whenever I found her in one of my small study groups, I was relieved.

Hersha also understood my difficulty with English. When I could not understand a colloquial expression, she always explained the term or the meaning of the sentence to me. When I said something incorrectly in English, she kindly corrected me.

Hersha had such an open heart. She was the only person I could feel free to talk to whenever I needed someone to talk with. If I called her, she would always call me back and give me thoughtful advice, even when she was busy. When I heard the news of her death, I looked at my cell phone's calling history; her name popped up first. It was difficult for me to accept the reality of her death at that time.

Because Hersha and I were in the biomedical science program, we worked together. We shared the same goal, which was to become good doctors and serve according to God's plan for us. Although she did not have the opportunity to reach this goal, her spirit is always with me.

What I learned from Hersha are Christian traits that I think are very admirable. She was not afraid to offer sound advice or be helpful, she was willing to listen, and she found time for our friendship. By reaching out to me, she created a bond that I will forever cherish as I try to demonstrate her excellent qualities to others. Perhaps people come into our lives, even if briefly, to show us how we should live the Christian life.

John Kioka, LLUSM class of 2009, was born in the United States but grew up in Tokyo, Japan. He received a BS degree in physics from Rikkyo University in Japan. June 14 is the day Hersha King was tragically killed.

June 15

Teach me thy way, O LORD, and lead me in a plain path. Psalm 27:11, KJV

Teach me, dear Lord, that the hypertrophy of the head is more deadly than the hypertrophy of the heart, that the hyperacidity of unforgiveness is more distressing than the "heartburn" of an ulcer.

Help me to live so that I can lie down and sleep each night, with a clear conscience, without bromide or barbiturate, and unhaunted by the faces of those to whom I have charged fees.

Grant, I beseech Thee, the power to focus my eyes on the distant goal of heaven—eyes undimmed by the blurring myopia of fame or fortune. Keep my ears alert to the call of duty, undeafened by the clinking of polluted dollars.

Guide my mind and hand as I administer healing potions to suffering patients; [and] help me to remember that the hypodermic needles should be tempered with the therapy of sympathy; the tonics enhanced by the stimulant of kindness; the transfusions aided by the nourishment of tenderness.

And then, when the last patient has been comforted, when the stethoscope, journals, and books have been laid aside, may my last call be Thy call, as I rest in [the] peace which Thou only can send. Amen.

Wilfred J. Snodgrass (1913-1981), LLUSM class of 1938, was a family practitioner in Santa Monica, California. He was LLUSM Alumni Association president from 1975 to 1976 and was LLUSM Alumni Association 1982 Alumnus of the Year. This devotional originally appeared in the April-June 1982 issue of the LLUSM Alumni Association Alumni Journal.

June 16

Jesus wept. John 11:35, KJV

I was now, finally, an intern. It was my first month on the wards at the fabled Loma Linda University Medical Center. Earlier, as a medical student, walking up from the basic science campus, I often gazed at the top of the medical center's parapets, imagining a castle, feeling as if I needed to assail it to be included. And now, here I was, finally on the inside. I was now a defender of that castle, repelling the enemies: disease, pain, suffering, and death.

The problem was I knew I wasn't that much different from a few weeks prior. Signing the patients' charts before had required the co-signature of an MD. Now, I was the co-signer. Yet, I did not feel any different than I had as a medical student, as far as my doctoring capabilities were concerned. I was completely overwhelmed those first few weeks by my responsibilities; and this was just the general medicine service, rather than a subspecialty service!

One of my first memorable patients was a male in his 70s who had been perfectly healthy all his life and was admitted for persistent abdominal pain. The computed tomography (CT) report showed a pancreatic mass, most certainly a malignant cancer. I was his doctor. I was the one who had to inform him and his wife of the diagnosis and his probable impending demise.

My feelings of inadequacy intruded into my awareness again, though I did not inform others of my plight. I had never had to tell someone they had cancer. I wasn't sure I had seen appropriate methods modeled for me. I had no idea how to engage in a conversation about this, and I did not recall any lectures on this topic.

I blundered my way through the interaction—essentially blurting out his diagnosis and prognosis without finesse, felt emotionally overwrought as a result, and moments later found myself in the ward's restroom, crying. After a few minutes, I was struck by the thought that I was at a crossroads in my emotional life. This was a very painful experience, which I did not like; and I knew that I did not have to feel this way. I knew I could avoid these feelings either through suppression, gallows humor, distraction, alcohol, or Valium.

I knew it was possible to turn off these feelings; but then I realized that if I did, I might then lose the capacity to re-access my emotions when I needed to in other relationships. Which direction to take was now my choice. I decided to stay present with my feelings, regardless of the accompanying discomfort. Rather than fearing or avoiding the discomfort of my feelings, I remained on the "learning curve," which, over time, taught me that my discomfort was a guide to my patient's needs.

All of us in the medical profession have developed our intellect, and some of us have accomplished this at the expense of our emotional self. Every good trait unbalanced by other good traits becomes a liability. Professional development is a daily and lifelong process. May my goal be to stay open to all that I am, no matter the discomfort it might bring, so that my impact on others has a greater beneficial range.

Mickey Ask, LLUSM class of 1979-A, is assistant professor in LLUSM departments of medicine and of preventive medicine. He is an addictionologist.

June 17

Commit to the LORD whatever you do, and your plans will succeed. Proverbs 16:3, NIV

I was surprised by how much harder the second year of medical school was than the first. After the second year got off to a rocky start, I began to question the calling that I had so strongly felt before going into medical school and even felt during my first year.

During this doubtful period, I attended a small service in Fontana, California, and was prayed for following the service. After praying for me, the pastor felt impressed that I needed to read the book of Joshua, as God had something special for me there. This grabbed my attention because a few months earlier, a visitor at my church—someone I didn't know—had told me the exact same thing, but I never took the time to read it.

Now with a confirmation, I took God up on His message and sat down to read Joshua. I was struck by how Joshua's radical obedience to God was rewarded with success after success on the battlefield. With all my recent doubts about success in my own life, Joshua, especially chapter 1, verse 7 (NIV) spoke directly to me. "Be careful to obey all the law my servant Moses gave you; do not turn from it to the right or to the left, that you may be successful wherever you go."

As if He was not direct enough, the following Sabbath the pastor at church had picked Joshua 1:1-9 to preach on, again emphasizing Joshua's obedience. After the sermon, I prayed, "Okay, Lord this is the third time recently that you've brought me to Joshua. I get that you want me to obey, but how?"

It didn't take long for God to answer. Three days later, Chaplain Silva, filling in for my religion class, began by passing out a "pop-out" Bible verse to each of us. I popped mine open and realized God and I had entered a conversation, as inside was Proverbs 16:3 (NIV), "Commit to the LORD whatever you do, and your plans will succeed." That was what He wanted, for me to commit my plans to Him!

With two weeks remaining until finals, I decided to take God up on His word and obey. I changed my study style by devoting a portion of my normal study time to time with God. During that time, I would study His word, rereading Proverbs and Joshua, and committing medical school and my life plans to God.

Leading into and throughout finals, I didn't feel as prepared as usual. However, I had surrendered them to God, and He gave me an unusual peace, free from the anxiousness and worries that usually accompanied exam week. A week after exams, I was stunned when I received my scores. Despite less time studying, I had the best test week of my life, with my grades a standard deviation above normal. As I continue to commit my plans to Him throughout my second year, He has astonished me again and again with His grace and faithfulness.

Corey Fuller, LLUSM class of 2010—for which he was sophomore class co-pastor—is from Redlands, California. He and Juliana (Hayton), a nurse at LLUMC, were married on June 17, 2007. He is a deferred mission appointee, and they are excited about future mission work.

But he who is greatest among you shall be your servant. And whoever exalts himself will be humbled, and he who humbles himself will be exalted. Matthew 23:11-12, NKJV

I had never really sensed a call to general surgery or to any of its subspecialties. Not surprisingly, of all the rotations required during the junior year of medical school, I was most apprehensive about the surgery rotation. I knew that it would be a difficult rotation for me; and when the time came, I found the mental and physical demands more challenging than anticipated.

Regretfully, I was also privy to a few interactions during which the attending surgeons' behavior was less than courteous. It was during such interactions that I found myself being particularly reminded that Loma Linda University School of Medicine is God's medical school unlike any other, and has been from its inception. I was also reminded of my own shortcomings and how, despite them, the love of our Lord and Savior remains.

After six weeks of general surgery, four weeks of subspecialty surgery, and two weeks of anesthesia, by the grace of God, I found myself awaiting the start of the last surgery of the rotation. The patient and the attending surgeon had already arrived in the operating room. I marked the time. The resident was running late. Realizing that each passing moment could be worsening what potentially was an already bad situation, I found myself growing increasingly uneasy for the resident. When he did arrive, I was fearful that he might be unduly chastised for his tardiness. And then a peculiar sight unfolded before me.

Neither a harsh rebuke nor an unkind word was uttered by this attending surgeon. Not only that, but the attending also helped gown and glove the resident! I was stunned. This scene ran so contrary to what I had thought would likely happen that it took several moments for me to process what I had just observed. Then, like a warm comforter on a dark chilly night, I felt the love of God envelope me, as I realized what a wonderful blessing it was for me to have my surgery rotation end like this.

My surgery rotation reassured me of God's plan for me and for Loma Linda by allowing me to witness firsthand the love of God expressed through a willing servant. I was also reminded of the words of our Master regarding greatness, as found in Matthew 23:11-12.

Is the reader wondering about the identity of that Christian attending surgeon? It was none other than the world-renowned cardiothoracic surgeon, Leonard Bailey, LLUSM class of 1969.

Clifford Cabansag, LLUSM class of 2008, is a resident in internal medicine at Kettering Medical Center in Kettering, Ohio. He and his wife, Kathleen, were married on June 18.

June 19

He has shown you, O man, what is good; And what does the LORD require of you But to do justly, To love mercy, And to walk humbly with your God? Micah 6:8, NKJV

As you start your day, think of the many people that God will allow you to touch today. Will your actions strengthen them in their daily struggles? Will the radiance of Christ shine through your presence in their lives?

Mother Theresa said we are all called to do small things with great love. Pray that your actions today reflect what Micah said. Treat each person that you encounter as special and unique. Remember that Christ exhorted us that "whatsoever we do for the least of his children, we do unto Him."

In the healthcare arena, we often deal with people who are suffering and in need of healing. We must remember that our ability to help is God-given; and often the greatest comfort we can give is spiritual, not physical. Take time today to reflect on how your actions either strengthen or weaken the Body of Christ.

Do small things with great kindness. Try to see the goodness in each and every person you encounter today. We are all on the same journey, and all of us need help along the way at some time. Take the time to reach out and validate the other person's importance and worth; and in so doing, you will validate your own purpose in life. Do these things quietly, without seeking recognition for your actions.

Be just in your actions, show mercy and forgiveness, and remember that it is the Lord's work you are doing, not your own. And thus you will be blessed all the days of your life.

Austin Colohan is professor in and chair of LLUSM department of neurosurgery. He received his MD degree from McMaster University in Hamilton, Ontario, Canada, in 1978.

June 20

A truthful witness saves lives. Proverbs 14:25, NIV

It is an early Thursday evening. The last remaining winter daylight from the south-facing window has faded, and only institutional fluorescent tubes light the room. My senior resident and I sit across from each other at an old mahogany desk. As a faculty member, I sometimes take the extra step to discuss spiritual things with certain residents, in order to connect in a way that transcends the usual grind. This time, Tom, and I share our personal journeys of growing up in the Seventh-day Adventist tradition.

Tom tells me how he has struggled with the question of God; now, religion is no longer real to him. He reads Bible stories to his kids because they are good stories, but that's about all. I tell Tom about a book I recently read. John B. Wong, LLUSM class of 1960, had given me Lee Strobel's *The Case for Christ*; but its unappealing journalistic style led to several failed attempts to read the book. After finally plowing through the first two chapters by sheer determination, I found the book to be captivating. That evening, I hand my copy to Tom. "Here's something you might like. I had a hard time getting started on it, but it's a really good book."

A few months go by. June 20, 2004, is a festive Sunday for the graduating residents. The dining area, now lit by the late vernal sun's filtered warm glow, is decorated for the graduation of four orthopaedic residents and two hand fellows. I am sitting at one of the fourteen round dinner tables, having a wonderful time with great company before dinner. I feel a tap on my shoulder. Turning around, I see Tom.

"My wife has something for you," Tom says with a smile.

"Okay . . .? Cherie has something for me?"

"Yeah," Tom replied and pulls out a 4"x5½" ivory Hallmark envelope and hands it to me.

I take it, and he returns to his table. I carefully open the gold sticker seal to find a matching thank you card.

Dear Danny,

Tom is wanting to say thank you for lots & lots of things—so I bought these great cards for him. But Danny, I have more than you know to thank you for. Your friendship with Tom has had *great* impact on me and on our family.

Tom & I have had more discussions about aspects of career—and most important, relationships with God. It's the first time Tom has expressed many of his thoughts—and I think he's been able to clarify in his own mind many ideas. He has said you are the first person he has been able to talk to about God and actually relate to. I can't help but love ya, Danny! *Thank you.* [signed] Cherie

I slowly put the card back in its envelope. After the February discussion in my office, I wasn't expecting any major impact—just a little ripple, maybe. I walk over to Cherie, give her a hug, and tell her that I was really touched by her note and honored to have played a little part in their lives.

Reflecting on that series of events, I can't help but think about how God can use such a little part to work out everything for the good of them that love Him.

M. Danny Wongworawat, LLUSM class of 1996, is associate professor in and assistant chair of LLUSM department of orthopaedic surgery.

June 21

I have set the LORD always before me: because he is at my right hand, I shall not be moved. Psalm 16:8, KJV

We were younger then, full of vitality and eager to face life's challenges. In 1950, I had graduated from the College of Medical Evangelists in medicine; and my wife, Helanejo, had also graduated in nursing. Having school debts to pay, we decided to make my home state, Michigan, our "mission field."

There was a need in rural central Michigan. After a few years, we built a medical center in the farming area around Ithaca. Family practice has always been on the forward edge of medicine, and we found ourselves doing everything. Soon we had a reputation of willingness to make home calls and do extra things for people.

Then, on a sunny day in the early fall, it happened. Farmers were harvesting grain-laden fields and filling silos for the winter. The phone rang and a most urgent voice pleaded for needed help—now! Learning with difficulty where they lived and not asking questions, I grabbed several sterile trays of instruments, intravenous lines, etc., and took one of my office nurses with me.

Arriving at the farm home, it was obvious that some kind of an accident had occurred. Several neighboring farmers were already gathering. I was ushered quickly to the back of the barn, where a forty-foot silo towered over my head. At the base of it was a huge tractor with an eight-inch drive belt attached to a monstrous iron silo-filling machine, which stood silent. A quick glance showed a middle-aged man on the back of an elevated farm wagon with his left leg, up to his groin, tightly locked in the massive auger of this huge machine.

He was in deep shock, still alive, and, of course, in pain. My quick, earnest prayer was, "Lord, help me save him [and] guide my mind and my hands." Immediately a plan flashed before me. His blood pressure was now very low, and he had no pulse. Starting the intravenous glucose with collapsed veins was a challenge. I administered morphine for pain, as well as antibiotics and tetanus toxoid.

During this time, I asked the gathering farmers to bring a metal cutting torch and pails of water. The dying man began to stabilize. Now, hopefully, we would be able to get him out of the machine. He had low blood pressure and a faint pulse. His crushed leg would have to come off. The farmer's workers were also beginning to help, giving me just enough room to do surgery.

Using large amounts of local anesthetics, I then felt another Hand steadying mine as I amputated his left leg, using my sterile instruments and drapes in the dirty area. That twenty-plus-mile ambulance trip to the hospital seemed like a year that day, but the operating personnel and surgeon on call were ready; and then the revision began. This farmer lived after one of the worst farm accidents in Gratiot County. Today, he can walk with a prosthesis. Truly, the Lord was before and at my right hand.

V. Lowell Sheline, LLUSM class of 1950, resides in Sedona, Arizona. He practiced family medicine for thirty-six years in Michigan. June 21, 2009 is the 60th anniversary of he and his wife, Helanejo.

Fear not, for I have redeemed you; I have summoned you by name; you are mine. When you pass through the waters, I will be with you; and when you pass through the rivers, they will not sweep over you. When you walk through the fire, you will not be burned; the flames will not set you ablaze. Isaiah 43:1-2, NIV

While working on my undergraduate degree, I remember an evening during winter quarter when I felt completely hopeless. I don't even remember what I felt hopeless about. Maybe it was an overwhelming class schedule, too many hours at work, or simply being a little too distant from the Lord. Whatever it was, I was desperate to make it go away. It was a cold winter night and I wanted to stay in, but I had promised friends I would meet them at the gym to watch a basketball game.

On my way to the game, the pressure on my chest seemed greater than ever. So out of total desperation to relieve the emotional tension, I started to pray. Mostly I remember just praying for a sign. I had never truly encountered the Lord, as some are so fortunate to do. That night I just had to know that there was a purpose for me, that He had a plan for me. I wanted to know that God truly is there, with us . . . always. I wanted proof that the Lord heard me and knew my sorrows.

I pulled up to the gym and was rather pleased with the parking spot. It was right in front of the doors, underneath a street light. I thought, "At least something good happened to me today." I don't remember anything about the basketball game, whom I was meeting there, or what team my school was playing against. All I know is that the Lord left a note on my windshield for me when I came out. The note didn't have my name on it; in fact it had someone else's name on it, a girl who drives the exact Jeep as mine, but in a different color. Perhaps the streetlight distorted the color of my car enough for it to be mistaken for the other one.

On one side of the note was written the girl's name, and on the other side was written, "Isaiah 43:1-2." I immediately rushed to my dorm room and flipped open my Bible to that verse. "I will be with you . . ." is what I read over and over again. I had given the Lord an ultimatum, demanding that I feel or find Him somehow; and sure enough I did. He answered my prayer in less time than a basketball game. I guess He really wanted me to know.

I think everyone has times of emptiness or loneliness, a time when they need something from the Lord that says, "I am with you." And sure enough, written for everyone to see, he says, "I have summoned you by name; you are mine." Someone once told me that what God calls you to do, He prepares you for. So, in your moments of desperation, when you feel like giving up, just remember a promise the Lord gave to us many, many years ago: "I am with you."

Kelli Andersen, LLUSM class of 2011, and her husband, Dane, LLUSD class of 2011, were married on June 22, 2008.

June 23

Then Jesus called for the children and said to the disciples, "Let the children come to me. Don't stop them! For the Kingdom of God belongs to those who are like these children. I tell you the truth, anyone who doesn't receive the Kingdom of God like a child will never enter it." Luke 18:16-17, NLT

It was early summer, and the two of us were driving back from an errand downtown, traveling along tree-shaded Normal Boulevard in Lincoln, Nebraska. Sitting close to me on the seat (years before child restraints) was my almost 5-year-old son, Toby. He looked so handsome, with his white-blond hair and dressed in his crisp little blue pants and complementary shirt. (His mother—my wife, Ruthita—always kept him fashionably dressed. Also, to this day she claims you can tell the quality of the mother by how clean her child is!)

We passed by a new playground the city had installed several months earlier. It was one of those greenish treated-lumber and coarse-sand areas—with tire swings, swinging bridges, and other "natural" elements so popular in the early 1980s. We had stopped there numerous times to play.

As we drove by, my son noticed it and said, "I like that place." I agreed that we always had a lot of fun there. And then I thought I'd take this opportunity to extol the virtues of another "play place," which we would soon be visiting on our summer vacation.

"Yes, Toby, that's a good place, but it's not nearly as much fun as Disney World!" I exclaimed. I must have sounded like a Disney marketing rep as I went on and on about all the exciting rides, new things to see, and glorious activities that awaited us there.

After what must have seemed to him like a very long and animated account about Walt Disney World, I concluded with, "Yeah, Toby, it's nice there, *really* nice!" And then those bright, innocent blue eyes looked up at me, and he said, "Yes, Daddy, but not as nice as heaven." I nodded and drove home in silence.

Sure, I felt as though I had been put in my place. But I was also thankful for all those mornings in Sabbath School. And I remembered the words of Jesus and thought about what He must have meant—knowing about childlike innocence, enthusiasm, and wonderment—when He said we should all be like little children.

Duane J. Fike is a copy editor and former English professor. He holds a PhD degree. He and his wife, Ruthita, reside in Redlands, California.

June 24

For I know the thoughts that I think toward you, saith the LORD, thoughts of peace, and not of evil, to give you an expected end. Then shall ye call upon me, and ye shall go and pray unto me, and I will hearken unto you. And ye shall seek me, and find me, when ye shall search for me with all your heart. Jeremiah 29:11-13, KJV

One of my very sick patients passed away today. She was a 36-year-old female, admitted for generalized weakness and fevers. She had a prior cervical lymph node biopsy highly suggestive of lymphoma, and had suddenly decompensated—becoming neutropenic and coagulopathic, in full-blown disseminated intravascular coagulation. Over the weekend, her blood pressure plummeted and she went into respiratory failure. Her hemoglobin dropped from 10 to 4; she was bleeding everywhere—vaginally, from her central line site, from the biopsy site, and from her stomach. Suddenly, at 2:00 p.m., I received a page; and an overhead intercom voice announced "Code Blue, Two South." I knew it was my patient. My co-intern and I ran to the code.

A few minutes into the effort, I was urged to find the patient's husband. He entered the intensive care unit looking dumbfounded, and I explained what was going on. He slowly walked into the room, now jam-packed with nurses, respiratory therapists, residents, and medical students—one of whom was performing chest compressions. The husband looked on in silence for what seemed like an eternity, then finally threw up his hands and said: "Okay, let's stop." A total of twelve minutes had passed since the code had begun, and the patient was declared dead. The patient's husband began weeping—a strange cry that was lacking in physical tears but full of agony—as he held the hand of his beloved, deceased wife, and the mother of his two children.

We allowed the husband time to mourn in solitude, after which I returned to speak with him. By this time, he was calm and collected. He proceeded to tell the nurse and me how much he appreciated what we had done for his wife, and how he knew we did everything in our power to keep her alive. He then turned to me, clutched my hand in his, and proceeded to tell me that he appreciated me and what I had done; and that as I grew older, I would gain more wisdom and learn how to help people all the more. Tears began to well up in my eyes as he was thanking and building others up during this most delicate moment of life. It took all of my energy to keep from crying, but somehow I managed to blink away the tears.

It was in this moment that I realized what a blessed opportunity every healthcare worker has to touch the lives of patients and their families. What a privilege it is, a God-given gift, to be entrusted with the care of the sick and dying. I realize that, as a future ophthalmologist, I will no longer be regularly involved in such critical life-death situations. But it is my deepest desire to learn to use my education and training for His glory, to lift others up in their time of need, and ultimately to lift up Jesus Christ. May this be your prayer as well.

Janie Yoo, LLUSM class of 2006—for which she was freshman class co-pastor—is a resident in ophthalmology at LLUMC. She and her husband, Paul, LLUSD class of 2008, were married June 24, 2007. They are both deferred mission appointees and look forward to serving as missionaries abroad when she finishes residency.

June 25

Be sober, be vigilant; because your adversary the devil walks about like a roaring lion, seeking whom he may devour. 1 Peter 5:8, NKJV

It had been one of those Saturday nights at Riverside General Hospital in Riverside, California: stabbings, gunshot wounds, emergencies all night long.

I was the anesthesiologist on duty; and just as the orange-red sun began peeking up over the eastern hills through a smoggy sky, I was ready to doff my scrub suit for street clothes. Then it happened: a young woman was rushed up from the emergency room—her right arm missing, with just a six-inch bloody stump of her humerus remaining.

She was a keeper and handler of exotic big cats for television shows; and that morning, perhaps doing something that she had done many times before, she stuck her arm through the fence enclosing the lions and leopards just to pet or say hello to her favorite big cat. Suddenly, the cat grabbed her arm, jerked it through the chain link fence until her shoulder was tight, and then bit her arm completely off. (Whether it ate the arm, I never found out.) All I could do was put her to sleep while the surgeons debrided and closed the skin over the stump.

The devil is like that cat, ready to pounce on any unsuspecting victim at the most inopportune time.

At a later time, while working at the Seventh-day Adventist Milimani Road Clinic in Nairobi, Kenya, we occasionally had opportunity to visit the fabulous game parks of East Africa. It was always a thrill to camp out among the magnificent wild life in the Masai Mara, Serengeti, Samburu, or Ngorongoro Crater parks and see the animals roaming wild and free. On a successful trip, we would see lions, cheetahs, and, occasionally, the elusive leopard.

One Sabbath, we stopped our vehicle to eat our lunch alongside a giant acacia tree. Not too far away, lolling in the shade, asleep on their backs with their feet pointed skyward, a pride of fifteen or more lions was the absolute picture of serenity and contentment. With their stomachs full from a good kill, they seemed to pose no threat to anyone.

I wondered: Could I open the sliding door just a bit and step out for a better picture? But then I remembered a young lady in Riverside with only one arm. With a giant leap, a lioness could knock me down, close her powerful jaws around my throat, and crush my trachea. It would all be over in one horrendous moment.

The devil is like that: just a little chink in our armor, a brief lapse in our judgment, and he is always waiting to catch us unawares and lead us down a road that ends in eternal destruction.

While visiting friends in Addis Ababa, Ethiopia, we were invited to Haile Selassie's palace by his housekeeper/caretaker, Mrs. Hansen. In his private zoo, we were privileged to hold a three-month old lion cub in our arms. He wiggled, squirmed, and seemed not a bit happy! But what a thrill for us! Some day soon, when the devil is forever banished to his well-deserved end and all the predators have become vegetarians, I want to kneel down beside my favorite big cat, gently pat his head, stroke his magnificent fur, and finally get the answer to a question I have had for so long—Can the big cats purr?

Lewis Hart, LLUSM class of 1949, was instructor in LLUSM department of anesthesiology. He is the father of Kenneth Hart, LLUSM class of 1969, and Richard Hart, LLUSM class of 1970. June 25 is his birthday.

Peace I leave with you, my peace I give unto you: not as the world giveth, give I unto you. Let not your heart be troubled, neither let it be afraid. John 14:27, KJV

I was a junior partner in the busy South Bay Ob-Gyn medical group in National City, California, in the early 1970s. We were called the "Three Fs:" Milton E. Fredricksen, LLUSM class of 1953-B; Forrest La Verne Fuller, LLUSM class of 1961; and myself. I was on call this particular weekend for the partnership; and it was very busy, as usual. In the midst of the hustle and bustle, I received a telephone call.

"Dr. Fisher?" "No I'm sorry, this is Dr. Fish." "Oh well, Dr. Fisher," (the name didn't compute with some of our patients) "this is Jennifer, and I'm 'wommicking' again." I knew Jennifer fairly well. She was an 18-year-old single woman, primigravida, who was in the early second trimester of her pregnancy. She had been admitted to the hospital on a couple of prior occasions with the diagnosis of hyperemesis gravidarum. In the background, I could hear yelling and screaming, plus loud music. "Go to the emergency room at the Paradise Valley Hospital, Jennifer. I'll meet you there." "Okay, Dr. Fisher."

From previous experience, I knew that Jennifer would have to be admitted to a quiet, darkened room, with no visitors or television, and that she would need intravenous fluids and gentle sedation. Her electrolytes were in normal balance this time, since she had been instructed to call immediately if she had a recurrence of her symptoms. After a couple of days of rest and a gentle reintroduction to a healthy diet, she was ready for discharge. She went on to term and delivered a normal child.

I thought about Jennifer's stressful life many times and the physical effects it had upon her. It led me to reassess my own stressful life. I recalled Ellen G. White's book, *In Heavenly Places.* The reading for August 30, 1968, was titled, "Christ's Legacy of Peace." In it she quoted John 14:27.

Certainly, any physician has stress, pressure, and perhaps not enough time for the important things in life: God, family, church, proper use of time, etc. But with that text in mind, I chose to renew my commitment to God, put Him first in my life, and recall His promises to all of us. I am retired now, but the commitment to put Him first still stands. I recommend it; it's good medicine!

Warren L. Fish, LLUSM class of 1961, is an obstetrician and gynecologist in Beaverton, Oregon. June 26 is his birthday.

June 27

God's voice thunders in marvelous ways; he does great things beyond our understanding. Job 37:5, NIV

The way we perceive our circumstances depends on our experiences.

It was another warm and humid June morning in Maryland. I was lamenting about having to wear my combat fatigues and boots, as I felt the sweat bead up on my neck at 0530 hours. My mind was inundated with financial concerns and work-related responsibilities that morning: the mortgage payment was approaching, food was eating through my bank account, childcare expenses continued, and my monthly work load reports were due.

As I backed out of the driveway, I glimpsed at a lawn that was begging for some attention. I was a first-year gastroenterology fellow in the twilight of an inpatient month, about the time when you're no longer sure if it's dawn or dusk. As I started rounding that morning, I remember being frustrated as an intern babbled his way through a patient presentation. And then I overheard a conversation in hushed tones.

They were saying one of my friends was currently en route via air, medevaced after suffering sudden cardiac death. How quickly my perspective changed—how ashamed I felt regarding my attitude! He was a Christian, an honorable husband, the father of two beautiful, young children, and a cardiology fellow of impeccable knowledge and skill.

When I ran down to the critical care unit, I saw "Big Tim" intubated and lifeless, his wife seemingly broken at his bedside. I tried to contemplate her feelings of helplessness and abandonment so I could offer some sort of comforting words. It is well known that the likelihood of recovery from ventricular fibrillation occurring outside of the hospital is beyond poor. I did what I was trained to do; and with tears pouring, I prayed with her for God's faithful mercy and grace. Five days later, with an implantable defibrillator in his chest, "Big Tim" walked out of that hospital with full mind, body, and spirit!

As a United States Army physician, I am ever reminded of the fragility of life, especially with all of the imaginable and unimaginable war injuries; and I am reminded of my need to deal with those who are unceasingly inflicted with things of the past that are so very present. These are palpable experiences that tend to provoke questions about life but have no answers. I also don't know why God heard my voice and answered my prayer that June morning. I am resigned that I just have to keep living, learning, and trusting in Christ . . . because my understanding is limited by my perspective.

Joseph Cheatham, LLUSM class of 2003—for which he was junior class president—is a gastroenterology fellow at Walter Reed Army Medical Center in Washington, D.C. He is a captain in the United States Army.

I will give you a new heart and put a new spirit in you; I will remove from you your heart of stone and give you a heart of flesh. Ezekiel 36:26, NIV

I have been witness to many miracles in my years as administrative director of Loma Linda University Medical Center's heart transplant program. Those of us who spend our lives "changing hearts" have often felt that we are merely instruments under God's direction; and that this complex process has so many components that cannot be planned for, predicted, or controlled.

In this context, I have often wondered what God has in store for some of our tiniest recipients. For instance, there is the story of Jose Marin that still delights me. Jose was born in 1989 in Los Angeles, California. He was the second child of his parents, and his birth was much anticipated. The family's joy was short-lived, however, when Jose went into shock at his home just twelve days after his birth, when his fetal circulation ceased.

He was rushed to the emergency room, where his fatal heart disease was diagnosed. Jose's parents were informed of the critical status of their son and faced a difficult decision: let him die, attempt palliative repairs, or opt for heart transplantation. His parents chose the transplant option, and the babe was transferred to Loma Linda University Children's Hospital. Jose had suffered serious neurologic and renal insults, and his life was fragile as he awaited a donor.

And then, on July 4, 1989, just two weeks after his eventful birth, a 2-day-old donor from eastern Canada was identified. Our transplant team left Loma Linda at 10:00 p.m. and returned to Loma Linda at 8:00 the following morning to begin the re-implantation operation. All went well, and Jose was discharged from the hospital in three weeks. Exactly one month later, Jose kept a scheduled appointment in the transplant clinic. His echocardiogram showed marked deterioration that was consistent with acute rejection.

Very dramatically, he had a cardiac arrest before our eyes. A heroic resuscitation effort began. Jose's heart function would not recover. However, as resuscitation continued, he seemed to respond to deep, painful stimulation. Then the dilemma—what to do? It just so happened that a donor, who shared Jose's blood type and weight, became available; but that donor's heart was intended for another infant. Nevertheless, that donor's heart was recovered from Oklahoma and placed emergently into Jose's chest while resuscitation continued. Fortunately, the other infant subsequently received another donor heart without incident.

There was always a concern that Jose would be neurologically impaired after such extraordinary intervention, but his recovery was uneventful. After several months at Loma Linda, the family returned home to Los Angeles.

I had occasion to speak with Jose's mother recently; and she told me how much joy Jose, now 19 years of age, brings to their family. He is attending community college, training to become a teacher. As the miracle of Jose's life continues to unfold, we celebrate God's hand in our efforts to give life.

Joyce Johnston Rusch was administrative director of LLUMC's heart transplant program and was also a nurse with the LLU Overseas Heart Surgery Team. She resides in Damascus, Oregon.

June 29

Being confident of this, that he who began a good work in you will carry it on to completion until the day of Christ Jesus. Philippians 1:6, NIV

It was the end of freshman year of medical school, and I was on my two-week elective in surgery at the Jerry L. Pettis Memorial Veterans Affairs Medical Center. As Elena, my third-year mentor, and I were making our daily rounds, we stopped as usual by Mr. J's room. In addition to asking him how he was doing and performing the physical exam, Elena opened Mr. J's colostomy bag while I assisted—handing her towels to wipe off any residuals. Needless to say, that particular task is never exactly the highlight of my day!

Mr. J usually didn't say much. While he didn't complain about anything, he seemed apathetic and expressionless. I was told he used to be very active and involved in church activities, as well as in volunteering his time and resources to help those less fortunate in his community. But as I stood there, it was hard for me to imagine him as anyone other than the person lying before me, slumped over in his hospital bed. That day, I had to do a modified history and physical exam; and Elena thought Mr. J would be the perfect patient for me.

After our initial entrance and greeting, Elena asked him whether I could examine him and listen to his heart and lungs. He stared at us for a couple of minutes and then said, "I'm glad you asked, before you started poking around." And then, in the next couple of minutes, Mr. J gave me one of the best pieces of advice anyone's ever given me. He emphasized the importance of seeking God's Spirit and asking Him to go before me into each room I am about to enter. Sure, he said, there are people who will yell, scream, and mistreat you doctors. But, he added, that with God going before us as we minister to each patient, we will leave the room knowing that we have helped them feel better than they did before.

Those words have always stuck with me. But even more moving was the image of Mr. J holding back tears as Elena leaned over and said, "Hang in there. God's not done with you yet."

I learned many things that day in Mr. J's room, the most important of which was that God brings people into our lives to teach us how to become better people. Furthermore, when we, like Mr. J, may think that we've been broken by time and circumstance, God's voice reminds us that "He who began a good work in you will be faithful to complete it until the day of Christ Jesus."

Anna Leigh Ursales, LLUSM class of 2009, emigrated from the Philippines to the United States in 1998. She is also a deferred mission appointee. June 29 is the date she received her acceptance into medical school.

He will wipe away every tear from their eyes, and there will be no more death, sadness, crying, or pain, because all the old ways are gone. Revelation 21:4, NCV

Jesus was clear about His mission on this earth. He understood what He was delivering to those around Him. Jesus said in John 10:10 (KJV): "I am come that they might have life, and that they might have it more abundantly." However, He didn't always do it in the time frame or manner that was expected.

Recall how He was chided for coming late to Mary and Martha's home after Lazarus had died. Seeing how troubled and upset the family was, Jesus cried with them, such that the Jews said in John 11:36 (KJV), "Behold how he loved him!" Others have thought that Jesus cried not just for Lazarus or his family, but for all of us who don't understand why He came to this sinful earth.

Though my early years of practice for patients were filled with scientific treatments of everything I had been taught, I soon realized that patients wanted someone who really cared, even if the outcome wasn't what they thought it would be. Though outcomes are important, they can be disappointing at times. But if we exercise our true altruism for our patients, they will ingratiate us with their gratitude.

I recall one incident in which a patient with pelvic and abdominal pain demonstrated a work-up with no obvious findings of organic pathology. Looking eye to eye, I finally asked, "Mary, what's going on at home?" With that question, big gloppy tears began flowing down her reddening cheeks. "Oh doctor, you have no idea what I have to deal with!"

Her story opened up with a floodgate of tears as she began explaining how her marriage and family were falling apart. Her treatment needs were far different than what a simple prescription could fix. She needed an understanding ear, someone who cared, and godly counsel from additional members of the healthcare team. I knew that her life had been touched that day, and she was on her way to healing.

Healthcare is about much more than just healthcare. It's about "people care"—or, as we say at Loma Linda, "whole-person care." Late in my career, Julie, my receptionist, and I began to recognize a pattern of success. We felt we had a good day, based on the number of patients expressing tears at the end of their visit—tears of relief, tears of joy, and, yes, I believe, tears of healing.

Revelation 21:4 (NKJV) says Jesus "will wipe away every tear from their eyes." I look forward to that day when the old ways are gone, the tears of healing have done their job, and we can learn at the feet of the One who cried the ultimate tears of healing on the cross.

Clifford Walters, LLUSM class of 1974, is associate clinical professor in LLUSM department of gynecology and obstetrics. He was LLUSM Alumni Association president from 2003 to 2004. June 30 signifies the end of an academic year.

July 1

When Jesus saw him lie, and knew that he had been now a long time in that case, he saith unto him, Wilt thou be made whole? John 5:6, KJV

"To make man whole" is the well-known motto of Loma Linda University. The key concept of achieving wholeness in spiritual, mental, emotional, and physical realms is taught to students, patients, and guests. Recently, I was reflecting on this notion and recalled two situations that occurred while I was in medical school.

As a third-year medical student, one of my rotations had devotional time set aside every morning for the staff to meditate on a brief thought presented by the chaplain. Something about that seemed interesting to me, but I didn't understand what it was or why. The second situation occurred when I was a fourth-year student when one of my electives was whole-person care. One "assignment" was to set aside some time just for myself. Interestingly, this was one of the hardest assignments during that rotation. I had no idea what I was going to do or where I would go. Then I started thinking that this was going to take a lot of effort and time, and what was the point anyway?

I ended up going to Oak Glen, California—a quiet area not too far from campus—and spending time there in the crisp mountain air, in the silence of a little park I found. Time seemed to slow down and pass by intentionally. It was difficult to be there and be still. My mind was elsewhere, thinking of other things that I could be doing, and how long would I have to stay there to satisfy the requirement. After about thirty-to-forty minutes, I headed back. Even though my experience was somewhat sabotaged by my own distracting thoughts, as I drove down the mountain, I was refreshed and surprised that I had benefited from my time in Oak Glen.

Now, as a resident, I think back to these experiences and realize the importance of wholeness. Many times in the medical profession, we tell our patients to eat right, exercise, find ways to reduce stress, etc.; but how much of our own advice do we also follow? Doctors and healthcare providers in general are notorious for missing sleep, skipping meals, and disregarding exercise or time for reflection on spiritual themes. What was striking to me about the above experiences was that we had been encouraged to take care of our own needs, too, and were taught that it was okay to do so. "Time out" was not selfish or self-centered; it was healthy.

It is interesting to note that Jesus also took time to take care of Himself. Of course, He spent a significant amount of time meeting the needs of others by preaching, healing, and teaching. Yet, He would find time for communion with His Father. He recharged Himself. He spent time with His family, with His disciples. He worked as a carpenter, which likely afforded him adequate exercise. If Jesus is the example that we should follow, then we should also follow His footsteps in pursuit of wholeness. He implores us: "Wilt thou be made whole?" (John 5:6, KJV).

Ana Gomez, LLUSM class of 2007, is a resident in psychiatry at University of Louisville Hospital in Louisville, Kentucky. She is a deferred faculty appointee. July 1 was the first day of her residency.

For ye shall not go out with haste, nor go by flight: for the Lord will go before you; and the God of Israel will be your [rear guard]. Isaiah 52:12, KJV

World War II was winding down. I had just completed a tour of duty and was hoping for my discharge from the service. However, instead of a discharge, I received orders to fly to Greenland to serve as the medical officer at the Grondal Navy refueling base. There were only about sixty men at the base, and I was given quarters in a Quonset hut with the dentist, the paymaster, and the radioman.

No great amount of medical work was needed, so I was assigned to keep the books for the canteen and to take charge of the mail. Here I was in Greenland, rather than in an orthopaedic surgery residency in Seattle, Washington.

One day a letter arrived from Washington, D.C., stating I was eligible for discharge from the service and could return to the United States on the first available governmental transportation. That was great news! I knew that I would need to clear this with Captain Charles Thomas, commander of the Greenland Patrol. I asked the radioman to send a message to Captain Thomas, requesting my departure on the basis of the letter. He answered promptly: "Your request, affirmative." I hoped to leave soon.

The following day Captain Thomas landed in Greenland. His first task was to send an officer to tell me that he had changed his mind and I could not leave. He spent some time visiting with several men just outside the Quonset, and I watched, hoping for a chance to see him and perhaps change his mind so that I could leave.

He left the group, walked toward the Quonset hut occupied by the base commander, and entered it. This appeared to be a good time to see him. I walked to the commander's Quonset and attempted to knock on the wooden door. I raised my clenched fist to knock at the door, but could not strike it. Again, I tried, and again I just could not hit the door.

I said to myself, there is something strange going on here, and quickly returned to my quarters. I dropped to my knees at the side of my bunk and asked the Lord to please let me know what was happening. My Bible was already on my bunk, and I opened it. Without paging through it, I just opened it and read the very first verse that struck my eyes: Isaiah 52:12. Reading the passage "cooled my heels."

Captain Thomas spent that night in a nearby village. He returned to base the next morning and I had no problem having a visit with him. He told me that he saw no reason why I could not leave. I could go with him on a Coast Guard cutter the following evening, and then catch a plane for the States.

We sailed out at midnight and arrived at Narsarsuaq the following afternoon, just in time to see "my" B-17 fly low over our heads en route to the States. At the airport office, I was told no plane was expected for a week. I was assigned quarters, but in about an hour a Navy crew arrived in a large bomber and was assigned the same quarters. I told them of my situation, and they suggested that I fly with them to Iceland the following day.

Upon arrival at Keflavic, Iceland, the next day, we received word that the B-17 that I so narrowly missed had crashed on Mt. Tom in Massachusetts and all aboard had been killed. I was shocked. While I never saw Captain Thomas again, I did say goodbye to his wife when we stopped in Greenland before heading south. She said that the Captain didn't know why he had changed my orders, but that "now we know: God didn't want you to die."

Arthur C. Miller, LLUSM class of 1942, was assistant professor at LLUSM department of surgery. He is a thoracic surgeon in Days Creek, Oregon.

July 3

And he said: "I tell you the truth, unless you change and become like little children, you will never enter the kingdom of heaven." Matthew 18:3, NIV

I lost our son, Michael, at church one Sabbath when he was only 12 years old. After the service, my wife and I had chatted with friends for a while. As we bade our goodbyes and started toward the car, we realized that Michael was missing!

"I will make this a teaching moment," I thought. "He needs to understand what I mean when I say, 'Stay close by and don't let me have to find you when we are ready to leave!'" True to my intent, I decided not to go looking for him. "He will have to walk home today," I told my wife. "The one-mile walk will not only be good for him, but he will have learned a valuable lesson."

Thirty minutes later, my wife spoke up as she prepared the Sabbath meal. "What if he gets mobbed on the way home? What if . . . ? What if . . . ?" So, I did what any good father would have done under the same circumstance. I sent our older son out to the street, to see if Michael was coming. He came back and reported no sighting.

It had now been more than an hour since I last saw Michael. In the interest of saving our nineteen-year marriage, I yielded to my wife's request to go back to church and find our son. However, I would be searching for him on my terms. I would drive around the church once and not get out of the car. After all, he needed to learn a lesson, and this was the perfect circumstance. I drove slowly around the church, peering as best as I could through windows and opened doors.

I was about to conclude the final lap, when I saw him. He was calmly walking toward me, with drinks and snacks in hand. The lack of urgency in his demeanor just about served to top the limits of a father's sabbatical tirade. He opened the door to the car and was greeted by an indignant, "Michael, where have you been? Do you realize that church ended over an hour ago?"

"Daddy," he replied, with the innocence only 12 year olds can muster, "I was at Teen Bible Study with Pastor D!" I drove home, again, in silence. I do not understand this anymore than Jesus' parents did (see Luke 2:48-50). Michael has not yet been baptized. However, he has ministered to a father's heart more than he will understand any time soon. I pray that he, too, will grow "in wisdom and stature, and in favor with God and men" (Luke 2:52, NKJV).

Dave Lawrence serves as LLU controller and is assistant professor in LLUSPH department of health policy and management. He has an MBA degree and an EdS degree. July 3 is the birthday of his son, Michael.

July 4

And we know that all things work together for good to them that love God, to them who are the called according to his purpose. Romans 8:28, KJV

I knew that a triplet pregnancy almost always delivered prematurely, but not this early! Mary was only sixteen weeks along and was in active labor, with her cervix 5 cm dilated. She had previously undergone an evaluation for infertility and was placed on cloiphene induction of ovulation. This can result in a double ovulation in about ten percent of the cases. In Mary's case, she ended up with trizygotic triplets! She was seeing me, as a maternal-fetal medicine specialist, for prenatal care.

In spite of my best efforts to stop the contractions, she progressed in labor to complete dilation and delivered an immature stillborn fetus. What a tragedy! I knew it was just a matter of time before the other two fetuses would also deliver!

Imagine my astonishment, however, when after the first baby had delivered, the contractions began spacing out and eventually disappeared. I trimmed off the umbilical cord as close to the cervix as possible and waited. Over the next few days, at bed rest, Mary's cervix gradually closed and reversed its effacement. It was as if labor had never occurred.

I had never seen a case like this before; I could hardly believe it! Mary eventually inquired, "Since I'm not doing anything here in the hospital, why can't I do the same thing at home?" Dumbfounded, I replied, "I guess so." Over the next weeks and months, at repeated outpatient prenatal visits, I was able to document that the remaining two fetuses were thriving and growing in the safety of Mary's uterus. Perhaps she would go to term! But it was not to be.

Seventy-four days later, at twenty-seven weeks gestation, with urgency in her voice, Mary called me again. "Doctor, I think I am in labor again!" "Come to the hospital immediately and I'll meet you there," I responded. She was again 5 cm dilated, but for the second time; and it was clear to me this pregnancy was coming to its final end.

I took Mary to the operating room and prepared her for cesarean delivery. This event happened twenty years ago, so, at this early gestational age, survival was not guaranteed. As I made the incision, I prayed: "Lord, if it be Your will, please allow these two remaining babies to survive!" Mary's twin daughters weighed 900 grams (2 pounds 0 ounces) and 980 grams (2 pounds 2 ounces), both with one- and five-minute Apgar scores of 4 and 7. After sixty days, Mary took her remaining twin daughters home from the neonatal intensive care nursery at LLUMC.

A few years ago, at a wedding, I met Mary, her husband, and her twin daughters. What a privilege to unexpectedly meet these two beautiful young women, completely normal and doing well, a miraculous testimony to the great God we serve!

Elmar P. Sakala, LLUSM class of 1973-B, is professor in LLUSM department of gynecology and obstetrics. He also has an MPH degree. He was LLUSM Teacher of the Year in 1996. July 4 is his birthday.

July 5

Be still, and know that I am God. Psalm 46:10, KJV

The 5-year-old boy lying in front of me looked just like the thousands of other children I had treated during my residency. Just three days prior, he had been running, playing, and acting like any other spirited child his age. Today, however, his parents brought him in because he was having difficulty breathing and was increasingly lethargic.

Initially, we thought that this was a simple infection; but his diagnostic tests were peculiar, and he was admitted to the hospital. Soon after, his health steadily declined and he coded repeatedly. I still remember vividly working furiously throughout the night to stabilize his illness and prolong his life. Inotropic agents, vasoactive drugs, ventilatory support, fluids, the entire gamut of medicines tried and failed. Eventually, despite our best efforts, he succumbed to his illness.

Soon after his death, as I sat by myself emotionally and physically exhausted, I could hear the pitiful crying of the boy's parents; and I wondered what we could have done differently. I even audaciously questioned why God would take away the life of someone so young and innocent. It was then that a short passage of Scripture pervaded my thoughts. "Be still, and know that I am God" (Psalm 46:10, KJV).

It has been many years since my encounter with that little boy, and since then I have seen my share of death. And yet there has been no single tragedy during my profession as a doctor that has affected me more than the death of that small child. It was during that time that God humbled me by reminding me that no matter what, He, and He alone, is in control.

As clinicians, we are so proud of our abilities, our intellect, and our education. We quickly credit ourselves whenever we achieve successes and just as quickly blame God when we meet failures and tragedies. We forget that our God is an omnipotent God who is, above all, sovereign. He is always in charge; and no matter what tragedy there is in life, we can always find respite in the promise given in Romans 8:28 (NASB): "And we know that God causes all things to work together for good to those who love God, to those who are called according to His purpose."

We must also remember to "be still"—not only because we serve a perfect God who is infinite, but also because we as humans are finite and fallible. This is especially humbling for us as clinicians because we do not ultimately control our own destinies nor those of our patients. But as fallible as we are, isn't it comforting to know that we serve an infallible God who is in control? The world may crumble around us; but we can rest on the hope of an immutable, sovereign God who loves us and is always there for us.

Benny Hau, LLUSM class of 1991, is medical director for the physician assistant program at LLUSAHP. July 5 is the wedding anniversary of his parents, Jonathan and Ada.

July 6

Therefore, if you are offering your gift at the altar and there remember that your brother has something against you, leave your gift there in front of the altar. First go and be reconciled to your brother; then come and offer your gift. Matthew 5:23-24, NIV

The passage in Matthew 5:23-24 does not say if *you* have something against your brother, go and be reconciled; it says if *your brother* has something against you! I think this passage reveals some important concepts: primarily that Christ puts a very specific responsibility on our shoulders.

Christ also said that unless our righteousness exceeds that of the Pharisees and teachers of the law, we will certainly not enter the kingdom of God. This passage tells me that He holds us to a high standard.

When someone hurts us, our natural response is to become angry, but Christ is acutely interested in how we deal with our anger. Very often, sustained anger is disabling to us. We may feel justified in being angry when we are treated unfairly, but there is a cost to our mind, body, and soul. On the other hand, if someone has done something against us and we choose to forgive, it helps us become free from the negative emotions of anger and hatred. Forgiveness does not mean forgetting the unfair treatment or condoning a behavior. Forgiving helps deal with your anger and be reconciled in your own soul. There was a time in my life when I had to set myself free from a debilitating anger.

In 1983, due to civil war in Sri Lanka, my family was hurt in many ways. One night in July we found ourselves running through paddy fields with only the clothes on our backs and our children clutched tightly to us. We were running from people who were determined to harm us and destroy our homes and possessions. That night we were faced with severe physical and emotional hurt. The anger of being displaced and physically hurt would consume me day after day and night after night for years.

My three children were infants when we left Sri Lanka, and as they grew, I often looked into their eyes and gradually decided that I would not leave a legacy of anger and hatred for my children. I had to choose to leave a legacy of love and forgiveness. I wanted to teach my children not to hold on to anger, and the best way to teach them was by being an example. With much prayer and reflection, I forgave the people who had hurt us. This was a patient process that resulted in a significant and marked release from the bonds of anger.

Mahatma Gandhi once said, "The weak can never forgive. Forgiveness is the attribute of the strong." Mark Twain added to that sentiment, "Forgiveness is the fragrance that the violet sheds on the heel that has crushed it." Forgiveness is, interestingly enough, a weapon God gives us to nourish our lives and spread an important "fragrance," as Mark Twain so appropriately puts it, to the world.

I strongly believe forgiveness is a gift you give yourself and a legacy that you will leave for the next generation. "Jesus said, 'Father, forgive them, for they do not know what they are doing'" (Luke 23:34, NIV). He left a legacy of forgiveness by His example. We can do the same.

Padmini Davamony is executive director for information services and decision support services at LLUHC. She has an MBA degree from La Sierra University in Riverside, California, and an MHIS degree from LLU.

July 7

A wise youth harvests in the summer, but one who sleeps during harvest is a disgrace. Proverbs 10:5, NLT

I relish summer. The joy I find in summer is not solely due to the blue sky or the temporary break in mental activities, but primarily because I return home to Iowa. Who I am, that is, my character and personality, has been shaped by my family—Mom, Dad, five brothers, two sisters, and me.

My parents adopted four children from Honduras and two from Vietnam. Each personality adds color, texture, and dimension to our family mural. There's Edward, the charmer; Samuel, the fix-it-man; and Benjamin, the . . . well, if you need something broken thoroughly, go to him.

Then there is Robert, the traveler. At 18, he has been to Japan, Mexico, and over much of the United States. Carl, always a big brother to me, is now working as a physician's assistant. Sonia and Ana, birth sisters, exhibit a unique ying-yang type relationship.

Being the oldest one at home, I have the privilege of first choice of the chores and the responsibility for finishing unclaimed tasks. The farm's endless "To-do list" prevents idle hands during the daylight hours. Cooking is my special outlet. I go through withdrawal at school; but in a large family, regardless of what I fix, a meal is greeted with enthusiasm.

Cooking doesn't consume my whole day; so I can enjoy one of the most enjoyable farm activities—haymaking. A barn full of freshly cut alfalfa hay embodies the essence of summer; one can almost feel the golden drops of sunshine in the presence of the green perfume. Each summer I manage to find time to lie out in the middle of a field and look up into the sky at eternity.

But other chores besides hay await me when I'm home from college. By then, my dad has the crops planted; but that still leaves fences and cattle. Fences—the free spirits of Iowa—wander along prairies, through woods, and beside streams. Upkeep of fences is important, unless one enjoys the art of herding cattle back into their pasture!

At night, I do my serious thinking. From the time I listened for the heartbeat of my doll, Jane, with Mom's old stethoscope, until now, medical school has been my aim. The farm has taught me patience, endurance, and cooperation. Medical school offers a challenge that I have not met previously, a challenge requiring all of the skills life has taught me thus far.

I want to go to medical school for several reasons. First, it requires an individual to continue learning throughout their education and career (and I have a need to discover the "why's" of the world). Second, medical care is an area that is an essential component in serving others, a need that will always exist. Third, it gives me an opportunity to apply my God-given abilities that will push me to reach my full potential.

Yes, being raised on a farm has taught me a lot about life. The feeling of exhaustion after a day's work is sweetened by the sense of accomplishment and the strengthening of social bonds formed. In the cool of my bedroom, underneath the newly risen moon, I can smile and whimsically wonder, "Is this heaven?" Then I remember, "No, just Iowa."

Carrie Marie Carr, LLUSM class of 2007, is a resident in diagnostic radiology at Mayo School of Graduate Medical Education in Rochester, Minnesota. This devotional was adapted from the personal statement portion of her medical school application.

Treat others in the same way that you would want them to treat you. Luke 6:31, NET

I met him by mere coincidence, on an outing I had been resenting. Our first encounter lasted fifteen minutes, and I thought that would be the end of it. One year later, his secretary called me at home on a rare occasion when I was too sick to go to work. (I wondered how she got my home number.) Quickly, he picked up the line and asked, "Can you come and work with me?"

I began to think of all the reasons I would say, "No." He was a stranger in cowboy boots, working in the middle of nowhere, a desert unknown to me called Loma Linda. I told him I was still in training; he said he would talk to my program director. And so I started working for him on a trial basis, one day a week, for one entire year, until I finally said, "Yes."

Over the fourteen years that I worked with him at Loma Linda University, I learned something new every day as I watched him. I saw how he led by love, how he served in humility, how he forgave those who trespassed against him, and how he inspired by random acts of kindness and planted words of wisdom. Not infrequently, he would write me a letter, thanking me for the work I do—although we saw each other on a daily basis.

Since I had come from institutions where this would have been unheard of, I had no doubt by then that this man had a secret road to God. He did not need to talk about Jesus, but it was crystal clear to me that Jesus was his role model and life-long inspiration. He had not published his mission statement, though it was already carved on his forehead—glaring to those who cared to notice. His whole life was centered on God and love of his fellow human beings.

The most amazing aspect of his personality was his tolerance. Whether it was the inefficient secretary, the ungrateful student, or the arrogant junior colleague, he maintained a smile and was willing to help each of them be the best they could be. Whenever I think about Loma Linda, I think of him, and of how special this place must be if such a man as this chose to make it his home for the past thirty years.

Eba Hathout is professor in LLUSM department of pediatrics and is head of division of pediatric endocrinology. She received her medical degree from Kuwait University Faculty of Medicine in Safat, Kuwait.

July 9

O taste and see that the LORD is good; How blessed is the man who takes refuge in Him! Psalm 34:8, NASB

Every life has distinctive moments. Often they are not the ones that explode like fireworks, but are subtle—sometimes missed in the present and rediscovered in hindsight. In June of 2006, I was fortunate enough to participate in a medical trip to Ecuador. I came back, not with stories of valiant effort, but with something more valuable: the calm comfort of the Presence of the Lord.

As a junior in undergraduate school applying for medical school, I had many questions about what I should do with my life. I possessed a strong desire to be a physician; yet, at the same time, I could not help but wonder if I was making the correct career choice. Was medicine right for me?

A ten-hour plane ride usually takes you to unfamiliar conditions, but this trip to Ecuador brought me to my center. I had never met any of the people with whom I was working; but when I arrived, I was drawn into a community formed by colleagues. They knew my passions and understood my driving forces, and I felt close to them.

When I began serving in the clinic there, I was at ease because I was doing something for which I was created. It was as comfortable to me as being in my own house. Latex gloves and concrete floors or pajamas and my living room, I felt no difference. I heard Him say, "I know the plans that I have for you" (Jeremiah 29:11, NASB). And then I knew that He would lead me to the place for which He had created me.

I had no experience and very little knowledge about working in health clinics. Yet, hundreds of patients received medical care and more than 100 people came to know Him through our team; and He said to me, "You can do all things through Me when I strengthen you" (Philippians 4:13, author's paraphrase).

No one had ever told me medical school or being a doctor would be easy. I knew it would be difficult. When combined with the pressure the world puts on Christians—that is, being a physician who practices for the Lord—the challenge would be even harder. But my determination began to form in small ways. One day in Ecuador, I looked out the window and saw children who had come to our clinic playing soccer with some team members. They were laughing and shouting, and I felt the deep joy that comes when you serve in His name. And He reminded me, "Better is one day in My courts than thousands elsewhere" (Psalm 84:10, author's paraphrase).

Though I heard no fireworks when I boarded that plane for home, the experiences there still affect me greatly. The Lord drew near to me and showed me that His hand was upon my life. I felt His desire to use me. He will show Himself to all His children in His own way, specially made for each one of us. And we will "taste and see that the LORD is good" (Psalm 34:8, NASB).

Bethany Cluskey, LLUSM class of 2011, is from Princeville, Illinois. July 9 is the birthday of her mother, Ellen. Her mother has given major support for all her daughter has done.

Ask, and it shall be given you; seek, and ye shall find; knock, and it shall be opened unto you. Matthew 7:7, KJV

Looking back over the sixty-six years since my graduation from medical school, I am thankful for God's guidance along the way. If we accept Christ, we can be assured that, as we ask Him in faith to guide us in making decisions, He will do so. As a young student working my own way through college, I didn't see any possibility of getting training in the medical field. However, that changed when I was drafted into the United States Army during World War II.

I was a dental technician, and one Sunday I was working alone in an army dental lab in San Francisco, using steel wool pads to scrub plaster of Paris off brass denture molds. And then it happened. Now I didn't hear God speak or have any dreams, but I felt very impressed to go back to college, finish pre-med, and apply for medical school. Three years later I had completed my goal, and, with God's help, GI tuition support, and a working wife, I was able to complete medical school. I am indebted to the Seventh-day Adventist Church and Loma Linda University for an excellent Christian and medical education.

After graduation, I spent three years in general practice in a small Washington state town, four-and-a-half years in mission service in the Philippines, and then another four years training in internal medicine and cardiology. I then joined the LLU faculty in Loma Linda as the school was making its transition from Los Angeles, California. Through answered prayer and open doors, I feel God has helped me make decisions all along the route.

One such example of God showing me the value of prayer and His ability to guide me came when I was a member of the LLU Overseas Heart Surgery team in Greece. During our time there, the Greek press reported our excellent results in the major Athens newspapers. The news articles stated that the results were so good because, while part of the team was in the operating room doing surgery, the other team members were in a room praying. We can never overestimate the importance of our influence and God's direction.

We are faced with many decisions in our lifetime, and it is comforting to know that God is always available to help us. Can we still make wrong decisions? Certainly, and we do, especially when we try to make them by our own feeble reasoning. But we have the assurance that if we make bad decisions, we can sincerely pray to Christ for forgiveness and our request will be granted. We may live with the consequences of a wrong decision, but it will help us when we use those experiences to do better in the future.

Roy V. Jutzy, LLUSM class of 1952, is emeritus professor in LLUSM department of medicine, division of cardiology. He was president of the Walter E. Macpherson Society from 1986 to 1987 and was LLUSM Alumni Association president from 1967 to 1968. He was named LLUSM Alumni Association 2002 Alumnus of the Year, received the LLU Distinguished Service Award in 1998, and was named LLU Alumnus of the Year in 2002.

July 11

Trust ye in the LORD for ever: for in the LORD JEHOVAH is everlasting strength.
Isaiah 26:4, KJV

Shortly after completing my fellowship, I encountered a particularly complicated neurology case and dropped by the office of my senior colleague, Robert "Bob" Shields, to ask for advice. Bob, trained by the prominent American neurologist, Maurice Victor, related a story from his residency days at Metrohealth Hospitals in Cleveland, Ohio.

Back then, hospitalized patients were followed (cared for) by the resident student doctors and only the most difficult or interesting cases were presented to the attending physician. One day, Bob encountered a patient with a complex neurological problem. He decided that the case warranted an opinion from the all-knowing Dr. Victor.

After Bob presented the details of the case, Dr. Victor thought for a while, then leaned back in his chair, shrugged his shoulders, and said, "Well, Bob, this case is too tough for me!" That was it; one of the foremost neurologists had considered all the diagnostic possibilities within his vast knowledge base and had come up short.

At the time, Bob's story made me feel a little better about not knowing the answer to everything. Since then, I have come to appreciate that getting the right diagnosis is only one part of a physician's duty. Medicine doesn't always provide us with clear-cut choices, and medicine isn't just about being right or wrong. It's also about establishing a trusting relationship with our patients, so we can walk side-by-side down the path of life and share in the good and bad times together. To do this effectively, we must have the same faith-based relationship with our healthcare colleagues, and most importantly, with God.

Intelligence, diligent study, and advances in modern medicine may carry us far, but they are finite. Thus, it's natural at times to feel "things are too tough for me." It's safe to say that in the course of our lives, we will inevitably face—either with a patient, a loved one, or even ourselves—an incurable or relentless disease.

Fortunately, we have an eternal promise from the ultimate Healer that, if we place the lives of our patients and ourselves into His hands, we have nothing to fear. His answer will be to heal, either in this world or the next. All we have to do is ask and trust and He will carry us through the difficult times; nothing is too tough for Him.

Bryan Tsao, LLUSM class of 1996, is associate professor in and chair of LLUSM department of neurology.

And we know that in all things God works for the good of those who love him, who have been called according to his purpose. Romans 8:28, NIV

The Beeve Foundation, in 1991, started serving Fiji at Turtle Island Resort, seventy miles north of Fiji in the South Pacific Ocean. Now in Savusavu, at the Jean-Michel Cousteau Resort, total eye care continues with examinations, glasses, and major eye surgery, all for no charge. As of February 2008, 2.7 percent of the population of Fiji has been served with eighteen successful missions. At the end of the eleventh mission, out of twenty volunteers from around the world, only my wife, I, and Kate from Australia were left to pack and store items for the following year.

Suddenly, a Fijian mom of six children appeared with her moribund 9-year-old boy. He was mortally septic, dehydrated, and unable to stand up by himself. His right jaw was extensively swollen from his neck to his forehead. He had large cavities in adjoining bicuspids of his right upper jaw and a fever of more than 106°F. This abscess was about to take his life. But I am an ophthalmologist, not a dentist.

Because this boy would not take water, I decided to start an intravenous line to administer penicillin. And then I knew I had to pull both teeth without breaking them. I did not know which one was causing this problem. With his blood pressure dropping, his tiny darkly pigmented dehydrated arm, and a very poor selection of old dental instruments, it was totally impossible for me. I could not do it.

God would not bring this boy to me to die. My dad was a dentist, and I have two brothers-in-law who are dentists. But that was no help now. I only knew that young people have strong dentate ligaments and that the teeth tend to break with attempted extraction, even with an experienced dentist. The boy and I were desperate. We needed help. I found a private spot so I could ask the Lord for help—to be in my arm and hands—and for God and me to do this together. A penicillin shot was given, and we went to lunch while we hoped his body would absorb the antibiotic.

The pontoon aircraft that had taken the last of our group to mainland Fiji had returned with two couples, both on honeymoon. They were the first guests on the island following our week of surgery. One of the couples walked right up and introduced themselves as they prepared to join the three of us for lunch. I was surprised and taken aback at his forthright boldness, especially as he admitted they were on their honeymoon. *He was a dentist from Seattle, Washington!* When my wife, Dorothy, and I first visited this island in 1989, we only knew the first names of some of the guests. Their relationship and occupation were never mentioned.

I found 500 ccs of Ringer's lactate and started the intravenous therapy with antibiotics added, *on the first try!* The dentist took the tooth out in about twenty minutes, after much struggling. Three days later, this boy and I were playing catch with a football on the beach as we waited for our pontoon aircraft!

As I left, I gave this now healthy boy and his mother copies of three books by Ellen G. White—*Steps to Christ*, *The Desire of Ages*, and *The Great Controversy*—and greatly thanked our Lord for His help.

Jerold E. Beeve, LLUSM class of 1967, is an ophthalmologist in Glendale, California. He and his wife, Dorothy, were married on July 12.

July 13

Dearly beloved, avenge not yourselves, but rather give place unto wrath: for it is written, Vengeance is mine; I will repay, saith the Lord. Therefore if thine enemy hunger, feed him; if he thirst, give him drink: for in so doing thou shalt heap coals of fire on his head. Romans 12:19-20, KJV

While on general surgery rotation during my third year of medical school, I was called down to the trauma bay at Arrowhead Regional Medical Center, in San Bernardino, California. A 23-year-old man had been partying late at night and became involved in a brawl with four men. One of these men broke a bottle and used it to slash open the patient's right forearm. It was my privilege to spend the next couple of hours with him, cleaning the wounds and placing numerous sutures.

During the course of time, I approached the subject of the fight. "I knew I shouldn't have gone out tonight," he exclaimed, as he proceeded to tell me the night's events. He explained that he had been dancing at a nightclub with a girl that was someone else's girlfriend. That man's friends had seen him and became very angry. They started a fight in the club but were kicked out by the bouncers.

While outside, the four men "jumped" him and shredded his forearm with the glass bottle. I asked him what he was planning to do now. He said he knew the man who had the girlfriend and had already called him; they were having "breakfast" the next morning. I asked, "Are you having breakfast or revenge?" Grinning, he responded, "I gotta get him back."

In keeping with whole-person care, I started to explore his religious beliefs. He said that he had been a Christian for a while. "I was happier then," he muttered reflectively. I asked him what he thought Jesus would do if He were in the same situation. He said, "So I guess I shouldn't get the guy back, huh?"

I explained that the cycle of violence would never end if he repaid evil with evil; and that it would take a bigger, stronger man to resist the urge to "get back at him." I do not know what happened after he left that night, but I prayed that he was able to be the bigger man and did not make his breakfast appointment.

This event impressed me that we are not to take revenge but must let God lead in our lives. If we cultivate a character like Christ's, we will be able to endure whatever is thrown our way and not take matters into our own hands.

Amber Strother, LLUSM class of 2009, is from Hendersonville, North Carolina. She and her husband, Bradley, met as students at Mount Pisgah Academy in Candler, North Carolina, and were married on July 13, 2003.

The LORD gives strength to his people; the LORD blesses his people with peace.
Psalm 29:11, NIV

I could hear the anxiety in her voice as she sat in my office. She said, "I'm not sure I'll know what to do with a baby." She laughed nervously. I glanced at her chart—39 years old, first pregnancy. A PhD degree horticulturist at a local university, she looked bookish. "I guess I'm going to find out," she said sheepishly. "We weren't really trying . . . and then this happened."

"Let's go take a look at the baby," I suggested. The first look at their unborn baby, even in grainy black and white, turns even stoic moms to mush. As I studied the tiny image, however, I felt that aching feeling that always rises in my stomach when I have to give bad news. There would be no more congratulations for this couple—for the tiny embryo on the screen had no pulsing blip where the heart beat should have been.

After the initial gregarious exchange, my tone grew serious, as I tried to find the best way to break the news. I could see the thoughts racing in her eyes and her furrowed brow—followed by a wash of tears. "When can we try again?" she asked, as if this sudden denial made it all the more irresistible.

They did try again, returning with a look of cautious optimism, tempered with a measure of innocence lost. But, again, there was disappointment. The second miscarriage led to a work-up with a dearth of helpful results. She tried to rationalize. "Maybe I'm not meant to be a mom," she whispered, knowing her window was closing.

Four months later, I found a note on my desk: "Mrs. S, + home preg 5wks ago, light bleeding, plz advise." I asked my nurse to order an hCG level and an ultrasound. This time the findings were even more disappointing than a failed pregnancy. With an hCG of 145,000 and a "snowstorm" pattern on the ultrasound, a hydatidiform mole rather than a normal pregnancy was almost certain. This meant surgery for evacuation of the pregnancy, followed by at least a year of contraception and blood tests to ensure a complete cure.

The disappointment was palpable when I related the bad news and discussed the fertility implications of the likely diagnosis. After arranging for surgery, she then said the last thing I expected to hear at that moment. "One more thing, Dr. Balli . . . I don't know if you're a spiritual person, but I wanted you to know that my husband and I have been praying for you."

I was blown away! Here I was, with three healthy kids, working in a Christian hospital, laying out this devastating news. And in the hour of her trials, she was lifting me up in prayer. Would I have done the same? Was I praying for her? Was I praying for any of my patients?

As I think back on that conversation, I'm struck by how the quiet voice of God comes into our lives—often when we're not expecting Him. I am reminded again that, despite our successes or failures as physicians, it is only our connection with Christ that can bring true inner peace—both to us and the patients we care for. In each busy, sometimes stressful, often overbooked day, may we never fail to point our patients to the Great Physician, the true Source of healing and the Giver of peace.

Kevin Charles Balli, LLUSM class of 1998, is assistant professor in LLUSM department of gynecology and obstetrics and is clerkship director for gynecology and obstetrics at LLUSM. He received the LLUMC Physician Whole-Person Care Award in 2007.

July 15

Humble yourselves in the sight of the Lord, and he shall lift you up. James 4:10, KJV

G rowing up, I witnessed my dad, Louis Smith, LLUSM class of 1949, challenging himself to become the best he could for "the school"—what he always called Loma Linda University. His parents valued education, and he determined to follow their example. After graduating from medical school, he immersed himself in a surgical residency at Los Angeles County-USC Medical Center in Los Angeles, California.

Dad went on to complete a fellowship at Harvard University in Massachusetts, where he was part of the team that performed the first successful liver transplant in a dog. He returned to Loma Linda to become a professor of surgery, training many students and residents in the art of surgery.

Other than his academic accomplishments, what is it the staff and students who worked with Dr. Smith remember? Yes, they remember he was a great surgeon; but they love to recall that he would take the time to pull a patient up in the bed, straighten the covers, and make sure the patient was comfortable, as he would address the complexities of the patient's treatment.

He would also remind the nurses and residents, "*Always* cut the tape," when putting on a dressing. "If the patient sees you did a careful and neat job on the outside, they will know you did a careful job on the inside as well," he would explain. While stitching in a new aorta or removing a dangerous plaque from a carotid artery, he never forgot to have the nurses call the family members in the waiting room. He remembered that they would be anxiously waiting for any news of their loved one.

His daily life was full of habits that revealed his care for patient concerns, not just surgical needs. Whether it was prayer in the vulnerable moments before a patient was wheeled into the operating room or picking up trash in the hallways of the medical center, he never wavered from his meticulous attention to detail. He never left a task undone.

Today, we call this "whole-patient care"; but to this pioneer of vascular/transplant surgery, it was just doing what Jesus modeled while on earth. Jesus showed us to wash the tired feet of His children. By caring for the whole person, my father was following his role model to the best of his ability.

As Henry Van Dyke said, "There is a loftier ambition than merely to stand high in the world. It is to stoop down and lift mankind a little higher."

Patti Catalano, LLUSN class of 1976, is an operating room nurse with the LLUMC heart team. Her father, Louis L. Smith, was LLUSM Alumni Association president from 1986 to 1987. He was named LLUSM Alumni Association Alumnus of the Year in 2000 and LLUSM Alumnus of the Year in 1993; and was recipient of the LLUSM Distinguished Service Award in 2003.

The eye is the lamp of the body. If your eyes are good, your whole body will be full of light. Matthew 6:22, NIV

Someone once said, "Life is not measured by the number of breaths we take, but by the moments that take our breath away." I am an active octogenarian and have time to reflect on the state of current affairs and the paradox of how our lives have changed over time.

I saw a passage recently where someone said, "We've added years to life, but not life to years. We've been all the way to the moon and back, but have trouble crossing the street to meet a new neighbor. We have multiplied our possessions, but reduced our values. We've conquered outer space but not inner space."

In today's world, we often take on more responsibilities than we can comfortably manage to fit into each day, creating angst and stress in our lives. This stress is a contributing cause of many illnesses, broken relationships, and depression, as well as the breakdown of our families.

In the Sermon on the Mount, God, through Christ, revealed many important life lessons. One of my favorite parts is found in Matthew 6:22, where Christ said "the eye is the lamp of the body." This metaphor is the "attitude" we need to pray for each morning. No matter how bad things seem to be, we must begin our morning prayer with an "attitude of gratitude."

Remember: God has a master plan for each of us, and an attitude of gratitude will be transmitted to everyone with whom we come into contact. I believe that expressions of gratitude for the gifts God has given us will better reflect His love for all mankind.

Joseph J. Verska, LLUSM class of 1955, is a thoracic surgeon in Sun Valley, Idaho. He was president of the Walter E. Macpherson Society from 1994 to 1995, and was LLUSM Alumni Association president from 1969 to 1970.

July 17

Praise be to the God and Father of our Lord Jesus Christ! In his great mercy he has given us new birth into a living hope through the resurrection of Jesus Christ from the dead. 1 Peter 1:3, NIV

It was a quiet Sabbath afternoon when my mother passed away. Although she wasn't always a Christian or a Sabbath observer, after her conversion she grew to love the sacredness of the Sabbath. In her last, pain-filled days, she often prayed that God would allow her to fall asleep on a Sabbath. And He did.

Now I've conducted many funerals in my more than two decades of parish ministry; but no amount of familiarity with grief and acquaintance with mourners prepared me for my personal encounter with our great enemy, death. Up until then, I told myself that I knew precisely how I would grieve. Being sanguine-choleric, it would definitely include drama balanced with the decorum becoming to a pastor.

But when the day came, it was nothing like I had planned or anticipated. There were a few highly controlled tears as I gave the homily. There were restrained sobs at the graveside as I conducted the committal service—perhaps due more to the ordeal of a long flight and tension from an even longer drive to the church, where I arrived moments before the service began. Maybe it was because I felt compelled to be strong for my grieving family and friends. Whatever the reason, I felt no overpowering sorrow.

Soon after the funeral, I congratulated myself on dodging the presence of the unwanted guest named grief. But come it did—with a vengeance that overwhelmed my strength and sabotaged my health. I couldn't leave my bed for a week as the floodgates of emotions finally opened and I sobbed uncontrollably. I was at the end of my wits when I remembered, *"For I know the plans I have for you,"* declares the LORD, *"plans to prosper you and not to harm you, plans to give you hope and a [good] future"* (Jeremiah 29:11, NIV).

In New Testament Greek, *hope* is defined as a "favorable and confident expectation regarding the unseen future." For when we feel trapped in a dark tunnel of despair or discouragement, and exhaustion is tempting us to quit, hope steps in, lifts our spirit, and points us to the light at the end, shouting: "You can make it. Yes you can!" When we struggle with a crippling disease or terminal illness and fear the worst, hope rises to the occasion and inspires us to persevere beyond the pain by reminding us that the wind and the rain still obey God's will and through Christ we will make it—yes we will!

When we feel rejected, abandoned, and alone, when we can't find a job or money to pay our bills, when we are forced to watch our dreams fade away—hope gives us patience to keep on trusting that this, too, shall pass and we will survive.

Hope isn't just another nice word or easy option that temporarily gets us out of a bind or a bad situation. It is an earnest attitude and attribute of the heart, soul, and mind. Regardless of the global economy or ground-zero emotions, in Christ we have a living hope as 1 Peter 1:3 confirms. It is His divine gift-wrap for the promise of a good future.

Hyveth Williams is senior pastor of the Campus Hill Church of Seventh-day Adventists in Loma Linda, California, and is assistant professor in LLUSR. She received an MDiv degree from Andrews University in Berrien Springs, Michigan, in 1989; and a DMin degree from Boston University in Boston, Massachusetts, in 1998. She was born on July 17 in Jamaica and was reared in London, England.

I have set you an example that you should do as I have done for you. John 13:15, NIV

B eing an example is, perhaps, the most powerful form of communication. Christ is the example most of us want to follow. But many other Christian individuals, by their example, can have a profound and positive influence on us.

One individual whose example had a major impact on my life was Dr. Everett N. Dick, professor of history at Union College in Lincoln, Nebraska, from 1932 to 1960. He was a mentor and influenced me to become a history major at Union College. Later, I came to more fully recognize what an outstanding individual and able scholar he was.

Everett Dick was the sort of person that many of us would like to be; but few of us possess his insights, drive, and talent. He wrote numerous books and articles on the history of the American frontier.

As testimony to his exceptional research and writing skills, Dr. Dick was given a leave of absence from Union College and awarded a Rockefeller Foundation grant to write *The Dixie Frontier* (published by Alfred A. Knopf in 1948). It was unusual to receive this kind of financial support prior to publication.

Dr. Dick had an exceptional ability to bring history to life in his lectures, regaling his students with vivid and entertaining stories about the American frontier. He had a passion for sharing history that made his students want to learn and understand more.

While serving in the military during World War I, he came under harassment and even did time in the brig, due to his unfailing commitment to keep the seventh-day Sabbath and not bear arms. This led, in 1934, to Union College beginning to give its young men military medical training (as Dr. Dick noted in his 1955 *The Medical Cadet Corps Training Manual*). Following that program, in 1936, the College of Medical Evangelists organized a medical training unit, the Medical Cadet Corps, led by Cyril Courville, LLUSM class of 1925.

It is likely that Dr. Dick was unaware of the positive impact he had on me, both professionally and personally. But his example as a scholar, a historian, a Christian, and a leader inspired me to learn from his experiences, and think about my words and actions and how they might influence others.

My desire is to be a good example, an inspiration to others, and to leave the world a better place for those who are on this journey with me and for those who follow. I want to always remember that sometimes it's my example, even in small ways, that may have the biggest and most lasting impact on others.

I have been inspired and blessed by the exemplary life of Christ and the lives of many people with whom I have had contact, including Everett Dick. A favorite quote of mine (paraphrased) from Mrs. A. J. "Bessie" Stanley (from the 1905 *Lincoln Sentinel*), sums up my thoughts:

"He has achieved success who has lived well, laughed often and loved much;
who has gained the respect of intelligent men . . . ;
who has always looked for the best in others and given them the best he had;
whose life was an inspiration and an example worthy of emulation;
whose memory a benediction."

Norman J. Woods, who began working at LLU in 1966, was president from 1984 to 1990. He received a PhD degree in the psychology of group and individual differences from University of Oregon. He lives in Lake Oswego, Oregon. In 1992, he received the LLU Distinguished Service Award.

July 19

He has delivered us from the power of darkness and conveyed us into the kingdom of the Son of His love, in whom we have redemption through His blood, the forgiveness of sins. Colossians 1:13-14, NKJV

The young woman was lying on the stretcher, in obvious pain, with blood staining the bright green wrapper she wore around her waist. She had been bleeding for three hours, and she no longer felt fetal movements. Her conjunctiva, lips, and hands were very pale, showing she must be terribly anemic. I wheeled her to the ultrasound room and confirmed fetal demise due to placenta previa and probable abruption. We'd have to take her to surgery.

I rushed down to the laboratory. Blood was obviously going to be a problem. Her hemoglobin was 5, only a third of normal. I did the math; we would need at least four pints of blood to adequately stabilize her.

To make matters worse, her blood type was O+, and the lab had only one pint of compatible blood left. Blood is scarce in West Africa, mostly because of a strong resistance to blood donation, due to a deep belief that it will make the donor weak or even die. After much convincing, her husband agreed to donate; unfortunately he was type A.

"I'm O+. I'll donate," I told the tech, as I sat down, ready for a blood check. My hemoglobin was an acceptable 13; and after a prolonged wait, as the blood slowly dripped into the bag, we finally got a pint of fresh, dark red blood, ready to use. That made two pints—at least enough to proceed to surgery, while someone else recruited two nursing students to donate blood to save a life.

We rushed the patient back and gave her spinal anesthesia after our usual prayer. I briefly looked up to see the blood I had just donated, still warm, now hanging from the intravenous pole, flowing into the patient's arm. I started the surgery as per routine, quickly slicing through skin, fat, fascia, and peritoneum. I cut into the uterus and found the placenta covering the incision I had made. I removed it, only to find a dead fetus, along with at least two cups of coagulated blood, evidence of the abruption that killed the fetus.

I worked quickly to avoid losing any more precious blood, closed the uterus, closed the fascia, and closed the skin. Still, she had lost a full liter of blood, which meant that even in the best-case scenario, we were only two pints ahead. We would have to monitor her closely to make sure she remained stable.

I sat down to write orders and caught a glimpse of the red puncture wound on my left arm. It reminded me of the importance of blood—the pint I had given, plus the pints three other people donated to save this woman. What a small price I had to pay. It made me think of the blood that Jesus shed for me, way back on Calvary . . . the blood that gives me strength from day to day . . . the blood that saves—not just from dying during surgery, but from the power of sin and from eternal death.

Maria Belen Lohr, LLUSM class of 2001, is assistant professor in LLUSM department of family medicine. She and her husband, Jason, LLUSM class of 2001, both family practitioners, are serving at Ile Ife Adventist Hospital in Ile Ife, Nigeria. They have two children, Michaela and Joshua.

July 20

Then they sat on the ground with him for seven days and nights. No one said a word to Job, for they saw that his suffering was too great for words. Job 2:13, NLT

Our 13-year-old son Stephen had been battling an aggressive muscle tumor for the last seven months. He'd won many battles with this cancer; but in spite of chemotherapy, radiation therapy, and surgery, we'd just learned that the cancer had spread to Stephen's meninges, the lining of his brain.

There was not a cure for this development; there was not even an effective treatment. Stephen would be coming home with us on hospice care. He would be coming home to die. He was now semicomatose, unable to participate in a conversation. I wasn't sure if I was going to ever hear his voice again.

My heart was devastated—ravaged like a landscape after a tornado. It had been a hard, exhausting seven months. And now it felt all too final. The hope I'd insisted on holding to so tightly was slipping inexorably out of my hands.

One of the nurses on the pediatric oncology ward was the mother of one of Stephen's best friends. She hadn't been assigned to Stephen much during his numerous hospital stays for chemotherapy, treatment of infections, and recovery from surgery. But whenever she was working and Stephen was in the hospital, she stopped by to say "hi."

This day, when she came in to work, she learned of the progression of Stephen's cancer. She came in to say hello. Stephen was sleeping. My wife was at home taking a quick shower, so it was just me.

As soon as I saw her, I began to cry. She walked over. I stood up. She extended her arms. I collapsed into them, sobbing. At that moment, every part of my life seemed unbearable. The next steps were unfathomable. The future choices were cruel, wrong, and unacceptable.

But I was being held while I cried.

I'm not sure how long that lasted. It felt like a very long time, but I suspect it was no more than a few minutes. I do know that several times the tears would slow down, only to be followed by a new wave of pain, fear, and despair, and a new flood of tears. And each time those arms were holding me. There weren't words. There weren't attempts to make me feel better. There was just holding.

I have many memories of great nurses, doctors, dieticians, physical therapists, and others who helped in the care of Stephen during his illness. My greatest lasting memory, however, will be being held; when life seemed impossible, being embraced as I cried. At a medical center like Loma Linda, miracles of technology, skill, and knowledge occur every day. But no miracle is as great as the miracle of caring, of just being there with those in pain, of holding another as they cry.

Wayne Dysinger, LLUSM class of 1986, is associate professor in and chair of LLUSM department of preventive medicine. He is clerkship director for preventive and community medicine at LLUSM. July 20 is the day Stephen died.

July 21

Blessed are the meek: for they shall inherit the earth. Matthew 5:5, KJV

I had to smile when I walked into the room.

Not because a large man with a ponytail and wearing dark leather pants was pacing the room. Not because he had a leather belt with a buckle identifying him as a member of a motorcycle group. Not because he was wearing a sleeveless, tight undershirt and had tattoos covering his muscle-filled biceps.

No, I smiled because sitting next to him on the bed was a 6-year-old boy dressed just like him.

The boy's undershirt didn't fit so well. His little thin arms poked out like a stick-man drawing. But he had the requisite ponytail and leather pants.

His undershirt was blood-stained from a forehead wound. A quick evaluation of the wound verified that he needed stitches. "This is something we can fix. I expect things to heal up just fine," I said, trying to put them at ease. They both looked at me, wanting to trust that I could make things okay.

I described how I would wash out the wound, make it numb, and then work on the sutures. The little boy looked worried, and, despite my verbal assurances, I wasn't sure he would be able to hold still for the procedure. I explained that a nurse might be needed to help him cooperate.

"That won't be necessary. I'll hold him," the man said. Skeptical, I set up the tray of supplies. I made sure a nurse was close by.

As I started to wash out the wound, the boy whimpered. I braced myself for a difficult job. The motorcycle man leaned across the boy's chest. He offered soothing words: "It's okay; she knows what she's doing. You'll be fine." I had to adjust the drape as the man's ponytail was close to my sterile field.

I decided that I wouldn't call the nurse. It soon became clear that his holding of the boy was more for comfort than restraint. Amazed at the tenderness, I kept working. The boy's fingers grabbed tightly to the muscle-filled arm, making tiny red dents among the tattoos.

I finished the job. The little boy reached up and hugged the motorcycle man. They both had tears in their eyes. Touched, I said, "You are really good with your son."

"Oh, he's not my son," he corrected. "He is just a kid from the neighborhood we took in. His momma is high on cocaine most of the time when she's not turning tricks to buy more. We never saw his old man. My wife and I just kinda look out for him."

I was quiet a minute, then I realized that it was my turn to talk. "That is wonderful," I said. "What a difference you are making!"

He looked at me with unexpected shyness and said, "Oh, this is nothing. It's not like I am saving the world or something like you, Doc."

"Oh, but you are," I said.

Kathleen Clem, LLUSM class of 1989, is associate professor in and chair of LLUSM department of emergency medicine. She is also the first woman to chair a department at LLUSM.

July 22

Before they call, I will answer; And while they are still speaking, I will hear.
Isaiah 65:24, NKJV

Several years ago, I established a scholarship fund for needy Canadian students in medical school. I felt compelled to start the fund because I had such a difficult time finding money to pay my own tuition when I was in medical school. Back then, before I even started my classes, a physician promised to pay for my first year. But when I arrived in Loma Linda, I was informed that my benefactor was only able to give me two hundred dollars.

My wife and I both worked, and we had a nine-month-old daughter to support; so life was not easy. I wrote to anyone I could think of to ask for money to allow me to stay in medical school. Two Seventh-day Adventist elementary school teachers from Winnipeg, Manitoba, Canada, sent me a little money; and a Seventh-day Adventist farmer from North Dakota, whom I hadn't seen since I was six years old, helped me—as did his daughter, a Loma Linda University graduate of medicine. I was also grateful to receive help from Drs. E. Crawford and Lindgren.

At that time, no loans or scholarships were available to Canadians studying in the United States. And that is why I set up endowments for Canadian students at Loma Linda University School of Medicine and two or three other Seventh-day Adventist schools. The scholarship fund that I set up at LLUSM was small and had not been used much, but it sat quietly growing interest.

One day I called the School of Medicine regarding another issue, and we started talking about the Miller Scholarship Fund for Canadian students. Two weeks later I heard "the rest of the story." It seems that after this phone conversation with the assistant dean for development, she walked over to the student affairs office and joined in a hallway conversation about a good, but needy student. She was in such extreme financial difficulty that she had spent much of the blazing hot summer with her electricity turned off, in order to save money for the start of her junior year.

Then the development officer with whom I had spoken remarked: "If only she were a Canadian student, I would have good news. I just found out about some money in the Miller Fund for worthy *Canadian* students." The mouths of the others present dropped open, and one quietly said, "But she IS a Canadian student!" From what I was told, they stood with tears in their eyes and thanked the Lord for this wonderful coincidence, which they knew wasn't a coincidence at all!

Leroy Miller, LLUSM class of 1958, is an obstetrician and gynecologist in San Diego, California.

203

July 23

Trust in the LORD with all thine heart; and lean not unto thine own understanding. In all ways acknowledge him, and he shall direct thy paths.
Proverbs 3:5-6, KJV

In 1895, I graduated from the Collegiate Course at Union College, [Lincoln,] Nebraska. At that time, our denominational medical school, the American Medical Missionary College at Battle Creek [Michigan] and Chicago was just being organized. . . . I entered the first class in the school and took three years of my medical course there. . . .

My fourth year in medical school was taken at Cornell University Medical College in New York City [New York]. The idea at the time in my taking one year of work in one of the larger and best recognized schools was that I might possibly be better able to help in the teaching in our own school. At the time when I graduated in New York City, I was greatly tempted to spend a period of years in New York, as I had very flattering opportunities offered me there. After weeks of indecision and counsel and prayer in the matter, I finally decided to go back and to connect with our own institution, our own medical school.

After remaining with the work of the school and sanitarium for five years, conditions arose which made it seem advisable for me to take up self-supporting, independent work. I therefore removed to Kentucky and spent three years in private practice. Following that, I spent three teaching at the State University Medical Department in Tennessee. Conditions then arose which made it seem advisable for me to take up private practice again, which I did.

At the end of three years, I was finally persuaded that it was my duty to [re]connect with the work here in Loma Linda. In coming to this final decision, the determining influence in the matter was believing that the school was of divine origin. This belief was based on the conviction that instruction for the school's founding came to our people through the Spirit of Prophecy.

And, in moving to Loma Linda, this conviction, that the work has been established in line with the direct purpose of God and that in taking up the work here we must step out upon faith alone, became the uppermost thought in my mind. This conviction has remained with me and is the determining influence in all of our decisions. . . .

As I look back over the experiences of my life during the last twenty years or more, notwithstanding the fact that I have not had any particular financial prosperity or advantages, I have, as it seems to me now, been led in every time of decision to do that thing which my conscience told me to do, often the thing which was entirely contrary to my own desires and leading away from what seemed to be the path of prosperity.

Newton G. Evans (1874-1945) was president of CME from 1914 to 1927 and professor of pathology for LLUSM. He was dean of LLUSM from 1944 to 1945. This adapted devotional is from a July 23, 1916, letter he wrote a prospective medical student. The Medical Evangelist remembered Dr. Evans as the "giver of self."

The person who has the power to give a blessing is greater than the one who is blessed. Hebrews 7:7, NLT

Winston Churchill's words, "We make a living by what we earn, but we make a life by what we give," were demonstrated to me by ten Loma Linda University School of Dentistry students on a recent trip to El Salvador. I became interested in El Salvador when I saw a World Vision program depicting the hardships of street children in that country. When I learned that Robert Weaver, a practicing dentist, was considering a trip to an orphanage in El Salvador, I signed on and began planning for the trip.

Once on site, the team of ten worked together extremely well in the available clinic, where Dr. Weaver paired second-year dental students with more advanced students to achieve maximum mentoring. In addition to their dental care, two hygiene students did a great job of calming the younger orphans during initial exams and cleaning. This gentle introduction to dentistry eased the restorative tasks for the dental students.

During full treatment days, we saw many patients—including all the staff and children at the orphanage. The students achieved varied experience in dealing with impacted wisdom teeth and abscessed teeth; they accomplished diastema closures and sealed numerous permanent molars. But what made this trip memorable was the students' giving attitude—always willing to see one more patient, and on the final day working through lunch to ensure treatment for everyone. But their finest hour was yet to come.

One of the orphans, Rosita, had come to the clinic with severe orthodontia needs. A local orthodontist had estimated that he could treat her for $780US. Of course, the orphanage budget could not encompass this expenditure.

Toward the end of our trip, Dr. Weaver found that, by careful shopping, the general fund for the trip was ending with a surplus. He informed them that each student would be receiving a rebate of $140 as part of the excess from their trip payment. They received their money with no strings attached.

When the team discussed again the case of Rosita, Dr. Weaver announced that he was placing an envelope atop a bookcase. This would be the students' opportunity to contribute to her care. Retrieving the envelope the final Saturday night, we found that the students' gifts totaled exactly $780 for Rosita's orthodontia! The Lord had impressed the students over the course of the weekend to individually place in the envelope an amount totaling the cost of Rosita's treatment.

By the time of our departure, some of the students had laid plans to sponsor a child at the orphanage. The interaction I had with these students made me realize that Loma Linda University School of Dentistry, like the other schools within Loma Linda University, is intentional about training mission-minded, caring professionals.

Don Horricks, LLUSD class of 1980, related this devotional to Fred Kasischke, who is associate dean for administration and service learning for LLUSD.

July 25

Rejoice in hope, be patient in suffering, persevere in prayer. Contribute to the needs of the saints; extend hospitality to strangers. Romans 12:12-13, NRSV

Brilliant red clay caked the soles of my hiking books as my translator, Bulla, and I descended upon the last hut of the day. My interest as a public health researcher had brought me to West Wollega, Ethiopia. We were there to interview mothers as part of an effort to understand why a large percentage of the children residing around Gimbie Adventist Hospital, also in Ethiopia, die prior to their fifth birthday.

A slender, weathered woman met us at the door and invited us to join her and her daughter in the traditional earth-constructed, smoke-filled East African home. My eyes, momentarily paralyzed from smoldering eucalyptus, sought to make out shapes in the dimly lit room. One female figure immediately came into focus.

A lethargic, 12-year-old girl, staring vacantly at the earthen floor beneath her, was seated at the edge of a small, hand-crafted bed. Her swollen belly, spindly arms, and loose skin folds were consistent with marasmus, possibly complicated by intestinal parasites. The preteen barely acknowledged our presence, as her 30-year-old mother offered us coffee and a place to rest. It was all she had.

I listened intently as the mother—impoverished, abandoned by her husband, and supporting her girls by selling charcoal in the street—described the deaths of several of her children. Her anguish was palpable, but at the same time there was no sense of bitterness or resentment in her voice. Perhaps what troubled me most was that this woman appeared genuinely more distraught over the fact that she could do so little to make our stay more comfortable. Bulla and I declined her beverage, completed our inquiry, and promptly departed.

The memory of that interview has etched a lasting impression on me. This is particularly true on days when endless email and text messages, many containing grievances about the contemporary workplace, cascade down from satellites above. On those days, I find myself asking what is important, why I work here, and how I can make a difference.

Then I think about that woman, that single mother in an earthen hut so far away. She had every earthly reason to be angry at her plight; but, contrary to my expectations, she was not. At the same time, she generously offered her visitors every comfort she could extend, requesting nothing in return. I aspire one day to be just like her. I would embrace the world with all of its imperfections—to be of service without expectation of reciprocity, and to be troubled by any lack of complete generosity. One day I pray I will possess the courage and faith to be like that Ethiopian woman—to give all I have.

David Dyjack is associate professor in LLUSM department of preventive medicine. He has a DrPH degree and is dean of LLU School of Public Health.

July 26

Then saith he unto his disciples, The harvest truly is plenteous, but the laborers are few; Pray ye therefore the Lord of the harvest, that he will send forth labourers into his harvest. Matthew 9:37-38, KJV

The scene is still unforgettable: the disheveled, fearful patient; the expectant, unsuspecting family; the chaos of the county emergency department; and the symptoms, as told by my middle-aged patient. He had unexplained nosebleeds for one week, shortness of breath, recent weight loss, decreased appetite, and a long history of smoking. All these conditions made me very suspicious of fulminant occult malignancy.

"My doctor told me my platelets were very low," he said, with energetic misapprehension.

"Do you smoke, sir?" I routinely questioned.

"I just quit." It was difficult to believe the convincing resolution in his voice.

"Do you consider yourself a spiritual person?"

"There's no hope left for me, if you only knew the things that I have done. . . ." He was clearly despondent regarding his eternal future.

"There is always hope. God will always take you back," I said. But he was not convinced.

I finished the initial interview, listened to his heart and lungs, wrote my notes, and he was admitted to the hospital. His platelet count was 7,000 (very low), his chest x-ray showed pneumonia, and on his peripheral smear he had a large percent of nucleated red blood cells, indicating that his bone marrow was likely involved in his presumptive neoplastic process. Very interesting . . . very sad. I spent the night reading about leukoerythroblastosis and thrombocytopenia and praying for my patient.

When I saw him next, I asked, "Sam, do you have any kids?"

"I have three, and I love them to death." He exuded a light I had not seen before.

"Have they ever messed up?"

"Oh yeah, my boy is in jail for murder." So sad, so profound, such a perfect illustration.

"Would you ever think about taking him back?"

"In an instant. I wouldn't think twice."

"Sam, you know the heart of God. He will always take you back. You are His child." The illustration caught him off guard. He remained pensive and quiet.

The next morning: "Good morning, Sam, sorry to wake you up. How are you?"

"No problem, I wasn't sleeping. I couldn't sleep all night." This caught my attention. Sleep reflects the state of the mind, and something was going on. "I've been thinking all night about what you said, and I was wondering . . . I was wondering if you would help me give my life back to Christ."

My eyes watered, my heart pounded. "Of course, Sam, I would be honored."

Sam had metastatic small-cell carcinoma of the lung. His medical prognosis was measured in weeks at best, but his spirit was healed; and I was reminded why I went to medical school.

Jamie Crounse, LLUSM class of 2007, is a resident in family medicine and preventive medicine at LLUMC. He is a deferred mission appointee. In 2007, he received the Wil Alexander Whole-Person Care Award.

July 27

Answer my prayers, O Lord, for your unfailing love is wonderful. Take care of me, for your mercy is so plentiful. Psalm 69:16, NLT

I love going to work every day of the week. I have never regretted the decision to become a physician. As a faculty member in Loma Linda University School of Medicine, I have the privilege of caring for patients as their primary care physician and to participate in the education of young men and women training to become physicians. This diversity of activities brings opportunities on a daily basis.

I have learned that patients look to their physicians to help them in making the important decisions that affect their lives tremendously. My philosophy of caring for patients has been the idea that, perhaps two or three times in one's life, an individual will truly need their physician to get them through a crisis. All physicians have experienced that satisfaction in making the diagnosis that answers the question of what is causing this or that problem.

Yes, that diagnosis may be grave or even terminal; but a clear answer to unexplained symptoms will ultimately allow people to deal with the present and future, once it is known what the true issues are. Sometimes, a physician can help, even if there is no cure available. I recall once caring for a patient who had developed Alzheimer's dementia. His physical health had declined so significantly that it was taking a terrible toll on his wife. She was guided by the promise made years ago that she would not place him into a nursing home.

But it was obvious that she was wearing down from the stress and strain of caring for him. This was affecting her both emotionally and physically in a tremendous way. I was aware of an opening in a local board-and-care home. I knew the owners would provide the loving and concerned daily care that her husband deserved. She could spend the entire day with him, but then return home at night to get rest and preserve her own health.

Over many years, I had developed a relationship of trust with her and strongly encouraged her to consider this as an option. Her decision to allow her husband to move out of their home occurred partly because of that relationship. It was a burden that was lifted from her, as she received the permission she needed to act before an acute crisis developed that would have thrown her world into chaos. Medicine is not always about diagnosing and treating disease; but it is always about caring for fellow human beings, and being right there when you are needed the most.

Raymond Wong, LLUSM class of 1979-B, is associate professor in LLUSM department of medicine. He is clerkship director for internal medicine at LLUSM. He was president of the Walter E. Macpherson Society from 2003 to 2006.

Bring ye all the tithes into the storehouse, that there may be meat in mine house, and prove me now herewith, saith the LORD of hosts, if I will not open you the windows of heaven, and pour you out a blessing, that there shall not be room enough to receive it. Malachi 3:10, KJV

A number of years ago while my wife and I were missionaries in Singapore, we personally experienced the proverb: "You can never 'out give' the Lord."

We were mentoring a small Seventh-day Adventist church in the satellite city of Queenstown, Singapore. This little branch church, planted by young people from the large Balestier Road Church, met in a small noisy shop in a cul-de-sac between a clattering print shop and a bakery that emitted delicious smells at sermon time. We badly needed a more suitable place to meet, and a private residence for sale nearby would be just the place for a "home church." The problem was how our congregation, composed mostly of students living "on a shoestring," could raise the purchase price of $60,000.

My wife and I longed to make a substantial contribution toward the purchase of a new venue for the Queenstown church but couldn't see how we could do that on our limited mission salary. One Sabbath, we invited a fellow missionary family to join us for lunch just before their scheduled permanent return to the United States. A concern of theirs was how to dispose of their family car, an older Australian Holden that had not sold because of its age and its high gas consumption. Gasoline in Singapore at that time was four dollars a gallon.

My wife and I talked it over and decided to put our newer Vauxhall car up for sale and buy our friends' Holden. We could contribute the sizable difference in profit to the Queenstown project because we needed a car only until our own departure in two years.

We asked the Lord for a sign—sell our Vauxhall in a week, thus indicating we should purchase the Holden. Our car did sell in a few days for a good price, and our friends gladly accepted our offer of $200 for the Holden. We were pleased that we could then contribute a substantial amount to the Queenstown church project.

The old Holden ran perfectly for the next two years. Then it came time for us to leave for our homeland. We wondered what we could do with the old Holden. Singapore, a very small country with too many cars on its roads, had recently passed a law that new cars could be purchased only with the trade in of an old car. I asked the Mercedes-Benz dealership if they had a need for old cars for "trade in" purposes. "Yes, we do," they replied.

I offered to show them the old Holden, which I needed to dispose of. They said, "We don't need to see it; we will give you $1,200 for it as it is. You drive it until the day before you leave, then bring it in, and we'll give you the $1,200!" Just before we left, and true to their promise, they gave us $1,200—an amount six times what we had paid for the car!

Truly, when God makes a promise, He keeps it, and pours out a blessing as He promised (Malachi 3:10). What a wonderful God we serve!

Galen H. Coffin, LLUSM class of 1949, resides in Gresham, Oregon. July 28 is his birthday.

July 29

And this is life eternal, that they might know thee the only true God, and Jesus Christ, whom thou hast sent. John 17:3, KJV

Character

Reputation is determined by what a man does; character by what he won't do.

Ability helps a man to get to the top; character will keep him there.

Character is not made in a crisis; it is only exhibited then.

Discipline

A lazy man is of no more use than a dead man, and he takes up more room.

It is easier to raise objection than it is to get busy.

Some folks are like blisters—they only show up when the work is done.

Intelligence

A wise man has his afterthoughts first.

Blessed are they who have nothing to say and cannot be persuaded to say it.

Great minds discuss ideas. Average minds discuss events. Little minds discuss people.

Humility

It is human to bow to a superior; it is divine to bow to an inferior.

People who hold their heads too high miss a lot of the good things in life.

The branch that bends the lowest bears the most fruit.

Joy

Contentment consists not in great wealth, but in few wants.

Don't spoil the life in making the living.

Some people get up bright and early, and some just get up early.

Kindness, Love, and Friendship

Faults are thick where love is thin.

Kindness is a language that the deaf can hear and the dumb can understand.

Positive Thinking

A man may fail many times, but isn't a failure until he begins to blame someone else.

A pessimist is afraid that success will walk in while he is present.

Success

Successful men forget yesterday, respect today, and anticipate tomorrow.

The thing about dreams is that you have to stay awake to make them come true.

The largest room in the world is the room for improvement.

Truthfulness

A lie does not become the truth by frequent repetition.

A lie travels by lightning express; truth comes by stagecoach.

Religion

To know Christ, and to make Him known, is our business here.

Christianity is not a cloak put on, but a life put on.

The best way to live for another world is to live life in this one for others.

The cream of the Bible is never found by skimming the surface.

Be an "amen" Christian, but don't shout it louder than you live it.

Walter B. Clark (1906-2000) served LLU as dean of students from 1947 to 1965 and as dean of admissions from 1963 to 1970. From 1970 to 1971, he was associate dean for admissions and student affairs for LLUSM. He and his wife, Lucile, were married on July 29. Some of his favorite sayings were compiled by Charles G. Graves Jr., LLUSM class of 1953-B, from which this devotional was excerpted.

A merry heart doeth good like a medicine. Proverbs 17:22, KJV

The pathologist's words dropped like a huge bolder right onto the shoulders of his physician/colleague listening on the telephone. "The biopsy shows that you have cancer." The physician was in the prime of his career, with children in high school and with many professional responsibilities. The prognosis for survival with this incurable cancer was about five years, assuming a good response to chemotherapy.

Even with a supportive wife, the cloud of depression he felt was profound. He did not want to die. It just was not fair! After struggling with the reality of his diagnosis for several weeks, he determined, with the help of supportive friends and family, to make the best of what time he had; he would turn the outcome over to God. So, he filled his life with things that inspired him and made him happy—including time spent with family and friends, music, sporting activities, and creative projects at work.

Being a patient now, he identified with his patients in a new and empathetic way. Since the cancer was slow growing, his oncologist wanted to try a promising new research treatment protocol that was going to start in a few months. It was decided to wait for a while to start treatment. Meanwhile, with hope in the new treatment, the physician/patient adhered to his program of positive, stimulating thoughts and activities.

With several delays in initiating the protocol, a year passed. When the time came to start on the new cancer treatment protocol, and to the surprise and amazement of the oncologist and his patient, all the tests, scans and x-rays showed that the cancer was gone. The oncologist then found, with testing in his research laboratory, that his patient had developed, internally, a unique cell line that destroyed the cancer cells.

Although it is not provable, it is very likely that an upbeat attitude and trust in a "Higher Power" contributed to keeping this physician going seventeen years at present—still waiting to start treatment—after the diagnosis of an incurable cancer. Truly, "a merry heart doeth good like a medicine" as the medical literature and most healthcare personnel can attest. Patients who develop an optimistic spirit, in spite of their diseases—and in contrast to those with a "victim" mentality (who become bitter, depressed, and angry)—tend to do much better coping with and surviving serious illnesses.

The quality of life when happiness dominates one's state of mind makes it worthwhile to go on, regardless of how much or little of life we have left. We are responsible for our own happiness, regardless of our situation in life. One can be in a concentration camp, a bad family situation, in the midst of a tragedy, and still be basically a happy person. Trust in a Supreme Being adds immeasurably to having a "merry heart." It is up to us to choose to be this kind of person.

Keith K. Colburn, LLUSM class of 1970, is professor in LLUSM department of medicine and head of division of rheumatology.

July 31

May the God of peace himself sanctify you wholly; and may your spirit and soul and body be kept sound and blameless at the coming of our Lord Jesus Christ.
I Thessalonians 5:23, RSV

I recently attended professional meetings that included a session on integrative medicine (IM), during which presenters enthusiastically shared their commitment to incorporating IM into the medical school curriculum. They defined IM as "treating patients with compassionate care that addresses all aspects of health and wellness— physical, psychological, social, and spiritual."

As I listened, I realized how grateful I am to be part of LLUSM, where the mission has included "providing comprehensive, competent, and compassionate healthcare for the whole person through faculty, students, and alumni" since 1909. And while the IM and LLU definitions may sound similar, they are distinctly different.

The two are alike in the interpretation of what it means to be whole. The word "whole" is derived from the old Germanic root *"hael,"* meaning "movement toward wholeness." Dictionary definitions include words like "restored" or "healed," "entire" or "altogether." The implication here is that there is a multidimensional emphasis in being "whole," whereby all the interrelated parts become complete or united.

As much as the definitions are similar, the context in which wholeness is practiced is very different. The LLU mission is very specific in identifying whose pattern we must follow—to "participate in **Christ's** ministry 'To make man whole.'" We are commissioned to integrate Christ-centered values into our personal and professional lives.

Medical professionals at LLU are prepared for service in the context of seven highly esteemed attributes of Christ, which have been adopted as the core values of LLU: 1) compassion to engage with the needs and suffering of others; 2) integrity to live a unified life in which one's convictions match one's actions; 3) excellence to exceed minimum standards and expectations; 4) freedom to make informed and accountable choices and to respect the freedom of others to do the same; 5) justice to treat others fairly and renounce all forms of unfair discrimination; 6) purity and self-control in all things; and 7) humility in serving others in a sacrificial manner. The practice of whole-person care through the demonstration of Christ-centered values should be the hallmark of LLU graduates.

Do we always achieve this lofty ideal in our personal and professional lives? Not always, but we must always try. LLUSM graduates consistently report that the area they most appreciate about their medical education is the emphasis on learning medicine in the context of caring for the whole person.

In 2006, a Petersdorf Scholar with the American Association of Medical Colleges visited the campus to interview administrators, medical students, and faculty regarding transformation culture and educating for professionalism. Here is one statement by the reviewer: "I experienced first-hand at LLU and the academic medical center, profound culture, environment and commitment to caring for the whole person. . . ."

My morning prayer is that God will stand by each one of us in this great task to represent Christ-centered values in the practice of whole-person care.

Loretta B. Johns is assistant dean for program development and evaluation for LLUSM. She received a PhD degree in business education from University of Maryland in 1986.

August 1

*"My grace is sufficient for you, for My strength is made perfect in weakness."
Therefore most gladly I will rather boast in my infirmities, that the power of
Christ may rest upon me. . . . For when I am weak, then I am strong.*
2 Corinthians 12:9-10, NKJV

"Warning: what comes next may challenge you and forever change the course
of an otherwise comfortable life." I wish some such sign somewhere had
offered that caution before I started medical school! The four years I
spent at Loma Linda University served to completely alter my own neat plan for life.
I started with a dream and vision that had been in some part inspired by the Lord—
although I had superimposed my own ideas of what was possible and had shrunk it down
into a little, doable, human thing. God spent four years softening my heart and expanding
my mind, and still He works on me daily.

Between my first and second years of medical school, I traveled to Ecuador. There
I felt the Lord nudging my heart toward a general surgery residency. I knew that of the
many specialties in medicine, this was not the one where I had the most intrinsic skill or
even the personality I thought one needed. After returning home, I spent months, which
became years, trying to explain to the Lord why I could not do this thing He was asking
me to do. But it became a gentle process.

He gradually showed me what was possible through Him. Did I catch that prolapsed
cord while on obstetrics rotation during one of my first nights of call ever as a third-year
student? Was it my ability that led a man struggling with post traumatic stress disorder
for decades to open up and let God's healing into his heart? How could my own strengths
allow me to balance extracurricular activities and a medical school education the way I
did? There is just so little evidence in my heart that points to me and so much that shows
He was behind it all. He was behind it ALL!

After dying to my pride again and again, God spoke to my heart one day. He reminded
me of all He had done and was doing for me, and He opened His Word to me in a new
light. All I knew came down to one thing—I was so completely weak on my own, but He
had more than enough strength for me.

I knew it. I had seen it. I could believe it. I did it. I pursued His lead, and He led me
through the toughest times I have ever known in my life so far. It seemed as if medical
school was mainly about learning to trust Him and a little bit about a medical education.
Residency, for me, is about continuing to trust Him—despite circumstances, feelings,
or any other form of evidence this world can produce. On those days when I am worn
out spiritually and emotionally—the hardest type of tired for me—I have enough left to
know only one thing: When I am weak, then He is strong in me. Together, WE can take
on anything.

*Kimberly (Arledge) Page, LLUSM class of 2005—for which she was co-pastor for the sophomore and
junior years—received the Leonard Marmor Award in 2005. August 1 recognizes a time in her life
when God was challenging her to trust Him in new ways. She completed three years of general surgery
residency at University of Utah prior to beginning a family medicine residency at St. Mark's Hospital in
Salt Lake City, Utah. She and her husband, Jimmy, live in Salt Lake City.*

August 2

Behold, I make all things new. Revelation 21:5, KJV

She was 73 years old but had an incredible vibrancy, a sharp wit, and a light in her eyes that made her seem younger. We laughed together in the intensive care unit. I was fascinated and enriched by the stories she told. No patient had ever touched my heart like this woman (we'll call her Mrs. Wagner).

Following a routine pancreatic biopsy, she developed severe pancreatitis. We did everything we could, but she slowly deteriorated. In horror, I watched this amazing woman—once full of humor and wisdom and life—gradually lose her ability to communicate. Two days before her death, however, the long squeeze she gave my hand said more than any words could have.

As a doctor, you enter medicine with a sense of awe at the power of modern technology. You learn pharmaceutical mechanisms of action, watch delicate surgery performed under a microscope, see astonishing anatomic detail on imaging studies, and start to think there is nothing you cannot diagnose and then cure or control.

Then you learn the truth. The hospital is a very different place than you imagined. Suffering happens. Bacteria develop antibiotic resistance. Some diseases remain incurable. People fight bravely but still lose their battles with illness.

I was bitter after Mrs. Wagner died. I questioned the goodness of God and even His very existence. I had prayed for her healing—how could He allow this flagrant injustice?

Over time, God, in His mercy, has led me to a better understanding of suffering. I would like to share two thoughts. First, in our accusation that God is not fair, we may assume an unfair stance toward God. We are quick to blame God for the bad but then give Him no credit for the good. We can recognize evil only because good exists as a frame of reference. Thoreau touches on this thought when he writes, "There is no odor as bad as that which arises from goodness tainted." The most terrible tragedies are those that damage the truest, purest, and most innocent.

Second, we are too preoccupied with this life. Our time here is given for one main purpose: to allow us the opportunity to accept the gift of Jesus—the gift of forgiveness and atonement that allows us to experience eternal life. It is about the choice, not the circumstances under which it is made. If our Lord, utterly sinless, suffered pain and an untimely death here on earth, how can sinners demand comfort—especially when comfort often leads us away from God?

The healing my friend receives will go far beyond the narrow constraints of my original prayer. When we meet again, I will encounter the consummation of the unique perfection God planned for her from before her birth—a heavenly being of whom I knew only a hint in that intensive care unit.

Robert Vaughan, LLUSM class of 1990, is a radiologist in Candler, North Carolina, where he resides with his wife, Tammy, and sons, Matt and Luke. August 2 is the date of their wedding anniversary.

August 3

I will instruct you and teach you in the way you should go; I will guide you with My eye. Psalm 32:8, NKJV

Consider this miraculous story of God's guidance: In the late 1990s, strong convictions led me to explore ways of becoming more aware of my patients' spiritual condition. A simple ten-point questionnaire of their spiritual journey that took less than a minute of their time to complete impressed me with how many considered their spiritual beliefs to be an integral component of their lives. So I decided to selectively seek permission from my patients for me to pray in their presence, especially when I found components that were particularly challenging or resistant to standard measures.

Harry and Lucy, an elderly couple, were always together for Lucy's appointments, although only she was my patient. During one visit, I expressed reservations regarding advisability of their proposed cross-country flight for a family emergency. My concern was for Lucy, as her hypertension was presenting difficult challenges. It was one of those times I sensed a strong need to pray. After receiving their permission, I offered a prayer in their presence for treatment guidance and their travel safety.

Some time later, Harry confided to me that praying for Lucy made him feel I was exaggerating the seriousness of her condition. However, I also learned that, through repeated dreams, Lucy had become convicted that they would soon be learning new spiritual truths leading to a change in Christian church denominations, even though they were actively involved in their current church. My praying in their presence influenced her to continue seeking my care.

Meanwhile, I became compelled to invite each of my patients to consider exploring often-misunderstood biblical concepts in greater depth, via video tapes, delivered either by mail or in person. Many accepted my offer. Being very hospitable, Harry and Lucy chose the personal home delivery method, which my wife and I were privileged to continue on a weekly basis for eight months. During our visits, they told us of having shared written copies of Lucy's dreams with friends and pastors, but these associates invariably brushed the writings aside as being perhaps interesting but rather eccentric.

However, to Harry and Lucy, the beautiful, profound, Christ-centered biblical insights and coherent understanding of prophecy were all part of dreams come true. They gladly accepted our invitation to attend church with us, and later Lucy declared that, upon first entering our sanctuary, she felt very impressed that this would be their new church home. Soon, Harry and Lucy joined our Chehalis, Washington, Seventh-day Adventist church by profession of faith. For the next five years, they added a tremendous vibrant, loving, caring component to our church fellowship in innumerable ways until they passed to their rest from sudden illnesses about three months apart.

My experience with Harry and Lucy is one of the most memorable illustrations of God's guidance in my medical practice, made possible through education at Loma Linda University, where the spiritual component of whole person care is given a high priority.

Helmuth Fritz, LLUSM class of 1973-B, is assistant clinical professor in LLUSM department of medicine. He resides in Chehalis, Washington.

August 4

And we know that in all things God works for the good of those who love him, who have been called according to his purpose. Romans 8:28, NIV

As I progressed through my training, I soon learned that not all healthcare institutions have whole-person care as their goal. Like animals, patients were herded though the system. During my nightly devotions, I prayed many times for the Lord to use me to reach my patients and let them know God cares for them.

It was in the evening, after a long day in the operating room with the typical rush of patients and procedures, that the Lord gave me an opportunity. I knocked on the door of 3326. A very pleasant African American female greeted me. She was sitting on the hospital bed. Her large round reading glasses quickly came off when she spotted me. Wearing the typical hospital gown, she was half covered with blankets. It almost seemed as if my patient had been crying. Her diagnosis of breast cancer must still have been fresh. It was then that I realized what this was. This particular moment in time was a "ball catching" event.

Moments like these present to a physician every day. During my training at Loma Linda, this scenario was described to me in a football analogy. Imagine with me that you are playing football, and a perfect pass is coming at you. Looking up at that beautiful spiral coming down at you, your only focus is "just don't drop the ball."

Back in the patient's room, I weighed this emotional problem in my head and commenced with the easy part. Behind my medical mask, I discussed expectations for the upcoming surgery, risks and benefits, and some of the complications. When I was about to leave the room, there was a pause in the discussion. During that pause, I asked God what I should do. "God," I silently prayed, "give me wisdom and strength to help this woman right now, emotionally and spiritually."

God did not take this request lightly. I noticed a little Bible lying open to the book of Romans. God inspired me to use this moment. I told her that I also was a Christian and liked to read the Bible because it comforted me in hard times. Then I gave her an assignment—to read Romans 8:28. After walking out of the room and shutting the door, it hit me: I had no idea what Romans 8:28 said! I vowed to look it up as soon as I had access to a Bible.

What blessed words to comfort someone the night before surgery. It is truly amazing how God works, if we only stop to ask Him. As you read this today, I hope you will find encouragement to identify and give strength during times when patients have deep emotional needs, and to consult God daily in prayer for wisdom and guidance. Last, but not least, remember the analogy and "just don't drop the ball."

Merlin Wehling, LLUSM class of 2001, lives in Kearney, Nebraska, with his wife, Chere. August 4 is their wedding anniversary.

August 5

Let your light so shine before men, that they may see your good works and glorify your Father in heaven. Matthew 5:16, NKJV

I vividly remember the day when our attending physician, Dr. Daniel Robitschek, paused during rounds at the Jerry L. Pettis Memorial Veterans Affairs (VA) Medical Center with the entire team and prayed with one of the patients. Although I do not know what happened to the patient afterwards, I remember that the attending physician had the courage to pray in front of all the staff assembled there to discuss the case.

This story reminds me of that attending physician's namesake, the prophet Daniel. When under King Darius' rule, some of the other princes—envious of Daniel's high position—tried to rid themselves of him. Now he could have changed his routine of praying before an open window toward Jerusalem, but he did not. This caused the "greatly beloved" prophet to be placed in the lion's den, but the lions had no power over him. The same was not true for the men who plotted against him.

Dr. Daniel and prophet Daniel's courage to pray before others has encouraged me to pray with my patients. On a mission trip to India, we held medical clinics in ten villages, and we would see about 200-to-300 patients per day. Of all the patients I saw, all agreed to have prayer except one. As a result of this work, as well as the evangelism teams that were working simultaneously, we saw many devote their lives to Jesus Christ.

In my own practice, I recall a 23-year-old woman who had been sexually abused as a young girl in Mexico. She was now separated from her husband and 4-year-old daughter, and was following a self-destructive course of drug use. I told her that the man who did this to her had, by his actions, made her believe the lie that she is of no value, that she could be used and then discarded.

I then explained that Christ died to dispel this lie. The truth is that even a drug addict is valuable enough for the King of the Universe to leave His throne and die to make it possible for that person to be saved. Whom do you choose to believe—an evil man or the King of the Universe? I told her that her choice would be known by what she chose to do with her life. I said that if she chose to accept the truth, she would no longer follow the same self-destructive path. During the next several weeks she made an amazing recovery and so far is still doing well.

I am hoping that the ripple effect of Dr. Daniel's prayer while on rounds at the VA Medical Center, as well as the prophet Daniel's prayer in the kingdom of Medo-Persia, will continue to benefit others through my sharing of this story. Thus, others will learn the truth that they are of such infinite value that the King of the Universe gave His life as a ransom for theirs.

Scott Ispirescu, LLUSM class of 1996, is a pediatric psychiatrist in Mission Viejo, California. August 5 is his birthday and is also the day he started medical school.

August 6

In my desperation I prayed, and the LORD listened; he saved me from all my troubles. Psalm 34:6, NLT

As a young flight surgeon on my first U.S. Navy operational tour, I could not wait for the opportunity to experience adventure and purpose. I was stationed in Guam, a small, remote island in the Pacific, where I was in charge of medical rescues in the 1.5 million square miles of the surrounding seas.

In mid-November 1996, we were shielding ourselves from Typhoon Dale, which had just missed Guam. In the late evening, I received a call from the U.S. Coast Guard. The USS *Guernsey Express*, a 200-foot vessel with twenty crewmen and more than 2,000 cows aboard, failed its attempt to escape the typhoon. The final signal transmitted by the captain of this vessel indicated that the ship had capsized. The Coast Guard wanted my decision whether a rescue should be launched.

The risk of losing an able Navy crew weighed heavily against the survival of twenty souls who faced certain death—if they were not already dead. This decision was almost too much for me, but my commanding officer expressed his complete faith in my decision. His words encouraged me; and the helicopter crew was willing to risk their lives, despite gusty eighty-five-knot winds and thirty-five-foot seas. We took off.

As we searched in the darkness, one of the crew members—wearing night-vision goggles—spotted a flare. The scene was unforgettable: floating dead cows, a ship capsized on its side, the yellow raft with fuzzy shadows of people inside, and descending flares. A rescue was nearly impossible. Just then, a large ocean swell pushed the life raft up, nearly horizontal from my line of sight. I caught a glimpse of the intense fear on the face of a survivor. It was at that moment that I became at peace and fear left me. I accepted God's will to take my life or spare it. Paralyzing fear turned into committed leadership. The calm steadiness of my voice appeared to soothe the crew.

By now, we had exhausted all of our reserve fuel, leaving only our auxiliary tank to take us back to Guam. I sent word to launch the other aircraft, if they were willing. We threw flares to the survivors and left them in the darkness.

Then fear reintroduced itself to us on our return to base. The auxiliary tank would not transfer its fuel. With only ten minutes of estimated fuel left, we began procedures to ditch the aircraft. The pilot started to put us in a hover to allow us to jump out safely. After the helicopter hit the water and started sinking, he would have time to escape from the cockpit. Just then, about twenty minutes of fuel transferred, and we flew on. This disconcerting sequence of events would repeat itself three times before we finally made it back.

The other helicopter crew had just as much difficulty in its rescue attempt as we did. For us, after nine hours of flying in these intense conditions, daylight allowed our pilot to find a stable hover, and we were able to hoist two survivors. The remaining survivors were rescued by the ship. So, finally, on the third attempt, between the two helicopters and one responding ship at sea, we were able to rescue all twenty survivors!

In reflection, I was given this *shield of faith* as a gift from God to give me success—not only for that mission, but also for future rescues, and countless life trials.

Troy Anderson, LLUSM class of 1994, is a neurologist and sleep specialist. He was a commander in the U.S. Navy; and for this rescue recounted in this devotional, he received the Navy and Marine Corps Medal—the highest peacetime medal awarded. He and his wife, Heather, and their children—Keoni, Brooklyn, and Blakely—reside in Buckeye, Arizona.

August 7

Now if God so clothes the grass of the field, which today is, and tomorrow is thrown into the oven, will He not much more clothe you, O you of little faith?
Matthew 6:30, NKJV

One of the first patients I saw while serving as interim surgeon at the Mugonero Mission Hospital in Rwanda was Nkwanda, a young lady recovering from complications of childbirth. Following extensive surgery for the removal of infected remnants of afterbirth and other dead and dying tissues, Nkwanda lay in a pool of urine on her bed, totally incontinent.

Each day as I made hospital rounds, Nkwanda begged me to do whatever was necessary to fix the problem; and each day I reminded her of the high risks involved and the unlikely possibility of obtaining a satisfactory result so soon after her previous surgery. However, I also knew that this was Nkwanda's only opportunity for help, without which she would spend the remainder of her days in misery. How could I refuse to give it my best shot?

Having committed her to God, and while pleading for wisdom and skill, I prepared for the nearly impossible task before me. Carefully, I searched through the collection of donated suture materials, catheters, and other supplies until I found something I thought might work. Meticulously, I dissected the still inflamed tissues, attempting to identify the anatomy and discover the true nature of the defect needing repair. After what seemed like hours, I was able to identify the large defect in the posterior wall of her bladder and to perform a tenuous closure.

The next morning on my rounds, Nkwanda was all smiles. While rejoicing with her and the staff at the apparently good outcome, I knew that she was still not out of the woods. My spirits were better when, on day two, Nkwanda was still dry, and the catheters were functioning as planned. Again on day three, our spirits soared! On day four, as I made my final rounds before my departure from Rwanda, I noticed that there was no urine in the collecting bag and that Nkwanda was again wet and sad.

I left Rwanda that day—dejected, discouraged, and wondering where was this God to Whom I had dedicated my life and services, the One I had believed could give complete healing to this poor lady, and into Whose care I had committed her.

I returned to my urban Chicago surgical practice but could not remove from my mind the sad disaster that had befallen this child of God in Rwanda, a land that so recently had been subjected to genocide.

Months later, I received an email from Mark—the student nurse who had been my interpreter and helper in Rwanda. "I saw your patient, Nkwanda, at the hospital. She is completely healed." The message was short and to the point.

Even as I write this story, now several years later, tears well up in my eyes as I recall the goodness of my God who knows every sparrow that falls.

Walter Thompson, LLUSM class of 1961, is a family practice surgeon in Lake Geneva, Wisconsin. He and his wife, Avonne, were married on August 7.

August 8

And the King shall answer and say unto them, "Verily I say unto you, inasmuch as ye have done it unto one of the least of these my brethren, ye have done it unto me." Matthew 25:40, KJV

In my thirty-five years of medical practice (residencies and beyond), I have been asked several times what it means to be a Christian (fashioned after Christ) doctor. Personally, I have asked the same question of my elders (those superior in knowledge, experience, education, and/or age). What is the *prima facie* case for a Christian doctor? How do I make the grade?

Providing high-quality healthcare, billing Medicare honestly, respecting patients and nurses, honoring one's teachers, and keeping up with continuing education may fulfill the physician licensure requirements. However, those activities are not enough to make the grade. Believing in God as the Supreme Being, and believing in a future heaven on earth will not make the grade either. Lucifer knows and believes in those facts, too; yet, he is unchanged.

I do not think that just going to church, paying tithe, keeping the Ten Commandments, being a good person, and committing no wrong or crimes will be sufficient either.

What was Christ's instruction? He commissioned His followers to pray daily: "Thy kingdom come. Thy will be done, on earth as it is in heaven" (Matthew 6:10, KJV). If God's will is done on earth, the hungry on earth will be fed, any thirst will be quenched, the homeless will be taken in, the naked will be clothed, and the sick and lonely will be visited.

As physicians, most of us live comfortable lives. And even though there is nothing wrong with being "comfortable," how do we carry out God's will on earth if we are detached from the world's sickness?

This earth is a laboratory in which followers of Christ have the opportunity to practice their faith. God places in our lives lost people who need our care. Are we to ignore His commission? In Matthew 25:40, we find Jesus' standard for heaven: How we care for these people, Christ's brethren, is the essence of a Christian doctor.

Fred F. Soeprono, LLUSM class of 1973-B, is assistant professor in LLUSM department of dermatology. He also has an MPH degree and a JD degree. August 8 is his birthday.

August 9

Pleasant words are like a honeycomb, sweetness to the soul and health to the body. Proverbs 16:24, NRSV

A favored author approaches the topic of the influence of the mind over the body from a number of directions. One such relates to Proverbs 16:24. Ellen G. White says, in *Education* (p. 197): "The influence of the mind on the body, as well as of the body on the mind, should be emphasized. . . . the marvelous life-giving power to be found in cheerfulness, unselfishness, gratitude, should . . . be shown." And there are others who extol the benefits of expressing gratitude.

Cicero: "Gratitude is not only the greatest of virtues, but the parent of all others."

Seneca: "Nothing is more honorable than a grateful heart."

Sarah Ban Breathnach: "Every time we remember to say thank you, we experience nothing less than heaven on earth."

Albert Schweitzer: "At times our own light goes out and is rekindled by a spark from another person. Each of us has cause to think with deep gratitude of those who have lighted the flame within us."

Alfred Painter: "Saying thank you is more than good manners. It is good spirituality."

We must admit that each of us is indebted to those who have gone before. We all have memories of grade school, high school, and college teachers, as well as professional school educators, who encouraged, commended, inspired, and lit the flame within us. These memories may, in turn, spur expressions of gratitude on our part.

And then there were coaches, relatives, or neighbors—the list goes on of those who have influenced our choices. Each deserves special pleasant words of commendation. Those words are life-giving to the sender and to the receiver. Science is beginning to discover that the flow of endorphins is prompted by pleasant words sent unselfishly and cheerfully.

Most of us relish words of gratitude directed toward us. How grateful we are to hear our children, our colleagues, family, and friends spontaneously drop a "thank you" in our direction. Science is finding endorphins that bring health to the body as a result of positive emotions generated by words. According to psychoneuroimmunology researcher, Lee Berk, DrPH, "We are beginning to realize the impact of thoughts and words on our own apothecary and its influence on the mind, body, and spirit."

Life-giving power comes through pleasant words of gratitude, sweet to the soul and health to the body. Today, find an excuse to pass on pleasant words of gratitude to someone in your life. Watch and wait for the "marvelous life-giving power found in cheerfulness, unselfishness, and gratitude. . . ."

Georgia E. Hodgkin is professor in and associate chair of LLUSAHP department of nutrition and dietetics. She received an EdD degree from LLU in 1991. She was president of the National Auxiliary to LLUSM Alumni Association from 2008 to 2009. August 9 is her birthday.

August 10

Let us run with endurance the race that is set before us, looking unto Jesus."
Hebrews 12:1-2, NKJV

The events that I loved most at the 2008 Olympic Summer Games in Beijing, China, were the distance races. The very idea that a human being could run at virtually full speed for 5,000 or 10,000 meters is simply mind-boggling! And while I loved the explosiveness of the 100-, 200-, and 400-meter sprints, there was something mystical about the distance races. Hebrews 12:1-2 invites us to enter the distance race known as the Christian life. One day while reading this text, a memory of something I had read on the Internet surfaced. I have paraphrased it into something like this. . .

"Every morning on the African plain; a gazelle wakes up and says to itself, 'I must outrun the fastest lion, or I will be killed.' And every morning, a lion wakes up and says to itself, 'I must outrun the slowest gazelle, or I will starve to death.' So you see, on the African plain, it doesn't matter whether I am a lion or a gazelle. When the sun comes up, I'd better be running."

Interestingly, Hebrews 12:1-2 says we must have the lithe, loping stride of the disciplined marathoner. Our Christian race is not a sprint. With this truth as a given, the writer proceeds to instruct us on how to run our race and win.

However, the race of faith did not begin with you and me, but with an earlier generation of runners, whose success in the faith invitational is chronicled and celebrated in Hebrews chapter 11. Imagine their post-race interviews:

Abel asserts, "I won my race when I chose to offer to God the sacrifice He requested."

Enoch says, "I won my race when by faith I walked with God right on up to His front porch, and He said, 'Enoch, you are closer to My home than yours. Why not just take up permanent residence.'"

Noah contends, "I won my race when I trusted that God would build an ark to save my entire household."

And Abraham reports, "I won my race when I trusted that God could resurrect my boy Isaac, even if I offered him as sacrifice."

While Moses says, "I won my race when I believed the suffering with the people of God was more valuable than the pleasures of sin for a season. I won my race when I refused sonship in Egypt's royal household."

And ladies, the hall of faith is no "boys only" club. That's why Sarah can say, "I won my race when I finally believed God would make me conceive, well past menopause."

That's why Rahab says, "I won my race when by faith I sheltered Joshua and Caleb."

These and legions of others entered the Christian race and finished their course. Were these runners perfect? No! Did they make mistakes? Yes! Did they stumble? Yes! But they ran and kept running by faith. So, run, Christian, because our lives are at stake.

But we do not run alone. The writer urges, "Looking unto Jesus, the author and finisher of our faith, who for the joy that was set before Him, endured the cross, despising the shame" (Hebrews 12:2, NKJV). With Jesus as our pacesetter, victory is guaranteed. He ran a flawless race. He knows the course. Run with Him at our side, and we will win. Now get ready, set, go!

Leslie N. Pollard is vice chancellor for community partnerships and diversity for LLU. He is also associate professor of theological studies in LLUSR. He holds the PhD degree, earned from Andrews University in Berrien Springs, Michigan, in 2007; as well as a DMin degree and an MBA degree.

"Teacher, which is the most important commandment in the law of Moses?" Jesus replied, "'You must love the Lord your God with all your heart, all your soul, and all your mind.' This is the first and greatest commandment. A second is equally important: 'Love your neighbor as yourself.' The entire law and all the demands of the prophets are based on these two commandments." Matthew 22:36-40, NLT

It was my first rotation on the wards as a third-year medical student, when on August 11, 1989, my attending physician, Harvey Elder, LLUSM class of 1957, said to me: "You have the gift of healing. You have the ability to learn this stuff; you enjoy it, and people are healed."

He seemed to be telling me that there was something about me, or something about what I was doing, that was causing people to get well—even though as a medical student my main job was simply doing admission histories and physicals. At the time I could not imagine what that "something" was; but I knew this was a key, insightful statement. I wrote it down in an important place. Work on the wards was unlike anything I had ever done before. And yet, as lost as I felt, apparently people were being healed.

As Christians, if we are honest, we know we are so very lost when it comes to what we are really supposed to be doing. We are supposed to emulate Christ; but we get so bogged down in the details, we just cannot seem to ever get it right. And as hard as we try, we never will get it "right," since we each have our own idea of what "right" is. It is only through the grace of Christ that any semblance of "getting it right" exists.

What is this "grace of Christ"? It is a realization of how overwhelmingly imperfect we are and how incredibly free His forgiveness is. It is an understanding of His total acceptance of us in our imperfect state. It is an awareness that He wants a relationship with us. It is knowing that He will work through us if we will turn all our efforts over to Him; and if we fully rely upon Him, just as He did on His Father when He was here. And then, as blundering as we are, Christ somehow shines through and is seen despite us.

While on those wards, I don't believe there were any "miraculous healings" taking place. Looking back, I think it was more an attitude of "I don't know it all, but I will try to help you understand what I do know to help you through this" that was bringing healing—despite continued illness, and despite me.

I also do not believe we will ever be completely perfect in our behavior or in all our thoughts; but we can have a perfect connection to Christ that gives us more an attitude of "I am not perfect; and I don't know it all, but I know One who really loves me, accepts me, and made things right in my life. Let me share Him with you in how I treat you as we interact today."

The bottom line is always love and relationship: Christ loves us; therefore, we love Him and have a relationship with Him. Out of this flows love for others and healing relationships.

Alison B. Carleton, LLUSM class of 1991, is a family practitioner in Nevada, Iowa. August 11 is the date this incident occurred.

August 12

Salvation belongs to the LORD; Your blessing be upon Your people! Psalm 3:8, NASB

After reading Rachel Naomi Remen's book, *My Grandfather's Blessings*, I was challenged to live each busy day as a medical professional with the goal of recognizing the spark of God in others. In the course of attending to the whole-person needs of my patients, I am afforded opportunities to touch and bless their lives by discovering ways to awaken or affirm their inner spark. Some days I remind myself that the anticipation of this awesome prospect is my reason for being on the road before dawn, heading to the hospital for another day of running between wards and patients and nurses, wondering if I will ever know enough to be a competent physician. Though I doubt whether I will actually be able to profoundly bless each patient in the way I might hope, there is something about taking a moment to acknowledge the need for blessing that gives me purpose on this journey toward becoming a physician.

While the solitude of my morning commute allows me to formulate lofty goals of compassionate interactions with my patients, the bustling hallways and mechanical hums and beeps of the hospital wards quickly drown out my silent reflections. Louder still are the cynical and frustrated comments of my colleagues as the day wears on and as the many medical and psychosocial needs of our patients build up around us.

At one point, I listened sadly to my colleagues' unconcerned conversation about a homeless patient who wanted to leave against medical advice—a man they had no intention of convincing otherwise. I recognize that one less patient on our busy team would lighten the daunting work load, but I cannot help but wonder if we failed this man by allowing him to leave with a problem that will inevitably bring him back in worse condition. More importantly, I worry that we have failed our calling as physicians by allowing ourselves to view this patient as a burden from which to free ourselves.

As I later reflect on this conversation and others like it, I realize that cynicism is a decision. Although I would like to think that the decision against cynicism is just as simple, I am increasingly aware of the pressure on medical professionals to adopt such perspectives about "difficult" patients. We are easily drawn into conversations and attitudes that are far from recognizing the spark of God in others.

Although I have yet to formulate the appropriate response to the cynicism in my colleagues, I feel more strongly every day that I want to be a doctor who sees each patient for the unique creation of God that he or she is. I want to combat the fatigue and discouragement that will inevitably come with this job by looking for how I can bless my patients and how they will bless me. Making the conscious decision to do this is the easy part—the challenge lies in living it out each day.

Gwen Gleason-Rohrer, LLUSM class of 2008, is a resident in family medicine at Harbor-UCLA Medical Center in Torrance, California.

August 13

How precious is your steadfast love, O God! All people may take refuge in the shadow of your wings. Psalm 36:7, NRSV

It was a warm summer evening in June. I was reviewing financial reports with the Mesa Grande Academy finance committee, in Calimesa, California, when my pager went off. As I continued to explain the wonders of unrestricted net assets, I peered down to take a look and it simply read, "It's time; we need to go to the hospital."

As I raced down those California hills, my thoughts were focused on the events of the last nine months and the pleasant realities of impending fatherhood. We had made all the preparations and gone through all the planning. The baby's room was painted, furnished, and stocked with enough supplies to open a neighborhood nursery. My wife had enjoyed an uneventful pregnancy; yet there was one nagging question that lingered in the back of her mind: How big would this baby be?

I was relieved as we walked into the medical center, turned ourselves over to the professionals, and began the process of labor and delivery. As my wife was being examined by the resident physician, she asked the one question that just couldn't wait, "How big do you think this baby is?" We were relieved as he assured us, "This baby is unimpressive."

Then the waiting began. With the hands of the clock inching forward, we waited and waited, watched "Jeopardy," and then waited some more. Finally, after nearly twenty-four hours, things began to happen in earnest. It became clear that this baby was "impressive" and needed to be delivered. His vital signs were degrading, and he was under stress. With the clock ticking, the attending physician did her best to explain the remaining options before emergency cesarean section to two first-time parents. The room began to fill with students and residents.

In the practiced and skillful hands of the doctor, the forceps did their work. As our nine-pound plus son made his debut, I eagerly waited to hear the first cry, only to see his limp body handed off immediately to the waiting neonatal intensive care-unit team. I watched with amazement and hope as they worked with machine-like precision to save our son.

After my wife had been "reconstructed," we found ourselves alone in the quietness of our room and without our son. It's impossible to describe the range of emotions that we felt, as we waited for news. We pleaded with the Lord to be very close to an innocent little boy, who seemed so very far from us and needed the watchful care and protection of his Maker.

You can imagine our joy when the door to our room opened at 2:00 a.m. as the nurse came in and announced, "Here's your baby!" As we peered into the crib of our precious son, we were overcome with thankfulness and joy to see him wrapped in his blanket and sleeping peacefully, with no tubes or monitors.

As I journey through life and at times wish for an Old Testament-style manifestation of God's power and protection, I can't forget the modern miracle I witnessed that summer evening. We witnessed the miracle of the God-given will to live and a life force that could not be quenched. We saw the wonder of life-saving technology in the hands of skilled professionals, and the miracle of how it all came together for a family that needed it in an institution ordained by God with a mission . . . *To make man whole.*

Rodney Neal is associate dean for finance and administration for LLUSM. He has an MBA degree. He and his wife, Kandi, were married on August 13.

225

August 14

And the peace of God, which passeth all understanding, shall keep your hearts and minds through Christ Jesus. Philippians 4:7, KJV

I was a senior anesthesiology resident; she was a 5-year-old patient with severe asthma. I will always remember the day we met. Let's call her Jill. She was a frequent visitor to Loma Linda University Medical Center emergency department because of uncontrollable asthma, and she had been admitted to the pediatric intensive care unit (PICU) many times in her short life. That day, I was called to help with an arterial line because Jill was again in the PICU; and, although she was doing better, she was still requiring repeat blood gases. As I walked in, I looked into her beautiful face with its shy smile looking up at me. She was sitting on her bed as big as life, with her legs tucked under her.

As we spoke, my wonder grew. Jill understood exactly why I was there and what I would be doing to her. As I sat beside her, getting everything together, she pulled a pillow onto her lap, laid her arm on it with her little wrist up and said to me, "It works best this way." While I worked, she never flinched and never cried out. She wouldn't watch, but she always had a calm expression on her face whenever I glanced up to see how she was doing. After the procedure, I could not help but take her small hand and squeeze it. I told her she had been so brave and that I hoped she would feel better soon. She just gave me her shy smile and I walked out, never to see her again; but I was forever changed.

Where do we get that kind of unshakable peace? We all desire it, we look for it in different ways, and yet few people I know have achieved the peace that I met in that small patient. As Philippians 4:7 says, the peace of God "shall keep your hearts and minds through Christ Jesus."

This young girl had been to LLUMC on numerous occasions and had experienced help in her times of need. From these experiences, a trust began to grow, a peace, a knowing, that when she could not breathe and needed help, kind people were there, ready to give her exactly what she needed. Sometimes pain was involved, but relief would come. God asks the same of us. "Prove me now, saith the LORD" (Malachi 3:10, KJV). By reaching out, with whatever level of trust/faith that we have, God meets us there, rewards our faith, and little by little our trust in Him grows.

I was the recipient of a little girl's trust, not because I was going to wave a magic wand and make her all better. No! In fact, I was going to hurt her and she knew it; but experience had taught her that LLUMC had kind people who only wanted good for her and who knew how to make her breathe easier.

Let's lean into the experiences that are put in front of us, and, in them, find a God we can trust.

Charles Cook, LLUSM class of 1983, is an anesthesiologist in Portland, Oregon.

August 15

Salvation is found in no one else, for there is no other name under heaven given to men by which we must be saved. Acts 4:12, NIV

I love road trips. The longer they are, the better. Every road trip is an opportunity to visit new places, listen to music, have deep discussions, and eat interesting food. What's not to love? In 2003, my best friend and I set out for Michigan. Neither one of us had ever attempted this trip before; so we looked forward to the adventure.

Unfortunately, I had to work the night before we left. "No problem," my friend assured me; "I'll drive first and you can rest." Of course, that "rest" did not happen. I was tired but much too excited to sleep. By late afternoon, it was my turn to take the wheel. As we drove along in the left lane, I felt something fall on my hand. Both my friend and I looked down to see what it was. The next thing I remember is my friend screaming. I had lost control of the car, and we ran off the road. I remember screaming, "Jesus, Jesus, Jesus!"

After what seemed like an eternity, we came to a stop on the opposite side of the highway, facing oncoming traffic. Amazingly, although it was the time of rush hour on this major highway, there was not a vehicle in sight. We sat in shock for a few seconds. By this time, we could see cars and trucks in the distance. I tried to start the car, but the engine refused to turn over. My friend began to unbuckle her seat belt. "Kim, forget it. It's just a car. Get out!" For some reason, all I could think about at that time was, "Oh no, my insurance company is going to drop me!"

I prayed, "Lord Jesus, please, I need this car to start." I tried again. This time the car roared to life and I drove on to the median. Almost immediately, a police car and a tow truck were on the scene. Their sudden appearance was interesting because we had not had time to make any phone calls and not even three minutes had passed! We assessed the damage. There wasn't much: one flat tire and a dent where we hit a small metal pole.

I retraced the path the car had taken across the median. It made no sense that we were even alive. We narrowly missed a large metal pole and a concrete embankment, either of which would have meant instant death. We stopped just a few yards shy of the drop off on the other side of the highway. It was as if unseen hands had guided the car. That day, I felt the power that is in the name of Jesus. I was more convinced than ever that He had plans for my life. I was grateful that God sent His angels to encamp around us and protect us.

Kimone Powell, LLUSM class of 2011, spent her childhood in Jamaica and New York City, New York. August 15 is the date this incident occurred.

August 16

If any of you lack wisdom, let him ask of God, that giveth to all men liberally, and upbraideth not; and it shall be given him. James 1:5, KJV

The humble family practitioner, who depends on his training and his God, can be given intuition and discernment that sometimes exceeds technology.

I practiced for more than forty years in a group practice in Wahpeton, North Dakota, a community with a population of about 14,000. One day an elderly lady came to my office, accompanied by her husband, who helped complete her history. She complained of having had several episodes of loss of consciousness, accompanied by what, according to the husband's observation, seemed to be fairly typical epileptic seizures. Appropriate diagnostic tests were done; and these, according to my recollection, included head x-rays and an electroencephalogram (EEG)—all of which were normal.

Not being sure of a diagnosis or just how to treat her, I observed her for a time; but the episodes continued. I became suspicious that her problem might be cardiac, with Stokes-Adams syndrome. This case happened in the early days of cardiac monitoring; so I hospitalized her for observation on the monitor, and the results proved to be completely normal. Furthermore, she did not have symptoms of any problems during this observation.

After reviewing her case with her and her husband, I told him that I was convinced that she was indeed having episodes of cardiac arrest and that she was in need of pacemaker implantation. I called a cardiologist, telling him of my convictions, stressing that I was certain that she needed this but that I had no documentation to support my feelings. I asked him to insert a pacemaker, even in the absence of proof of its indication.

She was sent fifty miles to see this consultant, where she was monitored for two or three days, again with no documentation of any abnormalities. Seeing no problems, and contrary to my request, he discharged her from the hospital. Fortunately for her, as she was preparing to leave, she had one of her episodes; and within an hour she had a pacemaker placed. She lived for years afterward with no return of symptoms.

Through the years, I have prayed daily that the Lord would give me wisdom to give my patients the care they needed. I firmly believe that He guided me in the care of this lady.

Glenn Wiltse, LLUSM class of 1947, is an internist in Albuquerque, New Mexico.

Trust in the LORD with all your heart; do not depend on your own understanding. Seek his will in all you do, and he will show you which path to take. Proverbs 3:5-6, NLT

We were living in a delightful country home in Deming, New Mexico, enjoying 360 good sunny days a year. My husband had decided to retire, and I did, too. But I was only 58. I thought, "Even though I am enjoying the counseling courses I am studying and our garden, I'm not using all the talents the Lord has given me." So, when we went out to Loma Linda to attend the Annual Postgraduate Convention, I inquired whether they needed anyone to teach family practice, which I had done when I lived in Loma Linda eighteen years before. They said, "You can practice here and teach one afternoon a week."

But I thought to myself, "I don't want to leave my lovely home and location to go back into that smog to teach one afternoon a week." We'd been back home about two weeks, when my husband asked, "Aren't you going to talk with that doctor in Loma Linda again?" That morning I prayed in desperation, "Lord, you know where you can use us most effectively. You know the future and what is best for each of us."

An hour later, the dean of LLUSM called and asked, "Would you be interested in teaching ambulatory care to senior medical students in a clinic we are planning to open in San Bernardino?" I speak Spanish fairly well and also realized that the job didn't involve getting up at night to deliver babies or taking care of emergencies, and I have always enjoyed teaching. So I accepted the offer.

We looked and looked for a house in California but couldn't find anything that began to compare with the home we left in New Mexico. Finally, we bought a tract house on a small lot in Loma Linda, but for five years we looked for a home with a lot large enough for a small garden and a view of the surrounding mountains. We eventually found one with room for a garden for flowers and vegetables. It also had room for a small orchard. But my husband's memory was beginning to fail; so we felt we shouldn't move, but that rather we should stay in Loma Linda, where he could find his way to the church and grocery store. He enjoyed the church fellowship and singing in the church choir. He and my two sisters, who later moved to Loma Linda, all developed some health challenges; and these required specialists' care. As it turned out, it was good we lived where we did, as there are so many specialists.

My husband and one sister have passed away now. I'm still enjoying gardening, traveling on mission trips, and studying the Bible with three groups of Cambodian friends. From this vantage point, I see how He showed us "which path to take."

Lois A. Ritchie-Ritter, LLUSM class of 1963, was assistant clinical professor in LLUSM department of family medicine.

August 18

[Felix] listened to Paul talk about believing in Christ Jesus. But Felix became afraid when Paul spoke about things like right living, self-control, and the time when God will judge the world. He said, "Go away now. When I have more time, I will call for you." Acts 24:24-25, ICB

On August 18, 1983, I was called for an obstetrical consultation for a patient in the intensive care unit. She had arrived at the emergency room (ER) the night before—unresponsive to commands, with shallow respiration and a rapid, thready pulse. An emergency brain scan revealed a massive hemorrhage in the left hemisphere. When I evaluated the patient—we will call her Teresa—she was on a respirator, and a dopamine drip was being administered.

Just a few days before I saw her, Teresa had moved to Fort Worth, Texas, from a small town in North Dakota. After completing high school, she reported to her parents that she was pregnant. Being somewhat embarrassed, they felt that it would be best if she quietly left and lived with her grandparents. She made the move; but late on the previous Thursday night, her grandmother heard a noise coming from the bathroom. Teresa was lying unresponsive on the floor in a pool of her own vomit.

An ambulance brought Teresa to our ER. The history from her grandmother placed her gestation to be approximately twenty-six-to-twenty-seven weeks. A fetal monitor verified a normal, reactive fetal heartbeat; but Teresa's clinical status continued to deteriorate. The neurologist and neurosurgeon had both agreed that Teresa's hemorrhage was too massive for intervention: the electroencephalogram (EEG) showed no brain activity—she was brain dead. A decision had to be made regarding the outcome of this pregnancy.

One option would be to do nothing, which would result not only in the death of Teresa but also of her unborn fetus. The second option was to deliver by cesarean section a premature infant whose birth at this point in the gestation diminished the prospect for a viable, healthy newborn. Teresa's grandparents decided on the latter option, and her parents were later able to take her healthy baby boy to live with them.

As the surgery team had transported Teresa to the operating area, I remember reflecting: I think I am going to be here next week. I am quite "sure" I am going to be here ten years from now. In reality, however, the only thing that I can be sure of is right now. One of the problems for young people today is they think that, after all, I am young; and once I get to be like grandmother, then I can develop a relationship with God. That's why she spends all that time in the rocking chair reading her Bible. In my experience, the growth in the Christian life begins *now*. This must include a daily study of God's Word, so that when a crisis does come, we won't even be tempted, because we will know what it means to trust in Jesus Christ.

Let us determine today to spend some time alone each day with Christ.

Robert Smith Jr., LLUSM class of 1969, is an obstetrician and gynecologist in Fort Worth, Texas.

You guide me with your counsel, and afterward you will receive me with honor.
Psalm 73:24, NRSV

I am retired now and have not been in practice for more than ten years. But while I was in practice, I had many occasions to see God's leading and guiding.

Of the many times, one particular incident stands out in my mind. During the three years my wife and I were serving as missionaries in Malaysia, I was working at Penang Mission Hospital. One day, as I was walking through the hospital, I met a Caucasian lady on the staircase. She turned to me and said, "Thank you, doctor, for saving my life!"

I was confused. She had not been one of my patients, and I hardly knew her. I remarked to the hospital staff what she said and inquired what she might be referring to. The surgery crew gave me the answer—resuscitation.

A few days prior to this unexpected encounter, I had read an article in a medical journal about resuscitation. It had mentioned several medications. Shortly after this, for some reason, I entered the hospital's surgery suite. There I was reminded by the surgery crew that I had found a certain amount of confusion. Off-handedly, I rattled off the names of the two or three medications that I had just read about. The crew, acting promptly on my suggestions, was able to save the patient's life. Evidently they had later informed the woman of my help. At the time, it seemed to be just another day at work.

How often do we do things that don't seem that important at the time? In this case, in retrospect, I now know that it was "the Great Providence" that guided us all that day.

Kai H. Pihl, LLUSM class of 1946, is an orthopaedic surgeon in Lincoln, California.

August 20

The prayer of faith will save the sick, and the Lord will raise them up; and anyone who has committed sins will be forgiven. Therefore confess your sins to one another, and pray for one another, so that you may be healed. The prayer of the righteous is powerful and effective. James 5:15-16, NRSV

During my first year of medical school, I spent two weeks in cardiology at a private hospital in Florida. I'll never forget a patient named Faith. She was an elderly woman dying of congestive heart failure. Two things struck me about Faith: first, her edematous legs were the most severe I had ever seen; and second, her tired, red eyes were windows of deep pain. The cardiology fellow told me Faith had been in the hospital for twenty-six days, and she would probably die there. He was aggravated because every time they would get ready to release her, she would avoid discharge and relapse.

During rounds one morning, I remember how Faith shared that she couldn't wait to get to heaven, so she could have a drink with her husband. The attending physician jokingly said, "I am not sure going out for drinks is possible in heaven." The attending then looked intently at Faith and asked, "What will it take to get you to go home this week?" Faith politely smiled and shrugged her shoulders.

Upon exiting the room, the fellow and the attending began discussing Faith's situation with frustration. They concluded that Faith was destined to die in the hospital. They didn't write it on her chart or say it verbally, but I could see it in their faces: they had given up on Faith.

The next day, while visiting Faith, I learned from her how afraid she was to die. She feared she wouldn't be going to heaven because she had taken God for granted and couldn't be forgiven. As I stood next to her bed, listening intently, I felt impressed to pray with her. Feelings of worry rushed over me. As a visiting medical student in a hospital that was not church affiliated, I was concerned that I could end up in trouble.

So I hesitated; but as I looked into her eyes, I felt God saying, "Go for it!" So I took a deep breath and asked Faith, "Would it be helpful if I prayed for you?" A shocked look came over her face. She exclaimed, "You would pray for me? You would do that?" I was beyond the point of no return and replied, "I would love to pray for you." She slid her bruised, frail hand across the bed and grabbed mine, then closed her eyes.

I began to pray, focusing on God's unconditional forgiveness and love. As I said, "Amen," I looked up at her face. Tears were freely flowing down her cheeks; and she squeezed my hand ever so tightly and whispered, "Thank you."

The following day, as we entered her room, something had changed! Faith emphatically declared, for the first time in over a month, that she was ready to go home. The attending didn't believe it when the fellow told him, so he had to ask Faith himself. Her reply was even more convincing the second time.

Sometimes we may be out of tests to run, or medicine to prescribe, or even convincing arguments to motivate change in patients' lives. However, we will never run out of our ability to provide hope and encouragement to our patients. The "power of prayer" and the "love of Jesus Christ" are two of the most powerful instruments of healing within a physician's reach.

Daniel Westerdahl, LLUSM class of 2010—for which he was freshman class pastor and sophomore class president—is the son of Howard and Judy, who were married on August 20.

August 21

Before they call I will answer. Isaiah 65:24, NIV

I was to give a lecture at 8:00 a.m. to the senior medical students at the White Memorial Hospital (now White Memorial Medical Center) in Los Angeles, California. I had thirty minutes to travel the last five miles when my right rear tire went flat. I pulled onto the shoulder, opened the trunk, and threw the spare tire on the pavement. With the bumper jack in place, and just as the flat tire was inching up off the pavement, I heard a snap in the jack and down went the wheel. I tried several times, but each time, as the tire was about to leave the pavement, the jack would give way. The jack was broken.

All I needed to do was to raise the jack an inch or so. What could I put under it? A board? I had none. I had just cleaned out the trunk. A book? I had brought none. I usually take along a book, but not that day. I checked the freeway for anything. It had been cleaned recently. I stood at the side of the freeway waving my hand, hoping someone would stop. But who would, on a busy freeway at twenty minutes to eight in the morning? And then the thought struck me: Why not ask God for help? I closed my eyes and offered up a petition for help. When I opened my eyes, an old car was moving onto the shoulder.

"I need a bumper jack," I said. The driver opened his trunk and pulled out a jack. It fit my bumper (a miracle in itself) and soon the flat was off. He was in a hurry, so I only used three lug nuts to hold the spare on. He was practically on his way as I threw his jack into his trunk. As I turned toward my car, I saw, to my horror, that the spare tire was as flat as a pancake! Two flat tires and time was running out. Once more I asked the Lord for help. When I opened my eyes there came a highway patrol car with its lights flashing. "Having trouble, young man?" the officer inquired.

"I surely am," and I told him my sad story.

"You are in trouble, aren't you?" And he laughed.

"And what is worse," I said, "There are a hundred medical students waiting at the White Hospital to whom I am to give a lecture in ten minutes!"

He thought for a moment and then asked, "When does your lecture end?"

"At nine," I replied.

"I tell you what, let's put the flat in my trunk. I'll take you to the lecture hall. While you're lecturing, I'll get the flat fixed, and then pick you up at nine, and bring you back here."

And that is what he did. God has a thousand ways to answer prayer that we can never think of. And to this day I ask myself, "Was the one who helped me a patrolman or was he an angel in a patrolman's uniform?"

Mervyn G. Hardinge, LLUSM class of 1942, also has a DrPH degree. He taught not only in LLUSM but also in LLUSPH, where he served as founding dean from 1967 to 1976. In 1967 he was named LLUSM Alumni Association Alumnus of the Year, and in 1997 he was named LLU Alumnus of the Year. He resides in Brewster, Washington.

August 22

The LORD bless you and keep you; the LORD make his face to shine upon you, and be gracious to you; the LORD lift up his countenance upon you, and give you peace. Numbers 6:24-26, NRSV

Let me share with you the story of a patient whose illness and recovery I ponder to this day. Mr. Hill was a healthy 54-year-old who developed fever, malaise, and headache. He thought he had the flu, but after he grew more ill, he came to the emergency department and was admitted with fever and confusion. Within a day or two, he was comatose and showed evidence of acute liver failure.

Each day, a group of us would visit him on rounds—a caring and hopeful team of students, residents, nurses, and respiratory therapists. Day after day, we reviewed Mr. Hill's laboratory tests, microbiology results, and a myriad of scans. A specific diagnosis eluded us. We applied ourselves to assuring his comfort and providing supportive care; but, sadly, with each passing day he appeared to slip further away.

I have always preferred to hold teaching rounds at the bedside. I would take Mr. Hill's hand in mine and tell him who I was and what we were doing at his bedside. I had no idea whether he could hear or sense us.

One day, without preamble, and much to our amazement, Mr. Hill opened his eyes and gazed at me intently for what seemed an eternity. A tentative smile changed his appearance dramatically. From that moment on, he improved each day and was discharged from the hospital within a week.

Although he had no lung problems, I asked him if he would see me in my pulmonary clinic in a few weeks. He said he would, and kept his word. When I saw him, he reported that he felt well and had returned to work. During the visit, we made a connection; and I asked him if he would mind seeing me again in six months. He readily agreed and six months later returned.

He told me he still felt well and wanted to share something important with me—his only recollection of his hospital stay. He explained that he was a man of strong Christian faith. He remembered clearly the day he "awoke" in the medical intensive care unit. He recalled me at his bedside—holding his hand and surrounded by a halo of light. He said that he saw the face of Jesus in mine and knew that he was healed.

You should know that I am Jewish. I think of myself as a spiritual individual, but Mr. Hill's experience was beyond my understanding and my system of belief. Mr. Hill thanked me for all our team had done. I told him that it was I who should be thanking him for reminding me of the power each of us has to heal by the reassuring sound of our voices, the comfort of our touch, and the force of our spirit—which is in our hearts.

The God I believe in is incorporeal. On most days I know that Mr. Hill's experience was a delusion brought about by his illness. And yet . . . ?

I believe that to be made in God's image means that the Spirit of holiness is within each of us. Perhaps that is what Mr. Hill saw that morning long ago in the medical intensive care unit. I pray that other patients will recognize that Spirit in all who work in a medical setting.

Philip M. Gold is professor in LLUSM department of medicine and is head of division of pulmonary and critical care medicine. He served as interim chair of LLUSM department of medicine in 2008. He and his wife, Roberta, have three children and six grandchildren. August 22 is the date of their wedding anniversary.

August 23

For if there be first a willing mind, it is accepted according to that a man hath, and not according to that he hath not. 2 Corinthians 8:12, KJV

We all found our way to the medical ward at Riverside General Hospital in Riverside, California. We were second-year students, feeling both proud and awkward in our barely used white coats. Nurses directed us to a small conference room containing a blackboard, an x-ray view box, chairs, and a slight old man with a thin mustache and a carefully pressed, but not new, suit.

He greeted us, speaking carefully and softly. "I'm Dr. Macpherson," he said; but his name held little significance to us then, since he was long retired. "Today," he said, "we will be learning to examine the chest. God has given us special senses and powers of observation and intelligence to interpret the information that we acquire through a careful examination. Let us pray that He guides us in learning and applying these skills."

He then led us from the conference room to a patient's bedside. He quietly introduced us to the patient, who, it soon became obvious, he had previously befriended. He then took a stethoscope from his coat pocket and carefully auscultated the chest—demonstrating to us the proper techniques of listening, using the bell and diaphragm. Having obtained the patient's permission, he asked each of us to listen and then describe what we had heard: rales. He then inquired if we heard sounds in all parts of the chest. Most of us were so focused on listening for sounds that we missed their absence.

He redirected us to a lung base so that we could listen again for absent sounds. With percussion, he outlined the area of dullness and then outlined it with colored marker. He percussed the contralateral chest and marked the diaphragm for comparison. He asked us to remember these markings, then thanked the patient for his kind assistance in teaching the young doctors, and led us back to the conference room. Here he pulled chest x-rays from their folder, placed them on the view box, and then pointed out to us the patient's basilar effusion and pulmonary congestion.

That afternoon, we discovered our professor had carefully selected and befriended several patients with different pathologies, reviewed each chart, examined each x-ray, and examined each patient in preparation for our instruction and his direction and refinement of our clumsy first attempts at chest examination. Dr. Macpherson allowed us each to feel that we were becoming skilled in physical diagnosis. Now, after many years as a medical school professor, I can appreciate the hours he spent preparing the patients, and organizing the medical records and the x-ray studies for this most memorable moment of instruction.

Walter E. Macpherson, LLUSM class of 1924, demonstrated that God has given us His gifts for helping our patients. He exemplified the highest ideals of medical education in their most elegant form. I often remember that particular day when I'm teaching medical students and house staff, and I pray that I can teach them as clearly and as well as Dr. Macpherson.

George T. Simpson, LLUSM class of 1973-A, is an otolaryngologist and a surgeon in Buffalo, New York. He also has an MPH degree. August 23 is his father's birthday.

August 24

For the LORD giveth wisdom: out of his mouth cometh knowledge and understanding. . . . Then shalt thou understand righteousness, and judgment, and equity; yea, every good path. When wisdom entereth into thine heart, and knowledge is pleasant unto thy soul. Proverbs 2:6, 9-10, KJV

The wisdom of God has been revealed to humankind through His Word, His creation, His messengers, and ultimately through His Son, Jesus Christ. It is His wisdom that has directed my path and guided me along the way. I am constantly reminded of those who have gone before me, blazing uncharted trails of life with the flaming sword of God's truth.

Even after thirty years of practicing medicine, I am overwhelmed with a sense of gratitude to the faithful men and women who have invested their lives in my dream of becoming a physician. I am indebted to those who shared their wisdom, which has enabled me to build a strong foundation for my faith and practice.

As I reflect on my medical education, there are several people who left a lasting mark on my life. These individuals exhibited faith and a commitment to Christ's ministry of healing. Among these is Chauncy Smith, LLUSM class of 1947. While attending medical school at Loma Linda University, I worked as a phlebotomist. In the early morning hours, I remember seeing Dr. Smith—sharply dressed and diligently making his daily rounds.

Another influence on me was Dr. Wil Alexander, with whom I first became acquainted while doing my undergraduate studies at Andrews University in Berrien Springs, Michigan. He exemplified a disciplined life through exercise, a practice that encouraged me to maintain a healthy lifestyle. Dr. Alexander remained disciplined even when he relocated to Loma Linda University.

Another mentor, Carrol Small, LLUSM class of 1934, my pathology teacher, would often give words of wisdom and encouragement while he lectured. He knew the pressures that physicians faced and the negative effect these pressures could have on the home and marriage. Dr. Small attributed his lack of stress in his home to his loving wife.

Two great religion professors strengthened my religious foundation. Jack Provonsha, LLUSM class of 1953-A, taught religion in a way that appealed to reason and understanding, and that challenged us to think for ourselves. Through his enthusiasm and passion, Dr. Graham Maxwell motivated students to dig deeper into God's Word.

Nothing could comfort an audience of young, insecure first-year students more than those role models who demonstrated kindness and a gentle spirit. I remember Walter H. Roberts, LLUSM class of 1939; W. Holmes Taylor, LLUSM class of 1932; and William Wagner, LLUSM class of 1944-B, in the anatomy department. These individuals invested time, patience, and kindness. Gordon Hadley, LLUSM class of 1944-B, dean of LLUSM, devoted hours of his personal time and attention to assure our success.

Time and space do not permit me to mention all of my recollections of the wise sages who walked the halls of Loma Linda University Medical Center. During this special anniversary of our alma mater, I pay tribute to the wisdom of these pioneers. By incorporating the physical, mental, and spiritual components of the healing ministry of Christ, these individuals not only prepared us academically; but they also passed on their words, deeds and character traits as a legacy built on God's wisdom.

Gideon G. Lewis, LLUSM class of 1975, is a family practitioner in Winter Park, Florida. August 24 is his birthday.

August 25

Dear friends, let us love one another, for love comes from God. Everyone who loves has been born of God and knows God. 1 John 4:7, NIV

"Unconditional positive regard." Dr. Leonard Werner, senior associate dean for medical student education for LLUSM, repeatedly said this phrase during the years he taught us. Not until halfway through my first year in rural family practice did I fully understand the value of "unconditional positive regard."

I was exhausted, having been up all night; and at the end of a long office day, I wanted to go home. But my nurse had one more patient I really needed to see: the schedule listed a patient, who was not known to me, with a chief complaint of "positive pregnancy test—wants to terminate."

I scolded my nurse, "Why are you putting her in my schedule? I can't and won't 'help' her with this. I won't even tell her where she can get 'help.' You know I don't agree with this!" Filled with righteous indignation, my mind was made up that I would let the patient know that this "problem" was something I did not believe in, and that I would not help her.

I was busy, tired, and had let myself be filled with condemnation. Then, Dr. Werner's voice went off inside my head: "unconditional positive regard." Must I maintain positive regard, even though I strongly disagreed with her plan? I was irritated and enjoying my righteous indignation. Nevertheless, I prayed. I asked God to come with me and guide me.

The patient was very matter-of-fact in her response to the usual question, "What brings you in?" She was pregnant, it was an accident, her husband did not even know, and she did not want to have the baby.

The next thing to happen was because of my prayer, because God was at work in the room. Instead of launching into my beliefs and my refusal to help her, I asked, "Why?"

"I can't do it."

"Can't do what?"

"Have another baby."

"Why?"

She had had terrible postpartum depression after the birth of her previous child and struggled with suicidal thoughts; she had not been a good mother or a good wife. She was afraid of even worse depression this time, and she still struggled with those feelings on a day-to-day basis. We talked for a long time. Eventually, she agreed to tell her husband; he agreed to work less and help her through this situation. We made medication adjustments, and she started counseling.

She did not have a procedure; she had a beautiful baby girl.

I am periodically reminded by a happy, beautiful, curly-haired 5-year-old of the importance of letting God love others through you. I clearly did not have it in me to do this on my own. First John 4:7 bids us to "love one another, for love comes from God." Without Christian training to show unconditional positive regard, I might not have invited God to guide me in that exam room. I am afraid to think of the outcome if I had walked in without that training.

Rick Marden, LLUSM class of 1999, is a rural family practitioner in Peru, Maine, where he resides with his wife and three daughters.

237

August 26

But encourage one another daily, as long as it is called Today, so that none of you may be hardened by sin's deceitfulness. We have come to share in Christ if we hold firmly till the end the confidence we had at first. Hebrews 3:13-14, NIV

With our first year of medical school behind us, my friends and I have been asking ourselves how we've been changed. The most obvious change is, of course, our knowledge of the human body. But an experience like medical school changes a person in much deeper ways. When we arrived here, we were regularly warned that, if we weren't careful, many of us would become cynical. We would forget our original spiritual reasons for coming to medical school.

As usual, I doubted that medical school could change me in such a way. But upon reflection, I am surprised by what I see. I think that the demands our coursework put on us can encourage a great degree of selfishness to grow. I have seen this in myself. Free time, when I wasn't studying, became so valuable to me that I would rarely think of seeking the Lord or of finding ways to serve others.

Instead, free time came to mean watching movies or occasionally exercising. I also have thought less about my original ideals than I did at the beginning of the year. Instead of dreaming of a future in missions, I've begun to dream of a higher rank in my class or the possibility of a more competitive residency.

When I told my friends these things, I also realized that, if it weren't for the various ministries I'm involved with, things could have been much worse. The accountability and edification I have found in our weekly Christian Medical and Dental Association meetings and Bible studies have been invaluable. Through those relationships, I've been given the opportunity to honestly share struggles, to seek the counsel of my colleagues and their prayers. Having a wonderful church family has also been very important.

Another conversation I've had with some of my classmates is a "what if" dialogue. We've pondered whether we would have gone to some of the other schools we applied to had we been accepted to them. And there was a time when I would have said "yes," and that if I had gotten into Harvard University in Cambridge, Massachusetts, or the Mayo Clinic in Rochester, Minnesota, then I would have gone there. But looking back on this year, and considering things with the eternal perspective of the importance of my soul, I would have to now say "no."

So, in spite of coming from a faith background other than Seventh-day Adventism, I have to say that this denomination has founded and nourished an institution where a Christian can become a doctor. This is a place where Christians can be affirmed and encouraged in their faith in Jesus Christ. For this fact, I am very thankful to my Seventh-day Adventist brothers and sisters.

Finally, I would say, to any Christian entering medical school, do not underestimate the trials that await you. Temptations that once may have looked dull because of the vibrancy of your spiritual life may gain a new and enticing luster. But if you can find fellow believers with whom to be open and honest, with whom to pray, and with whom to succeed and fail, you will make it through and be closer to God than when you began.

Matt Perkins, LLUSM class of 2011, is from Battle Ground, Washington. He attended Whitworth College in Spokane, Washington, and Ashbury Theological Seminary in Wilmore, Kentucky. He served as a youth pastor at a Methodist church in Battle Ground, Washington.

Blessed are the poor in spirit: for theirs is the kingdom of heaven. Matthew 5:3, KJV

"Is God good to you today?" The questioner was my friend Donald J. Hawecker, an amputee. In September 2000, at age 34, Donald had been struck by a truck while riding his bicycle. Rushed to a local hospital, Donald sustained injuries that required amputation of his left arm and leg, as well as multiple other surgeries. Fourteen pints of blood and three weeks later he regained consciousness. He remained hospitalized for more than six months. Following prolonged rehabilitation, Donald joined LLU Drayson Center's Team PossAbilities program. Currently, he spends several days a week volunteering in that program—buzzing around in his motorized wheelchair, assisting others, and inspiring all he meets with his sparkling enthusiasm for life.

Benedictus benedicat! This Latin prayer asks that the Blessed One may give a blessing. Sometimes expressed as a brief grace before partaking of a meal, this supplication reminds us of the Source of all blessings, the Giver of all goodness. Truly, we are blessed! Every new day is a gift from God. Life itself, health, strength, seeing the beauty of the world around us, hearing its sounds, feeling its touch—we are richly blessed beyond whatever we can imagine.

"To be blessed" means "to be favored by God." In the Torah, God promised Abraham that he would be blessed, and, in turn, would be a blessing to others (Genesis 12:1-2). In the opening verse of the Beatitudes in the Sermon on the Mount, quoted in the verse for this day, in addition to the poor in spirit, Jesus blessed those that mourn, the meek, those who hunger and thirst after righteousness, the merciful, the pure in heart: all of us who would be the children of God.

Despite his formidable limitations and infirmities, Donald spends much of each day not only pausing to praise the Lord for His manifold blessings of life, health, being on this earth; but also sharing these blessings with family and friends. Can we do less?

Lawrence D. Longo, LLUSM class of 1954, is distinguished professor in LLUSM departments of gynecology and obstetrics and of basic sciences, division of physiology; and is director of LLUSM Center for Perinatal Biology. He was LLUSM Alumni Association 1974 Alumnus of the Year, and received the LLU Distinguished Service Award in 1994. August 27 is Donald's birthday.

August 28

I will be glad and rejoice in your love, for you saw my affliction and knew the anguish of my soul. Psalm 31:7, NIV

It is never easy for a physician to lose a patient. We are trained to fix and cure and make people better. When a patient dies, we often feel a great sense of professional, as well as personal, failure. When I started doing palliative medicine, it helped me understand that our job goes far beyond just getting patients physically better.

While it may be that nothing we can do will cure someone's metastatic cancer or reverse a person's heart failure, there is much we can do to aid in spiritual and emotional healing, even when a patient is dying. And they often have more to offer us than we could ever imagine. Daniel was one such patient.

Daniel was only in his twenties when he first came into my office. His family brought him to me in a wheelchair, because he was too weak to make the walk. Daniel had been having abdominal pain and losing weight. But since he didn't have insurance, he ended up being seen in different emergency departments.

When I met him, he had been told that widely spread cancer had been found throughout his abdomen and chest. He was now waiting for biopsy results. I knew that no matter what type of cancer the biopsy revealed, Daniel's prognosis was not good. He had an appointment with the oncologist the following week to discuss his results and possible treatment options.

Daniel and his family wanted advice on how to proceed. I encouraged them to ask the oncologist what the goals of chemo would be—was it for cure or just to buy time? And how much time and at what cost? What would the side effects be? Did Daniel want to spend what might be his last few weeks or months of life in a hospital, and likely an intensive care unit, with little chance of getting better? Or, did he want to be at home with family?

When I saw him back in clinic a few weeks later, Daniel informed me that he had metastatic mesothelioma. This is not a common cancer, especially in someone so young. He had talked to his oncologist about benefits versus burdens of treatment and decided that pursuing chemo was not what he wanted to do with the little time he had left. Daniel decided to go home with hospice and enjoy being with his family. But he did not go home to die; he had some more living to do first!

Daniel had long been a fan of the Los Angeles Angels of Anaheim baseball team. His hospice team helped arrange to get him tickets to their game and meet all the players. I have a picture of Daniel wearing a jersey that all the Angels signed for him. Daniel was also a fan of Knott's Berry Farm, an amusement park in California. He wanted to spend a day there with his family. The one concern we had were the signs, prominently displayed, that warn: "If you have neck or back problems, are pregnant, or have other serious medical conditions, you should avoid this ride." Daniel looked ill, so I gave him a prescription that read: "This patient may go on any and all rides that he desires." He had a great time!

Daniel died a few weeks later. He was at home, comfortable, and surrounded by those who loved him most. It could have ended very differently. I'm glad it didn't.

Gina Jervey Mohr, LLUSM class of 1996, is assistant professor in LLUSM department of family medicine. In 2006, she received the LLUMC Physician Whole-Person Care Award. She and her husband, Lance, LLUSM class of 1996, live in Colton, California. Daniel was born on August 28.

August 29

He that overcometh, the same shall be clothed in white raiment; and I will not blot out his name out of the book of life, but I will confess his name before my Father, and before his angels. Revelation 3:5, KJV

In the years after World War II, many medical students spent their summers working. Some joined the U.S. Forest Service fire crews. A young man from Maine was a member of such a fire crew in the northern Sierra Nevada mountains. A sad event occurred during one of these forest fires. After placing a break around a fire, the crew moved in to take down trees, still showering sparks from their crowns. A loose branch (called a widow maker) fell, striking the medical student on his helmet and causing a thoracic spine fracture. He was evacuated first to Reno, Nevada, then to the White Memorial Hospital (now White Memorial Medical Center) in Los Angeles, California.

There, the neurosurgeon was unable to reverse the damage to his spinal cord, and he remained a paraplegic for the rest of his life. He returned to medical school in a wheelchair, was highest academically in his class for the remaining three years, and became our "permanent" class president, who worked to overcome the "cutthroat" culture. He arranged for old exams to be placed in the library for all to review, rather than being available only to a select few in a clique. He participated in small-group study sessions with those classmates who were struggling academically.

His classmates gave him a motorized wheel chair as a graduation present. He did a rotating internship at the White; and, during his obstetrics rotation, he was kidded about putting the forceps on and then putting his wheel chair in reverse! He completed a pathology residency and became the lab director at Rancho Los Amigos Hospital (now Rancho Los Amigos National Rehabilitation Center), in Downey, California—the rehabilitation hospital for a very large group of polio patients on respirators. He also worked with the pathology group at the Santa Fe Railroad Hospital in Boyle Heights, California.

After he became the medical director of Rancho Los Amigos, he added a spinal injury program, just as the polio patient population dwindled. He remained optimistic that new research would lead to an eventual cure for spinal injuries such as his. His good humor and positive outlook remain an inspiration to his classmates.

His deteriorating bowel function resulted in a series of operations that left him with an ileostomy. After his wife died from cancer, and shortly before he died, he called a classmate with cancer to advise him and to help his classmate learn how to care for his colostomy.

A life such as this provides an example of someone who has overcome difficulties while keeping his eyes focused on the goal. Let us keep our eyes focused on Jesus and remain overcomers to the end.

Rodney Willard, LLUSM class of 1956, is emeritus associate professor in LLUSM department of pathology and human anatomy. He was president of the Walter E. Macpherson Society from 2001 to 2002 and was an LLUSM Alumni Association 2001 Honored Alumnus.

August 30

Let not then your good be evil spoken of. Romans 14:16, KJV

Sometimes, if we are not alert to the implications, in our efforts to do good, we may inadvertently precipitate harm.

Perhaps I should have seen it coming, but there were reasons enough to distract me; and the tragedy caught me unaware. For one thing, I was a foreigner practicing medicine in a culture and language of which I was woefully unfamiliar and had only limited communication ability. For another, our recently completed mission hospital had just opened its doors to the community, and we were hurting for patients. To our advantage was the fact we were the newest and largest of the medical facilities in the valley, and being situated on the side of a mountain made our presence obvious to all.

The family of Mrs. T contacted us, requesting her transfer to our care. She was elderly and had fallen at home some weeks earlier, fracturing her hip. She was now languishing in a small hospital in the valley where "nothing was being done for her." In fact, the family had been told she would not likely survive. She was admitted to our hospital; and, in addition to her fracture, she was found to be suffering an advanced thyrotoxic state—causing her hip surgery to be postponed. However, she responded well to therapy and within a relatively short time underwent the successful pinning of her hip.

From the day of his wife's admission, Mr. T—with obvious anxiety—persisted in asking, "When is she going to die?" The repeated query was in spite of my repeated explanations and assurances to the contrary. As I had occasion to see Mr. T frequently, I observed a squamous cell carcinoma of some size on the side of his nose, and I stressed repeatedly the need for surgical intervention. He seemed unconcerned about the lesion on his nose and refused to be convinced his wife wasn't going to die soon.

I gave little thought to his odd behavior, ascribing it to ignorance or misunderstanding; but never once did I suspect the seeds of misfortune that were beginning to sprout. As Mrs. T had made a full recovery and did well in rehabilitation, she was discharged to go home, to be followed up as an outpatient. Three days later, a lifeless body was found half-hidden beneath the trees up on the mountain behind our hospital. Mr. T had committed suicide.

What were the dynamics of this tragedy, of this family? What was so intolerable to this man that he despaired of life? In some way, did the recovery of his wife dash his hopes? Did my informing him of his need for surgery play a part? Or was it simply that I failed to recognize sufficiently the symptoms of mental illness?

From this experience, I learned my professional efforts involve much more than the patient alone; they include the patient's family and culture. Sometimes our efforts to do good may precipitate unforeseen consequences.

Delmar Johnson, LLUSM class of 1954, is a surgeon in Loma Linda, California. He and his wife, Thelma, spent twenty-five years as missionaries in Japan and Singapore.

And this I pray, that your love may abound yet more and more in knowledge and in all judgment. Philippians 1:9, KJV

I came to Loma Linda, California, in 1942 from a very conservative Seventh-day Adventist home, where I was taught that God is love. Although He loved me, He and His angels were watching me very closely; and any slight error on my part would separate me from Him and result in eventual punishment. Allow me to share some of the things I've learned in the years since then:

First, God has helped me to understand that He didn't make rules to entrap me but for my benefit. If I stray, He is always there drawing me back and hoping I will return to Him.

Second, I have learned that we are each given a mix of heredity and experience. With these gifts, good or bad, we must make of life what we can. Life is full of ordinary days with no one to pat us on the back, no one to praise us, and no one to say how brave and noble we are. How we live these ordinary days is as important as our big moments. It is better to choose the positive, to believe in people, to give, to share and to make the most of every ordinary day. The important things of life depend on my attitude. If I look only to the past and have no plans, then I am old, even if only 25 years of age. But if I have plans and dreams, if I have love and family and friends, then I am young at any age.

Third, I have found that material things can be attractive, but that "things" are way down the list in importance.

I had this precept impressed on my mind forever one Tuesday morning in 1960. I was about halfway through serving my sixteen years in Africa, and a political revolution was in full swing. My family was already safe in another country, and I had been ordered by the United States government and the church to leave that day. As I drove away, I stopped on the hill across from Songa Mission and looked back at the hospital and my home, where almost everything I owned in it was being left to the whims of the rebels. Was it hard to leave my "things"? No, it was easy! The safety and security of my family were more important than anything!

I remember and share the thoughts of an old pastor in Africa, who attended a meeting where someone was promoting a return to his people's old animistic, fear-filled ways. He rose and said: "I once lived in that dark valley. But I have come up on the mountain top and will never go back down into that valley of fear." Those words spoke volumes and made me thankful I was raised in the sunshine of God's love—and He is still calling me to higher levels.

Marlowe H. Schaffner, LLUSM class of 1946, is a specialist in emergency medicine. He was LLUSM Alumni Association president from 1987 to 1988 and was an LLUSM Alumni Association 1962 Honored Alumnus. He resides in Canyon Lake, California.

September 1

Yea, though I walk through the valley of the shadow of death, I will fear no evil;
For You are with me; Your rod and Your staff, they comfort me. Psalm 23:4,
NKJV

Complicated ethical decisions are made daily in the field of medicine. But having to deal with my personal ethical dilemma was a new challenge. Shortly after becoming pregnant with twins, I, like many other soon-to-be moms, was faced with my first ethical decision. Should I have a blood test to screen my children for genetic diseases? Although I knew I would not terminate my pregnancy if the test was positive, I wanted to be informed. My screen was abnormal.

Our physician suggested I have an amniocentesis. My husband and I decided against it because it could potentially risk the life of both twins, another ethical decision. At nearly twenty-four-weeks gestation, the bombshell was dropped. The smaller twin was experiencing inconsistent blood flow. The obstetrician told us that it was unclear when the blood flow would stop.

This was the biggest ethical decision of all. Should we deliver the twins now, thus facing the complications of 23-week-old twins? (As a pediatrician, I know what complications premature children experience, a fact that made the decision even harder.) Should we hope and pray for each week we get and try to make it to twenty-eight weeks, thus increasing their chances of survival? How do you choose to risk the life of one twin to save the other? That was the choice we had. Baby B was doing fine, but Baby A had problems.

After much, much prayer we decided to wait till twenty-eight weeks. On the day of my final obstetrics visit prior to the scheduled delivery of the twins, we learned that Baby A had died. We were floored, but we had prayed. We just knew God would answer our prayers. There were family, friends, and friends of family and even friends of friends literally around the world praying for us. Why did He choose to save only one child instead of both?

Now, almost three years later, here is what I know. God was there the whole time. He helped us make the hardest decision of our lives. He stood there and dried our tears. He saved our now living son and delivered him in perfect health, although six weeks early. He allowed us to be the parents of twin sons in heaven; so while we will not get to see our son Eric grow up on Earth, we will see him grow in Heaven. We still don't know why he died, but we do know Who held our hands through the toughest time in our lives. We know that when Jesus returns, we will all be reunited. Sometimes, when our son Gabriel is playing, I long to see both of my boys together, but the greatest assurance is that in heaven I will, FOREVER. Thank you, Lord, for holding all of our hands and giving us comfort THROUGH IT ALL.

Kiesha Fraser Doh, LLUSM class of 2001, is a pediatrician in Cape Charles, Virginia, where she lives with her husband and son. September 1 was the birth and death date of Eric Michael Doh.

When they had crossed, Elijah said to Elisha, "Tell me, what can I do for you before I am taken from you?" "Let me inherit a double portion of your spirit," Elisha replied. 2 Kings 2:9, NIV

Having nursed my husband through a long, difficult, and lingering illness, I'm comforted by the story of Elisha. It's puzzling on the face of it. His predecessor, Elijah, is a colorful and powerful man of God who was translated to heaven by a whirlwind in a chariot of fire. As humble Elisha picks up Elijah's mantle, his only request of the great prophet is for a double portion of his spirit.

So what happened? Was his prayer answered? Elisha lived a pretty amazing life, but there were no Mt. Carmels, no blaze of glory, and no translation at the end. These two men could not have been more different. Elijah suddenly appeared—no family mentioned, just that he was a Tishbite. He probably resembled John the Baptist: coarse clothing, hair wild from days of travel, and suddenly standing before astonished King Ahab. Elisha, on the other hand, came from a wealthy family, lived in the city, and dressed appropriately. Still, he left everything to follow Elijah.

While Elijah's life was filled with dramatic messages of condemnation and judgment, Elisha—a gentle, kind man—became a prophet of peace. Following his prayers, bitter waters became sweet, a dropped ax head floated, and poisonous food became safe. Once, he even restored a dead boy to life, just as Elijah had once done.

Besides healing Naaman's leprosy, perhaps his most notable miracles occurred at the city of Dothan. With a hostile army surrounding the city, Elisha prayed for God to open his fearful servant's eyes to see the much larger army of angels guarding the city. When the hostile army entered the city, and following an answer to Elisha's prayer, they all became blind. Telling them they had the wrong city, Elisha led them to another, where their eyes opened to a lavish feast. The war was over.

But for me, Elisha's most significant experience came at the end of his life. We're told that the Lord permitted a lingering illness to afflict him. During the long hours of weakness, misery, and suffering, his faith took hold of the promises of God. He sensed around him heavenly messengers of comfort and peace, according to Ellen G. White's book, *Prophets and Kings*, pages 263 and 264. Elisha did not complain. He did not become depressed and ask God to let him die. His double portion of the Holy Spirit enabled his faith to endure to the end.

Sometimes we fail to recognize and appreciate the special grace and strength of the suffering among us. Elijah's stories are thrilling, but we can also draw strength and inspiration from Elisha's. It's often the ones who don't get well, lose their children, or live with serious handicaps who end up receiving double portions of grace from above. Paul expresses it well in Philippians 1:19 (KJV), "I know that this shall turn to my salvation through your prayer, and the supply of the Spirit of Jesus Christ."

Aileen Ludington, LLUSM class of 1948, is an anesthesiologist residing in Paradise, California. She was an LLUSM Alumni Association 2002 Honored Alumna.

September 3

One of his disciples said to him, "Lord, teach us to pray, just as John taught his disciples." Luke 11:1, NIV

In September 2006, as part of my LLU duties, I attended a site review of a facility in the Sierra Nevada mountains above Bishop, California, at an altitude of 12,470 feet, where breathing is difficult. Returning to Loma Linda, I was extremely fatigued, had a pronounced hyperacuity to odors, and had a wheezing sound coming from my right lung. Tests revealed two tumors within my brain, and my right lung was found to be full of numerous masses. Upon biopsy, I was diagnosed with melanoma, stage IV. A physician friend gave me thirty days to live. Another friend said that only 3 percent of people with my cancer live three years post-diagnosis, and that that was the best I could reasonably hope for.

I knew they were going to be wrong about these prognoses. After all, God was in heaven. He wouldn't let me die if only I would do my part and fight to survive. On the advice of my physician, we chose the most aggressive path to defeat this disease. Accordingly, my two brain tumors were removed during a ten-hour procedure; and my right lung was removed by my friend Leonard Bailey, LLUSM class of 1969, in an equally long and difficult procedure.

Dr. Bailey came to me as I was awakening after the surgery and explained that he felt the presence of Jesus with him throughout the procedure. He stated that they had nearly lost me several times due to complications where the exceptionally large tumor was wrapped around and in my pulmonary artery but that he was guided by our Lord.

Many people asked me about my relationship with God at this time. Perhaps the strangest question was, "Was I angry with God?" For me this was and continues to be the largest enigma I experienced. Why would one be angry with God? How could I possibly hold anger against Jesus, who died for my sins?

However, it was the later depression of thinking that my life would soon be over that affected me the most. The possibility that I would not be able to hold my wife or see my beautiful daughters grow further into adulthood took its terrible toll. After the successful surgeries, this depression became overwhelming; and I decided to stop eating and let go.

My wife caught on to this ridiculous plan and stopped it. She told me she loved me and would not let me die. She made me promise to start eating. God had given life to me, so now I needed to fight to keep it. I promised and had my first meal in several weeks. During this "recovery" period, I prayed to God every conscious minute. I prayed that he would forgive my foolish initial decision and help me survive.

I remembered that when asked by the disciples to "teach us [how] to pray" (Luke 11:1, NIV) Jesus answered by teaching them the Lord's Prayer. I have recited this prayer over and over, and to this day I repeat it silently to myself during waking hours.

I survived my cancer and am now four years in remission as of September 2008. Now I am among the 3 percent of melanoma survivors. I thank all those at LLU who have prayed so deeply and movingly for me. It continues to be an extremely humbling experience. Why God answered our prayers I will never know. All I can say is that prayer is a very powerful and real phenomenon. Use it. Keep using it! Never, never give up! We may never know when it will work, but we should be greatly satisfied to know and understand that it does work.

Michael Kirby is professor in LLUSM department of pathology and human anatomy. He is course director for neuroscience at LLUSM. He received a PhD degree in neuroscience from University of California, Riverside, in 1984.

September 4

The Lord is compassionate and gracious, slow to anger, abounding in love. He will not always accuse, nor will he harbor his anger forever; he does not treat us as our sins deserve or repay us according to our iniquities. . . . As a father has compassion on his children, so the Lord has compassion on those who fear him; for he knows how we are formed, he remembers that we are dust. Psalm 103:8-10, 13-14, NIV

I was a first-year medical student taking my last battery of tests before Christmas break. Not only was this test cycle brutal, because it was the only thing impeding me from going home for Christmas break, but it was also brutal for other reasons. The cycle covered the areas of respiratory physiology, immunology, anatomy of the abdomen and gastrointestinal tract, biochemistry, patient diagnosis, and cardiac auscultation.

Anatomy was the first test, and I really wanted to start the week off strong; so I hit the books. On examination day, I opened the test up, and, to my surprise, I realized that only half dealt with abdominal questions. The rest of the questions dealt with the larynx and the neck. "Uh oh," I said in my head, as I attempted to complete the test. I finished the test and walked home, confident that I had passed.

Surprisingly, the anatomy department had our grades ready that night, and I apprehensively went to check them. I was expecting either a low B or a high C, because before, even when I felt that I didn't do well, the Lord had always helped me come through with an acceptable grade. So I logged onto the Internet and checked my grade. I failed the test with flying colors, with a grade of 61 percent. I FAILED A TEST!

How could I ever be a good doctor and fail a test in medical school? I had already been studying all day for my upcoming immunology test, and the combined stresses of no sleep, hard studying, and a failed test took its toll on me . . . tears started to fall. Yes, I—a 6'5" tall man—started to cry. I couldn't even fake my wife into thinking it was my allergies.

Failure was the worst possible thing that could happen to me. Most medical students aren't used to failure; they are accustomed to being at the very top of their class . . . with ease. But I learned from this situation that it is important to differentiate between having a failure and being a failure. I know that I am not alone in saying that my walk with God can be summarized as a continuous series of failures. I try and try and try to be the upstanding Christian man that Christ would have me to be, but often my efforts fail.

I praise the Lord, though, that the Bible gives me hope. I praise the Lord that I tend to come down on myself harder for my failures than Christ does. I praise the Lord that He does not equate our value with our failures. Remember that Jesus knows that we are but dust; He knows how fragile we are, and He certainly knows the struggles we deal with every day. His Word says that as far as the east is from the west, that is how far He has removed our transgressions from us. That means that we don't have to fail anymore! We don't have to continually give into the temptation that so easily besets us. When we truly give all of our mess to Christ, our failures turn into successes. Never forget that we serve a loving and forgiving God, Who is slow to anger and Who understands our failures. When we fall, He is there to catch us.

Jaysson Brooks, LLUSM class of 2011—for which he was freshman class web coordinator—was born and reared in Maryland and attended Takoma Academy in Takoma Park, Maryland, where he met his future wife, Brittany, LLUSM class of 2011. He is a deferred mission appointee. September 4 is his birthday.

247

September 5

I will instruct thee and teach thee in the way which thou shalt go: I will guide thee with mine eye. Psalm 32:8, KJV

A series of miracles, beginning many years before, continues to be supplemented to this day. To just touch on some of the earliest ones will show their importance to me and to my family.

Miracle Number One: My parents were sent to Africa as missionaries in 1911, before any of their four sons were born. But malaria and its complications nearly ended my father's life within a year, and my parents were sent back home. It was a life-saving event. He began a remarkable recovery while on the ship sailing for England.

Number Two: My parents were providentially guided in the choice of ships sailing back to the United States. They sailed on a smaller ship, rather than waiting for a much larger and newer ship, which they would have preferred. Time forbade them from waiting extra days; thus, they avoided the catastrophe of sailing on the *Titanic*.

Number Three: Several years later, after homesteading in Saskatchewan, Canada, my parents accepted positions at the old Battleford Academy in Saskatchewan, where their four children began regular schooling. After serving for three years, they decided to return to the U.S. The difficulties seemed insurmountable with the immigration officials. Then, God opened a way; and the family moved to the state of Washington.

Number Four: My parents were able to obtain teaching certificates in Washington after only one year of college, having had enough college credits at Union College in Lincoln, Nebraska, to qualify them in that short time.

Number Five: The depression of the 1930s threatened to jeopardize my parents hopes of giving their sons a college education, but another miracle took place. Father had learned the broom-making trade while in South Dakota and was able to obtain some old broom-making machinery. He taught us to make brooms. This skill paved the way for our college education at Walla Walla College (now Walla Walla University) in College Place, Washington.

Number Six: Medical school? We were in no way capable of earning that amount of money needed, it seemed. And yet, in the autumn of 1935, my oldest brother, Glenn, enrolled at Loma Linda, and with the financial help of a dedicated spouse and the co-op system, was able to graduate in 1940. My wife of two years was also willing to commit herself to the task of supporting us while I was studying.

Number Seven: I narrowly escaped death in a fearful auto accident, but that is a story in itself.

Number Eight: The day drew near for my first appointment as a medical student at 7:00 a.m., on September 5, 1938. But another miracle was about to occur. It was nearly midnight on September 4 when my wife, Marjorie, went into labor. She was admitted to the hospital and delivered our first child, a precious little girl, at 6:25 a.m. Since then, I have never participated in the birth of a newborn child without being in awe of God's amazing design of the human being. What a Designer! Yes, that day was the most momentous day of my life.

We shall never cease to be grateful for God's guidance during those early times and the many years that have followed. And yes, He fulfilled His promise.

Robert Earl Bolton, LLUSM class of 1943, is a family practitioner in Wenatchee, Washington. September 5 was the day he began medical school and is also the birthday of his first child, Elsie Mae.

September 6

Blessed are those who mourn, for they will be comforted. Matthew 5:4, NIV

She is 28 years old and works at the Nordstrom corporate office in downtown Seattle, Washington. He is 29 years old and engaged in real estate business. They have a beautiful, polite, friendly 4-year-old daughter, who is very excited about her new sister—due to arrive in the summer. My pregnant patient is at twenty-nine-weeks gestation.

I receive the call on a Tuesday morning that she hadn't felt the baby move the previous day, so we bring her in for an "NST" (nonstress test to monitor fetal well-being). We cannot get a heartbeat. I bring in the handheld ultrasound machine to search for a heartbeat but there is none. It is a stillbirth.

It is one of those moments when you are about to relay tragic news and you are struck with the enormity of what you are about to say. I wonder if I can say it without sobbing myself. I try to prepare for the torrent of tears and sadness and "whys." It crosses my mind that I really just want to be a gardener. Through my own tears, I convey the news. We make some calls for the young mother and wait until her husband comes to take her home.

On Wednesday, both parents arrive in the early morning so the mother can begin the misoprostol induction. They are admitted to a room at the far end of a hallway, where a little hanging rainbow marks the room. I check in throughout the day; finally, the next day, about midafternoon, a tiny, nearly perfect little sister is born. The parents did not think they could look at her, but they do. We wrap the baby in a soft blanket, even add a little hat, and they hold her. They tell me that in the last forty hours they have grown so much closer and they have felt loved. They hold her and tell me they feel an unexpected sense of peace.

Their pastor comes back to see them again. Their close friends and divorced parents join in harmony to grieve with them and support them. All the nurses from shifts in the previous thirty-six hours stop by to express their condolences.

I keep thinking I went into obstetrics and gynecology because it is such a happy corner of medicine. But I also realize the sad moments have taught me the most.

Karen Wells, LLUSM class of 1993—for which she was senior class president—is an obstetrician and gynecologist in Kirkland, Washington.

249

September 7

My flesh and my heart may fail, but God is the strength of my heart and my portion forever. Psalm 73:26, NIV

Overwhelmed, anxious, and angry—these are words that described me seventeen years ago. For, you see, my husband had just been arrested for a crime I didn't know he had committed, leaving me a single mother with a young son and a baby on the way. Overnight I went from using an American Express Gold card to being on welfare.

On September 7, 1991, I gave birth to a precious baby girl. On her second day of life, my daughter, Christina, was diagnosed with hypoplastic left heart syndrome—a fatal heart defect. I thought, "This cannot be happening!" God (who I wasn't sure really existed) must be playing a terrible joke on me. Broken-hearted, I watched as Christina was put in an ambulance and taken to Loma Linda University Medical Center, where she was placed on the transplant waiting list. Then, on October 27, Christina received her new heart.

The next few years did not get any easier. I added more words to describe myself—depressed, frantic, and unsure. By the time Christina was three years old, she had gone through heart rejection, endured three massive strokes, and had more sicknesses, hospital stays, and clinic visits than I care to recount. I found myself crying continually and barely able to put one foot in front of the other. I had sunk into the lowest, deepest, darkest pit of my life.

In this pit of despair, Christina's nurse, Helene, became my friend and shared the love of Christ with me. It was in this place that I began to look up and hear the gentle calling of my Lord, Jesus Christ. Everywhere I turned at Loma Linda, people would speak His name. My eyes had been opened and I knew that Jesus Christ was God Almighty Himself. I became beautifully and wonderfully saved! He lifted me out of that miry pit and gently began to restore me. I now had glorious new words to describe myself—love, joy, and peace—the fruits of the Spirit.

Christina grew up. She was amazingly witty and bright. Continually captivating others, she bubbled with joy. She LOVED Jesus. But on March 6, 2001, my 9-year-old daughter passed away.

The next few years proved to be even more difficult. Though I had a perfect peace and could even rejoice in seeing all that God had done, my son, Norman, became angry and sullen. Through Norman's pain, the Lord remained faithful. Today, my 18-year-old son serves the Lord with all of his heart, as the Lord sends him on missions across the globe, helping children in need.

I still look back on those first days and remember Loma Linda with fondness. I can see now how God used the doctors, nurses, and staff to be His hands that lovingly pointed me to the cross. Not only did my daughter receive a heart transplant, but my son and I received beautiful new hearts as well.

Christy Lindsey is the mother of a heart-transplant recipient. She resides in Murrieta, California.

September 8

Before they call I will answer; while they are still speaking I will hear. Isaiah 65:24, NIV

In the mid-1980s, while taking an obstetrics-gynecology call at a large HMO in northern California, I had an unforgettable experience. After delivering a patient, I discovered she had multiple lacerations extending the full length of the vagina that were bleeding profusely.

It was about 1:30 a.m., and I started suturing with a will. The patient was bleeding so heavily that I could hardly see what I was doing. I adjusted the light, got an assistant to suction, and continued to suture as fast as I could. By now I was feeling faint from the long hours, the hot light just behind my back, and the fear that things were getting out of control.

We started giving blood and cross-matched for more. At times, I would pack a large sponge into her vagina to stop the flood while I caught my breath. This was the woman's second child. What would I tell her husband? A hysterectomy wouldn't stop this deluge. I started wishing I had chosen another profession!

About five minutes before 2:00 a.m., I heard the words in my mind, "Have the nurse call your wife to pray for you." Not wanting the staff to think I was "losing it," I prayed in my mind for help and kept on working. At 2:00 a.m. I heard the same command again. This time I obeyed. I also had the nurse call in some extra help. It happened to be Robert Rusche, LLUSM class of 1973-B. We finally got the bleeding stopped around 3:00 a.m. The patient had lost about ten units of blood but went on to make a full recovery.

When my wife was awakened at 2:00 a.m., she immediately called her friend Peggy for more prayer. Peggy and her husband were in a prayer group with us. When my wife called, Peggy was wide awake. "I'm already praying for Gary," she said. "The Lord told me to get up and pray for him, even though I was sure he was getting more sleep than I was."

I was astounded at this news when I got home the next morning. The next time I saw Peggy, I asked her when she had started praying. "Oh, about 1:30," she said. When did she quit? "About 3:00." I was blown away! I had really heard from God. So had Peggy. If I hadn't obeyed the prompting, I would have missed out on a wonderful blessing. Truly, the Scripture is clear: "Before they call, I will answer; while they are still speaking, I will hear."

Gary Watts, LLUSM class of 1976-A, is an obstetrician and gynecologist in Paradise, California. September 8 is the birthday of his wife, Cyndee.

September 9

And I heard a loud voice from the throne saying, "Now the dwelling of God is with men, and he will live with them. They will be his people, and God himself will be with them and be their God. He will wipe every tear from their eyes. There will be no more death or mourning or crying or pain, for the old order of things has passed away." Revelation 21:3-4, NIV

He was a young man in his late twenties who has been admitted to our hospital. Five months prior, he had completed his first marathon at a respectable pace. He was married, had two young children, and was dying in our intensive care unit. He had a tooth extracted earlier in the year, and the socket did not heal well. Further examinations and biopsy revealed the horrible and unexpected news: he had a poorly differentiated carcinoma involving the jaw and surrounding soft tissues.

Chemotherapy was instituted at a local cancer center. Despite aggressive therapy, the cancer continued to spread, causing progressive swelling. It was not unusual for him to become fatigued; and the afternoon he was admitted, he had fallen asleep on the couch. His wife, knowing how tired he was, let him rest and kept the children occupied. Late in the afternoon, she became concerned because he usually did not sleep that long. She tried to rouse him, but he would not awaken.

The cancer had spread to the point that the patient could no longer protect his airway. The combination of pain medication and malignancy extension had reached a critical point, and he had suffered a respiratory arrest. He was quickly resuscitated and placed on ventilator support in the emergency department. Still, he did not awaken. It wasn't clear exactly how long he had been without oxygen.

The family knew of his poor prognosis but did not expect the end would come so soon. He was carefully watched throughout the evening. As the on-call resident, I was heavily involved with caring for this gentleman and comforting family members. His room was overflowing with loved ones, and I quickly became part of their extended family. Unfortunately, he wasn't expected to awaken.

I remember commenting that I would be the second happiest person, only behind his family, if he did awaken; and soon that happiness abounded! His family commented to me that they thought the sequential compression devices on his legs were bothering him and could they please come off. With the sound of Velcro coming apart, he opened his eyes. He quickly became oriented and was able to breathe on his own. Ventilator support was removed, and he was able to speak and visit with his family and friends.

It was beautiful to watch God's miracle all evening as he visited and said goodbye. Neither he nor his family wanted to continue further treatment, have a tracheotomy performed, or have him placed back on the ventilator. It was likely that the next time he fell asleep without support, he would not awaken. In the very early morning hours of the next day, I cried with his mother and his best friend as I made the death pronouncement. The sadness I felt was mixed with awe of what a wonderful God we serve—that He blessed this family with time for them to say, "I love you and goodbye."

Lisa G. Umphrey, LLUSM class of 2004—for which she was senior-year community service coordinator—is a cardiology fellow at University of North Carolina at Chapel Hill. In 2004, she received the LLU Chancellor's Award.

And the people, when they knew it, followed him: and he received them, and spake unto them of the kingdom of God, and healed them that had need of healing. Luke 9:11, KJV

God does the healing; we do the cooperating. Jesus had commissioned the disciples to go preach the gospel and heal the sick. When they returned and reported their success privately to Jesus, the people heard about it and came to join the celebration recorded in Luke 9. For more than 100 years, Seventh-day Adventist medical education has promoted that same teaching/healing model given to the disciples by Christ.

With the advent of "miracle drugs" and other modern medical advances, it is easy to forget the true source of healing. For example, all the antibiotics in the world will be of no benefit if the immune system designed by our Creator is not working (as when it is suppressed by poor nutrition or the use of alcohol or tobacco). The principle that "God does the healing, we do the cooperating" is important to remember and apply whenever illness occurs. The case of Marty exemplifies the value of this understanding.

Marty developed joint pain when he was just 4 years old, but it was not diagnosed as rheumatoid arthritis until several years later. By the time I saw him during his teenage years, he had severe swelling and pain in many of his joints, as well as damage to surrounding tissue. Fortunately, with the use of medication, he gradually improved and was able to graduate from high school. Then I didn't see him for several years, and I assumed he was doing well. However, fifteen years later he showed up one day in my office in a wheel chair, unable to stand without assistance.

I told Marty that new medicine was available that might help him to walk again; but he would have to take a weekly injection and work hard with physical therapy, including pool exercises. I also told him about the research showing it is best to avoid red meat and cigarette smoke for patients with rheumatoid arthritis. He was willing to do his part in the healing process. When I saw him again recently, he was so grateful to be walking and able to drive his truck. He said, "You gave me my life back!" I had to tell Marty I couldn't take the credit since "God does the healing, we do the cooperating!"

Edwin H. Krick, LLUSM class of 1961, is associate professor in LLUSM department of medicine, division of rheumatology. He was LLUSM Alumni Association president from 1979 to 1980 and was LLUSM Alumni Association 1988 Alumnus of the Year. September 10 is dedicated to his uncle, Roy B. Parsons Sr., LLUSM class of 1929, who served for fifty years as a missionary in Africa. Inspired by his uncle to take medicine, he later became a missionary to Japan, where he served for eight years and was the third American to pass medical boards in Japanese.

September 11

Comfort the fainthearted, uphold the weak, be patient with all. . . . always pursue what is good both for yourselves and for all. 1 Thessalonians 5:14-15, NKJV

Giving advice is usually a thankless business and I'll not venture far in that direction. I have always tried to keep in mind the unconsciously profound summation written by a young schoolgirl: "Socrates," she wrote, "was a Greek philosopher who went about giving people good advice. They poisoned him!" More about advice will be shared later.

Since the mid-1980s, I have written a number of articles for publication in the LLUSM Alumni Association *Alumni Journal*. Permit me, if you will, to share the essence of one of those articles. I titled it "Reminiscence Reborn," and it related to my being able to share some memorable medical school experiences with two of my sons—Gregory, LLUSM class of 1987, and Barry, LLUSM class of 1993. Both, when the article was written, had graduated and were either in residency or private practice.

Funny thing about memory, I mused. You can recall specific events, keenly, at times, and sometimes even remember the most vague of memories. Occasionally, there are accidental reflections that just pop into your awareness for no particular reason. However, the emotion, the poignancy, of those intense moments that often punctuated the medical school experience cannot ordinarily be revisited . . . or so I thought.

But then I became aware that my two sons were traveling some of the same paths as I had, some twenty-five or more years before! As I have listened to these young men recount some of their most vivid and exciting moments, it has brought back and refocused with exquisite clarity some events that otherwise might have been lost forever.

I thank them for that rebirth of memory that allowed me the luxury of reliving important and perhaps critical times in my life. To me . . . some of these moments have, without a doubt, been a spiritual experience. Certainly spirituality comes in many different forms, but these have been special for me in a distinctive and meaningful way.

One of my favorite quotations is from Oliver Wendell Holmes: "Man's mind once stretched by a new idea, never regains its original dimensions." Imagine that! And it happens to all of us at Loma Linda. To me, that is also a spiritual experience.

Finally, I offer a reminder from a letter written by Benjamin Franklin. This letter was written toward the last days of a long and incredibly productive life. It was written to the Reverend Ezra Stiles, who had asked about Dr. Franklin's religious beliefs. His spirituality is expressed very eloquently and succinctly. He wrote, "I believe in one God. The creator of the universe. That He governs it by His providence. That He ought to be worshipped. That the most acceptable service we render to Him is doing good to His other children."

To me, those words are just as true today as when they were written on March 9, 1790, more than 219 years ago. Think about it and notice this—I have carefully avoided advising you to live your life as Benjamin Franklin suggested. I know the inherent danger. But there is an incandescent truth here, and I think it's a good idea!

Hubert C. Watkins, LLUSM class of 1962, is associate clinical professor LLUSM department of dermatology. He was LLUSM Alumni Association president from 1984 to 1985. September 11 is his birthday.

September 12

So now, O Israel, what does the LORD your God require of you? Only to fear the LORD your God, to walk in all his ways, to love him, to serve the LORD your God with all your heart and with all your soul. Deuteronomy 10:12, NRSV

Varner J. Johns Jr., LLUSM class of 1945, was chair of medicine and chief of cardiology for many years during the development and growth of Loma Linda University during the 1950s and through the 1980s. Many medical students and house officers had the opportunity to observe and learn during teaching rounds with Dr. Johns on cardiology service. I was fortunate to be one of them.

Dr. Johns was a devotee of the art of physical diagnosis, as well as a talented teacher. His observational skills at the bedside were legendary, leading to frequently organized trainee attempts to trick him by enlisting the aid of patients in producing false historical and/or physical evidence. But I was never aware of any successful attempts at leading him astray. He always took such things in good humor and turned these events into teaching points. This approach tended to turn rounds into a friendly competition, leading to enhanced learning.

He always followed daily rounds by retiring to a small conference room on the unit to discuss a carefully prepared topic of his choosing. The most memorable topic from these morning meetings, and one that has stayed with me all these years, was his discussion of "professionalism."

He asked, "What is it that sets the professional person apart from the tradesman, craftsman, businessman, salesman, industrialist, or skilled laborer? It is not the important basic personal attributes such as honesty, integrity, industry, dependability, perseverance, intelligence, or initiative—traits that may be common to all.

"There are, however, crucial differences that set the professions apart from all other fields of endeavor. The first is the long and intensive academic preparation that is required. The second is selfless service. There must be a willingness to serve without regard for personal comfort or convenience and, at times, without monetary or material rewards.

"A third characteristic that sets the professions apart is the devotion to scholarship. There is a perpetual search for truth and a sincere desire to share this truth—in contrast to the business world, where there is frequently a competitive hoarding of knowledge for selfish benefit. The professional has an insatiable thirst for shared knowledge and truth that results in a life-long quest.

"The Christian, who is also a member of one of the professions, should have a deep yearning to introduce God to his fellow man. Those who know God will love Him, and those who love Him will also serve Him. This knowledge of God will not be imparted by sermons, but by the demonstration of dedication to loving care, in the life of the professional person, for those he serves with superior skill. In such a life, the character and teachings of Christ will be reflected and will provide a dynamic and an impelling Christian witness."

David B. Hinshaw Jr., LLUSM class of 1971, is professor in and chair of LLUSM department of radiology.

September 13

For where two or three come together in my name, there am I with them.
Matthew 18:20, NIV

Our Loma Linda University School of Medicine class of 1970 was not large by today's standards, just eighty-six students. We knew each other well, and many of us were newly married. These new relationships as couples were an important step in developing lifelong friendships. So it hit us hard when one of our own classmates, Nancy Simpson, developed serious cancer of the neck. Her husband, Jim, and brother-in-law David Wilkins, were also in our class; and word of Nancy's diagnosis spread quickly like a cold fog among all of our classmates.

As new physicians, we were just becoming used to facing bad news with our own developing patient skills, but this was too close to home. Through multiple surgeries and radiation, we all followed Nancy's course carefully, assisting her and Jim as we could, and keeping them in our prayers. Fortunately, Nancy lived many more years and raised a family, before finally succumbing to her disease.

At the same time, we supported one of our other classmates, George Williams, who hailed from the little country of Guyana. He was quiet and reserved in his relationships. When word drifted out that George was engaged to a sweetheart from home, we were all excited for him. It soon became clear that any wedding was going to be difficult, though, without any family members around. So the class took on George's wedding as our class project. We planned the event, rented the room, organized the details, and quite literally became his surrogate family for this important milestone.

These two events have always symbolized for me the value of personal relationships that Loma Linda excels in so well. One was on the bad side of the ledger, the other on the good. But both equally evoked a response of pulling together, surrounding each other, and providing support. While we were all competitive, it was clear that these issues of the heart were much more important than any scaled score or class standing.

Keeping priorities in balance was an important lesson for those years and throughout life. Many of us have drifted apart by now, but class reunions still evoke a sense of companionship, of coming together for each other's good. That is a gift we can continue to give back. Thank you, Loma Linda, for providing that kind of environment, where we could mature together into the kind of friends and professionals that embody those values.

Richard Hart, LLUSM class of 1970, is president of LLUAHSC and president of LLU. He received a DrPH degree from Johns Hopkins University in Baltimore, Maryland, in 1977. He was an LLUSM Alumni Association 1994 Honored Alumnus.

He hath shewed thee, O man, what is good; and what doth the LORD require
of thee, but to do justly, and to love mercy, and to walk humbly with thy God?
Micah 6:8, KJV

Micah's list seems short enough. The problem for students is that there are all those other lists from teachers, spouses, parents, and offspring. Still, if we are creatures, then our Creator's expectations deserve a fairly elevated position in the list of things we should be doing. This is particularly true for students: your minds are expanding, new ideas are arriving daily, hourly; and decisions are being made that will affect your entire lives from this point forward. Today is not only the first day of the rest of your life (an observation that is always the case and for all people) but, for you—the scholar—it may well involve decisions that will affect your entire life in major ways. So do I have any "rules of thumb" to suggest? I do—two of them.

Keep Sabbath inviolate for the three "Fs,"—family, friends and (f)ilosophy (or time set apart for thinking about meaning in life if you prefer). During your student days, your mental capacity will grow more rapidly than at any other time in your life. If you don't allow your ideas of God and Creation some time to keep up with that growth, then all sorts of not-so-pleasant things are very likely to intrude into your future. Either your moral, ethical, and religious capacity will keep pace with your growth in intellectual capacity or it won't, and that is an outcome too painful to contemplate. So be sure, throughout your student career, that you "walk humbly with God."

Do justly in your relationships. In times to come, your relationships will be largely with your patients. For now, they will be mostly with your classmates. If you come into possession of information that you know would be helpful to the rest of your class—share it. If you are tempted to cheat or cut corners or excuse some action that falls below the standard of action of a lady or a gentleman, don't do it—even if no one but you will ever find out. Remember, you will be spending the rest of your life living with yourself; and you will know about it. Love mercy—offer help where help is needed. Take notes for a classmate who is ill. Tutor a fellow student who is having trouble.

Remember that if God is Creator God, then you are a creature in His sight. Carry yourself as such. As God is at work in the world for good, you, created in His image, should be doing likewise. You were created for a purpose. You owe something to the world. Your sphere of influence may be narrow now, but that won't always be the case.

Do justly, love mercy, and walk humbly with your God.

Brian Bull, LLUSM class of 1961, is professor in and chair of LLUSM department of pathology and human anatomy. He is immediate past dean of LLUSM, serving from 1994 to 2002. In 2003 he was named recipient of the LLU Distinguished Service Award. He first delivered this devotional to a group of sophomore medical students. September 14 is his birthday.

September 15

Jesus wept. John 11:35, KJV

I knew the young teacher since he was a boy. He played sports in the church league, water-skied, rock climbed, and camped with our kids. He went to church school and then to college, learned to play music, and wrote many songs about his personal relationship with God. He married a sweet girl and made a happy home. When he was notified by mail that he had passed his California Basic Education Skills Test (CBEST), he danced about the house in his pajamas because now he was a teacher. He began teaching in a private church school and immediately found a place in the hearts of his teenage students. He was a happy man with a future.

But the young teacher became weak and lost most of his normal blood cells because his bone marrow was completely replaced by acute leukemia. Several courses of chemotherapy made him bald and nudged him as close as possible to death in order to kill the tumor cells. We all prayed a lot and hoped a lot. When he recovered, I repeated the marrow test and, to my great joy, found that the tumor cells were gone! It was a precious moment. He was in remission.

The young teacher and his band celebrated by giving a concert. When the concert began, he smiled at the crowd and said, "Guess what? I'm in remission!" And then he praised God and life with music. His leukemia, however, returned a year-and-a-half later. He died in spite of therapy, prayer, and anointing with oil. Why? I just do not know. Sometimes God's will does not make sense to me. All that I know is that God has agreed to be responsible and will make it right someday.

And so his wife, family, friends, students, and pathologist all wept. Jesus wept, too. We wept because tender memories, promises, and a hope were all that remained of the young teacher's beautiful soul. Why does Jesus mourn with us? He knows that the young teacher will live again. Why did Jesus weep with Mary and Martha when Lazarus would so soon step out of the tomb? He did so because He loved them then, as He loves us now.

We will never appreciate how much the waste, the senseless and unnecessary waste of humanity resulting from Eden's fall, saddens God—a sadness that emerges when humans suffer. Jesus loves us so much that He remains with us in our warped dimension and also suffers. Being God makes Him more, not less, sensitive to our pain. When we hurt, He cannot help but also hurt. So, His tears now mean that we are in His hands. They comfort us as we wait, sometimes it seems for such a long time, for the final joys of eternity.

Jeff Cao, LLUSM class of 1971, is professor in LLUSM department of pathology and human anatomy and course director for pathology at LLUSM. He was president of the Walter E. Macpherson Society from 1998 to 1999 and LLUSM Alumni Association president from 2005 to 2006. He was LLUSM Teacher of the Year in 1999 and 2007 and was an LLUSM Alumni Association 2008 Honored Alumnus.

September 16

When they knew God, they glorified him not as God . . . but became vain in their imaginations, and their foolish heart was darkened. Who changed the truth of God into a lie, and worshipped and served the creature more than the Creator, who is blessed for ever. Romans 1:21, 25, KJV

Pride in human wisdom—the worship of "the creature more than the Creator"—leads us down some slippery paths. Let us note an example or two.

Faced with the fundamental question, "What is there in the universe apart from humankind that can provide solace, guidance, or support for humankind?" some philosophers have concluded that there is nothing. (I decline to quote Psalm 14:1 here, but leave it to you to look it up later.) Is this the kind of solace you intend to offer distraught people you meet in your office or on the hospital ward?

Is that *little* faith all that you will have to offer your patients? This abandonment of the God of the Bible leads, all too often, to a denial of the ethics of the Bible. And, indeed, it dismisses any other effective code of conduct—except, perhaps, the code presently favored by some CEOs in the news: "If it's not illegal, let's go ahead!

Can it be that undue dependence on human intellectual breakthroughs—such as antibiotics, whole-body scans, chemotherapy, and artificial hearts—has led us to ignore the Creator and worship the creature more? Or to deny the Creator's absolute truths and to rely instead on our own, ever-shifting, approximations?

What *shall* we believe? Can we have any *fixed points* in philosophy and theology? Upon what is our faith to be based?

It is not, in many quarters, fashionable to announce firm answers to these questions? We are more often told, "The quest for wisdom is the thing; the goals are unattainable. Do not expect ever to reach them."

In his day, John Dewey was considered a great thought leader. Here is how he viewed "absolute truth": "The only truth worth having is not truth in any absolute or final sense but rather 'truth made'—truth provisional, truth for the time being . . . There are no eternal verities and no final answers . . . Moral and other values, therefore, have nothing of the abiding and eternal about them."

How does that compare with the assertion of the Psalmist, "For ever, O LORD, thy word is settled in heaven" (Psalm 119:89, KJV) or of Isaiah, "The grass withereth, the flower fadeth: but the word of our God shall stand for ever" (Isaiah 40:8, KJV). On which authority shall we depend for guidance?

When your professional careers come to an end, will you say to yourself, "I gave my patients the best that I could offer: endoscopes, antibiotics, CT scans, the tenderest of humanist philosophies, but no part of God's Word or of Christ as Savior—for I trusted the creature more than the Creator."

Or will you conclude, "I gave my patients the best I had—modern medicine, skillfully administered, plus the good news of God's love and His healing and saving power. I trusted and followed not the creature, but the divine Creator."

Carrol S. Small (1910-1997), LLUSM class of 1934, served as LLUSM Alumni Association president from 1946 to 1947 and was LLUSM Alumni Association 1982 Alumnus of the Year. He received the LLU Distinguished Service Award in 1984 and was LLU Alumnus of the Year in 1995. September 16 was his birthday. This devotional, adapted by Brian Bull, LLUSM class of 1961, was originally a commencement address to graduating medical students.

September 17

I will give you a new heart and put a new spirit in you; I will remove from you your heart of stone and give you a heart of flesh. Ezekiel 36:26, NIV

Cynical and jaded, I look in the mirror at a familiar face but note an unfamiliar heart. What has happened to me?

In medical school, I led out in worships and participated in spiritual-care practicums, learning how to address the spiritual needs of my patients. I attended a summer workshop on how to compassionately address patients' physical, emotional, and spiritual needs. I planned on being a "super" physician who understood, cared, and met all my patients' needs.

But I have changed. My attitude stinks. Sometimes I see the patient as a puzzle that needs to be figured out. Other times, I view the patient as annoying or, worse yet, despise him. What happened to the compassion I possessed when I first started on this journey? Is not this patient God's special child? Did He not come to this earth and live a life perfected by unimaginable suffering—even facing the prospect of eternal loss—just for this patient?

I realize I have slipped away from God and the ideals that He placed in my heart. I have built walls around my heart to protect myself from pain; and these same walls have trapped the pain inside, preventing me from letting it go. My heart was once alive, but now it is bitter, cold, lifeless. I need a heart transplant.

As the overwhelming hopelessness of my situation and my utter inability to do anything about it floods over me, I fall to my knees in tears. A flood of pain wells up from the depths of my heart. I feel the abandonment of my parents' divorce, the self-hatred of years of moral failure, and the pain of rejection. I cry, and cry, and cry.

After what seems like an eternity of pain, I realize that strong arms are holding me. I am on God's lap and He is holding me close to His heart. Here is safety and peace. There are no words about my failures, no expression of disapproval. I only see indescribable love and compassion.

I hear, "My child, I love you. I will never leave you nor forsake you. I will give you a new heart and put a new spirit in you; I will remove from you your heart of stone and give you a heart of flesh. And I will put my Spirit within you." I see Him reach into His chest and remove His heart and place it in my chest.

In awe, I see the transformation. The bitterness is wiped away. Peace and joy return to my heart. I see that only in my brokenness could God perform that painful heart transplant. I realize that each day must begin with time on God's lap, enjoying open-heart communion.

I realize that I need healing before I can help my patients heal. God gave me the greatest gift—His heart. I can now share it with my patients.

Mark Sandoval, LLUSM class of 2005, is a resident at Synergy Medical Education Alliance in Saginaw, Michigan. He is a deferred mission appointee. In 2005, he received the Wil Alexander Whole-Person Care Award.

September 18

Therefore, since we are receiving a kingdom that cannot be shaken, let us be thankful, and so worship God acceptably with reverence and awe. Hebrews 12:28, NIV

It was my first morning in China. As I emerged from the Landscape Hotel in Dali Old City, I was greeted by the crisp, cool morning air as I beheld the majestic Cangshan Mountains, literally pressed against the city. My teammates and I on the medical mission team stared in awe at the mist and clouds that covered the seemingly endless range of mountains. As the clouds rolled and moved swiftly at the peaks, I began to think of the relationship between the clouds and the mountains—which defined which?

Of course, the mountains were stationary testaments, towering over all that man had made for millennia. And yet, there was the swirling mist and the clouds that were perpetually there, yet always on the move. Although the clouds gave the mountains their aura and mystique, it was the mountains that determined their course. This scene of dependent beauty resonated in my mind and brought forth praise of God's creation from my mouth.

Weeks later, I found myself on another mission team and once again beholding Cangshan's beauty. The local high school kids had decided to take us for a day hike, and it was at the foot of these mountains that we entered a temple. The kids led us to the incense-filled main temple room, where a pantheon of idols resided. The idols were carved to be larger than any man and wore expressions of wrath.

One by one, the kids made an offering before bowing down to each of the idols. There was a feeling of intense sorrow as we watched our kids kneel before these man-made images. As I pointed to the chief idol, I asked one of the kids, Herbert, to whom he was bowing. His answer: "I don't know the name of that god." Here were kids, who, though subject to these idols did not even know the name of that which they worshipped. The scene of blind bondage was distressing.

There are parallel acts of worship within these two instances, but they could not be any further apart from one another. One involved the observation of creation, and that led to a spontaneous overflow of praise for the Creator. The other involved the observation of a creature worshipping a man-made creation. It was in that moment that I realized that all creatures were created to worship. It was not a question of whether or not to worship, but a question of who or what to worship.

Currently in the United States, our struggles reside not primarily in the worship of carved idols. Our primary idolatry is not even in the realm of finances or comfort or glory. Our main idolatry is a man-made view of God. We have indeed reduced God to our own notions, rather than magnifying God to who He is, as revealed by His Word. Let us resolve today to learn more of the complete character of God and, in so doing, appropriate worship will fill our hearts.

Andrew Wai, LLUSM class of 2010—for which he was sophomore class pastor, junior class co-pastor, and LLUSM senate chaplain—is from Orange, California. This devotional is dedicated to his parents, George and Sue. September 18 is his father's birthday.

September 19

So he set off and went to his father. But while he was still far off, his father saw him and was filled with compassion; he ran and put his arms around him and kissed him. Then the son said to him, "Father, I have sinned against heaven and before you; I am no longer worthy to be called your son." But the father said to his slaves, "Quickly, bring out a robe—the best one—and put it on him; put a ring on his finger and sandals on his feet. And get the fatted calf and kill it, and let us eat and celebrate; for this son of mine was dead and is alive again; he was lost and is found!" And they began to celebrate. Luke 15:20-24, NRSV

I tell the story of the Prodigal Son (Luke 15:11-32) to a group of about twenty boys at San Bernardino (California) Juvenile Hall every other week. The parable, as told by Jesus, is about a son who asks for his share of his inheritance, before his father dies. The son, of course, wastes it on prodigal living and ends up feeding pigs, perhaps the lowest possible job in that day and culture. At this point in his journey, he came to himself and felt how lost he really was. His "true idea" was to return to his father, beg for forgiveness, and ask to be his servant.

I can imagine his father seeing him in the distance, as the son walks towards home. His father had been waiting and watching, and, upon seeing him, runs to him and embraces his son. As the son begs for forgiveness, his father forgives, but when the son asks for servanthood, his father gives him the clothes of a son.

Psychoanalyst Sigmund Freud said that we project the image of our earthly father into what we think God is like. For example, if we had an absent father, then it would be our tendency to think that God is absent and distant. But the father in this story represents what God is really like: compassionate, trustworthy, and waiting to restore a relationship and make us sons and daughters.

The times of shipwreck in my life have defined me. I imagine that everyone has those moments, like the Prodigal Son feeding swine—moments when each of us realizes our desire to return to God, to kill our pride, to ask for forgiveness, and to be a servant. In other words, we come to ideas that take us out of our ego, out of our own reality. As Christian writer C. S. Lewis wrote in *Mere Christianity*, in order to find your true personality, you must submit all your desires, all your life, and everything you are and have to God.

David Puder, LLUSM class of 2010—for which he was freshman class president—is from Cupertino, California. He attended University of California, Berkeley. He is currently a juvenile hall chaplain and is a leader of the LLUSM class of 2010 Haiti Project.

September 20

The LORD is gracious and compassionate, slow to anger and rich in love. Psalm 145:8, NIV

"**I**f my father has any complications from this surgery, I'm going to sue you, and everyone else involved in his case!"

I talked with the son on the phone for a few more minutes, biting back the retaliatory remarks that were bubbling on the tip of my brain. We're here to take care of the patient, I told myself over and over again, not the angry, pain-in-the neck family member.

Mr. Ramirez was 67 years old and had been in the hospital more than two weeks. When he had first shown up in the emergency room, he was hovering on the edge of death, and none of us expected him to make it. Now, two weeks later, he needed definitive surgery to fix his broken legs. I entered his room, and here was a kind, elderly man whose face lit up with a smile as I walked through the door. I explained the surgery to him and told him his son wasn't very happy right now. He patted me on the hand and gazed into my eyes, "It's okay, doctor," he said with his broken accent, "I know you will do your best, and don't mind my son; he is just worried for me."

The surgery was long, but went well. Afterward, I went to the waiting room, called out the family name, and cringed inside. Now I would have to talk to the abrasive son in person. There was no answer in the waiting room, so I reluctantly called him on his cell phone. I reached him just as he was pulling into the hospital parking lot.

I waited in the hall as a man in his mid-40s stopped in front of me. His eyes were puffy and had dark circles under them. The lines of stress were deeply etched in his face. I began talking with him; and without much coercion, I found out that the night of the accident, his mother was also in the car. She was at another area hospital in critical condition, and it didn't look like she was going to make it.

I also learned that his parents had adopted his drug-addicted sister's children just a year before, and now this man and his wife had taken them in. To make matters worse, he lived over an hour away and was about to lose his job if he didn't go back to work the next week. My eyes got misty as he told me his story. A wave of shame washed over me for the things I had been thinking about this man, a man who was doing everything he could just to hang on.

Chad Harbour, LLUSM class of 2004, is a resident in orthopaedic surgery at LLUMC.

September 21

But my God shall supply all your need according to his riches in glory by Christ Jesus. Philippians 4:19, KJV

In 1956, I was asked by the Seventh-day Adventist headquarters, the General Conference, to fill a call for the Ethiopian Union in Dessie, Ethiopia. The hospital in Dessie had been destroyed during the Italian Occupation. A special Sabbath offering had been designated for the rebuilding of the hospital.

When we arrived, there were only seven rooms in the building that could be used. After the construction was completed, we had capacity for a fifty-five-bed hospital. But there was almost no equipment to furnish the hospital, and the equipment we did have needed to be replaced. We needed a surgical table, a surgical light, x-ray machine, and certain other basics to make this building a hospital.

For instance, once, while delivering a baby, the portable army table that held the patient, collapsed, and my arm was caught in the metal side. Fortunately, help was present and my arm was released without being permanently harmed.

We prayed at a prayer meeting with the hospital workers for help from above. Just a few days later, a letter arrived from a former mentor, Dr. Howard Knott, from Seattle (Washington) General Hospital, where I had interned. He expressed that he had heard I had married and had accepted a position at a mission hospital. He asked if there was anything he could do to help us. I immediately wrote back, telling him of our needs.

Writing again from Palm Springs, California, he indicated that he and some friends would like to help and asked how much money we needed. At the time, we could purchase items from Europe less expensively than having equipment shipped from the United States, so I told him we needed $12,000. A few weeks later, we received a check for $15,000. We had a wonderful prayer meeting of praise with our workers; and I wrote a letter thanking him for his wonderful gift, truly an answer to prayer.

Sadly, our letter arrived back in California the day of his funeral. His widow wrote that he had such joy in giving his gift and that he felt it was the best thing that he had ever done. We purchased the items needed and had the only well-equipped hospital in an area of over two million people. God had provided in a most wonderful way.

The story doesn't end there. Dr. Knott's wife, through her friends, continued to give funds; and we were able to have a water well drilled to provide all the water that we needed for the hospital. We were also able to fund a clinic for the Danakil tribe in the desert town of Asaita. We spent five years at this mission hospital and have often said they were the happiest years of our lives.

This account is only one of innumerable stories of answered prayer during those years—years in which we found that God does truly supply our needs.

Alex P. Bokovoy, LLUSM class of 1946, is a surgeon and resides with his wife, Sandi, in Denton, Texas.

And he shall turn the heart of the fathers to the children, and the heart of the children to their fathers. Malachi 4:6, KJV

"There is a collect call from Dave Brooks; will you accept it?" I was Dave's father and a clinical faculty member of CME. It was Sabbath morning, and my wife and I were about to leave for church when the phone rang. The voice on the other end said, "Dad, will you call the hospital and tell them I am sick and cannot be on duty today?" My son's voice was thick and the words ran together. He should have already been at the hospital; he was the surgical intern on call. But he was in Las Vegas and couldn't get home in time.

"But, Dave, I can't be your cat's paw* to get you out of trouble when you are not really sick," I replied, saying words I have wished a thousand times had not been said! Dave was sick. He knew it, but I did not. His response was immediate, "I'm going to hit a Diesel." I did not understand. Just like I had not understood him for many years. Then there was the clang of the receiver and silence.

During church, my thoughts were on my conversation with Dave. Was his call a cry for help from one who had reached a crisis in his life; had I failed to help him? Dave had never before intimated he wanted to make the final escape from life; but he had made numerous temporary escapes—tranquilizers, sedatives, alcohol, long hours driving in his car.

Dave was interested in things that did not interest me—things that to me were superfluous and unimportant. No, I had not been a companion to Dave. So, that morning, in church, I determined that I was going to be more available to him. I was going to understand Dave, and I was going to be involved in his activities.

The sermon ended. We drove home as usual. Dave's wife, who was due to give birth in five weeks, was waiting for us. Had she heard any more from Dave? No, not a word. We looked out the front window and saw the sheriff walking toward the front door. After a brief inquiry, he said, "Call the Highway Patrol at San Bernardino."

"There has been a fiery crash between a sports car and a truck on the highway about one mile north of Baker," the Highway Patrolman informed me. "The occupant of the car was burned beyond recognition, but we found a piece of the registration certificate with your street address on it. Do you know who the driver of the car might be?"

Oh, why had I spoken those words to him that morning—the last ones he would ever hear from me? He was desperate and was crying for help. Why did I not help him in this crisis? My words had goaded him into making that final desperate decision—and . . . my actions and attitude through the years. I felt responsible for his tragic end.

In the midst of my sorrow, I vowed I would be there for my remaining children. Maybe I could be involved in some way in the interests of my grandchildren and other young people who would need guidance. Yes, I learned the hard way, through a parent's worst nightmare, that being there for one's family should be one of the highest priorities. As the end of my life approaches, if someone has learned from my mistakes and is wiser and happier by my having lived, then my life will not have been in vain.

*Slang for "covering" for someone

Roger W. Barnes (1897-1982), LLUSM class of 1922, was LLUSM Alumni Association president from 1932 to 1933, and was LLUSM Alumni Association 1952 Alumnus of the Year. This adapted devotional, originally written anonymously about his son, Richard, LLUSM class of 1958, appeared in the August 1, 1974, issue of the Review and Herald, *fifteen years after his son's suicide.*

September 23

Then the Lord spoke to Moses, saying, "This shall be the law of the leper for the day of his cleansing: He shall be brought to the priest. And the priest shall go out of the camp, and the priest shall examine him; and indeed, if the leprosy is healed in the leper, then the priest shall command to take for him who is to be cleansed two living and clean birds, cedar wood, scarlet, and hyssop. And the priest shall command that one of the birds be killed in an earthen vessel over running water. As for the living bird, he shall take it, the cedar wood and the scarlet and the hyssop, and dip them and the living bird in the blood of the bird that was killed over the running water. And he shall sprinkle it seven times on him who is to be cleansed from the leprosy, and shall pronounce him clean, and shall let the living bird loose in the open field." Leviticus 14:1-7, NKJV

The Israelites were given strict orders regarding infectious diseases, especially leprosy. When one reads chapters 13 and 14 of the book of Leviticus, one gets the impression that God was very particular about the health of His children.

But beyond the level of diseases as they existed, He clearly wanted them to see the dangers of spiritual diseases and how to avoid them. In case they did contract them, He wanted them to see the source of correction and healing that would be available.

Leprosy stands out *par excellence* as a surrogate name for sin. Among the Hebrews, the cleansing of a leper was carefully attended to. Two birds were chosen; one was killed while the other was bathed in the blood of the sacrificed bird. The live bird was then let loose to fly away—hence the expression, "Let the live bird go free."

Jesus paid extraordinary attention to those diseased, especially to the despised lepers of His time. He spent much time in the home of the famous leper, Simon. In Matthew 8:2, a leper came and pleaded for help. Although it was common practice not to touch a leprous person, Jesus went beyond protocol. He touched the leper and healed him!

Is this not what He does for all of us? He also might softly say to each of us as He touches us, "Go now, and let the live bird go free."

Do you remember on one occasion when He healed *ten* lepers? If so, then you also remember that only one of them, the one least expected to show appreciation, returned to tell Him thanks. Let us not forget to return to Him to tell Him thanks after He says to us, "Let the live bird, washed in blood, go free."

Hear how Joseph Parker said it in his 1886 *The People's Bible*: "'Blessed is the man whose sin is covered'—and sin can only be covered or hidden in one way. No cloth of human weaving can ever conceal it; it will rise and show its figure before the vision of the world though all the silk and purple ever thrown upon it. There is an appointed covering; have we accepted it? Observe, this is the law of all life."

God looks down from heaven and sees us engaged in the continual endeavor to cover our sin. He says, "It cannot be done; you have undertaken something impossible; that miracle does not lie within the compass of human invention or mortal strength. But you are right in the endeavoring to cover it. You are working according to the law, the full operation of which you do not understand." And then Jesus says, "I will provide the covering."

Lloyd A. Dayes, LLUSM class of 1959, is emeritus professor in LLUSM department of neurosurgery. He is also a specialist in forensic medicine who holds the PhD, DMin, DD, DTh, and MBA degrees. In 2001, he was named LLU Alumnus of the Year.

Let integrity and uprightness preserve me. Psalm 25:21, KJV

The email message on my screen had only two words in the subject line. In bright blue letters it read, "My mistake." I could see that it had come via the online bioethics forum to which I subscribed. The author was an acquaintance of mine, a physician who teaches at a medical school in the Midwest. While I get far too many email messages from such sources to read them all, I was too curious to ignore this one.

The message opened this way: "Let me tell you all a story. I injected the patellar bursa of a young man who had bursitis there. I reached for the Depo-Medrol (a type of injectable steroid) but came up with Depo-Provera instead (a female hormone). The injection went well, and I wrote my note and went up to the office."

Later that day, according to his account, the physician got to thinking about what he had done. He went back to check his notes and realized that he had carefully documented his mistake. He resisted the temptation to change the note. Instead, he called a urologist to ask for advice and was told that one injection of Depo-Provera would probably not seriously affect the patient.

A week later the patient returned. The knee was less painful but still not completely improved. This time the doctor injected the correct medicine. He ended his email account of the story this way: "I tried to tell him of the mistake, but the words just wouldn't come out. The knee is all better now. My mistake is still documented in the chart. Should I still tell my patient that I injected him with a female hormone?"

This simple little story touched off a long and sometimes sharp debate among members of the online forum. A few argued that it was obvious that the doctor should tell. Many others argued that there was no point in telling since there was no obvious harm to the patient.

It was a long time before I finally learned what the physician decided. Meanwhile, I reflected on the fact that so much of medicine, just like the rest of life, depends on trust. In his book, *Trust*, Francis Fukuyama shows how the prosperity of societies is critically dependent on the shared level of trust. The most time-honored element of traditional codes of medical ethics, all the way back to Hippocrates, has been the protection of trust.

Scripture often links integrity to preservation and prosperity. Integrity is the result of living in accordance with our own well-considered convictions. In other words, integrity means knowing what we believe and then being willing to act accordingly. Just as an integer is a whole number, a person of integrity is a whole person, not shattered by duplicity or insincerity. Trust is the result of believing in each other's integrity. As one who is the recipient of medical care, I do count on the integrity—the wholeness—of my caregivers for the preservation of my own wholeness.

So how did the story end? A couple of years later, I saw that the physician who had written the email confession had published a book of his poetry. I bought the book, *House Calls, Rounds, and Healings* by David L. Schiedermayer. In it, I found a short poem titled "Female Hormones." It revealed that a year after the incident, the physician had admitted his mistake to the patient and had apologized. The patient had graciously assured the physician that it was "no big deal."

Gerald R. Winslow is professor of ethical studies in LLUSR and is also associate scholar for LLU Center for Christian Bioethics. He received a PhD degree from Graduate Theological Union in Berkeley, California, in 1979.

September 25

And you will be my witnesses, telling people about me everywhere. Acts 1:8, NLT

Shortly after beginning to work on the oncology unit, I met Mrs. Hughes. She was in her late 50s and had breast cancer. She and her husband had three adult daughters. Once a month, she would be admitted for chemotherapy, and I gradually formed a strong bond with her and her family. She lived life with gusto and approached her cancer with an optimistic spirit that was contagious. We had many opportunities to chat about her children, her charity work, and her zest for life.

One thing we didn't discuss was spiritual issues. I had previously worked with a woman who believed God had called her to pray with every patient she encountered. While it sometimes went well and was much appreciated, I also observed times when the patients were offended and disturbed by the prayer. Rather than risk repeating those scenarios, I decided that prayer would never be part of my treatment plan. I would simply be a cheerful, compassionate person, and, hopefully, others would notice and ask why I was different. I would then explain that I was a Christian and that God made a difference in my life.

Unfortunately, the chemo wasn't effective for Mrs. Hughes, and the doctors shared the sad news with her. Now, when she was admitted, it was because she had an infection or needed better pain control. The cancer had spread to her lungs and she had difficulty breathing.

I arrived at work one morning and learned that Mrs. Hughes had been admitted during the night and was not expected to live long. I got a quick report, then headed straight for her room. There, huddled around her bed, was her family. I slipped in and listened as they shared stories of family vacations, Christmas gifts, and practical jokes. Realizing I had some memories to share myself, I quietly stepped forward as they welcomed me into their circle. I told them what an inspiration she had been to me—how I admired her indomitable spirit.

Soon, I realized I must go and check on my other patients, but I struggled to leave. "Would it be okay if I said a prayer with you?" The words were out of my mouth before I even thought, and I immediately regretted them. However, the group seemed grateful; so I offered a short prayer, then excused myself to make rounds.

One of the daughters followed me out into the hallway and grabbed me by both arms. "Kathy," she exclaimed with amazement, "We didn't know you were a Christian!" She was thrilled . . . I was devastated! Here was a family that I had known for nearly a year while working in a faith-based hospital, and they had no idea I was a Christian.

"Let your light shine" took on new meaning for me as I realized I would always be more intentional about my faith after meeting Mrs. Hughes.

Kathy McMillan is director of LLUMC department of employee spiritual care. She has an MA degree and is a registered nurse.

Cast your bread upon the waters, for after many days you will find it again.
Ecclesiastes 11:1, NIV

In August 2008, I received an email from a Vietnamese woman's son, who was writing on her behalf. The email had been forwarded to me because they were inquiring about a team of American heart surgeons who were in Vietnam in 1974. The team had performed open-heart surgery there on the writer's mother when she was only a teenager.

My heart skipped a beat. Not only did I know about Loma Linda University Overseas Heart Surgery Team and their trip in 1974, *but I was a senior medical student who had the rare and wonderful opportunity to accompany the team to Vietnam that year!*

I immediately returned an email and attached a group picture of the fifty-two patients on whom the team had done surgery in Vietnam in 1974. The next day I received a response from the woman's husband. He conveyed that his wife was delighted to see the picture and, yes, she could identify herself in the group! He continued: "She always wanted to tell you all about how she came to feel alive after her heart got fixed by your team of doctors. It was only in reading a magazine article given to her by a friend that we learned that it was a team of Seventh-day Adventist physicians."

Attached to the husband's email was a note written by the patient. Hers was a heart-touching message and began: "I have been thinking of you all the time and wishing someday to see you all again. You all are my saviors. Thanks for the picture. I can't tell you how happy I am to see myself in it—that was 34 years ago! Years go by, and I have been busy with life, but I never forgot all of you who saved my life."

She continued: "In 1987 I escaped (from Vietnam), got caught, escaped again, and was in a refugee camp for three years. I came to Canada in 1990. After three years, I met my husband. We work at home (run a bed and breakfast and I am a hairstylist), have two children, and are doing just fine. I have a happy marriage, we all are healthy, and we have good children. Life is like heaven to me. I appreciate everything I have and thank God every day.

"At 14 years old in Vietnam, I did not know the names of anybody with your team or the organization you belonged to. I was talking about my story to one of my clients one day, and he knew about the Loma Linda heart team. He is the one who helped me find you.

"If it is possible, could you send me a picture of the team? I would like to know which one you are in the picture, because, at 14, I did notice the good looking ones! Just a reminder—if any of you ever have a chance to come to Victoria, don't get a haircut first. I will do it with pleasure and will guarantee my work. God bless you all."

I stared at my computer screen and pondered the story that had just unfolded. How many others around the globe have untold stories as a result of our institution's mission work? And how many of these people actively pray for our university and its healthcare providers? As I contemplated these and other questions, I felt humbled, yet blessed, to be part of something that is so much larger than myself.

H. Roger Hadley, LLUSM class of 1974, has been dean of LLUSM since 2003. He is professor in and former chair of LLUSM department of urology. He and his wife, Donna, were married on September 26.

September 27

Go with confidence. The LORD will be with you on your mission. Judges 18:6, NET

M rs. Pettis and I once had the pleasure of having as our guest Dr. Edward R. Annis, president of the American Medical Association (AMA) and president-elect of the World Medical Association. During his stay in southern California, Dr. Annis visited the Loma Linda University campus. He met with teachers and students and saw plans for the School of Medicine's consolidation at Loma Linda.

As we drove back to the airport for our flight to Los Angeles, California, he made some comments, which I would like to pass on, editorially:

This is a nice location. I'd like to be a medical student in an atmosphere like this .... Loma Linda University students should be greatly inspired by those who have gone before them, serving their country and their church in such exemplary and humanitarian fashion throughout the world.

I like the design for your new Loma Linda [University] Medical Center. It is one of the best plans I've seen....

One of the most inspiring experiences I've had since becoming an officer of the AMA was a meeting with members of the National Association of Seventh-day Adventist Dentists several months ago in Florida. These men were more than well-trained dentists—they were professional people with a significant purpose in life ... and to my mind, this joy of living and commitment to humanitarian goals is best inculcated by religiously oriented universities....

Your graduates serving primitive peoples unselfishly in many lands comprised a peace corps long before the idea gained political popularity.

I hope I may come back when your physical plant is completed. I like what you are setting about to do here.

This sort of spontaneous enthusiasm for our program and objectives encourages me. It reminds me of the many nice things Vice President Lyndon Johnson said when he visited the west coast recently.

Our University does have a great past and, in my book, it has an even greater future. I'd far rather share the optimism of such than join the "crepe hangers" who find the challenge of change and growth disturbing.

Loma Linda University is a great institution with a wonderful mission. Give it a little faith, love, confidence, and a lot of hard work and it will be even greater. What do you think?

Jerry L. Pettis (1916-1975) served as LLU vice president for public relations and development. He was the first Seventh-day Adventist to serve in the United States House of Representatives and represented California from 1967 until his death in 1975. This devotional originally appeared in the September 27, 1963, issue of LLU Scope.

September 28

Being confident of this, that he who began a good work in you will carry it on to completion until the day of Christ Jesus. Philippians 1:6, NIV

It was crunch time and I was desperate. My performance on the first set of exams was dismal. Now it was the day before our second set of exams, and I was feeling hopeless. I had studied as hard as I could, but it was still not good enough. College was not so difficult for me because even if I was a little behind I could cram the night before an exam and usually do just fine. But medical school was different. The sheer volume of information to learn prevented cramming for tests.

So, here it was the night before our second set of exams, and I felt as if I were going to fail. As I sat at my desk praying for wisdom and God's grace to help me through these exams, a song came to mind. I remembered that it talked about God beginning a good work and being faithful to complete it. As that melody kept playing in my mind, I tried to find the Bible verse that inspired the lyrics. I needed to claim its promise so I could be confident of my success the next day.

I tried but couldn't locate the verse in my Bible. Fortunately, my study partner found it in Philippians 1:6. This verse showed me that God did not bring me all the way to medical school to let me fail. He not only brought me here, but He is also faithful to complete it! Of course, I had to cooperate and do my part; but there was no longer any despair. I had confidence that He would help me succeed. Yes, the next day my exams went well.

During my first year of ophthalmology residency, I felt lost again. Everything was new; and it was similar to going through early medical school all over again. There was so much information to assimilate, and everyone else seemed to learn it much faster than I did. Then that verse came to me again, "He who began a good work in you...." God had brought me into this residency, and He would be faithful to help me succeed.

With this assurance, I was able to settle down and study hard knowing that, eventually, I would learn what I needed to know. Residency training did go well. Today, I am happily working in a Christian ophthalmology group practice.

Stressful situations and challenging cases still come up periodically, but I know that God will help me through them all. We are not meant for failure here! He will be faithful to give us the courage, wisdom, and endurance necessary to complete our tasks until the day of Jesus Christ. May the promise of Philippians 1:6 always stay close to you in whatever difficulties you may encounter. Our only job is to faithfully remain close to Jesus.

Paul Y. Chung, LLUSM class of 1991, is an ophthalmologist who resides with his wife, Iris, LLUSM class of 1995, in Chehalis, Washington.

September 29

While he was saying these things to them, suddenly a leader of the synagogue came in and knelt before him, saying, "My daughter has just died; but come and lay your hand on her, and she will live." . . . But when the crowd had been put outside, he went in and took her by the hand, and the girl got up. Matthew 9:18, 25, NRSV

Many God-ordained miracles and experiences we witnessed while working in Zambia, Malawi, and Botswana (1976 to 1985) have made lasting impressions on my family and me: One that stands out perhaps the most happened while we were in Kanye, Botswana. It involved Gopalong, a 9-year-old girl, who showed up at our hospital in the back of an old Bedford truck.

From a bank of earth, she and her two friends were digging out a special clay, which is used for plastering their houses. Suddenly, a cave-in crushed all three of them. She was the only one alive when the villagers dug them out. She was covered with dirt and had mud in her eyes, nose, and mouth—just everywhere. Yet she was alert and talking. A quick check showed that her lungs and heart were okay, but the abdomen was empty, just skin draped over the spine. The small bowel was between her thighs, all covered with mud, crushed, and full of holes. Her pelvis was crushed and she had an obvious left tibia-fibula fracture.

I called the trauma team together—two nursing students, one nursing instructor, and one enrolled (LPN) nurse. We also alerted the entire mission to pray for this girl and us. We started intravenous fluids and gave her some ketamine and pethidine (Demerol). I washed and cleaned the bowels, while the nurses cleaned up the rest of her. When the abdomen was prepped and opened, we found that the small bowel had entered the dome of the bladder, exited the left side of the bladder, tunneled along the left side of the vagina through the left femoral ring and the fascia to emerge externally by the left upper thigh.

The pelvis was crushed and broken in several places, and the pelvic floor muscles were shredded. After several hand-stitched small bowel resections and hole patches were completed, the bowel looked okay. The bladder holes were closed, and the crushed pelvis shards were placed in near anatomic position. Her tibia-fibula fractures were set and cast. Six hours later we took her to the intensive care unit, placing her bed nearest to the nurses' station in a thirty-bed ward.

She did not develop infection and was always happy and cheerful. After a month, she began to walk with crutches. However, she was incontinent of urine. Since her pelvic floor was so destroyed, there was no adequate bladder support. After considerable thought and prayer, God impressed me to form a sling with strips of rectus abdominus fascia to give support for the bladder. It worked—Gopalong was dry! She and her family were very thankful and happy. So, three months later, a little girl, who should have died in the African bush, walked out of a humble mission hospital. Once again, God showed up in a mighty way and healed His precious child.

John Rogers, LLUSM class of 1974, is a family practitioner in Caliente, Nevada. Gopalong came to their hospital toward the end of September.

September 30

Happiness lies more in giving than in receiving. Acts 20:35, NEB

During my residency at Loma Linda University Medical Center, my wife, Pat, and I often took our two little boys, David and Michael, to the beautiful Jerry L. Pettis Memorial Veterans Affairs (VA) Medical Center grounds on weekends. They loved to feed the ducks! They would split a loaf of bread and feed all the ducks as fairly as they could. This sometimes meant squatting down carefully on the steep grassy banks in order to reach some "less lucky" ducks.

We sent one photo of such a scene to their grandmother, my mother. She posted the photo onto a larger piece of paper and added a caption on the top portion with the words from Acts 20:35 (NEB), "Happiness lies more in giving than in receiving," written in English and Chinese. She then mailed this piece of art back to the grandsons.

This framed picture has been sitting on top of a counter at home since then, serving as a constant reminder of happiness in sharing. (Years later, grandma donated her body to a medical school as another act of sharing.)

From time to time, at the dinner table or during family devotion time, the four of us would talk about serious topics like, "What is the purpose of life?" Gradually we felt, most likely, that the pursuit of happiness is the purpose of life.

Over the years, we also pondered the essence of true happiness. We concluded that happiness comes through sharing. When we share the most valuable (and invaluable) possessions with people around us, we experience genuine happiness. For example, Robinson Crusoe found more happiness after he rescued Tuesday and Friday and shared his island with them. We may share time, love, talent, money, etc., and, of course, the gospel!

A similar thought is that in order to share something with others, we have to acquire it first. We can only share what already belongs to us. It may take years of dedication to acquire something valuable; and, yet, sometimes we focus so much on acquiring, that we lose sight of sharing—much like the rich young ruler in the New Testament. Happiness then will elude us.

Now, by God's grace, I am still practicing internal medicine. Pat is the office manager and dietician. David, LLUSM class of 2001, and Michael, LLUSM class of 2007, have gone through the VA Medical Center grounds and Loma Linda University Medical Center campus several thousand more times during their medical training. We are all sharing with people much more than a loaf of bread every day.

We all have received so much from the medical community at Loma Linda. May the Lord lead us in every way to share the gospel and the art of healing so those who receive and those who give will all enjoy abundant true happiness in Him. Amen.

Peter Y. Chang was a resident in internal medicine at LLUMC from 1979 to 1982. He also has a PhD degree in chemistry from Princeton University in Princeton, New Jersey, and an MD degree from University of Miami in Coral Gables, Florida. He is an internist in Riverside, California. September 30 was the birthday of his late mother, Chen Chih Wu Chang.

October 1

He will wipe every tear from their eyes. There will be no more death or mourning or crying or pain, for the old order of things has passed away. Revelation 21:4, NIV

Heartbreak! Yes, heartbreak for the devoted mother, the dying child, and the dedicated resident doctor. Three lives, woven together for almost a year, again this evening battling a disease unresponsive to available therapy. Tears overflowed. Tears of overwhelming despair of a young mother whose dreams of a bright future in a new land had been shattered by her only daughter's deadly disease. Tears of pain of a trusting 3-year old, lying motionless on the treatment table—her body now prematurely aged and emaciated by the ravages of leukemia and the poisonous treatments available in the 1960s.

And there were tears of defeat, coming from the resident. She was exhausted from the endless hours of work; emotionally drained from the futility of yet another attempt to reverse the relentless progress of this disease. She felt spiritually desiccated by unanswered personal prayers for the healing of this beloved child.

That night, four decades ago, was, for me, a time of professional and spiritual crisis. The passion to bring health and healing to humanity had been born within me, early in life, during a year-long serious childhood illness. After a total recovery, I began the journey to respond to an inner calling to "healthcare ministry"—a blending together of the spiritual nurture of my patients along with state-of-the-art, professional care.

What followed were years of faithful study and rigorous preparation, but nothing had prepared me to confront the profound pain and loss I felt that night. How could I comfort anyone when unanswered questions rocked my own soul? Where was God? Why would He allow an innocent child to experience such extreme suffering? Why was He so unresponsive to my petitions for restored health? My naïve view of life was shattered.

My quest to find the answers has continued through the last four decades. It propelled me to deeper spiritual study. It fueled my commitment to ensure that graduates of Loma Linda University School of Medicine are prepared to face the real world of pain and suffering, to provide whole-person care, and to preserve their own wholeness.

The brief life of that little girl, years ago, and in a land far from Loma Linda, is responsible for my dedication to this unique place of learning. We have an incredible privilege of living our mission here to continue "the healing and teaching ministry of Jesus Christ, 'to make man whole'" thereby "transforming lives"—not just here, but for eternity.

B. Lyn Behrens is emerita professor in LLUSM department of pediatrics and is a specialist in pulmonology. She received her medical degree from Sydney (Australia) University in 1964. Before retiring in 2008, she served as founding president of LLUAHSC; as president of LLU beginning in 1990; and as dean of LLUSM from 1986 to 1991. She was named LLUSM Alumni Association 1996 Alumna of the Year and was also recipient of the LLUSM Distinguished Service Award in 1992. She chose this date because on October 1, 1909, Ellen G. White, one of the founders of the Seventh-day Adventist Church and a key individual in the founding of LLU, wrote on the necessity and character of the educational work to be conducted at Loma Linda.

Do not gloat over me, my enemy! Though I have fallen, I will rise. Though I sit in darkness, the LORD will be my light. Micah 7:8, NIV

It's 9:00 p.m. I am lying in bed, looking out the window at the twinkling lights peppering the nearby peninsula. I haven't slept in two days. Five doctors are exiting my hospital room after breaking the news to me that my eight-and-a-half pound son, who was born at 5:00 a.m., was finally diagnosed with multiple heart defects, including hypoplastic left heart syndrome. The defect is fatal; a transplant would be our best option for survival. "Would you like a sedative?" they asked, "You really need to rest."

I said, "No, thank you—I'm going to pray."

In the blackness of the midnight sky with a big autumn moon, I asked God for more light, more clarity to help me understand. I never asked WHY, surprisingly. In my prayer, I said "WOW! You chose ME to be the mommy of a baby so weak and fragile? He looks so big and strong on the outside—how could he be so sick? How will we know how to care for him with two other small children? When will he come home?"

We had so many questions, with no sensible answers. As my prayers continued, I felt empowered, honored, a surge of strength filling me to follow His will and to stop questioning. "Just LISTEN! Follow MY lead," the Lord said to me. "You will be blessed." As if to give me a tangible earthly symbol, and probably due to my intense fatigue after giving birth without rest, I imagined the enormous job board at the University of California, Los Angeles, which takes up the entire length of the career office wall. The best, most highly qualified jobs were way at the top, needing a stepstool to reach. Other, lower-status jobs covered the remainder of the board.

That night, in my pitch-black hospital room, I was spiritually raised to the top of that job board, completely feeling empowered by the Holy Spirit to take the highest ranking job of my life—to be the mother of a special-needs, fragile child. I was being asked to follow not my own, but the Lord's path, lit by His love and going in His direction. My husband and I always, ALWAYS made decisions for our son PRAYERFULLY, never relying on our own understanding; but just putting him in God's hands, knowing every day is wrapped in a bow—a GIFT!

Steven received his new heart at Loma Linda twelve-and-a-half weeks later, only to reveal numerous midline deformities down his body that impaired his development in so many ways. But he fought and fought to LIVE through so many hard strikes against every system of his body. There were so many doctors and specialists, scratching their heads with doubt. And so many days with dark messages, hopeless prognoses, more meds, more admits to the hospital—yet another setback along with poor development.

But, through it all, now seventeen years later, Steven laughs, smiles, and with limited speech he brightens everyone's day. Our family never said, "WHY US?" We said, by the grace of God, "WOW! US?!" We truly believe, as Christians, that we were never promised an easy road, but it is what we do with our trials that glorifies God. Steven has ILLUMINATED our lives. He helps us shine God's light on what is truly important in life. We thank the many medical professionals who have counseled us, prayed with us, and helped our son's light continue to shine, whether it is here on earth or from above.

Renee Holdridge is the mother of Steven, who received a heart transplant as an infant. She resides in Los Angeles, California. October 2 is Steven's birthday.

October 3

And I will ask the Father, and he will give you another Counselor to be with you forever—the Spirit of truth. The world cannot accept him, because it neither sees him nor knows him. But you know him, for he lives with you and will be in you. John 14:16-17, NIV

I have dreamed of becoming a doctor since I was a little girl, but my road to medical school had many challenges. I struggled with the Medical College Admission Test and had to retake it twice. My low initial scores prevented me from being accepted to medical school right after college. That detour led to the development of doubts. I doubted my ability to succeed, even if I reapplied to medical school; and I questioned whether I had correctly heard God call me to medical missions.

These doubts were short-lived, however, as I was quickly assured of my call from God; and, with diligence and support from my family, I was finally accepted to Loma Linda. Since the path to medical school was not as easy as I had hoped, I thought for sure that, once I started, things would easily fall into place, as I finally got to study how to help and heal people. And, of course, I have learned many things. But what I couldn't possibly see when I started was that life does not stop just because I am studying to be a doctor.

When I entered my freshman year, I had several challenging but fulfilling roles. I was a pastor's wife, a new role as my husband was starting his first pastorate. I was also very involved with my family and am blessed with my roles as daughter, sister, and granddaughter. But I continued to add roles in my first two years. I became a mother at the beginning of my sophomore year. The challenges that I thought would not be present, once I finally got into medical school, began to accumulate.

Individually, all of these roles bring purpose and importance to my life. But interwoven together, my life is at times overwhelming and confusing. When I stand back and look at all the things I am trying to accomplish at once, I often wonder how I will make it another day, week, month, or year.

But God has taught me much through these challenges, both before and after entering medical school. I have found peace and guidance in the midst of my life's storms, a peace that can only be from God. Whenever I begin to feel overwhelmed or start to doubt my call, I sense a calming deep within me that encourages me to keep going.

Through many years of having an intimate relationship with God, I have learned that the Holy Spirit sent to dwell within me is always there. All I need to do is stop and listen. When we do stop, we will find the answers for which we are searching, or a gentle embrace in times of sorrow, or a firm nudge to take life's next step. It's not easy being pulled in what feels like a million directions at once, but we have assurance that God is always with us and gives us the strength to face any doubt or challenge.

Rikki Martinez, LLUSM class of 2009, is from Fountain Valley, California. She and her husband, Steve, have a son, Dietrich. October 3 is her son's birthday.

October 4

As God's chosen ones, holy and beloved, clothe yourselves with compassion, kindness, humility, meekness, and patience. Bear with one another and, if anyone has a complaint against another, forgive each other; just as the Lord has forgiven you, so you also must forgive. Above all, clothe yourselves with love, which binds everything together in perfect harmony. Colossians 3:12-14, NRSV

Not long ago, in my late 30s, I realized that I had some anger issues that needed resolution. I contemplated where the anger was coming from and decided that I needed to start resolving those issues by forgiveness. Looking back, I realized that the first person I needed to forgive was a little boy from my childhood.

I was a preacher's kid, and we moved all over the country. When I was in second grade, we lived in a Minnesota town that had no Seventh-day Adventist church school. So, I went to the local public school. One summer, I went to a playground to play with some friends from my class. There were also some boys playing there, and they started teasing us. My response was, "Sticks and stones may break my bones, but names will never hurt me." And I ran off to swing.

I leaned back on the swing, pulled up, and SMACK, a rock hit me square on the forehead. I was shocked, but I knew who threw it. Quickly, there was blood everywhere. A neighbor lady saw what had happened, brought a towel, and called my mother. I was taken to the emergency room, where the wound was cleaned and I had stitches placed. Later, the wound became infected and I became quite ill, but eventually healed.

My father was called to a new location, and we moved shortly after that. I never saw that little boy again. Now, as an adult, I realized I was still unhappy with this incident and decided the boy needed to be forgiven. After reading all the verses in the Bible concordance on forgiveness, I prayed a prayer of forgiveness for this little boy, Danny.

The next day after this prayer, I worked my shift in the emergency department (ED) in southern Oregon, where I now live. I was treating a family that had been involved in a car accident. Frequently, law enforcement officers come in with the patients to get more information about the accident. I began to talk with the sheriff involved in this case. I glanced down at his name badge and thought the name sounded familiar, although I had never seen him in the ED before. So I asked him, "Is your first name Danny?" He replied yes. My heart began to pound. I asked, "Did you used to live in Minnesota?" He again replied yes. Now, I also had goose bumps. He was wondering why I was asking these questions and who I was. So I blurted out, "Do you remember throwing a rock at a little girl when you were in second grade?"

His eyes flew open wide and he said, "Was that YOU?" Although I was barely able to speak, I got out the word "yes." He said, "I have felt bad about that my whole life. Were you ok?" I replied jokingly, "Well, I became a doctor." Danny, now the sheriff, said to me, "I am sorry." And my response, from the bottom of my heart was, "I forgive you."

I have since seen Danny a few times around town and have told him that I had prayed for forgiveness for him just the day before we so unexpectedly ran into each other after thirty years. He is not a practicing Christian at this time, but I am hoping, after hearing the evolution of the miracle that can come only from God, he will realize the amazing blessings of a life with Christ.

Tamara Stewart, LLUSM class of 1994, is a specialist in emergency medicine in Ashland, Oregon. October 4 is the birthday of her daughter, Heather.

October 5

My soul waiteth for the Lord more than they that watch for the morning: I say, more than they that watch for the morning. Psalm 130:6, KJV

As I write this, I am taking general surgery call in the last month of my second year of residency. It's a Friday night, and I'm on call again on Sunday. I've had a busy week and will have many more to come. It's been a tough year spiritually. Finding time to spend with God takes some extra effort. I am still enjoying my career, but I don't want to have my career become so important that it drowns out my line to God.

I haven't had any dramatic spiritual encounters to write about during medical school or residency. I'm sure that they will come at some point. I'm still growing. In fact, sometimes I am just so tired that the only thing I can do is wait. Wait to feel God's presence, wait to start another day where I might feel more spiritually alive as well.

And right now, I'm just waiting for tomorrow morning to come so that I can go to church and give the Sabbath School lesson—something that nourishes me as much as the class. I can definitely identify with Psalm 130:6—there are many times I just watch for morning!

I'm waiting for consults to come in and for traumas to inundate us tonight, right now. But, really, I'm also waiting for the morning to come. Not just tomorrow morning, but the morning when we wake up and there are no more traumas. That special morning when there is no more need for a physician. The morning when I will meet the Great Physician face to face, instead of just waiting for Him.

Isaiah 25:9 (KJV) says, "And it shall be said in that day, Lo, this is our God; we have waited for him, and he will save us: this is the LORD; we have waited for him, we will be glad and rejoice in his salvation."

Elizabeth Johnston, LLUSM class of 2006, is a resident at University of Nebraska Medical Center in Omaha, Nebraska. She and her husband, Michael, LLUSM class of 2006, live in Omaha, Nebraska.

*On the way to Jerusalem he was passing along between Samaria and Galilee.
And as he entered a village, he was met by ten lepers, who stood at a distance and
lifted up their voices and said, "Jesus, Master, have mercy on us."
When he saw them he said to them, "Go and show yourselves to the priests."
And as they went they were cleansed. Then one of them, when he saw that he was
healed, turned back, praising God with a loud voice; and he fell on his face at
Jesus' feet, giving him thanks. Now he was a Samaritan. Then said Jesus, "Were
not ten cleansed? Where are the nine? Was no one found to return and give
praise to God except this foreigner?" And he said to him, "Rise and go your way;
your faith has made you well." Luke 17:11-19, RSV*

That last sentence (Luke 17:19, RSV), "Rise and go your way; your faith has made you well," has always been interesting to me. Did we not read previously, "And as they—the ten—went, they were healed"? That means the Samaritan who fell at Jesus' feet had already been healed! So why did he need to be "made well." Why would Jesus declare a second healing?

To me, that last comment by Jesus means that physical healing is not sufficient to accomplish total and permanent healing. There must also occur a spiritual healing to complete it and make the person whole. That same approach is a major part of the teaching at Loma Linda University. To me, the instructors try to follow the divine pattern of total healing—cure the body of physical disease, but follow up by paying attention to the mind and soul.

There was a pattern of healing in every instance of Jesus' healing ministry. It was:

Your sins are forgiven.

Your faith makes you whole.

Go and sin no more.

Faith, or matters of the spirit, is important for the patient. Thus, we make man whole.

I found that this "second healing" was at the core of my training to be a physician at Loma Linda University. We were led to follow the divine pattern of total healing—rid the body of physical disease and follow with the tuning of the mind and soul for the healing of the whole being. That legacy I have carried with me throughout my professional life. Hence, my medical experience turned my profession into a calling.

Naor U. Stoehr, LLUSM class of 1957, is an obstetrician and gynecologist in Takoma Park, Maryland.

October 7

Love each other with genuine affection, and take delight in honoring each other.
Romans 12:10, NLT

Emotion often takes a back seat to reason and objective analysis in clinical medicine—a calm approach easy to understand for those of us who are occasionally carried away. However, might emotion be a positive element in the matrix of moral decision making in the care of patients?

On occasion, I tag along with colleagues who practice medicine. As an outsider, I try not to ask too many dumb questions. I listen closely along the way. One morning on rounds, the medical team was torn by debate about whether or not to order kidney dialysis for their patient. A 42-year-old male was suffering from multiple organ failure.

Some on the team felt that if they could get the kidney working again, there might be a good chance for recovery. The nephrologists, however, did not feel the patient was a good candidate for dialysis. We turned our attention to other patients, moving on to other rooms that were laid out in a circle on this floor, without resolving the matter of whether or not to order dialysis.

Six patients later, standing just opposite the room our patient was in, the attending physician grabbed all our attention with a raised, pointing finger. "Look over there," he said. "If that picture doesn't change your mind and tip the balance in favor of ordering dialysis, there is something wrong with you!"

We looked, and, standing next to his unconscious father, holding his hand, was a boy still in his winter coat. Likely about 8 years old, the boy, seen next to his father, was indeed compelling. Our emotions do often compel us to move in directions we might not normally move. If we can manage the delicate balance of emotion and reason, then clinical moral decision making becomes a whole-person event.

Temperance is the virtue we exercise in the balance of emotion. It is not practiced in the effort to quell our emotions, but rather to help us manage well those things that move us. Passions are managed and moderated by temperance; and, when practiced well, we integrate our emotion into each and every clinical context.

In particularly difficult cases fraught with moral issues, instead of being carried away by emotions, we are actually more humane and decent because of them. In fact, the great Christian theologian Thomas Aquinas argued that, without including emotion tempered by virtue, a person is not really engaged in human decision making.

The great clinician William Osler called it *aequanimitas*: the ability to truly engage your emotions in clinical settings to thoroughly understand the situation, while bringing to bear the full force of your medical knowledge. Some have wrongly thought that Osler meant for physicians to be cold and stern through the practice of *aequanimitas*. One of my favorite Osler passages tells of how he envied the close connection that the nurses in his facility had with the patients—a connection established and bonded from the more human, emotion-oriented art of medicine and less focused on the cold, hard science of medicine.

I never found out if the picture of father and son compelled the medical team to order dialysis for our patient, but I did discover an attending physician who understood the fine art of practicing medicine.

Mark F. Carr is professor of ethical studies in LLUSR and is director of the Center for Christian Bioethics at LLU. He received a PhD degree from University of Virginia in 1998, and also has an MDiv degree.

October 8

Seek the LORD, all you humble of the land, who do his commands; seek righteousness, seek humility. Zephaniah 2:3, NRSV

It's easy to remember Loma Linda University's core values of Justice, Compassion, Humility, Excellence, Integrity, Freedom and Self-control/Purity—just remember "J CHIEFS." Of all these values, many philosophers have called humility the solid foundation of all virtues. Humility, or humbleness, is being courteously respectful of others. It is the opposite of aggressiveness, arrogance, boastfulness, and vanity. Rather than "Me first," humility allows us to say, "No, you first."

Humility also allows us to go more than halfway to meet the needs and demands of others. To be educated and knowledgeable—complete with degrees and clinical specialties—is one thing; and, yet, we need to be quietly confident, not boastful, as we serve others. Humility is all about quietly acknowledging our shared accomplishments, but without arrogance or the self-congratulatory isolation that leads to pride.

Here are a few of my suggestions for practicing humility:
- "Listen" to others.
- Give credit to others.
- Practice using these phrases: "You are right" or "What do you think?"
- Correct yourself, not others.

Baseball great Yogi Berra, known for his off-hand comments, once remarked that you can "observe a lot by watching." Have you ever observed that the higher people rise, i.e., the more they have accomplished, the higher their humility index? Those who achieve the most, brag the least.

At Loma Linda University, I am surrounded by colleagues who have the ability to get the job done without drawing attention to themselves. And I see students who, in spite of busy schedules, routinely give the anonymous donation of their time in service to others. I observe administrative leaders who are humble servants. I witness random acts of humility extended to all, regardless of position.

Yogi was right; we can observe a lot just by watching! So, weave humility into the fabric of your life—someone's watching!

Billy Hughes is associate professor in LLUSM department of pathology and human anatomy and is dean of LLUSP. He received a PhD degree in biology from LLU in 1978.

281

October 9

You see me when I travel and when I rest at home. You know everything I do. You know what I am going to say even before I say it, LORD. . . . You saw me before I was born. Every day of my life was recorded in your book. Every moment was laid out before a single day had passed. Psalm 139:3-4, 16, NLT

God has visibly guided and blessed my life at a most intimate level. I know that He changes clinical outcomes and lives. He changed mine.

Between my second and third year of medical school, I completed basic science research in the LLU perinatal biology laboratory, studying how interstitial fluid pressures were controlled in the body. We published our results in the *American Journal of Physiology*. When I returned to clinical rotations, I quickly began to forget about the implications of my research. But God had a different plan.

Twenty-five years later, I had a successful practice in ophthalmology. One day a young teacher presented with one of the worst postoperative complications in refractive surgery. Both eyes appeared to be blinded with necrotic scars in the visual axis. It was a textbook case, although I had never seen such a complication personally.

Over the years, I had made it a habit to begin each surgery with prayer. I fervently prayed over this young lady. I took her to the operating room for emergency surgery. I was stunned. Nothing I was witnessing under the microscope agreed with the medical literature. Over the next few days, it was clear that her clinical course did not match what any medical books described.

And then one day, as I was examining the patient, I suddenly realized what was happening. In an instant, God opened my mind so that I could see that my patient did not suffer from tissue necrosis, but rather from a severe form of localized corneal edema. I immediately changed her medical regimen. But the treatment went against everything I had been taught. Based on conventional wisdom, my plan was completely wrong.

She immediately began to improve and eventually recovered perfect 20/20 vision in each eye. To my knowledge, an outcome like this had never been reported. Her recovery and visual outcome were nothing less than miraculous. Later, I saw seven more eyes with the same problem and with treatment the same perfect result.

With much prayer and study, I realized that the cause of these complications was a disruption of forces that control interstitial fluid pressures in the cornea. More than twenty-five years before, God opened the door to expose me to this obscure topic in physiology. His purpose was to prepare me for clinical challenges decades later—challenges that had not even been imagined in 1983. This etiology had never been considered.

As a result of this early work, my observations irreversibly altered our profession's understanding of this disease and the factors that control fluid dynamics in the cornea. These discoveries propelled me to become a world-recognized authority on this important topic. For some unknown reason, God determined to make me a vehicle to communicate to the world just how incredible His design and creation can be.

Ellen G. White wrote in her book *Education* (p. 17), "It is the work of true education . . . to train the youth to be thinkers, and not mere reflectors of other men's thought." Reliance on His power, combined with a Godly education provided by God-fearing teachers and mentors, can change the world. It changed mine.

Brian R. Will, LLUSM class of 1985, is adjunct assistant professor in LLUSM department of ophthalmology. He resides in Battle Ground, Washington.

October 10

And God will wipe away every tear from their eyes; there shall be no more death, nor sorrow, nor crying. There shall be no more pain, for the former things have passed away. Revelation 21:4, NKJV

The shrill jangle of the telephone woke me out of a deep slumber early one morning. It was my sister Waylene. "Goong Goong [our grandfather] was admitted to the hospital last night. He was intubated this morning." I cleared the fog from my brain, and thought, "It can't be—I just talked with him yesterday afternoon." But with his advanced age and history of cardiac disease, this scenario was clearly a reality.

I woke my husband, Jim; we cleared our schedules for the day and drove to the hospital. The next several days were a roller coaster of emotions for all of the family. Goong Goong would make small strides forward, only to fall back even further. As his condition deteriorated, our prayers grew more desperate and pleading. Two weeks after his intubation, his pupils became fixed and dilated, and I had to tell my mother that his brain was dead. It was the most heart-rending conversation I have ever had with her. We buried our grandfather with heavy hearts but were thankful that God had given him a long and happy life.

So often, both inside and outside the hospital, we see suffering, pain, and death in those who seem too young to deserve it. I think of Ethan,* who has Hurler's syndrome. He has lived ten difficult years, is ventilator-dependent, and is deteriorating rapidly. His mother has devoted the prime years of her life to his exhausting care. Then there's Nicole,* age 4, with Cornelia de Lange syndrome. She wears hearing aids, glasses, is unable to walk or talk, and has the mental and physical development of an 8-month old. I think of Roy,* whose maxillary sinus cancer recurred after extensive surgery, chemotherapy, and radiation. He and his wife were sobbing in my office, wondering how to tell their 13-year-old daughter that her father would not live to see her grow up.

As physicians, we are supposed to comfort, to heal, and to give hope to people who are hurting; but too frequently we have to give messages of despair. To be sure, with God's grace we can help and even cure many patients of their physical ailments. But in this life, there are too many that we cannot. What hope can we give to those who need help the most? Only the hope of Christ, the great Healer, and His promise of the earth made new, a place without tears, sorrow, death, or suffering. My family is looking forward to heaven, where our grandparents will be young and healthy again. Ethan will be rid of his tracheotomy and ventilator. Nicole will be able to see, hear, walk, and talk. Roy will be reunited with his family. What a great promise of hope for all of us!

*Names have been changed

Marilene Wang, LLUSM class of 1986, is a head and neck surgeon in Los Angeles, California. October 10 is the birthday of her grandfather, Joseph R. Hwang.

October 11

The generous soul will be made rich, And he who waters will also be watered himself. Proverbs 11:25, NKJV

The year was 1975. The Vietnam War was finally over, after having dragged on from 1961 to January of 1973. But the effects of the war were still very much alive. Communism, which was to have been stopped by American intervention, had come to South Vietnam. Part of that variety of communism was a philosophy that intellectuals were dangerous to the common people and must be eradicated. This thinking meant that the lives of professionals or those training to be professionals were in grave danger.

The medical schools of the United States opened their doors to Vietnamese medical students who could escape their native country. Loma Linda University took in ten students in the years around 1974. These students had begun their studies using English textbooks. But, as we know, if you have studied in a foreign language, and then have to listen to that language spoken by a national, there is an enormous difference between textbook English and spoken English. In this case, all of the applicants had to first spend time at Loma Linda University's Riverside campus (now La Sierra University), trying to become more proficient in this new language.

Many of the Loma Linda University students went out of their way to help their Vietnamese classmates, and those classmates were grateful for that help. Because of the culture shock, the difference of the new curriculum, and the language barrier, they needed all the help they could get.

One of these Vietnamese students was facing a particularly difficult time in her new environment. Somewhat older than her classmates, she had been torn from her husband and was the mother and guardian of two children. Her escape from her native country had been hazardous in the extreme. In addition to the cost of schooling, she had to come up with living expenses for herself and her children.

A young medical student couple, both members of the same class, took a special interest in this Vietnamese girl. They made themselves available to answer questions when the lecture was not clear to her, invited her and her family to share meals, and did what they could to explain American ways.

National Boards Part I came at the end of the second year. Facing National Boards is intimidating for the best-prepared student; it was positively traumatic for the Vietnamese, who had so little background in spoken English. The American couple talked together and made a decision. He would loan his notes from the past two years to their protégé, and he and she would study together for boards.

They took their boards. When the results were posted, the Vietnamese girl with American notes was the only one of her group who passed the boards on the first try. The wife topped all the women in her class, and her husband had the highest of any California medical student for that year.

This act of generosity proved the words of Proverbs 11:25 and demonstrated the spirit of Loma Linda University by helping not only patients but also fellow students and all who need a helping hand.

Ruth Giem Edwards is the mother of David Giem, LLUSM class of 1972; Paul Giem, LLUSM class of 1977-B; and James Giem, LLUSM class of 1982. She resides in Spirit Lake, Idaho. October 11 is Paul's birthday.

October 12

Are not five sparrows sold for two pennies? Yet not one of them is forgotten in God's sight. Luke 12:6, NRSV

My forte is listening; my speech is far from eloquent. However, within the last year, I have experienced something that has clarified my prospective in every direction—but especially upward.

It was Sabbath evening, October 6, 2007, and I chose to stay home, while my wife and 9-year-old twin girls, Alexandra and Madelynn, went to eat and do other girl things. I again complained of being tired and not up to it. After they left, I began to feel short of breath.

In spite of relaxing in my special chair, the breathing did not improve. I became worried after thirty minutes, as two or three prior episodes in as many months had always stopped within that time. I went outside into the cool fresh air but felt no essential change. After some time, my family returned and I was so distressed that I suggested we go to the nearby regional medical center.

I was soon stabilized from a blood pressure of 250/180 and admitted. The cardiologist consultant informed my wife and me that I needed surgery, or otherwise I would die. I never knew that I even had a cardiac problem. The diagnosis was aortic stenosis.

My wife, Jacquelynn, made arrangements for transfer to Loma Linda University Medical Center, and I was admitted by October 9. I found myself relaxed and also impressed with how quickly the diagnostic testing was done. A valve replacement was done on October 12, just six days after my original bout. Words cannot convey how uplifted my wife and I were by the words and prayers shared with us by Anees Razzouk, LLUSM class of 1982.

The facts were that I had been in end-stage cardiovascular failure. The good doctor had never seen such a severely fused valve (ejection fraction had been less than 20 percent). He could not believe that I had not been diagnosed earlier, or that I had survived so long without complication, i.e., stroke or myocardial infarction. Kenneth Jutzy, LLUSM class of 1977-A, is now monitoring my hypertension medications and looking into a possible need for a pacemaker for bradycardia.

I am overwhelmed by the awareness of how closely God's eyes have been on me all my life. I am so very thankful for a God whose eyes are on the sparrows (and others).

Donald E. Paden Jr., LLUSM class of 1972, is a psychiatrist in Corona, California. He now volunteers with Mended Hearts at LLUMC.

October 13

Be careful for nothing; but in every thing by prayer and supplication with thanksgiving let your requests be made known unto God. Philippians 4:6, KJV

For a 10-year-old child, the impression was profound. On one of our walks home from a weekly church service, it was very clear that something dramatic was about to happen. The dark angry clouds had just completed their assembly in the skies above us. Peering in the distance behind us, we could see that the torrential showers had already begun. It was at that moment I heard my mother pray, asking the Lord to hold the rain until we were safely home.

Less than a minute after reaching home, the thunderous downpour started and continued for more than two hours. This "life-changing moment" in the mind of a young child was proof enough that our Heavenly Father—who created this world, who could part the Red Sea for safe passage of the children of Israel, and who could still raging waters—was still engaged and interested in the affairs of our daily lives.

Since my childhood, the road through life has been more complex. The journey has included rocky, unpaved country roads, flooded valley gorges, steep climbs on the rough side of a mountain, dead-end streets, mountaintop lookout views, and quiet brook retreats. Sometimes, the challenges have led to anxiety, then uncertainty, and eventually stress. But always the principle of the "life-changing moment" seems to bring peace.

My best days have been those where my partnership with the Lord was clearly established and renewed. Proverbs 3:6 (KJV) says, "In all thy ways acknowledge him, and he shall direct thy paths." Clearly, this is a proven strategy for the way forward. This path will lead to success; it will lead to happiness; it will lead to peace that will pass all understanding. But, more importantly, it will lead to eternal life.

Let your prayer for today be: "Lord, I acknowledge you as my Creator, Sustainer, and Redeemer. Plant my steps today in the pathway of righteousness. Order them with Your words and anoint me with Your will. Lead me and guide me as I make a difference in the lives of people You will place in my path. If there is any disappointment today, help me to understand that it's only an opportunity for a blessing. Thank You for this new day and a new opportunity for service. Bless me I pray. Amen."

Hansel M. Fletcher is professor in LLUSM department of basic sciences, division of microbiology. He is course director for microbiology and immunology at LLUSM. In 1990, he received a PhD degree in microbiology and immunology from Temple University in Philadelphia, Pennsylvania.

He is your praise; he is your God, who performed for you those great and awesome wonders you saw with your own eyes. Deuteronomy 10:21, NIV

The words of a popular country song "I saw God today" remind me of the many ways and places I see God in my practice. However, as the business and "busyness" of my practice and life increase, it becomes easier to overlook the impressive things I see every day. The following are only two examples of extreme courage.

An 18-year-old boy with muscular dystrophy has just come into the emergency room. He has a terminal disease, is in a wheelchair, and uses a ventilator at night when he sleeps. He has attended high school this way, and his senior prom is tonight. Unfortunately, his caretaker slipped when transferring him from his wheelchair, and the boy fell to the ground. His work-up reveals bilateral tibiofibular fractures.

As I tell him about his injuries, he lies on the bed with two tears slowly streaking his face. The "unfairness" of it all overwhelms me as I think of the few life experiences he has left. When his pain and fractures are stabilized, I call the orthopaedist and together we work out a plan that will allow the patient to attend the prom. I think of how every one of this young man's days is filled with more courage than I exhibit on my best days!

A 55-year-old mentally retarded woman, accompanied by her mother, arrived by ambulance. The woman had difficulty breathing; it was found that she had pneumonia. The patient was placed on oxygen and treated. I spoke with her mother regarding her treatment options, should her condition deteriorate. I particularly asked the mother about assistance from a ventilator. The patient's 80-year-old mother, who had cared for her child for 55 years, spoke quietly and said, "She has been with me for her whole life and she is all I have left." I asked the mother if there was anyone for her to call, and she said no. The patient's clinical condition worsened, and the time for a resuscitation decision came sooner than anticipated. The patient's mother stood next to her daughter and said she didn't want her child to suffer any longer. I was touched by the courage of a mother who made the most difficult choice for her child because she loved her. When I stop to look, I see moments of courage; I see the grace and beauty of the human spirit; and I see God . . . today.

Tamara Thomas, LLUSM class of 1987, is professor in LLUSM department of emergency medicine and is associate dean for faculty development for LLUSM.

October 15

Wherefore the LORD God of Israel saith, I said indeed that thy house, and the house of thy father, should walk before me for ever: but now the LORD saith, Be it far from me; for them that honour me I will honour, and they that despise me shall be lightly esteemed. 1 Samuel 2:30, KJV

When I was a teenager, I had my tonsils removed. The surgeon was my father, John O. Ford, LLUSM class of 1953-B. Just before the anesthesia, he asked me if I would like him to pray. Gratefully, I accepted his offer and have long cherished the memory of that experience. Since then, I have found that when faced with illness or a critical medical procedure, most people appreciate prayer.

Throughout my entire career as an ophthalmologist, I have been offering my patients the option of having a word of prayer said for them prior to surgery—and it has proven a rich blessing! My motivation is the guiding principle of my life—"Them that honor me I will honor" (1 Samuel 2:30). And what better way to honor God than to recognize Him as the Great Physician before surgery.

In my practice, all my surgery patients are conscious during their procedures. After greeting the patient, and just before starting, I tell them that I like to begin all my surgeries with prayer. I ask them if they would be comfortable with that. Ninety-nine percent say yes, often with strong expressions of appreciation. The remaining 1 percent express ambivalence or, rarely, some more negative response.

Interestingly, in one large secular city where I operate mostly on younger patients, I noticed that prior to 9/11, the percentage of those who declined was about 5 percent. After 9/11, it changed to 1 percent, similar to the percentage in other cities where I work.

My prayers are short, positive, and cheerful. A typical one is—"Dear Father, thank you for the privilege of helping John see better. Please bless our efforts. In Jesus' name I pray. Amen."

For some patients, this may be the first prayer they have participated in for a long time, or the only healthy prayer they have ever heard. Those who seem reluctant are the ones I am most happy for, because I assume their image of God is distorted and I have been given a precious opportunity to help improve it. At the end of the procedure, some are especially grateful and specifically thank me for the prayer.

I still have my share of surgical complications, including some due to my own failures. But the prayer helps me keep calm, courageous, and full of faith that God will bring ultimate good out of whatever happens.

I encourage every doctor and surgeon to adopt some version of this practice—it is a blessing not only to patients, staff, and observers, but also to other physicians.

Robert O. Ford, LLUSM class of 1974, is an ophthalmologist in Chehalis, Washington.

October 16

So it is not the will of your Father in heaven that one of these little ones should be lost. Matthew 18:14, NRSV

An author once wrote, "At times we feel 'invisible.' But those who fight for children—for their safety and their health—are building great cathedrals. We cannot be seen if we are doing it right. And one day, it is very possible that the world will marvel, not only at what we have built, but at the beauty that has been added to the world by the sacrifices of invisible people."

On October 16, more than twenty years ago, a pediatric attending physician, fresh out of residency, was called for a consult. Many might think it bad luck that this new attending doctor had come to be known as an expert in cases of suspected child abuse. Such expertise might seem particularly unfortunate, given the fact that, twenty years ago, these cases were far more under recognized and even more difficult to prove.

On that day, Dr. Clare Sheridan-Matney evaluated a tiny infant that had been badly injured. The child had numerous injuries. The history provided by the caretakers in no way explained the severity of what she was noting. She then did what she has been doing for the past twenty-plus years—she became the voice for the child. Although at that time few were willing to do this, she stood up and called this case "child abuse." She forwarded her report to the authorities, whose job it would be to take the next step.

Twenty years later, that same child was admitted to Loma Linda University Medical Center. Profoundly delayed, underweight, and very sick, she had been in the care of those same caretakers during the intervening twenty years. This would likely cause any doctor to pause and reevaluate the past twenty years of service. Some might even see this case as a failure. But for all of us—the doctors, social workers, and staff who have worked with Dr. Sheridan-Matney—we look at this case and see the cathedral she has been building for more than two decades.

No matter the case, however difficult or heartbreaking, she has continued to fight. Quietly, with little praise and no promises of great reward, she has been building this work—brick-by-brick. She has saved thousands of children and perhaps, at times, has felt invisible. Few children are likely to have even known what she has done, being too small and young to know the face of the person who saved them.

When I asked her once what prompted her to take up this crusade, she told me that she saw the horrors of child abuse and that she felt a responsibility. Imagine how this world would be for children if we all felt this responsibility. As a famous author once said, few cathedrals have ever been built because so few people are willing to sacrifice to that degree. For twenty years, Dr. Sheridan-Matney has been working and building something she will never see finished. If at times she has felt invisible, she needs to know that we all see her; and the eyes of God see everything.

Amy Young-Snodgrass, LLUSM class of 2001, is a specialist in forensic pediatrics in Loma Linda, California.

October 17

Remember the Sabbath day, to keep it holy. Exodus 20:8, NKJV

"What part of the nation would nobody miss?" This question is likely what our nation's leadership asked before placing a good share of their nuclear missiles in the prairies surrounding Knob Noster, Missouri. It was an exceptionally boring Air Force base—nothing of consequence ever flew in or out of our base (thankfully). But, in any case, I, Captain Richard Faiola, USAF-MC, along with eight or ten others on the medical staff, defended our nation within the walls of what is currently a dinky, decommissioned hospital and clinic at Whiteman Air Force Base in Missouri.

I wasn't supposed to be there. Like many of my generation, I had just assumed that my church would train me for three to four years and then send me as a missionary to some exotic place for seven or more years. It did not quite work that way: The deferred mission program would only provide partial financial help—and not be available until the last two years.

My fellow LLUSM class members of 1976-A were among the first recruits in the nation to the far more generous and timely Military Health Professions Scholarship Program. I entered with letters only from the Air Force, assuring me that medical personnel were not expected to bear arms and that my Sabbaths would be protected.

The years 1979 to 1981 were relatively quiet. But Iraq had recently invaded Iran, the Russians were in Afghanistan, and Libya was at war with Chad; there was the usual "unrest" in Angola, Ethiopia, Haiti, and Liberia. So, somebody in the military decided that ALL units had to be field ready.

The first weekend training exercise, I convinced myself, was a legitimate, vital, necessity—even on the Sabbath hours. Who knows, I might learn something necessary to save a life in a real situation. However, it proved so utterly useless, clinically, that I could not accommodate myself to the next opportunity.

I explained my position both in person and in writing to my commander. I reproduced copies of my pre-recruitment correspondence and offered to take emergency department duty. To his thinking, none of that mattered. I had to be at the next training exercise or be arrested as AWOL (absent without leave) and spend my time in the two-cell brig until my court marshal. I made it clear that I was prepared for that possibility.

The next Friday afternoon, I sat in the auditorium with probably 200 others in full field gear and equipment as ordered. As sunset approached, I checked my watch frequently. Finally, I began to gather my things for a discrete departure. I had no sense of being watched; but at the very last moment, before I took my own action, the head of nursing, by rank second in command, planted herself in front of me, addressed me formally, and simply ordered: "Captain Faiola, dismissed." She smoked and she drank too much. Rumors floated about a possible inappropriate relationship between her and the hospital commander. But to me, she remains an angel.

Richard Faiola, LLUSM class of 1976-A, is a family practitioner in Olympia, Washington.

I knew you before I formed you in your mother's womb. Before you were born I set you apart and appointed you as my prophet to the nations. Jeremiah 1:5, NLT

I was recently asked by a young mother who was entering medical school, "Would you do it all over again? Now that you know what it takes, would you still become a doctor?"

My first thought was, "Are you crazy? I just finished the twenty-sixth grade. I can't imagine starting over!" I quickly tucked my sarcasm into my back pocket and reached for some thoughtful insight. "There will be many envelopes," I said. "You will frequently find yourself staring at them with sweaty palms, a dry mouth, and fearful thoughts of failure."

My initial encounter with this combination of emotions came with my first disappointing envelope. It was obvious that I needed to beef-up my reading comprehension for the second attempt at the Medical College Admission Tests (MCAT). Would I be good enough to make the cut? Insecurity escorted me to the post office as I sent off my medical school applications. In my mailbox arrived more envelopes, accompanied by . . . oh, yes, the sweaty palms and dry mouth.

Medical school was quite similar to childbirth. I remember it being fairly unpleasant but can't remember the specifics that would keep me from doing it again. The time passed eventually and the match for residency was upon me. Cue the sweaty palms and dry mouth, because here comes another envelope, informing me where I would be going.

I traded my tattered, short, white lab coat for a crisp coat that brushed the back of my knees. I would walk through the breezeway postcall and stop to watch the sunrise. I found comfort in the fact that the fresh brains, those who had slept in the past twenty-four hours, would soon return for rounds.

Over time, envelopes began to arrive for all sorts of things. There was the envelope that contained the results of my final United States Medical Licensing Examination (USMLE), another contained the results of the pediatric specialty board exam, and yet another contained an invitation to interview for a fellowship. Each envelope carried an element of uncertainty, a degree of sacrifice from my family, and a large dose of fear. But I took solace in Jeremiah 1:5.

Would I do it all over again? Well . . . this is what I do know. After a long day in the emergency department, my mind has been challenged and my body is tired; but I work in an utterly satisfying profession for which I have no regrets.

Andrea Thorp, LLUSM class of 2001, is instructor in LLUSM department of emergency medicine. She and her husband have two sons.

October 19

Cast thy burden upon the LORD, and he shall sustain thee. Psalm 55:22, KJV

It was a busy afternoon and my four kids were in a large hot tub in the back yard. They were swimming and diving under water. My wife and I were inside, about 20 feet away, taking care of some business. We were "watching" out the open door, when I noticed two of our boys laughing, trying to pick up Cooper, our middle son. I walked out to the tub. Cooper was floating face down on top of the water. I picked him up, thinking he was playing. He was not. He was cyanotic and breathless.

I put him down and started CPR. I was terrified. I prayed for God to revive him. After the paramedics arrived and I had a chance to "relax," I could hear Jesus saying that whatever happens, "My grace is sufficient for you, for My strength is made perfect in weakness" (2 Corinthians 12:9, NKJV). I was truly weak. By this time, Cooper's oxygen saturation was about 70 percent, and he was having some respirations. My prayer for his life was being answered.

I thanked God but was scared about having to raise a near-drowned child. I continued to trust Him and went "boldly to the throne of grace . . . [to] obtain mercy and find grace to help in time of need" (Hebrews 4:16, NKJV). My wife Kathy and Cooper were taken to the hospital. I arrived later to find them in the intensive care unit. Cooper was awake but restless and grunting.

On the way to the hospital, I called our physician, Dr. Walsh, who said that he would come pray with us. When he came, he prayed for God to help our shakened belief and spoke some uplifting Spirit-filled words. A friend, Dawn Banks, sent me a text message: "Remember, God loves Cooper more than you do," which brought even more tears to my eyes. Shortly after Dr. Walsh left, Cooper was able to sit up and started answering simple questions. The doctors were amazed at the miracle! Within twenty-four hours, our son was back to normal.

Why did God heal Cooper and not your child or your friends? I don't know. God sees the big picture; and if we are receptive, we recognize His sustaining grace. I do know that He has used this experience to deepen my faith and that of many others, and also to heighten my appreciation of the gift of life, whether it be mine or that of others.

I remember this quote by Ellen G. White: "The Lord does not press on anyone burdens too heavy to be borne. He estimates every weight before He allows it to rest upon the hearts of those who are laborers together with Him. To every one of His workers our loving heavenly Father says, 'Cast thy burden upon the Lord, and He shall sustain thee.' (Psalm 55:22). Let the burden bearers believe that He will carry every load, great or small" (*Testimonies for the Church*, vol. 7, p. 297).

Mark Sutton, LLUSM class of 1990, is assistant professor in LLUSM department of family medicine. October 19 is the date this incident occurred.

October 20

Are not sparrows two a penny? Yet without your Father's leave not one of them can fall to the ground. Matthew 10:29, NEB

Providence watches over us in small and large ways. In this case it was midsized . . . a midsized Australian shepherd. It began with my husband reading the local section of the newspaper. What brought this on? Normally his interest in news articles runs toward global events and major league sports. Maybe God was nudging him. In any case, there was a small announcement that a formerly abused dog, described in a previous news item, was now available for adoption.

"We need to get a dog," declared my husband. "Okay . . . if that's what you want," I responded. Don called the animal shelter and was informed that there was so much interest in the dog that a drawing would be held at the animal shelter on the upcoming Saturday. We were going to be gone that weekend, but at least we knew he would get a good home. When we got back Sunday afternoon, Don called the shelter to confirm that the drawing had gone off as planned. "No. No one showed up," they said.

Monday morning we were at the shelter before it opened. As we sat in the parking lot, we could feel the pall of sadness and death that often pervades such places, regardless of how well-intentioned the people are who run them. I looked down the rows of kennels behind the chain-link fences and saw sad, dispirited, lifeless animals. Here were dogs that had already given up hope—except one.

One dog was alive, vibrant, active, and aware of all that was going on around him. "No," I told myself, "I will not bond with another dog. We're here to adopt Pedro." We went into the shelter office and announced our intention to adopt Pedro, the dog featured in the newspaper. They gave us the number of his kennel, we found it, and there he was . . . the dog to which I had already given my heart. He jumped up and embraced me. We had clearly found each other.

Since that time, Pedro has grown in sweetness and devotion. He is my husband's constant companion. He senses when anyone—family, friend, or stranger—needs a little extra comfort, and offers it gently. He provides love, joy, enthusiasm, and much-needed exercise.

As Jesus said in Matthew 10:29, God is aware of all living things. Providence watches over us in big ways and in small—and in midsized ways. Pedro is our miracle doggie. He's always there—giving us love and comfort, and reminding us that small coincidences can change our lives, if we let them.

Resa L. Chase, LLUSM class of 1976-B, is professor in LLUSM department of pathology and human anatomy, division of pathology. She is course director for cell structure and function at LLUSM. She was LLUSM Teacher of the Year in 2003. She is married to Donald, LLUSM class of 1976-B.

293

October 21

Jesus said, "Father, forgive them, for they do not know what they are doing."
Luke 23:34, NIV

Forgiving is an active virtue, which was practiced and advocated by the Founder of our Faith. Forgiving can transform human relationships in dramatic and unexpected ways. The model of forgiving most thought of by Christians is the behavior of our Lord on the Cross of torture and shame, a cross that became the symbol of the glory of Christianity.

The Cross tells us that, in the face of cruelty, torture, barbarism, or simple unkindness, forgiving those who have hurt us is one of the most important activities in which a Christian can engage. Doing so may be unnatural; it may be regarded as weakness. And yet, this act was the immediate response of our Lord to horrible physical abuse and ridicule.

Forgiveness was not deserved by the religious authorities, who arranged for the crucifixion of Christ, nor the deranged mob that demanded His execution. And forgiveness was not expected by the professional soldiers who were doing their murderous duty. Our Lord's willingness to forgive was so powerful and surprising to those professional killers that they proclaimed, "Surely this man was the Son of God" (Mark 15:39, NIV). When practiced, forgiving will lead others to recognize: "This person must be Christ-like."

Opportunities to forgive are as common as the daily stresses and tensions of life. Forgiving enriches and preserves marriages, friendships, and family relationships. Those who are closest to us require the balm of forgiveness most. Forgiving your partner for being different than you in temperament, habit, or behavior may be the best thing you can do to nourish and preserve this most intimate and important relationship.

A burden of chronic bitterness and unhappiness is the fruit of failing to forgive. Even and especially when one has been victimized by serious sins, such as physical or sexual abuse or infidelity, forgiving the offender is a part of necessary healing, whether or not the marriage or other relationship continues.

It has been said, "To err is human, to forgive divine." It may be better to say that to forgive is to join with the Divine in an action that brings healing to our hearts and to our homes. To the Christian, the experience of being forgiven by our Lord should lead us to become more forgiving and consequently happier individuals.

Bruce N. Anderson, LLUSM class of 1964, is a psychiatrist in Deer Park, California. October 21 was the birthday of his father, Charles L. Anderson, LLUSM class of 1941.

But sanctify the Lord God in your hearts: and be ready always to give an answer to every man that asketh you a reason of the hope that is in you with meekness and fear. 1 Peter 3:15, KJV

It was a call day, one of many during a rigorous residency, as I walked into "Mr. Smith's" room. Here was a patient to whom, the day before, I had delivered the news that there were no options remaining for his metastatic melanoma. "Is your pain controlled? How did you sleep?" I inquired. As he answered, he seemed despondent. "Is there anything you'd like to discuss?" I inquired.

For a while, we discussed his surprise over his prognosis. Finally, I asked, "Are you a man of faith, Mr. Smith? Do you believe in a life after this one?" "I think that there is probably a god out there," he replied, "but there is no way we can ever know for certain—or know how to reach him." A conversation about the assurance of salvation through Jesus ensued, but Mr. Smith insisted that there was no way to be certain of how to reach God.

That night, the ward (and my pager) fell under a rare silence. Even the nurses' station was tranquil, without the din of ringing phones or "call" lights. I went to check on a patient I had admitted earlier that evening. "Mr. Johnson," also a cancer patient, was admitted for pain control in the setting of widely metastatic prostate cancer. Upon entering the room, I noticed a worn Bible on the bed stand.

After a few minutes, I ventured, "I notice you keep a Bible next to your bed. Are you a believer?" Mr. Johnson's face lit up, and he answered, "Oh yes. Ever since I was a child, I have followed the Lord." We began to discuss Mr. Johnson's life of faith and his anticipation of meeting the Lord face-to-face. To him, death was opening the door to a reunion with the dearest of friends.

Later, in a moment of solitude, I contemplated my interactions with each of these two patients. Although both men were facing death, one man was racked with uncertainty, while the other looked to death with certainty, hope, and expectation.

As medical professionals, there are many demands of our time. There is always an unending stack of journals and medical records. In the midst of becoming competent physicians, it is so easy to lose track of the only thing of eternal value—our hope in Jesus and His gift of eternal life. Whether it is in sixty years or sixty hours—will we face death with the joy and anticipation of meeting a dear Friend? Will we have spent the time necessary to call Jesus our best Friend? And even before that moment, will we have sufficiently equipped ourselves to give an explanation for our "hope within" to our patients, friends, and family?

In the midst of a busy schedule and countless patients, or whatever our work may be, let us not forget to dedicate time and energy to the only certainty of life—our hope of eternal life through Christ Jesus.

Renee Prins, LLUSM class of 2006, is a resident in internal medicine at Oregon Health and Science University in Portland, Oregon. In 2006, she received the Leonard Marmor Award. October 22 is the birthday of her grandfather, Tony Prins.

October 23

But my God shall supply all your need according to his riches in glory by Christ Jesus. Philippians 4:19, KJV

In the late fall of 1911, Nathan P. Colwell, MD, secretary of the Council on Medical Education, visited the College of Medical Evangelists to make a preliminary assessment of its standing with the American Medical Association. He seemed pleased with CME's progress in teaching basic sciences, yet could not make a report because the school was conducting classes in but three of its five-year curriculum.

Colwell then asked, "Why are you starting a new school, when there are already 150 medical schools in the United States? Don't you know we are endeavoring to reduce the number of such colleges by cutting out the small schools that are not well prepared to give medical training?"

CME President Wells A. Ruble, MD, responded with CME's objectives for the new school:

To prepare medical missionaries to go into foreign lands to preach the gospel.

To provide a school where we can educate our own Seventh-day Adventist young people for our own work.

To give to young people a training in the special lines of treatment that we pursue in our denominational institutions, which are scattered throughout the world.

To throw around our students an influence tending to keep them true to their determination to prepare themselves for medical missionary work.

To provide a first-class medical college where our young people may get a medical education without being obliged to violate their consciences by engaging in work on the seventh day of the week.

Colwell expressed his full sympathy and said that he saw the need for such a school. After examining the school and conferring with its faculty, he met with business manager John Burden. Funding seemed to be his greatest concern. "What is the financial backing of this school?"

Burden replied that the church's 110,000 members made up any deficits in its mission and educational programs. He further explained how church members had successfully supported various financial projects, which had seemed, to all human appearances, doomed to failure. Burden then described the unique physical, mental, and spiritual emphasis of the church's international missionary program. He added, "Will you tell me, doctor, to what school can we send our young people to equip them for this world mission work with this threefold preparation?"

Colwell replied, "There is no such school in existence."

Burden then asked, "Do you propose to destroy this little medical school . . . that is in no way competing with your endowed medical colleges but is our only means for supplying our missionary program?"

Colwell answered indirectly. "Mr. Burden, when I took my medical course, it was to become a medical missionary. . . . The medical got me, and the mission lost out." From that day on, Colwell befriended CME. He understood its purposes and appreciated its objectives. As for his contributions to CME, John Burden not only co-founded the Sanitarium but also played a vital role in establishing the School of Medicine.

Richard A. Schaefer is LLU historian. He is former director of LLUMC community relations and has been working for LLU and LLUMC for forty-two years.

We love because he [God] first loved us. 1 John 4:19, NRSV

During the clinical years, medical students begin the process of gradually transforming themselves into the types of physicians they will eventually become. In large part, this transformation occurs through modeling themselves after other physicians. For example, the thoughtful history and examination performed by an internist may highlight the importance of meticulous attention to detail. Or the tender care by an infectious disease specialist, working in an HIV clinic, may stimulate a desire within the student to incorporate the same type of compassion toward each patient, regardless of social standing.

Or, again, the time spent by a pediatric neurologist caring for a severely mentally retarded child may trigger the conviction that all life is of great value. By contrast, the encounter with a physician who is gruff, short-tempered, and arrogant, will, ideally, cause the student to decide, "I don't want to be like that!"

In many ways, Jesus lived the life of a physician, probably spending more of His time healing and caring for the sick than preaching. I believe that we should ultimately pattern every aspect of our life as physicians after the greatest Physician of all. For example, among the social outcasts of Jesus' day were those afflicted with leprosy. The compassion of Jesus toward these suffering individuals is very obvious in one account.

"A man with leprosy came and knelt in front of Jesus, begging to be healed. 'If you are willing, you can heal me and make me clean,' he said. Moved with compassion, Jesus reached out and touched him. 'I am willing,' he said. 'Be healed!'" (Mark 1:40-41, NLT).

The phrase "moved with compassion" is used several times to describe the face of Jesus toward the sick and suffering. "And when Jesus went out, He saw a great multitude; and He was moved with compassion for them, and healed their sick" (Matthew 14:14, NKJV).

Sometime later, Jesus came across a funeral processional. "A funeral procession was coming out as he approached the village gate. The young man who had died was a widow's only son, and a large crowd from the village was with her. When the Lord saw her, his heart overflowed with compassion. 'Don't cry!' he said" (Luke 7:12-13, NLT).

Of course, Jesus had the power every physician would envy, the ability to raise the boy from death; yet notice that his initial response toward the mother was to be "overflowed with compassion" and then to act from that heart of love.

The bottom line: The life of Jesus does not consist merely of words recorded on a page. For each physician, the life of Jesus may become a transforming and living reality within. When patients encounter such a physician, they will leave with the sense that they have experienced goodness, compassion, mercy, and hope. In short, the patient-physician encounter has the tremendous potential to reveal the love of God to a dying world—a bright reflection of God to lighten a darkened world.

Brad Cole, LLUSM class of 1992, is assistant professor in LLUSM department of neurology. He is course director for neuroscience at LLUSM. In 2005, he was LLUSM Teacher of the Year. He and his wife, Dorothee, LLUSM class of 1994, reside in Redlands, California.

October 25

Those who know your name will trust in you, for you, LORD, have never forsaken those who seek you. Psalm 9:10, NIV

In no other place have I experienced the words of Philippians 4:19 ring truer than during a trip to the Solomon Islands between my first and second year of medical school. The verse says, "And my God will meet all your needs according to his glorious riches in Christ Jesus" (NIV). En route to Papua New Guinea for a month-long mission trip, from mid-July to August 2007, I had stopped in the Solomon Islands, as the country had recently been through a natural disaster. On April 2, 2007, a tsunami had struck Gizo, an island in the western province of the Solomon Islands, destroying many homes and injuring or killing scores of people.

At Gizo Hospital, I met a young Seventh-day Adventist physician, native to the Solomon Islands, named Gregory Jilini, who serves as health director for the Western Province of the Solomon Islands and as director of Gizo Hospital. During our conversations, I learned that Dr. Jilini and one other physician at Gizo Hospital were responsible for the care of more than 70,000 people who inhabit the Western Province.

With a staff of 250 (100 being hospital workers), Dr. Jilini managed the care for the region during the time of the tsunami. A total of fifty-four people died, many more were injured, and more than thirty of his staffs' homes were destroyed. A large portion of the hospital had also been swept away by the ocean's powerful surge. Dr. Jilini recounted how he and his staff literally had to carry patients to the highest point on the island in order to secure their safety. For about one week, patients were sheltered under makeshift tents and hospital mattresses laid on top of the grass.

Running between emergency meetings with local government officials, treating sick patients with limited medicines, and caring for his own family—while aftershocks continued to rock the island—Dr. Jilini reached the point of physical exhaustion. Of this experience, Dr. Jilini says, "I sometimes almost gave up, as the responsibilities on my shoulders were just draining me physically. I believe my faith in God, knowing that He is right beside me all the way, gave me the strength to carry on."

With technological advances and seemingly endless supplies of medicines and instruments in the developed world, it is easy to forget how much we should depend upon our Heavenly Father. We serve a God who longs to be involved in our daily lives, providing for our every need; yet we lose sight of this wonderful experience as we rely on our own "strengths" to make it through. Patiently, our Father waits for us to seek His help in those times when all our efforts have been to no avail and we finally realize that we cannot succeed on our own.

May we learn to trust and depend on God to direct us through life's twists and turns. Isaiah 26:4 (NIV) states, "Trust in the LORD forever, for the LORD, the LORD, is the Rock eternal." Indeed, our God is a Rock eternal, never forsaking those who put their trust in Him.

Alexandros Coutsoumpos, LLUSM class of 2010, is from Silver Spring, Maryland. He is a deferred mission appointee. October 25 is his birthday.

Yet who knows whether you have come to the kingdom for such a time as this?
Esther 4:14, NKJV

On this day, October 26, 1984, the world was captivated by a tiny baby girl known as Baby Fae. All watched the nightly news for medical updates. Her now-famous photo, with the dark brown incision down her chest and a phone held to her ear, was shown nationally and internationally.

Baby Fae was born with a lethal heart defect known as hypoplastic left heart syndrome. She had been transferred to Loma Linda University Medical Center, where her parents were told of the serious nature of the disease. Her parents took her home to die, unaware that the now world-famous Leonard Bailey, LLUSM class of 1969, had been researching xenografts (cross-species heart transplants) in the animal lab in an attempt to save newborns with just such defects.

Dr. Bailey believed the research should be put into practice, and the internal review board agreed. So, after the parents were informed thoroughly regarding what would be an experimental operation, Baby Fae's diseased heart was removed and the heart of a baboon was placed into her tiny chest.

Those of us who cared for Baby Fae were caught up in a huge media event. We were proud and honored to be part of this history-making procedure. Reporters clamored for any piece of news; television vans, with their antennae probing the microwaves, surrounded the hospital. Security was very tight.

Not everyone was impressed with the initial success of the operation. Animal rights activists and many in the medical world were critical of this experimental operation. Some thought of Dr. Bailey as an attention-seeking maverick, unaware of the years of research done in preparation for this day. In contrast, stuffed toys, flowers, and messages of congratulations and hope flooded in as the baby girl was weaned off support and bottled and burped, soothed and cuddled, just as all babies are.

Baby Fae lived an amazing twenty-one days but died of graft rejection. The world then grieved the sweet little girl that had captivated its heart as it anxiously watched her progress on the nightly news. Her memorial service, held at Loma Linda University Church of Seventh-day Adventists, was packed with family, and now extended staff-family and friends, and some of Dr. Bailey's patients who attended to support him. Cameras clicked and flashed continuously as reporters documented the celebration of life in a tiny little girl and the courage of a loving mother who took such a huge leap of faith for the love of her child.

Baby Fae's legacy lives on. The following year, Baby Moses received an orthotopic heart transplant (same-species transplant) then Baby Eve, Baby Nicholas, Baby Jessie, Baby Rudy, Baby Rachel, and on and on. Now, twenty-five years after that now-famous surgery, more than 650 pediatric and adult heart transplants have been performed at Loma Linda University Medical Center.

Dr. Bailey, humble surgeon, and Baby Fae, the helplessly-ill child—together "for such a time as this."

Janette Whittaker-Allen is a registered nurse and pediatric heart transplant outpatient coordinator at LLUMC.

October 27

For he shall give his angels charge over thee, to keep thee in all thy ways. Psalm 91:11, KJV

"Cast your seed in the furrow of the world's need and watch it grow," challenged Dr. Arthur Bietz, senior pastor of White Memorial Church of Seventh-day Adventists in Los Angeles, California. He was speaking years ago during a chapel service to me and to a throng of medical students, including seniors, who would be graduating in a few short weeks.

For many in Los Angeles in those days, and probably today, here was the lure of a world metropolis, "the City of Lost Angels"—with its millions of people from everywhere, drawn by the magic of the city's climate, estate, and promise. It can be an irresistible tide to which people are drawn into a future without an anchor.

My journey began in the vast grain fields of Western Canada, snug up to the eternal snows of the jutting Rocky Mountains. On a broiling August harvest day, while gulping half a gallon of cold water, I paused to reflect upon my future. As I sat in the bunkhouse at the ranch headquarters, I was thinking about Harvard University and a dean's invitation. I was mentally comparing all of the prestige, wealth, and fame of Harvard, versus an upstart College of Medical Evangelists—a missionary medical school with an unknown future in California, 3,000 miles in the opposite direction.

What kind of future could I expect at CME? Perhaps a lifetime perspective of a soul per year won to Christ and even building a few churches in far-off, needy places would suffice. Maybe service in many lands, surgeries under all kinds of conditions, strange places and people. And, finally, death on some lonely tropical atoll, being buried by the ants but ... then a home in heaven—such would be the life of a medical evangelist. The Great Father must have slapped his thigh in Western fashion and pronounced, "This cowboy is in for a real ride!"

But I made my choice and my saga began; and the years rolled by, with prayers at sunup and sundown, carrying a red leather Bible, and feeling the guiding Spirit all along. There was no looking back. And, yes, there was missionary work, in a dozen nations and innumerable settings—from the Arctic to the steaming tropics—providing service, surgery, and sermons unending. So it's true: Each of us is given the responsibility of carrying on the Lord's work, at home or abroad—here, there, and everywhere there is a need. We are children of the Most High, stewards and servants in the place of Jesus, endowed, empowered, and inspired.

Through tide, tempest, and tornado; through trials, tribulations, testing, and even tragedy—the steady hand of God is always there. Strange names, strange places, and strange circumstances test the fiber of the soul to the core; but a thousand miracles and more attest to the angel by your side to bring you through, and to a God who will never let you down.

I have found that God is always there, letting us know, from time-to-time, that He is in command, in charge, and can save to the uttermost. As Psalm 91:11 says, keeping "thee in all thy ways."

Charles Mason von Henner, LLUSM class of 1951, is a family practitioner, general and trauma surgeon, and plastic and reconstructive surgeon. He also has an MPH degree. He resides in San Marcos, Texas.

Now faith is being sure of what we hope for and certain of what we do not see. This is what the ancients were commended for. By faith we understand that the universe was formed at God's command, so that what is seen was not made out of what was visible. Hebrews 11:1-3, NIV

The seed of Loma Linda University Medical Center was planted in November 1905 as the College of Evangelists. Later, in December 1909, it was chartered as the College of Medical Evangelists, a story with miracles of its own. It grew into Loma Linda University, the institution from which I graduated in 1976—with me becoming an anesthesiology resident, eventually a professor, and finally department chair. I have witnessed many things that most people can only imagine, and that those who are untrained might consider miraculous. Yet, I am human—differentiated only by medical education, trained in techniques of high specialization—nothing else.

It is easy to imagine, arguably, that many may be convinced that the human mind can learn transcendentally—explaining *any* conjecture. In my opinion, individuals who become more educated also become more susceptible to this delusion. We have our medical textbooks infusing knowledge, our mentors teaching expertise, and ourselves performing seeming miracles; these are all tools from which miracles bloom.

In October 1987, Paul Holc—a baby not yet born at Loma Linda—had a death sentence awaiting his birth: hypoplastic left heart syndrome. The trained human mind constructed a solution—heart transplantation. Baby Paul was to be the youngest child to receive a heart transplant. He was only three hours old. Finding a suitable donor heart would be miraculous. An anencephalic baby girl, Gabriel, was the answer. Identified less than four days earlier, her location, Ontario, Canada, presented a problem. However, medical air transport and "life support," up to the time of procurement, allowed the historic operation to proceed.

Being the attending anesthesiologist for Paul's transplant, my training was integral in keeping baby Paul alive. Paul survives to this day, receiving routine medical examinations.

Is God present in any of these situations, or is this all human invention and existential tragedy? The human mind cannot causally know a fact to be true *a priori*—an impossible Aristotelian proposition because causation is not an experience. What then is to be construed about the existence of God? On articles of faith, skeptics always seem to have the upper hand. It is impossible to disprove a negative proposition, given the domain of Deity.

Christians claim experience, notably through Scriptures, that God is extant, that He exists. Unsatisfactorily, for the skeptic and intellectual, the issue is far too simple. But no large libraries or sophisticated textbooks are required. For the believer, the thought is clear—his mind assured and intelligent, by faith. God called all things into existence. The universe did not produce itself; it is a creation acted upon by imposed law. It is God who has spoken with authority.

God's word is efficacious. He speaks; and what was not, now is. Once God becomes part of the intellectual equation, all things become simplified. Shut Him out, and man is lost in his efforts and imaginations. He can neither create nor arrive at the knowledge of a Creator. Man, a creation, cannot comprehend his Creator, except by faith.

Robert Martin, LLUSM class of 1976-A, is professor in and chair of LLUSM department of anesthesiology.

October 29

He presented another parable to them, saying, "The kingdom of heaven is like a mustard seed, which a man took and sowed in his field; and this is smaller than all other seeds; but when it is full grown, it is larger than the garden plants and becomes a tree, so that the birds of the air come and nest in its branches."
Matthew 13:31-32, NASB

Two of the most important times in my life required a deep faith-based relationship with God. The first incident was when I was diagnosed with Hodgkin's disease. Among the difficulties with which I had to deal were the surgical and radiation therapy complications, the disruption on my life, and the stress on my family.

The second event (sixteen years later) was when my wife and I felt compelled to start the Minority Introduction to the Health Sciences (MITHS) program, now in its tenth year. The program, sponsored by Loma Linda University through the School of Medicine, offers high school students a first-hand opportunity to experience what happens on a health-sciences campus. There are many sacrifices associated with maintaining the program at a high level. Thus, both of these experiences have tested and shaped my faith.

The development of a strong faith that matures into real trust in God can only occur as a result of a refining experience with Him—one that allows for significant growth of faith. In the fiery, refining process, we are tempted either to give up (if we are in the throes of a tough experience) or not to start down a tough road in the first place. In our impatience and subsequent discouragement (both ploys of the enemy), we are tempted to say, "If I only had more faith! My faith just isn't big enough!" As if everything depended on the size of our faith.

In the parable of the mustard seed, Jesus sought to teach His disciples *and us* that it is not the size of our faith that counts, but it is the immensity of God's power and His plan for our lives that makes the difference!

Lloyd John Ogilvie, in his book *The Autobiography of God*, puts it this way, "Christ lifts our inverted attention off our own insufficient faith to the immensity of God's resources for growth and change. All we are to do is plant the seed and leave the results to God. . . . He wants to make us His miracle for the world to see what He can do." Thus, the tiny mustard seed can grow into a large mustard tree that can be the perch for those around us in need of hope and encouragement.

The first of my life-changing experiences allowed me the privilege of learning the valuable lesson of entrusting the results of seed-sowing to God. In the second experience, I am privileged to practice what I learned. The second could not have occurred without the first.

I urge you to look for the lesson found in each of your refining experiences with God, rather than have the "why me" attitude. Let God's sweet Spirit empower you to use your difficult, life-altering experiences to raise your sights above yourself, so that you can grow into a mustard tree that will provide hope, encouragement, and healing to all those you see on morning rounds.

Leroy A. Reese, LLUSM class of 1972, is assistant professor in LLUSM department of gynecology and obstetrics and is associate dean for the Los Angeles Programs for LLUSM. He was an LLUSM Alumni Association 2001 Honored Alumnus. In 1999, he received the LLU Distinguished Service Award.

Now therefore hearken, O Israel, unto the statutes and unto the judgments,
which I teach you, for to do them, that ye may live. Deuteronomy 4:1, KJV

Sunday, April 15 [1906], the beautiful buildings and grounds of the Loma Linda Sanitarium were solemnly dedicated to the service of God.... During the exercises, the people were told of the remarkable providences that had attended every step taken to secure the property.... [I] spoke ... for nearly half an hour....

I tried to make it plain that sanitarium physicians and helpers were to cooperate with God in combating disease not only through the use of the natural remedial agencies He has placed within our reach, but also by encouraging their patients to lay hold on divine strength through obedience to the commandments of God....

Physicians and ministers are to unite in an effort to lead men and women to obey God's commandments. They need to study the intimate relationship . . . between obedience and health. Solemn is the responsibility resting upon medical missionaries. They are to be missionaries in the true sense of the term. The sick and the suffering who entrust themselves to the care of the helpers in our medical institutions must not be disappointed. They are to be taught how to live in harmony with heaven. As they learn to obey God's law, they will be richly blessed in body and in spirit....

In an article published in the *Review* of April 6, 1905, I wrote: "On our way back to Redlands [California], as our train passed through miles of orange groves, I thought of the efforts that should be made in this beautiful valley to proclaim the truth for this time. I recognized this section of southern California as one of the places that ... should have a fully equipped sanitarium.

"Why have such fields . . . been left almost un-worked? As I looked from the car window, and saw the trees laden with fruit, I thought, Would not earnest, Christlike efforts have brought forth just as abundant a harvest in spiritual lines? . . .

"We are called upon by God to present the truth ... to those who ... come to southern California from all parts of America. Workers who can speak to the multitudes are to be located where they can meet the people, and give them the warning message." ...

How thankful I am to the Lord ... for this place ... for us to use to the honor and glory of his name! . . . more important than magnificent scenery and beautiful buildings and spacious grounds, is the close proximity of this institution to a densely populated district, and the opportunity ... of communicating ... a knowledge of the third angel's message.... Let us remember that one most important agency is our medical missionary work. Never are we to lose sight of the great object for which our sanitariums are established—the advancement of God's closing work in the earth.

Loma Linda is to be not only a sanitarium, but an educational center. With the possession of this place comes the weighty responsibility of making the work of the institution educational in character. A school is to be established here for the training of gospel medical missionary evangelists.

Much is involved in this work, and it is very essential that a right beginning be made. The Lord has a special work to be done in this part of the field.... the Lord will go before them, preparing the way.

Ellen G. White (1827-1915) was one of the founders of the Seventh-day Adventist Church and was instrumental in the founding of LLU. This devotional first appeared in the June 21, 1906, Advent Review and Sabbath Herald.

October 31

Then he took his staff in his hand, chose five smooth stones from the stream, put them in the pouch of his shepherd's bag and, with his sling in his hand, approached the Philistine. . . . As the Philistine moved closer to attack him, David ran quickly toward the battle line to meet him. Reaching into his bag and taking out a stone, he slung it and struck the Philistine on the forehead. The stone sank into his forehead, and he fell facedown on the ground. So David triumphed over the Philistine with a sling and a stone; without a sword in his hand he struck down the Philistine and killed him. 1 Samuel 17:40, 48-50, NIV

It seems to me that God is especially extraordinary when we do our part. God loves when we are proactive. The Bible gives us countless examples, but I can reflect on my own life as a testimony to this. He has proven to me that if I do my part, no matter how small, He will make up the rest.

When I enrolled at Oakwood College (now Oakwood University) in Huntsville, Alabama, my career goal was to be a physician. I never considered Loma Linda University for many reasons. Every year I had actually avoided the dean of admissions' visit to our campus, until my last year, when my friend (now my wife) strongly encouraged me to interview and take advantage of the opportunity. I had also realized that getting into a medical school was not easy, after I received what seemed like hundreds of rejection letters. I am convinced now that had I not taken the small step of going for an interview, I would not be a physician today.

I wanted to be an obstetrician and gynecologist after my first two years of medical school, but changed my mind during my second rotation. Then I had a brief but life-changing meeting with Dr. Able Torres. He encouraged me to consider surgery. I was surprised by his advice because my grades and board scores were average. I did not think I was competitive to do anything surgical. He told me simply to try.

During my senior year, I made arrangements for an audition urology elective at Emory University in Atlanta, Georgia. A few days before I departed for Atlanta, Emory pulled out of the match for the upcoming year. My options were to arrange for a late audition at another program or to continue with my audition elective at Emory. I was an average student, so a successful early audition was critical for me to match.

After praying about the situation, the Lord inspired me to go to Atlanta. I worked very hard during the rotation, even though I knew Emory was out of the match. As it turned out, I was the only medical student for urology. I had the opportunity to work very closely with the chief of urology. Later, while interviewing, I was told that I had a very strong recommendation letter from Emory. I believe that recommendation opened the door for me.

To make a long story short, I am a board-certified urologist. God took my efforts and performed what I consider to be a miracle. God promises to help us through whatever challenges we face. God does not need our help, but isn't it amazing to see how He can take our minute human efforts and give us divine superhuman results. Do your part today and let God do the rest.

L. Jonathan Bryant, LLUSM class of 1998, is a urologist. He and his wife, Anissa LaCount, LLUSM class of 2000, reside in Yucaipa, California.

Think upon me, my God, for good, according to all that I have done for this people. Nehemiah 5:19, KJV

On November 1, American medical schools issue evaluation letters for each of their graduating medical students. Formally called Medical School Performance Evaluation letters (better known as "dean's letters"), these are used by residency program directors to assess which applicants to invite for interviews for residency positions. It also ends up as part of a physician's application for state licensure or hospital medical staff membership.

Dean's letters contain all the accomplishments, beyond grades, that each student has achieved during medical school. They describe research published, humanitarian activities, mission trips, and honors achieved. As a result, each student emerges as a paragon of medical virtues: the altruism of Albert Schweitzer, the erudition of Sir William Osler, and the empathy of Marcus Welby.

Comments from each clinical rotation are also included, usually with a positive "spin." A student who took two hours to complete an admission physical exam might be termed "methodical." One who disappeared immediately after rounds might be termed "efficient in ward work." Struggling students are lauded for "improving rapidly," and shy students praised as "quiet, but with an impressive fund of knowledge when called upon."

Dean's letters also disclose negative information about the medical student, such as a failure in a class, a health problem that required a leave of absence, or even an episode of cheating. However, the deans who write these letters consistently frame such incidents in the most winsome and gracious manner possible. A dean might write, "During his father's hospitalization for a stroke, John devoted himself to supporting his family and as a result was unable to pass his biochemistry final exam. He performed up to his usual standards when he passed the exam two months later."

Along this same line, another dean might write, "Brittney's dedication to medicine and her perseverance are clearly demonstrated by her sitting for the United States Medical Licensing Examination step 1 seven times. Students with less character might not have persisted to achieve her dream of becoming a physician." Even health problems are disclosed in a positive manner: "Leslie has taken steps to assure patient safety by asking to be monitored by our Well Being Committee while undergoing treatment. This unflinching confrontation of the issues resulted in superlative evaluations during the past year." May we all live up to the picture our dean's letter paints of us!

I find it comforting to know God evaluates me as I am. He does not suffer from amnesia with respect to my sins but does not allow my sins to foreclose on our further relationship. That is the difference between forgiving and forgetting. I can count on God's evaluation of me to include everything I have done, but He has consistently demonstrated Himself to be even more winsome and gracious than a medical school dean.

Daniel Giang, LLUSM class of 1983, is professor in and former chair of LLUSM department of neurology. He is associate dean for graduate medical education for LLUSM. November 1 is the day dean's letters are sent out.

November 2

To every thing there is a season, and a time to every purpose under the heaven.
Ecclesiastes 3:1, KJV

Ah, internship—the beginning of a new sense of responsibility, enthusiasm, altruism—until the fifth month of rotation, that is. By then, I was already burning out—perhaps due to the two months of depressing oncology; followed by two months of chronically-ill patients at a nearby affiliate hospital. Or, maybe my spirits were low because I knew that two days off in four months just wasn't going to cut it for me. Whatever the reason, by the time I started my general internal medicine phase on the 6100 unit, saving the world wasn't exactly on the top of my list.

To make life more miserable, our new attending physician for the month was no Dr. Patch Adams. He carried himself aloof and critical. Whatever he discussed during rounds usually consisted of what I felt were worthless topics. One morning he was trying to explain to us how to derive the Bayes' Theorem (the formula for Positive Predictive Value—a crucial concept in disease screening). I was steaming inside. Who cares about some irrelevant theorems? Quit wasting our precious time; we still have tons of patients to see, orders to write, notes to chart, conferences to attend, and need time to sleep!

While Dr. Attending was still rambling on, a third-year medical student abruptly interrupted him. "You are wrong, sir," he said. "This is not how you derive the Bayes' Theorem! I happen to have a master's degree in biostatistics." Oh, what a way to finally stop the drivel!

One time there was an elderly patient who was very displeased with me. He claimed that I kept changing his warfarin doses thus creating havoc with his International Normalized Ratio (INR—useful in monitoring the impact of "blood thinning" medicines). One morning, as the team moved on to the next patient, he signaled Dr. Attending to stay behind. No doubt he wanted to dish out a few grumbles about me. After rounds, Dr. Attending approached me regarding the matter. I defended myself by complaining that Mr. Elderly always fussed over this and that. I have lots of work to do. I don't have time for all his whining.

Dr. Attending paused thoughtfully. Then he said, "Time does not belong to us; it belongs to God." Indeed it does. When Christ was on earth, He spent most of His time healing, feeding, blessing, and ministering to others. Then He used the remaining time communing with God. He demonstrated to us how to be good stewards of God's time.

Yes, the irony of life. I probably learned very little from Dr. Attending when it came to internal medicine. And I still don't know how to derive the Bayes' Theorem. But his one short sentence, his reminder, still resonates throughout my career.

Wilfred Shiu, LLUSM class of 1990, is assistant clinical professor in LLUSM department of preventive medicine. This incident occurred in November.

And hope does not disappoint us, because God has poured out his love into our hearts by the Holy Spirit, whom he has given us. Romans 5:5, NIV

I believe that one of the most misunderstood words in the physician's vocabulary is the word "hope." Our patients or their families ask us, "Doctor, is there any hope?" How shall we answer? Do we answer from a helpless, passive, not really believing sense of, "I hope so"? Or can we answer from a place of confidence?

I remember sharing a midnight moment with the father of one of my patients. His son was desperately ill, but there had been a slight improvement in his condition. We rejoiced. We had HOPE! Twenty-four hours later his son was dead. Yet, his memorial service, though sad, was also an incredibly uplifting occasion.

Several weeks before, I had taken care of a 14-year-old girl who had had a fight with her parents and had broken up with her boyfriend. She decided to take a whole bottle of Tylenol. She suffered serious injury to her liver but fortunately recovered. She was in despair. She had lost hope.

What makes the difference in these two scenarios? It is the ability to have hope. Hope is a critical element of life. Proverbs 13:12 (NIV) says that "hope deferred makes the heart sick." I have seen this all too often.

But "What is hope?" you ask. We all know 1 Corinthians 13:13 (NIV): "And now these three remain: faith, hope and love. But the greatest of these is love." I agree that love is fundamental. And faith also gets a lot of attention. Righteousness by faith, faith of our fathers, faith to move mountains. Thus, this aspect is also a component of our walk with God.

But what of hope? It's the most neglected part of this holy trio. Most of us think of hope in this sense: "I hope I win the lottery." This is no more than wishful thinking. This is not the hope that Paul links with faith and love. No, God's hope is a joyful anticipation, a confident expectation based on a strong faith and evidence. Christian hope does not mean an ignoring of things as they are but rather an anticipation of things as they ought to be.

How do we get hope? We cannot buy it; we cannot earn it. No, we receive hope as a free gift from God. David says, in Psalm 62:5 (NIV), "Find rest, O my soul, in God alone; my hope comes from him." With the hope that God gives us, we can be confident in the future because of what God has done and is doing for us.

As physicians, we are called on to confront mortality, and in my specialty in particular the tragedy of illness and death in children. Believe me, this is never easy. But, I take comfort in the words of Job 19:25-26 (NIV): "I know that my Redeemer lives, and that in the end he will stand upon the earth. And after my skin has been destroyed, yet in my flesh I will see God."

This is the hope that allowed my patient's family to carry on—to see that there is more to this life than what we see here. And it's what caused Peter to declare, "Praise be to the God and Father of our Lord Jesus Christ! In his great mercy he has given us new birth into a living hope through the resurrection of Jesus Christ from the dead, and into an inheritance that can never perish, spoil or fade—kept in heaven for you" (1 Peter 1:3-4, NIV).

Richard Chinnock, LLUSM class of 1982, is professor in and chair of LLUSM department of pediatrics. November 3 is the birthday of his wife, Ruthie.

November 4

He hath shewed thee, O man, what is good; and what doth the LORD require of thee, but to do justly, and to love mercy, and to walk humbly with thy God? Micah 6:8, KJV

Micah 6:8 is one of my favorites because it gives a simple, straightforward, concise answer to a question that often concerns us: What does the Lord require of You? The answer in Micah is exemplified in the motto of Loma Linda University—"To make man whole."

For several years, the Loma Linda University Overseas Heart Surgery team worked in China with the National Heart Hospital of China. We would join them and go to different hospitals on each trip. After five or six of these trips, the head of the National Heart Hospital said he wanted to tell me what things our team had contributed to his country. I settled back like a proud parent, eager for him to shower us with accolades and descriptions of the skills and talents of the team.

He said, "Your team has made three significant contributions to cardiology and cardiac surgery in China." He continued, "The first contribution was that we soon learned that you Americans like things to be clean, not just in the surgery area, but in the rooms and halls—everywhere. We would send a team, one or two weeks in advance, to the hospital where we were to work. They would get the facility as clean as possible. The staff in these hospitals appreciated the new standard and decided to maintain the higher level of cleanliness, which they have done." Of course, I was glad the hospitals were cleaner, but I was waiting to hear about our unique skills and scientific efforts.

He went on to say, "Your second contribution was making our younger doctors realize that they must learn English. I have tried to encourage them by offering classes and tutors—but to no avail. Your people were willing to go to remote areas of China— places no English-speaking people had ever visited. Our people soon realized that if they were to fulfill their potential, they would need to read and speak English. The classes are now full of eager students, and we are extremely grateful."

I had hoped that we would be valued for something more than cleanliness and English, but he continued. He said, "The third contribution your people have made is to demonstrate the value of team work and how it is applied. This concept is completely foreign to us. We observed you working and how each person's opinion was heard and heeded. A nurse or a technician could make suggestions, and everyone listened and often action followed. Every member of the group was free to speak, knowing their idea would be considered. Thank you for your example."

He accepted the medical skills of our team as a given and valued what I thought of as a "given" to be the most significant. I realized that the things of most importance to them were to us simple by-products of a Loma Linda University School of Medicine education. A version of Micah came to mind—what doth your education require of you but to further cleanliness, communication, and to demonstrate equality and team work.

Joan Coggin, LLUSM class of 1953-A, also has an MPH degree. She is emerita professor in LLUSM department of medicine. A pediatric cardiologist residing in Loma Linda, California, she was co-founder of the LLU Overseas Heart Surgery Team. From 1978 to 1979, she served as LLUSM Alumni Association president and was named the association's 1997 Alumna of the Year. In 1990, she received the LLU Distinguished Service Award.

But he wanted to justify himself, so he asked Jesus, "And who is my neighbor?"
Luke 10:29, NIV

The world often associates the designation "Christian" with the notion of being the absolute opposite: looking down on sinners, attacking those with different beliefs, shunning those deemed ungodly. I obtained my medical school education in a Christian institution; however, I came into contact with a few individuals intolerant of drug users, homosexuals, prostitutes, and other "sinners." I think that is why I was so touched when I served one day in the HIV clinic in San Bernardino, California.

I remember arriving that day in the HIV clinic, not knowing what to expect. What were my patients going to be like? And, possibly more frightening, what was my attending physician going to be like? From the second I saw him, I was intimidated to the bone. My attending had white hair and a chiseled face, showing a combination of wisdom and intellect intertwined with a conservative, unbending attitude of practice. It was like meeting a long-serving deacon at church, who dictated the rights and wrongs of conduct in the house of God.

I was afraid to say anything—afraid of uttering something wrong and asking questions that might make me look as ignorant as I probably was. His face was stern like the pastor of a church. I felt that, sometime during the day, he was going to sit me down and start preaching to me about the righteous and unrighteous acts of life.

All of that changed, however, throughout the day when I saw him with his patients. There was the heroin addict, who had contracted HIV from sharing needles. There was the homosexual man, who needed his medications adjusted and some anal warts removed. There was also the noncompliant patient, who had been in and out of prison, whose only excuse was that she kept forgetting. It was remarkable to see the demeanor of this stern-appearing doctor melt into compassion and care as he dealt with these patients, with these "people."

He never condemned them for their practices, never looked down on them. He was only stern about what the patients had to do for their well-being. His one goal was simple—to get these souls to their next birthday. His arsenal was also very simple: anti-HIV drugs, education, and prayer. The prayer was the most profound to me.

For the first time in medical school, I felt that I was seeing the true love of God. He did not judge them. He did not even speak of the practices that brought them into this place. He met them where they were, trying to give them a second chance at life. That day I saw Jesus, and the place where all of us Christians should be.

Samuel McCash, LLUSM class of 2007, is a resident in pathology at Mount Sinai Hospital in New York City, New York. His wife, Sarah, raised money to help build an orphanage through their nonprofit organization, Project Comfort, by auctioning off her wedding ring. (The ring was returned to Sarah after the auction.) November 5 is the day he first asked Sarah out on a date.

November 6

The Lord is not slow in keeping his promise, as some understand slowness. He is patient with you, not wanting anyone to perish, but everyone to come to repentance. 2 Peter 3:9, NIV

"What is America like?" I asked my mom at a refugee camp in 1979. Among hundreds of thousands of Cambodian nationals who had fled their war-torn country, my family and I were now living in Kao I Dang refugee camp in peaceful Thailand. From the camp, many refugees were being sponsored into France, Australia, Canada, and the United States. Much to our tremendous joy, we had made contact with relatives who were living in Long Beach, California. We finally had our own sponsors!

"It will be paradise," my mom answered, with a tone of comfort and assurance. It already felt like paradise at the refugee camp, compared to the terrifying years in Cambodia. Could there be a world better than this? My mom's words created a great deal of imagination in me.

It took one-and-a-half years for my family's papers to clear. And for one-and-a-half years, I longed and longed for the world of my imagination. I would routinely watch many fortunate refugees board buses to leave for their respective new worlds. When our time finally came, the overwhelming joy would easily erase memories of sufferings in Cambodia. Taking those steps the day we boarded the bus was like walking into paradise.

Christian missionaries were at the refugee camp to teach English and Bible classes. I enjoyed the English classes very much; and with so much free time, I readily attended the Bible classes as well, hoping to learn more English there. Little did I foresee how much I would be drawn to the story of Creation, the story of Jesus, the story of the Cross, and the story of redemption. Curiosity got the better of me, and I attended regularly and even began to read the Bible on my own in the evenings.

At the conclusion of the course, the missionaries showed the *Jesus* film, and a large crowd showed up. Many were curious onlookers whom I had never seen in class. It was a very moving experience to see the stories in the Bible come alive on screen. Here I was, 9 years of age, and I felt the powerful presence of God. I began to worship Him daily.

After arriving in Long Beach, California, and adapting to a new way of life, by Providence I met Dr. and Mrs. Hyder, the parents of Linda Ferry, LLUSM class of 1979-B. They introduced me to the Seventh-day Adventist church in Long Beach. Mrs. Hyder generously drove my brothers and me to many church functions. Holidays were especially exciting. I increasingly saw that the Seventh-day Adventist set of beliefs was consistent with what I had learned on my own. I officially joined the church in baptism.

Although America did turn out to be paradise, as my mom had promised, it does pale in comparison to the paradise that Jesus has promised. There we will be living in holy communion with Him throughout eternity. What will that paradise be like? Even my mom couldn't answer this. But when the saints take off their crowns and fall to the ground in worship, we get a tiny glimpse (see Revelation 4:10).

May this destination be for every person, as God wants everyone to come to repentance and not perish, as is stated in 2 Peter 3:9. And on that glorious day, our Sponsor will personally come to pick us up. Whether it will be the next one-and-a-half years or a lifetime away, it is worth the wait. Let us long for that day!

Daniel Chan, LLUSM class of 1998, is a family practitioner in Los Alamitos, California.

November 7

Do not be anxious about anything, but in everything, by prayer and petition, with thanksgiving, present your requests to God. And the peace of God, which transcends all understanding, will guard your hearts and your mind in Christ Jesus. Finally, brothers, whatever is true, whatever is noble, whatever is right, whatever is pure, whatever is lovely, whatever is admirable—if anything is excellent or praiseworthy—think about such things. Philippians 4:6-8, NIV

My friend, Paul, a dedicated police officer assigned to our county's SWAT team, was participating in a physical training exercise, when he suddenly collapsed after traversing several obstacles on the course. As the team physician, I had just completed training—only two months earlier—all of the officers in basic first aid, CPR, and proper usage of the automatic external defibrillator (AED).

Their training took over as they flawlessly performed CPR, rescue breathing, and defibrillation to our friend and fellow officer, restoring blood flow to his brain and body. Four days later, he was released from the hospital neurologically intact.

Although he underwent an extensive evaluation by the cardiology service, there was no apparent explanation for his sudden cardiac death. He chose to heed the advice of his consulting physicians and had an automatic internal cardiac defibrillator (AICD) implanted in his chest, giving his heart "protection" from any future similar events.

Contrast that with a recent cardiac arrest in our emergency department (ED) of a 23-year-old male with severe dilated cardiomyopathy. All of us in that ED seemed to work especially hard to save this young life. In spite of multiple procedures and a valiant effort, he died.

After this death, his cardiologist stated that at every office visit he would ask this patient, "When are you getting that AICD put in? When?" The patient's reply was always, "Next time, doc . . ." This patient's heart had no "protection," and he paid for it with his life.

As Christians, our hearts are naturally "diseased." We are born sinners. In fact, God said in Genesis 6:5-6 that our every inclination is toward evil. Do you think that Christ, the Great Physician, has offered *your* hearts protection? I think we're given a big clue in Philippians 4:6-8.

But, do you believe that we are to do this ourselves? Would a patient be expected to implant his or her own defibrillator? Of course not, and, likewise, we should expect the Great Physician to give us help in gaining the peace of God that will guard, or "protect," our hearts.

Acts 15:8-9 (NIV) says: "God, who knows the heart, showed that he accepted them by giving the Holy Spirit to them, just as he did to us. He made no distinction between us and them, for he purified their hearts by faith."

I challenge you to invite the Holy Spirit into your life, thus affording your heart the protection it needs. Do not deny the Great Physician for the Peace of God can be yours.

David K. Tan, LLUSM class of 1997—for which he was senior class president—is a specialist in emergency medicine in St. Louis, Missouri.

311

November 8

"I have revealed and saved and proclaimed—I, and not some foreign god among you. You are my witnesses," declares the Lord, "that I am God." Isaiah 43:12, NIV

It was a beautiful day in November 1991, as my family and I drove to a nearby lake in Ethiopia. But it was about to change. Without warning, a man with a machine gun ran into the middle of the road and forcefully signaled my father to stop the car. As the car slowed to a stop, the man began walking toward us.

Then, with seemingly no provocation, he opened fire on our vehicle and began spraying the car with bullets. I remember the screams of my mother combined with the staccato of the machine gun fire. The smell of gunpowder wafted into the car as hundreds of small pieces of shattered glass rained down on me.

Somehow, eternity squeezed itself into a few fateful seconds. The robber took nothing more than a couple of watches and some containers of food. And as quickly as he appeared, he was gone.

It was then that I heard my mother scream again. I looked over to the passenger seat to see my mother cradling my father's head on her lap as blood spurted out the side of his neck. Then I heard her call to my brother, sister, and me: "Say goodbye to Daddy. He might still be able to hear you."

On November 8, 1991, my father's life was ripped away.

But the story does not end here.

One year after the ambush, the perpetrator was arrested. In many Ethiopian jails, food, clothing, and blankets are often not provided. This responsibility is left to the family and friends of the prisoners. My father—who had been a nurse—had helped people from the murderer's village, and the murderer's family knew and respected him. On finding out that their son was the assassin, the parents refused to help him. After hearing this, my mother decided to help my father's killer. She sent him food, clothing, and blankets.

I can never comprehend the anguish she must have felt as she helped her husband's killer. I can never feel the pain she struggled with as she cooked those meals for my father's murderer. I can never fully know how she overcame the agony she constantly relived in order to keep this man alive. But through her example, she showed me a love for God that was strong enough to reach out to a killer's soul. About two years after my father's death, my father's killer became a Christian and was baptized!

My mother allowed God to use her to bring the healing news of the gospel to a murderer, but He also used her as a living example of faith to heal the bitter anger within me. Her life became my healing. And because of her example, I strive to bring healing through my life as a medical student and eventually as a doctor. For now I understand that medical professionals are called to be reflections of the Great Healer.

Ardel William Gorospe, LLUSM class of 2010, grew up in various parts of Africa, where his parents were missionaries for more than twenty-four years. He is also a deferred mission appointee. November 8 is the date of the tragedy, but it also marked the beginning of the change in his heart.

November 9

Lord, make me to know my end, And what is the measure of my days, That I may know how frail I am. Psalm 39:4, NKJV

During rotations on the medicine service at Loma Linda University Medical Center East Campus "Community Hospital," family medicine interns are not only responsible for their internal medicine and medical intensive care unit patients, but also carry the Code Blue pager for the hospital. As an intern, I spent call nights dreading the sound of the code pager. (For some reason, our pager's chime tune was "Jingle Bells," and I've hated that song ever since.)

During a call one night early in my internship year, I spent the evening in intensive care unit room (ICU) 7 performing a thoracentesis on Mary, a middle-aged woman with breast cancer. After the successful "lung tap," she was breathing easier and was able to sleep. Her husband went home for the night, assuming, as did I, that she was stable now.

By midnight, I tucked in my patients and retreated to the call room. I slept until 4 a.m., waking to the electronic screech of "Jingle Bells." Rushing to the floor, I found 94-year-old Elsa in respiratory distress. A patient of another team, Elsa—very emaciated—was a stranger to me. As I began cardiopulmonary resuscitation (CPR), I cringed at how her prominent ribs flexed under my compressing hands.

We wheeled Elsa down to ICU room 6, where the Code Blue team and I intubated and defibrillated her. All of our efforts appeared futile, and after twenty-five minutes of ventricular fibrillation, punctuated by lengthening episodes of asystole, her family and I decided to cease resuscitation attempts. Contrary to custom, her heart monitor was not turned off; and after more than five minutes of asystole, Elsa's heart suddenly resumed an organized rhythm. She regained a pulse and stabilized on the ventilator. I was astonished and rather proud of myself for "saving" this lady's life.

Then, an ICU nurse quietly informed me that Mary, whom I had last seen sleeping peacefully after her thoracentesis, had died about ten minutes before. She was a "no code," so there had been no Code Blue alarm—her death had been quiet and calm.

I was completely devastated. I collapsed into a chair, weeping, trying to understand this juxtaposition: "Stable" Mary had died silently, while I stood next door, witnessing "fragile old" Elsa recover after a prolonged, and apparently futile, Code Blue. The emotional whiplash became worse when Mary's husband arrived, still expecting to greet his wife after a good night's sleep.

Time has passed. My patients die or live, sometimes regardless of my medical abilities. These experiences are still emotional; but I believe that a wiser Physician numbers each day of our lives, and He may intervene for reasons I cannot always understand. My goal now is to love and serve each Elsa and Mary with equal energy, always mindful that their lives, and mine, are but fleeting moments in God's hands.

Austin Bacchus, LLUSM class of 2004—for which he was sophomore class pastor—completed a residency in family medicine at LLUMC. He and his wife, Marie-Lys, live in Lake Geneva, Wisconsin. November 9 is his wife's birthday.

November 10

As he went ashore, he saw a great throng; and he had compassion on them, and healed their sick. Matthew 14:14, RSV

Searching for motivation after hours of staring at my textbooks, I stumbled across the Patrick Hughes' story on the Internet. Born without eyes and with a birth defect of tightening joints, Patrick plays trumpet for the University of Louisville (Kentucky) Cardinal team, with his dad pushing the wheelchair. That story of difficulty reminded me of Mr. S, who became a good friend and was the first customer at the Japanese food franchise business I owned. Mr. S was with the United States Air Force during World War II. He fought in the Pacific area, including Korea, where I was born. Little did I know then what this friendship would grow to be and that it would motivate me to change my career.

When I met him, Mr. S needed a companion, and I was interested in listening to his experiences. Mr. S and his troops were ordered to investigate the city of Hiroshima, Japan, the day after the atomic bomb detonated. Ever since that mission, metastasizing cancer had invaded much of his body. Sometimes he would show me one of his new synthetic body parts, such as an eyebrow with a spring in it or his knee bone where doctors had replaced a cancerous bone. He suffered insomnia over losing his comrades and seeing village people taking their own lives after hearing ill rumors about what American troops would do to them. He had an uplifting spirit, however, and demanded a strong hug from me every time we met.

Over the next three years his condition deteriorated. I would visit him in his apartment and bring with me some Miso soup. He was comfortable enough to ask me if we could pray for his daughter. I never fully understood what attracted us to each other, in light of our different ethnicity, age, language, religion, and culture. The only reason I can think of is need. I remember listening to Sigve Tonstad, MD, PhD, as he explained need-based healthcare during a healthcare debate.

It was need that drew us closer, and I find Jesus as the ultimate source of empathy. Ellen G. White describes Christ's childhood: "Jesus worked to relieve every case of suffering that He saw. He had little money to give. . . . To those who were in need He would give a cup of cold water, and would quietly place His own meal in their hands" (*The Desire of Ages*, p. 87).

Mr. S has passed away, but he has left me with the idea of caring for seniors and also helped me to decide to study medicine. I am also indebted to his comrades and many others who sacrificed their lives during the Korean War. Without Mr. S, I might not have become what I am, let alone be studying medicine.

Joo Kim, LLUSM class of 2012, is from South Korea, where he served in the military as an army detective.

November 11

The LORD does not look at the things man looks at. Man looks at the outward appearance, but the LORD looks at the heart. 1 Samuel 16:7, NIV

The sticky note on the front of the chart read: "Someone please talk to this patient (we'll call him Jose). He is very rude to the staff and uncooperative with his care." Who, me? I thought. I barely knew the patient. All I had seen of him was his shattered femur, stabilized in the operating room the day before. They had informed me he was a hefty Hispanic teenager, a member of a gang, and had suffered a gunshot wound to his thigh that splintered the bone. He had received numerous blood transfusions on arrival at the hospital.

So now what was I, a stranger and a third-year medical student, going to say to this teenage gang member about his attitude in the hospital! All I knew about gang members was the stereotype. What if I make him mad, I thought, and trembled a little.

I approached the door, cracked slightly open. Only his back was visible in the dark room. "Jose," I called out safely from the door. "Who is it?" he asked in a gruff voice. "I'm the student doctor. Listen, I know you've had a rough few days and everyone keeps disturbing you, but I'm just going to take a look at you since your surgery, okay?" Immediately his voice softened. "Yes," he grunted, and I walked in to where I could see his face.

"How *are* you?" I asked.

"Okay, I guess." He sighed and shifted onto his back.

"First time you've been shot at?"

"Yeah."

"How does it feel?" I expected him to shrug his shoulders, say it wasn't a big deal. Instead, "It's scary . . . nothing like this has ever happened to me before." A pained but thoughtful look was on his face.

"Wanna talk about it?"

"No," he shook his head.

"Okay. Well, you can always ask the staff if you want to talk about it later, okay?"

"Yeah."

"You've survived a lot so far. Someone must be watching out for you." I pointed up. He nodded.

"And the staff here has done a lot to get you where you are. They'll do everything they can to help you. What do you think?"

"Yeah." he said, and sighed again. "I know . . . I know."

After talking with him some more and examining him, I left the room. But I couldn't shake him off my mind the whole day. Humanity and suffering were actually underneath that big build and offensive attitude. I had gone in prepared to face steel—I discovered someone broken. I saw an angry gang member—God showed me a hurting teenager.

In that brief conversation, I was allowed a glimpse into his heart, the way God sees him. It was a reminder to me that God never labels anyone. He sees through every façade straight into the heart of a person, knowing and loving unconditionally. And He will go to the ends of the earth to fulfill the deep-set needs of that person.

God grant us the miracle to see and love each individual the way He does.

Dipika Pandit, LLUSM class of 2009—for which she was junior class pastor—is originally from Hendersonville, North Carolina. November 11 is the birthday of her sister, Mia. Through her own life example, Mia has taught her sister how to truly love and care.

November 12

Still others, like seed sown among thorns, hear the word; but the worries of this life, the deceitfulness of wealth and the desires for other things come in and choke the word, making it unfruitful. Mark 4:18-19, NIV

The phrase "worries of this life" can be literally translated as "the distractions of the age," and it refers to the preoccupation with temporal issues. There are many things that worry me, not the least of which involves the pursuit of academic success. Please don't misunderstand me; I definitely think God wants us to be responsible with our studies.

I am sure most of us desire to help others through medicine, but I will be the first to admit that part of my motivation stems from a few worldly desires: wanting people to think I am smart, getting into residency, and the hope of financial security. But God does not promise us these things, even if we follow hard after Him.

However, He does promise that He will never leave us or forsake us, and that He will carry out His purpose in our lives (Hebrews 13:5 and Romans 8:28, respectively). In response to seeking the praises of people, God says that we should be most concerned about His opinion over that of others. John 5:44 (NIV) states, "How can you believe if you accept praise from one another, yet make no effort to obtain the praise that comes from the only God?"

In response to our pursuit of a good life, the Bible explains that our well-being is dependent on God's plans and not our accomplishments. In Romans 8:28, Paul explains that God uses all things (even our apparent failures) to accomplish His purpose; because "in all things God works for the good of those who love him, who have been called according to his purpose" (NIV). However, do not mistake God for a spiritual genie that grants all our wishes.

No, God does not give us what we want in order to fulfill our desires; rather, He gives us what we need to accomplish His purpose. Interestingly, being in His will provides us with the utmost security and goodness in Him—the very things we wanted all along.

I am sure that as we go through medical school and continue with the rest of our lives, we will be tempted to give up God's Word for the empty promises of this world. But always remember that His will takes precedence over yours and that His plans for you are good, even though they might not be what you want at the time. For us who have been saved through the blood of Christ, we have been freed from the enslavement of our sin so that we no longer live for ourselves but now live for God. Submit to the Lord and allow His Word to bear fruit in your life. Do not let the preoccupation with temporal issues choke out that which is eternal.

Andre Cipta, LLUSM class of 2009—for which he was junior class co-pastor—is from Redlands, California, and is currently on a leave of absence attending the Master's Seminary in Sun Valley, California.

November 13

Have mercy on me, O God, have mercy! I look to you for protection. Psalm 57:1, NLT

My life's path, as it is for most people, has taken turns not anticipated. Through a series of unusual circumstances, I have become a hospital administrator. For more than twenty years, I have joined caregivers in this ministry. Balancing the needs of patients and physicians with the business portion of healthcare has been demanding but rewarding. Also, I have witnessed God's protection, love, and miraculous healing many times.

Of course, the job comes with stress. So, I have tried to include exercise in my regimen. A few years ago, my husband and I were serving the Seventh-day Adventist hospitals in the Denver, Colorado, area, when we experienced one of God's protective times. Our home there was in the foothills, near the beautiful Red Rocks Amphitheatre, which is surrounded by winding trails.

Our daughter had discovered a new trail in that area and had talked with me about checking it out, since it led to a prominent vista. So, one Sabbath afternoon I persuaded my reluctant husband to go with me on a several-mile hike along this new trail. We both believed the hike would be good, providing us a time to be together and take advantage of the natural beauty so close by.

As we were starting out, I began to narrate to my husband, Duane, an overview of our destination, as shared by our daughter. When I finished talking, we walked a few minutes in silence. Then, suddenly, I stopped. My husband was just ahead of me on the narrow trail, and, perplexed, he turned to look at me and inquired what was wrong. I told him, "I don't know."

"Are you sick?"

"No."

"Are you already tired?"

"No."

We continued to stand still, as we both pondered why my body refused to let me go any further. A minute or two later, three other people caught up to us and passed by. They walked no more than ten feet when we heard them gasp. They saw the tail end of a snake. We joined up with them and watched in horror as the largest rattlesnake either my husband or I had ever seen finished its slither across the path. At that point, the trail was very narrow, and scrub oak bushes grew close to the ground on each side. There was no way we would have seen the snake, and my open sandals would have left me vulnerable. Had we been there just a few seconds earlier. . . .

Duane and I looked into each other's eyes, realizing that we had just experienced something miraculous. It was so profound that, instead of continuing the hike, we returned home to reflect. We immediately looked up the text Psalm 57:1.

We both were grateful for God's loving protection on that day. But, just as remarkable, our family has seen other interventions from above. We share these when we need to be reminded that God is in control and that He loves us. We also feel blessed because serving at Loma Linda has allowed us to join a large family of believers, who have their own memories of miracles, regardless of the paths they have chosen.

Ruthita J. Fike is chief executive officer of LLUMC. She and her husband, Duane, have two children, Verinda and Tobias. November 13 is her birthday.

November 14

For through the law I died to the law, so that I might live to God. I have been crucified with Christ; and it is no longer I who live, but it is Christ who lives in me. And the life I now live in the flesh I live by faith in the Son of God, who loved me and gave himself for me. Galatians 2:19-20, NRSV

Halfway through my second year of medical school during a course I was taking, I experienced an eye-opening lesson that has changed my perception of myself and the meaning of Christianity. Psychopathology was a semester-long class and had only two exams: the midterm and the final. I did not pass the midterm and became worried as the final exam approached. I received a card in the mail, inviting me to attend a study session for that class; the class instructor was conducting the session.

When I arrived at the study session, I soon realized that only a few had been invited, those who had failed. Although we were all initially embarrassed, we all took comfort in knowing that more than one had failed. The instructor spent several hours explaining the basics slowly and patiently, until he felt that we understood. A few weeks later, we received the results of our mock board scores for the class. Not only had I passed the class but I had also received a 99th percentile on the national exam. I thanked God because I knew that it was a gift from Him, and I thanked the instructor for caring.

Two weeks later, while attending a Christian youth conference, I heard a preacher talk about surrendering to God. He asked the audience if there was anyone who had surrendered his or her life 100 percent to God. I was about to raise my hand, when I realized that no one else was raising a hand. I thought in my mind, "I have surrendered everything to You, Lord—my heart, my mind, my entire life."

Then, like a dam that gave way, a rush of thoughts flooded my head. Issues that had once bothered me, but that I had become numb to, came back with such a terrible sting: my careless use of His Sabbath, when I would speak my own thoughts and sleep through it as if it did not have a greater purpose; how I entertained unclean jokes, movies, songs, and chit chat that promoted sin and a skewed image of God's plan for man; and my negative and sinful thoughts that I justified because they were too sweet to give up. It all became very ugly in my mind.

I heard nothing else that the preacher said. I sat there with my face in my hands, crying uncontrollably. Then, another thought flooded me, "You were happy with 99 percent. I want 100 percent of you." I am still humbled when I think about it five years later. I vowed at that time to follow God 100 percent, but soon realized how difficult it is to be a Christian. It initially separated me from my family and friends because I could no longer do the things that I did before, however benign they once seemed.

So today, each day, I come to God in prayer: "Lord, I cannot do this myself. Only You, God, are good. Therefore, let it not be me today, but Christ who lives in me."

Mercedes Patee, LLUSM class of 2005—for which she was junior class pastor—is currently serving in Iraq as a naval flight surgeon. She is also a flight surgeon on NASA's emergency shuttle recovery team. She is married to Allen, LLUSM class of 2010.

November 15

Then I heard the voice of the Lord, saying, "Whom shall I send, and who will go for Us?" Then said I, "Here am I. Send me!" Isaiah 6:8, NASB

In the past fifty-some years of my life, I have heard these words time and time again. They always have seemed to refer to "the work" or "spreading the gospel to all the world." I guess, despite all the plethora of mission spotlights, evangelistic sermons, and missionary vespers, the real meaning of these words never seemed to impact me personally. It would take a far-away and unpopular war for me to truly connect with these words emotionally. Here is my story.

I live in the United States of America. In this country, we are blessed with so many freedoms and privileges that it is very easy to overlook their importance in our lives. We only seem to realize the true value of our God-given rights when something threatens to take them away.

Even though we have all these privileges, many of us seem to take them for granted. Turn on the radio, listen to your coworkers, surf through the Internet news community, and you will hear the message that, somehow, you are not getting what you deserve . . . what you are entitled to. But the reality is that God has blessed us and blessed our country far beyond what we deserve.

As a student of history, I have especially enjoyed witnessing God's Hand working in the establishment and development of our great country. Even so, when I was "asked" to deploy with the United States Marines to Iraq, I acquiesced grudgingly, only because of a sense of duty. I did not feel strongly that I personally owed anything to my country or my fellow citizens. But God had something to teach me about the spirit behind patriotism and service.

During my tour in Iraq, I worked both with United States citizens and with noncitizens, men and women, some young and some not so young. Day after day, I saw these individuals line up and volunteer to go out on missions, knowing that they might never return to the base . . . and some never did. They did this not necessarily for country, but for the ideals and freedoms that free countries represent—those same God-given rights that we have here at home.

I began to realize that they did not volunteer to serve out of obligation or desire for glory. They served in the midst of an unpopular war, out of a spirit of service for each other. They were inspired by what they believed in and wished to bring to others.

As I continued my tour of duty, seeing living examples of selfless service, I remembered Isaiah 6:8, a text that I had read and listened to my whole life. As I saw the willingness to serve displayed every day by the men and women in Iraq, I began to truly connect emotionally with the experience of Isaiah. Feeling a need to bring help and light to a world darkened by evil, he was willing to give of himself . . . even give his life . . . to bring life and hope to a troubled world.

And, as I truly understood in my heart, the experience behind those courageous words, I knew that I would never again be the same . . . because I had seen and now know deep inside the power behind the words, "Here am I; send me."

Gene R. Conley, LLUSM class of 1976-A, is a urologist and an internist. He and his wife, Annette, reside in Fresno, California.

November 16

For he shall give his angels charge over thee, to keep thee in all thy ways. They shall bear thee up in their hands, lest thou dash thy foot against a stone. Psalm 91:11-12, KJV

It was during the tragic civil war in Nigeria in the late 1960s that the eastern region separated from the Federal Republic of Nigeria. I was working as medical director of the Ahoada County Hospital near Port Harcourt, Nigeria. Because of the civil war, there were fears that law and order would break down at any time. We were in Biafra in the breakaway territory. Many countries were involved and participated in the work in that country.

It was during these tense days, when the beds of the hospital were filled, that a sleek, long, black limousine arrived at the entry gate of the hospital. In came the representative of the United States ambassador. He said he was just traveling in the area and stopped by to see how things were going. He asked me to call all the Americans to a meeting due to an "emergency situation."

Surprisingly, he then announced, "I appoint you a captain in the United States Army!" He told us we would be kept in touch by radio. In the event of an emergency, they would send in helicopters to take us out of Biafra.

Some time later, a group of Baptist missionary doctors came in to see me and exclaimed very excitedly, "Sam, let's get out of here!" I pondered a moment because there would be no doctor around, and the hospital was full of sick people. Should I leave these patients without any help? About that time, the Baptist doctors burst into tears, "Sam, we have got to leave now; let's go now!" However, I felt compelled to stay until help came.

Several months passed; but one night, as I lay down to rest, I had a dream—which I knew the Lord sent. I thought the Lord spoke to me and said, clearly, "LEAVE NOW!" I woke up and told my wife, "Let's get out of here immediately!" We hurriedly left the hospital within a very short time.

We then learned that we were only two hours ahead of the advancing army, ruthlessly destroying everything and everyone in their way. But God kept us alive and helped us miraculously to escape. We actually escaped by canoe across the great Niger River, at a point where it was three miles wide. That day in a war-torn country far from home, we experienced God's watchcare over us as promised in Psalm 91:11-12.

Samuel Lee DeShay, LLUSM class of 1959, also has an MA degree, an MPH degree, and a DMin degree. He and his wife, Bernice, reside in Columbia, Maryland. He was an LLUSM Alumni Association 1972 Honored Alumnus. November 16 is Bernice's birthday.

November 17

May you be made strong with all the strength that comes from his glorious power, and may you be prepared to endure everything with patience, while joyfully giving thanks to the Father, who has enabled you to share in the inheritance of the saints in the light. Colossians 1:11-12, NRSV

As a sapling emergency room (ER) attending physician, still green from residency, I was learning how to grow into my new single-doctor coverage in this "garden" of diseases—and I was far from blossoming. Frustrated patients were sprouting like weeds all around, and I was feverishly trying to tend to them all. Thus, I had no time to waste on patients that "didn't need to be here."

I found myself having to deal with various kinds of the "non-ill." These included first-time parents, who rushed babies to the ER because they were crying unnaturally; experienced bellyachers, who decided that tonight was the magical night that a random ER doctor would solve the mystery that their own gastrointestinal specialists could not; young, anxious, heart-murmur owners, who demanded that I investigate the possibility of a senile heart attack. These patients were simply not that sick! As the waiting room became crowded and ambulances steadily arrived, I felt these particular patients were wasting my time.

And then one day, I became a patient. I needed to see a specialist. I had a problem I did not fully understand. I had so many questions, and I was scared. As my doctor ushered me out of his office so that he could receive his next patient, I suddenly realized: I'm now the weed.

My problem may have been trivial to him, but it was the world to me. In essence, this was my crying baby, my unanswered bellyache, my anticipated heart attack. Standing at the clinic's exit, there were still so many things I sought to understand. I telephoned my doctor's office several times; not once did I receive a response. The unanswered questions that lingered within me stole days from my life.

Suffering as a patient transformed me into more of a doctor. My job necessitates efficiency, but I do force myself to pause now and again. I remember that I am the one with the answers. Providing reassurance and some hand-holding is not a waste of time. Sacrificing a speedy, patients-per-hour score is sometimes the appropriate thing to do, since compassion requires time. Every day, I endeavor to strike the right balance. I need to make an effort to see as many patients as possible. At the same time, I hope I am never guilty of stealing a day from one of my patients.

David Chang, LLUSM class of 2001, is a specialist in emergency medicine in Redlands, California. November 17 is his birthday.

November 18

I have told you these things so that in me you may have peace. In the world you have trouble and suffering, but take courage—I have conquered the world. John 16:33, NET

His name was Angel, and he needed a ride home to Yucaipa, California—a town about ten miles away. Well, not really, because he knew how to get home. He had arrived at 8:00 a.m. at LLU's Operation Fit Camp for Health by taking two buses, and he was planning to take two buses home that evening. Truth is, I needed to take Angel home because I wanted to hear his story. In a very quiet voice, full of confidence, he gave me glimpses of his life through answers to my questions.

"I began riding the bus by myself when I was 7 years old," he started. My eyebrows went up. "It is just what I had to do. You see, my mom is sick; and it is just the two of us living together. I am not afraid. We have no car as it is too expensive, and the bus works well.

"When I was 10 years old, we were almost homeless after my mother lost her job when she was diagnosed with rheumatoid arthritis and was unable to walk. I found her a doctor at Loma Linda University by looking in the yellow pages. And I found her a job in the *Green Sheet* and registered her for orientation at Wal-Mart. You see, she speaks no English; and at 10 years old, I was pretty good at English."

By this point in his account, I was beyond intrigued by his story of resilience. I asked him what his goals were and who his hero was. "I want to go to college and be a doctor, but I do not know if I have enough money. My hero? It is my mother; she never complains. My goal is to be around to help her if she is sick."

I left him at his home; and as I returned to my own home, I noticed all the buses that passed. How many of those buses were carrying other young children with huge dreams and courage?

Marti Baum Hardesty, LLUSM class of 1979-B, is assistant professor in LLUSM department of pediatrics. She and her husband, Robert, LLUSM class of 1978-A, reside in Redlands, California.

God works in different ways, but it is the same God who does the work in all of us. 1 Corinthians 12:6, NLT

As I emerged from an exam room in the family medicine clinic, I could tell Marty had already arrived for his appointment. The smell of warm, freshly-baked jalapeño bagels wafted down the hall, and the sound of happy chatter came from the team leaders' room in the back. This was going to be a good day in clinic.

Marty rarely arrived for an appointment without bringing fresh bagels for the staff. These he personally delivered with a cheery "Good morning" and a "God bless you," as he limped his way from desk to desk, leaning on his walker. Soon his thick chart appeared on the exam door, and I went in to see him.

Marty is a patient with traumatic brain injury. As a young man, he had a motor vehicle accident that left him with permanent mental and physical disabilities, including weakness and painful muscle contractures on one side of his body.

He was excited to show off his new walker, which had three wheels, handlebars, and brakes. He talked about how good God was to him and how much he loved Jesus. His cheerfulness and good humor radiated from his smiling face.

As I listened to him and refilled his prescriptions, it seemed as though my worries faded and gratitude for the goodness of life filled my heart. We finished the visit with prayer, and he went on his way. It was a very good day in clinic—a very good day.

John Testerman, LLUSM class of 1980-B, is associate professor in and chair of LLUSM department of family medicine. He received a PhD degree in biological sciences from University of California, Irvine, in 1971.

November 20

Be still, and know that I am God. Psalm 46:10, KJV

It seems that many people live in the fast lane of life, rushing from place to place, while thinking about or doing something else—such as talking on cell phones or listening to chatter on the radio or television. I once lived the noisy life on "Busy Street," and I was the self-designated Queen of Multitasking.

Then a series of health challenges focused my attention. I eventually realized that I would have to discontinue my work and seriously adjust my lifestyle. Being forced into the slow lane was discouraging, and I spent many quiet hours of reflection and reading spiritual pieces. As I looked inwards toward the Spirit, I became increasingly aware of the wonders of life.

Along the way, I discovered the beauty of silence. I began to understand the meaning of Psalm 46:10. It was amazing to me that, when I created a quiet atmosphere and acknowledged God, I found that He was present.

I now believe that God and I are partners in the necessary efforts for me to stay balanced, and I'm able to work again. I do my part, and He ensures that my actions are effective. It is fun to keep bumping into God throughout the day. My life has turned into a series of mini-miracles, and I just smile.

Albert Einstein once said, "There are only two ways to live your life. One as though nothing is a miracle. The other is as though everything is a miracle." I believe that everything is a miracle—from nature's beauty to finding a parking place at a convenient location.

As members of the healing arts, we know the importance of the LLU motto, "To make man whole," in the healing of our patients. Let us also apply that motto to our individual lives and seek unity of the body, mind, and spirit. Live gently, instead of fast. Listen for God's gentle whisper, and keep your eyes and mind open each day for His mini-miracles.

Peggy J. Fritzsche, LLUSM class of 1966, is clinical professor in LLUSM department of radiology. She was LLUSM Alumni Association 2008 Alumna of the Year and was an LLUSM Alumni Association 2005 Honored Alumna. She and her husband, Anton Hasso, LLUSM class of 1967, reside in Redlands, California.

I can do everything through him who gives me strength. Philippians 4:13, NIV

We were honored to have the leading general surgeon, residing in a nearby city, choose to come to Loma Linda University Medical Center for the surgical treatment of his coronary artery disease.

This man was highly regarded in his field. He was talented and was trained in the best institutions. After his successful coronary artery bypass surgery, there was the usual discussion about the causes and prevention of his disease. Among the lifestyle factors discussed was the necessity that he should give up cigarette smoking.

He said he had tried to stop in times past but had been unable to do so. He thanked us profusely for the good care he had received and said he would see what he could do. The last time I saw him, he was still smoking.

About the same time, we performed coronary artery surgery on a retired major in the United States Marines. He had seen heavy combat in Vietnam and Korea. Interestingly, he had been captured by the enemy in both Vietnam and Korea. In both instances, he had outmaneuvered and overpowered his guards and escaped.

In the postoperative interim, he was also counseled that he must stop smoking. With emphatic firmness in his voice and direct eye contact, he quickly replied, "That will be no problem." Later he told us he never smoked again. It is apparent that when this man made a decision, he was determined and accomplished it.

Statements from the fine book, *Christ's Object Lessons* by Ellen G. White, page 56, affirm the role of our choices combined with God's strength. "The power of choice is ours, and it rests with us what we will become." And on page 316, she wrote, "He expects us to overcome in His name."

The Christian often sees in his life many negative characteristics that must be overcome. God has promised supernatural aid to do this. As Paul testifies in Philippians 4:13, we can do anything through Christ's strength.

Ellsworth E. Wareham, LLUSM class of 1942, is a thoracic surgeon and emeritus professor in LLUSM department of surgery. He was co-founder of LLU Overseas Heart Surgery Team. In 2006, he was named LLUSM Alumni Association 2006 Alumnus of the Year; and in 1994, he was named LLU Alumnus of the Year.

November 22

Give your servant therefore an understanding mind. 1 Kings 3:9, NRSV

In 1965, my wife and I arrived in Loma Linda as students, coming from Maryland amid east coast warnings that we must not lose our faith, as others had done after going out West. I now realize that those forty-plus years since then have profoundly enhanced my understanding of how God can lead in our lives. Let me explain.

As a young new associate dean for student affairs for LLUSM, I once asked a student, who had an impressive story about God's leading in his life, to talk for chapel. He told his story about God answering his prayer when he hadn't really studied for a test and had done well. The reaction I heard from the medical student body was surprising but should have been predictable: Those who hadn't been the beneficiaries of God's special blessing on that test were angry. How dare he not study and ask God to circumvent natural results. The experience added to my journey of understanding.

Through the years there have been hundreds, and probably thousands, of struggling students trying to reconcile their absolute knowledge that God had brought them here with the current facts of their impending failure. Where is God when you really need Him? A new way of conceptualizing God's role in our lives awaited the clarity of many stories.

I began to see that God has a harder time working with us when we tell Him what we want Him to do. The alternative is so wonderful. Prayer always connects us closer to God when, instead of being all-knowing ourselves about what should be happening, we surrender the entire life project over to a Higher Power and allow things to occur as they must. At that point, God can cause incredible things to happen. We have gotten out of God's way!

I have seen more miracles occur when students begin asking for companionship rather than for results. This simple difference is life-changing, and I began incorporating it in my own life. I now know that my job is not so difficult. Micromanaging life doesn't work anyway—especially if it involves someone else's life.

We all know that bad things happen to good people. We, however, have a resource for support. We can get through those tough times, which we only push away when we take charge and ask for specific actions that may or may not be really what works for our lives.

Medical and dental students have given me a whole new invigorated view of God's interest, power, and commitment to His children. What a gift Loma Linda has given me! Thanks for all your stories; they helped form mine. Finally, allow me to share a favorite prayer.

The Serenity Prayer
God grant me the serenity to accept the things I cannot change,
Courage to change the things I can,
And the wisdom to know the difference.

Bill Hooker, associate professor in LLUSM department of pathology and human anatomy, earned a PhD degree in anatomy from LLU in 1969. After serving from 1977 to 1978 as assistant dean for student affairs for LLUSM, he was appointed associate dean and served in that position until 1993. From 1994 to 2008, he served as associate dean for student affairs for LLUSD. He received the LLU Distinguished Service Award in 2008.

In reply Jesus said: . . . "Which of these three do you think was a neighbor to the man who fell into the hands of robbers?" The expert in the law replied, "The one who had mercy on him." Jesus told him, "Go and do likewise." Luke 10:30, 36-37, NIV

"That object lying motionless in the middle of the road is a person," I exclaimed to my wife, as we sped past it on the dark, unlit, two-lane highway. It was a black, moonless night the evening we drove back to our home at Mountain View College from the port city of Cagayan de Oro on the island of Mindanao in the Philippines. We were on the major thoroughfare between the coast and the interior, where the college was located.

In 1984, when my wife and I were on the teaching faculty of the college, this road was no more than one lane in each direction, winding seventy-plus miles through the mountains. We were at the outskirts of a small town; and no houses were in sight—just a shelter at the side of the road, designed for those waiting for a bus.

Reports of the activity of the New People's Army (NPA), a grass-roots Communist insurgency, were common—with frequent skirmishes between them and local police or the Philippine army patrols that sought to subdue their activity. It was not uncommon for NPA groups to hold up passengers on buses or cars, robbing them of money or valuables. Warnings were given, especially to foreigners, not to be on the road after dark—and especially not to leave one's vehicle.

With these warnings in our minds, we viewed the motionless body. Had he been hit by a passing vehicle? Was he planted there by an NPA group to lure a passing vehicle into a trap? But if he were alive, he surely would need help. It was almost midnight; was it safe to stop? If he wasn't dead, and he stayed on the road, chances were good that he would be hit and killed.

We looked at each other for a few seconds and knew that we had to turn around and help. We parked and rushed over to the man. A quick assessment revealed a strong, bounding pulse and no signs of injury. As we carefully rolled him over, the strong smell of alcohol gave us a probable diagnosis—an inebriated man who had decided to sleep off his stupor in the center of the road!

We moved the man to the side of the road but were unable to flag down any of the passing vehicles. Eventually a Jeep pulled over, with a stately looking gentleman in the passenger seat. He assisted us in rousing the man enough for him to stumble over to the nearby bus stop shelter, where we left him to sleep off his drunkenness.

Many months later, while attending the college banquet, we were both amazed and humbled as the governor of Bukidnon Province, the invited guest of honor, shared a story of how he had witnessed two good Samaritan faculty members help a drunken villager along the dangerous highway. Vividly we were reminded that our Savior left the safety of His heavenly home to come down to this dangerous planet to rescue us who are drunk with sin. In response to this love, how could we have done otherwise?

Stephen Nyirady is associate dean for admissions for LLUSM and is associate professor in LLUSM department of basic sciences, division of microbiology. He received a PhD degree from LLU in 1972. He chaired and taught in Seventh-day Adventist college biology departments in the United States and abroad for thirty-three years before assuming his current position in 2004.

November 24

And I pray that you, being rooted and established in love, may have power, together with all the saints, to grasp how wide and long and high and deep is the love of Christ. Ephesians 3:17-18, NIV

It isn't easy being the parent of a child needing a heart transplant. First and foremost, you, as a parent, have a desperately-ill child, for whom you have to decide what is in his or her best interest. And complicating that decision, you may have to move across the country, take a leave of absence from your job, separate your family, and commit every moment of your life to caring for this new little one.

Amazingly, most parents choose to do whatever it takes to give their baby a chance at life. Regardless of race or family origin, and whether wealthy or poor, older or younger, and well-educated or not, parents and families commit their lives and resources toward giving this new life a chance. And most of them do not complain or think that they are doing anything extraordinary; they just act out of love they have for this newborn being.

There are many success stories from cardiac transplantation—children who excel academically, go to college, marry, some even have children. But there are also children who struggle—academically, socially, spiritually, physically. Having the privilege to watch these families and their children as they grow up gives a glimpse into the love Christ has for us.

The parents of the children who are successes are proud of their children's accomplishments, as are most parents of healthy children. But the amazing glimpse of Christ's love for us as doctors is how the parents of the children who struggle feel about their offspring. Some children are different, not able to learn much, maybe not able to walk, but their parents and families lovingly care for them day in and day out. Life, in whatever form and with whatever abilities given, is precious and loved by these parents.

Even the most profoundly disabled children have parents who advocate for them, make decisions on their behalf. Sometimes, those decisions may mean the child must undergo a procedure or a surgery. And sometimes, courageously, the decision is made to stop aggressive medical interventions.

Christ loves us in a similar fashion. When He created us, He made us perfect, beautiful, in His own image. Just as parents, in choosing a heart transplant, hope and dream that their baby will be successful or "normal," so Christ created us to be perfect. But sin entered in, and we are marred—different, so far from what He hoped for us to be. But, He loves us still, He advocates for us, He cares for us day in and day out.

And, eventually, He gave His all, in order to give us a chance again at life—the perfect, beautiful life that He had planned for us in the beginning. In the love and sacrifices the parents of children needing heart transplants give to their children, the love of Christ for us is glimpsed.

Tamara Shankel, LLUSM class of 1988, is associate professor in LLUSM departments of pediatrics and of medicine. She is associate dean for clinical education and is also course director for physical diagnosis at LLUSM. She and her husband, Ted, LLUSM class of 1988, reside in Calimesa, California.

He will regard the prayer of the destitute, and will not despise their prayer.
Psalm 102:17, NRSV

As a child- and adolescent-psychiatrist, I have seen and heard stories of both physical and emotional suffering and have thankfully witnessed many cases of positive transformation. Of these experiences, one incident stands out in my memory. A 12-year-old boy was admitted to Loma Linda University Behavioral Medicine Center for behavioral issues related to a traumatic brain injury. The boy, who I'll call David, exhibited impulsive aggression, and was verbally uninhibited, with marked articulation deficits.

These conditions were secondary to his traumatic brain injury, the result of being hit over the head with an aluminum baseball bat by his mother while she was under the influence of drugs and alcohol. David had been in the rehabilitation center for eight months dealing with the consequences of the head injury; however, he had been unable to continue on the rehab unit due to his disruptive behavior.

Arrangements were made for him to be transferred to the Behavioral Medicine Center's child inpatient psychiatry unit. Following admission, he was started on psychotropic medications. Additionally, a behavioral treatment plan was set, and he participated in group and individual counseling sessions. His progress was slow, however, and he continued his disruptive and inappropriate behavior.

Each day I make rounds in the morning with students and residents and often return to finish up the day's work in the evening. This day I was late, and it was nearing the children's bedtime. David had experienced a particularly out-of-control day. I stopped by his room to talk about his behavior just as he was getting ready to go to bed. Taking me somewhat by surprise, he asked if I would pray for him.

While willing to do that, I felt it could have a greater impact on him if he himself prayed, so I encouraged him to pray. He readily agreed, knelt by the bed, and started to pray. "Oh Lord, thank you Jesus…" in a Pentecostal manner. As he continued, he prayed for God's help with his own behavior, for his grandmother (who had taught him to pray), for his mother, for the staff, and for me by name.

Surprisingly, his thoughts and requests were organized and coherent, in contrast to his usually loose and disorganized thoughts and speech. The prayer was of real needs and was very emotionally charged. David finished his eloquent prayer, and I followed with a very brief and simple prayer by comparison.

Hiding the tears in my eyes as I told him good night, I quickly left his room. As I left the unit and drove home, once again I had my own silent prayer for my patients. I recognized that we could only provide a safe environment and age-level treatment for his emotional growth, but that David's prayer and mine to the Divine Healer is where man's power is turned over to God.

William Murdoch, LLUSM class of 1973-B, is associate professor in and interim chair of LLUSM department of psychiatry. He is also medical director of LLUBMC, as well as chief of child/adolescent psychiatry at LLUBMC.

November 26

Everything is possible to one who has faith. Mark 9:23, NEB

Those encouraging words were spoken to a desperate father whose son had been ill from birth. The evil spirit had attempted to throw the lad into the fire or drown him in water. It could just as well be a contemporary teenager, who, addicted to meth or alcohol, has dropped out of school with no job skills and no future. Helpless then or helpless now makes no difference.

In a desperate plea, the father says, "If it is at all possible for you, take pity upon us and help us" (Mark 9:22, NEB).

Jesus responds, "If it is possible?" (*Are you kidding? Let me tell you plainly, sir, I am not the variable. I am always with you. You are the variable.*) "Everything is possible to one who has faith." (*Or to the person who trusts Me to be present and helpful. You are the one who decides the future of your son by your trust and belief in Me.*)

"'I have faith,' cried the boy's father; 'help me where faith falls short'" (Mark 9:24, NEB). With that positive intentional affirmation, Jesus takes the lad by the hand and restores him to full health.

Let me be clear at this point. God created you and wired you to trust (have faith in) Him and to choose the way of positive choice, to survive in spite of the greatest of odds.

The annals of human experience continue to inspire us with the tenacity of the human spirit supported by a benevolent Creator. Few have stated it better than Dr. Bruno Bettelheim. Thrown into the horrors of the Dachau concentration camp, Dr. Bettelheim recalls being too weak to swallow food. A fellow prisoner, confined for years, counseled him, *It's up to you if you survive here. You won't like the stuff they serve for food. But to survive, you'll eat whatever it is, whenever it's served, revolting as it is. You'll monitor your body—defecate when you can, read when you can, sleep when you can. And decide to keep your mouth shut.* His subsequent writing, including *The Informed Heart*, clarifies the positive choices that permitted Dr. Bettelheim to endure and emerge from that camp.

We all can carry out some area of freedom of action and thought, however insignificant. Those prisoners who focused on what was unjust, wrong, and broken found exactly that. On the other hand, those prisoners who looked for what worked were utilizing the power of positive intention.

Remember what Jesus said to the father, *I'm the constant; you are the variable.* "Everything is possible to the one who has faith."

William Loveless is professor in LLUSD department of educational support. He is the immediate past senior pastor of Loma Linda University Church of Seventh-day Adventists, where he served from 1990 to 2000, and previously from 1970 to 1976. Between these two pastoral appointments, he served as president of Columbia Union College in Takoma Park, Maryland. He has an EdD degree from University of Maryland.

November 27

In fact, we felt sure that we were going to die. But this made us stop trusting in ourselves and start trusting God, who raises the dead to life. 2 Corinthians 1:9, CEV

Life's experiences and its challenges can be stepping stones or stumbling blocks. A penetrating question is, "Why and how do some people go through some of life's most agonizing experiences and still exhibit courage, dignity, and grace?" What is their secret?

It seemed like just another Wednesday evening support group meeting for cancer patients at Loma Linda University Medical Center. There were nearly 120 of them in attendance. Most of them believed that their tumors were being totally obliterated by protons during the eight-to-nine weeks they were in treatment. Each was on a journey—seeking hope, healing, and wholeness. They shared an experience that bound them together—emotionally, physically, and spiritually.

They were an interesting group of people, coming from all across the country and from around the world. Blue- and white-collar. Hindus. Buddhists. Christians from all denominations. Single and married. There were a few who claimed to be agnostic and one who openly said he was what would be considered an atheist. Even he acknowledged that there was something different and almost magical about the place.

The patient who addressed the group next had become acquainted with many in the room. He was soft-spoken, and it appeared to some as if he had carefully and prayerfully thought about each word he was about to share. Several knew that he was an emeritus bishop in the Catholic Church in the Midwest.

"Most of us have cancer," he began. "For me, it is the second time. I have had a reoccurrence. I want to share what has been happening to me. I believe we continue to experience healing in sharing. My testimony is really about my blessed Savior Jesus, and what He has taught me during the last few weeks. This has been a very special time for me here at Loma Linda. Thousands have cancer, but only a few come to Loma Linda.

"However, I am convinced that no one comes to this religious institution by accident. I have had a lot of extra time to reflect and pray during the last two months. I have been looking upward and heavenward. There is power in prayer and praise. God has helped me realize that my cancer is a gift. Life provides us with many challenges and opportunities to grow. I will never be the same. None of us will. I hope to be able to minister and relate to people in a more caring and compassionate manner.

"In addition to being treated for cancer and meeting so many of you wonderful people, I experienced another blessing. For the last several years, I have been taking medication for high blood pressure. Even then it has been borderline. After I had been on this campus for three weeks, I am pleased to share that my blood pressure has been normal for the first time in years. This medical center and its people are truly amazing. I believe I have been on Holy Ground, and God wants me to use this gift to His honor and glory. God also wants you to look up to Him."

Stepping stones or stumbling blocks? It all depends on the direction we are looking.

Lynn Martell is director of special services for radiation medicine at LLUMC. He was vice president for advancement for LLU from 1999 to 2006. He received a DMin degree from McCormick Theological Seminary in Chicago, Illinois, in 1990.

November 28

The king [David] was deeply moved, and went up to the chamber over the gate, and wept; and as he went, he said, "O my son Absalom, my son, my son Absalom! Would I had died instead of you, O Absalom, my son, my son!" 2 Samuel 18:33, NRSV

The tattooed, pierced, and unkempt 17-year-old man was accompanied by his parents and older sister. He had recently been diagnosed with testicular cancer. The patient had undergone chemotherapy and had come to see me for a consultation regarding surgical removal of his retroperitoneal lymph nodes. The young man was disrespectful to his parents and flippant about his clinical situation.

Following my review of the importance of regularly scheduled follow-ups, the mother and father were clearly concerned about how his behavior would affect his long-term prospects. After more discussion, it became clear that, in the view of this socially conservative family, the son was rebellious, had behaved irresponsibly, and had generally underachieved. Clearly there was tension and discontent in the relationship between the son and the parents.

After I had reviewed the options of management, the father asserted that cure was the most important thing. He indicated that, in spite of the possible problems related to surgery, maximum treatment with surgery—thus necessitating fewer future follow-ups—would be best. The father was emotional and said that he could not bear the thought of losing his son.

In a urologic cancer practice, most patients are older adults; it is uncommon that patients come for office visits accompanied by their parents. In my practice, it is usually the parent who has cancer, and the spouse and children are worried for their loved one. I have become accustomed to dealing with the dynamics of older patients and their families. The discontent and compensatory behaviors usually deal with disappointments and issues in the past. In this situation, however, the family tension was primarily over what would happen in the future and about how the son could reverse his course and fulfill his potential in life.

After possible lung metastasis had been excluded, the surgery was scheduled. Even when offered less invasive treatments, the family reaffirmed—given the rebellious nature of the patient—that the most definitive treatment would suit him best. The surgery removed cancer containing lymph nodes, and the family was by the young man's side throughout his entire hospitalization. In spite of his previous misbehavior and rebelliousness, the unconditional love of his parents for him was very obvious. Whatever disappointment he had caused was far outweighed by their love for him and belief in his potential.

I was struck by the depth of the parents' love for their son and by the forgiveness and reconciliation readily offered by them. It reminded me of 2 Samuel 18:33, when King David heard that his rebellious son Absalom, who was trying to overthrow his father, had been killed. These situations are a fitting reminder that the strong parental love that we see on this earth is a fraction of the love God has for his human children.

Herbert Ruckle, LLUSM class of 1986, is professor in and chair of LLUSM department of urology.

November 29

I know, O LORD, that a man's life is not his own; it is not for man to direct his steps. Jeremiah 10:23, NIV

I 1947, I came home from school, ran into our house, and made a "pronouncement" to my mother: "Mom, I am going to become a doctor." Mom, a former teacher, looked at me with a bit of disbelief in her demeanor and simply replied, "Well, if that is what you wish to do, then go for it."

So the pursuit of that goal began with God leading in ways I would not know or could have believed. My journey became a process of work to meet college expenses, including colporteuring; cleaning Halcyon Hall (a dormitory at Washington Missionary College [now Columbia Union College] in Takoma Park, Maryland); and being a lab assistant, as well as studying and keeping a single vision. I had no idea what I would do after graduating if I did not make it to medical school.

Only one medical school ever entered my thoughts: the College of Medical Evangelists in Loma Linda, California. How well I remember that interview with Dean Clark from the College. Nervous was not the word to describe how petrified I was remembering that C+ in physics, despite studying hard. (I am neither inclined to do abstract thinking, nor am I mechanically inclined.)

Then came that telephone call with the announcement that I had been accepted into the School of Medicine. I ran through the college dorm shouting and stopping everyone that I saw, announcing, "I am going to medical school, I am going to medical school, I am going..." Then reality set in. Just where did I think I was going to obtain money for tuition, living, and traveling expenses? In those days, there was no such thing as scholarships or places where one could obtain a loan.

So I had to come up with a plan. Howard Morse Jr., LLUSM class of 1958, and I were "competitor" friends—vying as to who could make the highest score on a test. Howard was a junior and also planning to enter medical school. His father, Howard Morse Sr., LLUSM class of 1929, was a family physician in Takoma Park, Maryland. Of course (in my *naiveté*), I would just go and ask Dr. and Mrs. Morse for money! Taking a bus to their home, I went in and asked. Rather surprised, they said that they would think about it.

I really prayed, because this was the only source of funds I knew. The next week, the answer came: Yes, but they would give the loan for tuition one semester at a time and charge 4 percent interest, starting at graduation. Sadly, my mom died in October 1952, not knowing the realization of my dream-come-true. But my dad promised that he would pay for my living expenses.

August 1953 found three classmates and me driving a car from Washington, D.C., to California—expenses paid. Could we have seen how God would direct each step—my specializing in obstetrics and gynecology, and eventually practicing in Brunswick, Maine? Or that I would meet Richard Spindler, my future husband, in South River, Ontario, Canada, at the house of Hilda Rainda Scheffler, LLUSM class of 1957? Or that there would be some mission time in Penang, Malaysia, Singapore, and Guam?

How we look forward to the time when I will meet my mom again, thank her for her encouragement, and tell her of the fulfillment of my dream. I will also thank my dad, Dr. and Mrs. Morse, and all those who had faith in a naive, simple West Virginian.

Alice N. Cunningham, LLUSM class of 1957, is an obstetrician and gynecologist. She and her husband, Richard Spindler, reside in Brunswick, Maine. November 29 is their wedding anniversary.

November 30

Present your bodies a living sacrifice, holy, acceptable unto God, which is your reasonable service. And be not conformed to this world: but be ye transformed by the renewing of your mind, that ye may prove what is that good, and acceptable, and perfect, will of God. Romans 12:1-2, KJV

"Please come to China and help us with our smoking problem," requested Dr. Tian Benchen, who—sponsored by China's Ministry of Health—was visiting the United States. He actually set a date, and our team was ready to go when a phone call from him stopped us. "Don't come," he said. We wondered why. That evening on television we learned why: Tiananmen Square. The Communist party leaders had rebuffed the "student" uprising.

But the Lord overruled, and the next word from China was, "Come!" So, on November 30, 1990, we found ourselves in Beijing, China. We presented papers on the Five-day Plan to Stop Smoking at the Second Annual Symposium on Smoking and Health at Beijing Medical University.

The auditorium was packed with two physician delegates from every of the thirty Chinese provinces. They came full of questions: "How did the Five-day Plan begin?" "Can the program be adapted to China?" "What is your success rate?"

The plan began in the 1938-39 school year, when I was a medical student. My classmate, John Petersen, LLUSM class of 1939, and I were conducting preventive medicine lectures to waiting patients at the White Memorial Hospital (now White Memorial Medical Center) Clinic in Los Angeles, California. "Tobacco and How to Stop Smoking in Five Days" stood high on the list. The smokers learned the importance of diet, exercise, proper breathing, water inside and out—with no alcohol, tea, or coffee. We told the Chinese our success rate was 33 percent, i.e., not smoking after one year.

That evening a delegation asked us to come to Shenyang and conduct a full Five-day Plan to Stop Smoking Program. We accepted. Among the Chinese doctors was our interpreter, Huang Yimin, who spoke excellent English. He wanted to learn how to conduct the program, but even more thrilling was his desire to study the Bible.

Each day he would come to my room. I would read from the Bible, *Ministry of Healing*, or *Steps to Christ*; and we would have prayer. It was not long before he asked to pray and asked God to direct him. He told me, "You have taught me that Christians love people. Thanks so much for coming to China." I watched him change from Communist to Christian.

I knew from that time on that the Lord was leading us and that the Five-day Plan would help open the doors of China. We counted on Drs. Benchen and Yimin to lead out in our work in China. They have surpassed our expectations.

On our trip to Sir Run Run Shaw Hospital, the Five-day Plan was carried as a program on the local television station. The nearby university hospital became a staunch supporter of the smoking-withdrawal program. They asked us to come back, and we have. We now have a major presence in all the capital cities of China.

The entire experience in China has strengthened my belief that God has a program that will not fail as long as we humbly pray for His guidance. The Lord has given us a great "entering wedge," the "right arm" to open hearts and minds.

J. Wayne McFarland, LLUSM class of 1939, was an LLUSM Alumni Association 1990 Honored Alumnus. He resides in Loma Linda, California. November 30 is the date of his first trip to China.

December 1

The LORD your God is with you, he is mighty to save. He will take great delight in you, he will quiet you with his love, he will rejoice over you with singing. Zephaniah 3:17, NIV

He is tired. Completely tired. Thoroughly exhausted.

Just a few hours before, standing atop Mount Carmel, he had proven to all that God is the God of Israel. But he is running now . . . running away from a queen who wants him dead. In his terror, he collapses and begins to pray: "God, I've had it. Take my life; I'm ready to die." He has nothing left to offer . . . or so he thinks.

In his exhaustion, he sleeps. But it isn't long before he finds himself shaken awake by an angel. "Get up, Elijah. Eat and drink." Twice the angel comes to him and bids him eat and drink, lest the journey be too much for him. Two meals fill Elijah with enough strength to travel for forty days and forty nights.

Forty days and forty nights. I counted. It's the exact number of days and nights in every test block, from the first lecture to the last exam.

Fall quarter had scarcely started when it caught up to me. The moments of frantic, late-night cramming before the first set of exams had given way to a sense of overwhelming exhaustion and blinding fear. There was far more demanding my attention than I had time for. And, despite everything I tried, I fell further and further behind. If I was having so much difficulty keeping up in the first few weeks, how was I going to make it through four years? Most crippling of all, these were not thoughts that I had ever dreamed myself capable of thinking. I felt like I had nothing left to offer.

I found myself reading Elijah's story one such morning. I wanted so badly to taste that bread. I longed for that kind of sustenance. And then a thrill crept into my mind as I thought something too wild to be true. I counted the days off the schedule: thirty-eight, thirty-nine, forty. And sure enough, there, under my finger was the last exam: physical diagnosis. And as I sat there, silent in awe, I heard His beautiful voice whispering in my heart: "Forty days and forty nights. I will sustain you. Just come. Eat and drink, lest the journey be too much for you."

There are many things that frighten us. There are many things that weigh us down. There are many times when all we can think of and all we can see is how exhausted we are. But even in the moments when the pieces are broken and small, God is with us. He will sustain us with His love. We will survive. For if God can give Elijah enough strength to travel hundreds of miles through a dusty desert for forty days, God can and will give us enough strength to learn the things that we need to in these forty days. So come. Eat of the fruit of His love and drink from the cup of His grace that you might have the strength for these forty days.

Priscilla Chee, LLUSM class of 2012, was born in Malaysia and reared in Loma Linda, California, and currently resides in Moreno Valley, California.

December 2

I listen carefully to what God the LORD is saying, for he speaks peace to his faithful people. Psalm 85:8, NLT

"I'm not doing so well, doc. I just can't sleep." That was the complaint of my first patient during my third year in medical school. I think we all probably remember our first patient—that sense of trepidation and fear as we realize that the rubber is about to meet the road. In an instant, we're supposed to transition from a bookworm with an anatomy atlas to a physician; and I was certain that this patient, Mr. R could see right through me.

All I possessed at that moment were the seven dimensions of a history and physical and my small lab book of normal values. Or, at least that's what I thought. As I entered the room, I couldn't shake the thought that I was in the wrong place; I wasn't ready for this. What did I have that Mr. R needed?

Immediately, his eyes locked on mine; and although I didn't know it then, they were searching. I'd like to say that I knew from the outset that I was in a special situation, but that awareness only struck me much later. In truth, as we began to discuss his difficulty sleeping, I was still thinking, "Hmm, this must be how he introduces himself to doctors."

As it turns out, Mr. R was a veteran of the Korean War, and he hadn't slept well since his return from Korea. Slowly, he began to unpack his history and his nightmare. In Korea, he'd accidentally killed a 12-year-old boy, someone he'd mistaken for an enemy combatant. There was no malice in his actions. It was purely a mistake made under a stressful situation, where it's your life or theirs.

In his mind, Mr. R knew it was an accident; but in his heart, he could never forgive himself. Every night, in his sleep, the image of that boy played out in his mind, making his sleep anything but restful. While I was still absorbing the gravity of his story, he spoke several words that would change my perspective regarding the required skills of a physician.

"You know," he said, "My doc's gonna wonder why I told you this, 'cause she doesn't even know about it. In fact, I've never told anyone else this, not even my wife. I'm just finally ready to get some help." This obviously wasn't his routine introduction to doctors.

As the rest of the visit played out, I kept wondering what I had done to help this gentleman open up. Ultimately, the answer was "nothing." When I entered that room, I was right in thinking that I possessed no special skills or talents. But I had God. The only one skill that was absolutely essential to becoming a physician was being open to God's surprises. At that moment I realized that when God uses you, it doesn't matter what your skill set is or how much experience you have. All that ultimately matters is that you open yourself up to His devices, and He'll wield you in ways you never thought possible.

Matthew Hiersche, LLUSM class of 2009—for which he was community service coordinator for the sophomore year—is from Redlands, California, and Ellensburg, Washington. He is a deferred mission appointee. December 2 was the birthday of the first physician in his family, his grandfather, Edward Kneeland Rebok, LLUSM class of 1948, whose love of people and their "story" reminds his grandson to always be eager to listen.

December 3

The King will reply, "I tell you the truth, whatever you did for one of the least of these brothers of mine, you did for me." Matthew 25:40, NIV

He could not have been more than 3 or 4 years old. His tummy protruded out in front of him as he walked down the sidewalk in his funny little white hospital gown. His face, arms, legs, and bare feet worked hard to carry that big tummy gracefully. In his hands he carried a big yellow banana. It was all he had.

At the mission hospital, meals can be purchased for a few cents, but his parents could not afford to buy them. So, they stayed in the noisy, smelly "family kitchen area" in the back of the hospital to prepare his food over a small open fire of sticks between three stones. White corn meal, cooked like mush (Nsema), was their staple food for all three meals. Onions, tomatoes, or bean leaves might be added for the sauce (Ndiwo), if available from the garden at home. Sometimes they would have red beans but seldom an egg or a piece of meat to flavor the sauce. Bananas, God's popsicles, are not very expensive in season here; and children love them the world around.

Today, long after morning rounds, I met Chico out there on the big sidewalk, his face all smiles. I could only say the usual greeting, "Moni, muli bwangi." He recognized me from daily rounds. He could not speak English; but, in his own way, he wanted to let me know he was grateful for the hospital and our care. He carefully broke his banana in half and, with a gleeful look, handed half to me. He shared what he had. My eyes filled with tears.

After he had gone, I took a picture of that banana half. Somehow it symbolizes what it meant to me to be out there, without many of the necessities of modern medicine, but with the love that he accepted. Without thinking about it, he understood Matthew 25:40. Oh, Father, have I done as much? I have our three healthy children, delivered in the mission in a clean delivery room. He was probably born on the earthen floor of his parents' hut. We also have plenty of nourishing food.

And, importantly, our water comes from a cistern and, except in very dry seasons, is abundant, chlorinated, and safe. He has Bilharzia, an infection from the local water that will ruin his liver and has already started its work in his small body. Poor nutrition further complicates his healing, even as he responds to the harsh medicines that may give him a slight hope of recovery. But he senses love, and his little heart responds to that love . . . even as our hearts unfold to Your love.

How we long for Your coming, Lord. Help us to be Your hands and Your voice and a reflection of Your love to these, Your little children.

Rheeta Stecker, LLUSM class of 1963, is a family practitioner and lives with her husband, Elton Stecker Jr., LLUSM class of 1963, in Hot Springs, Arkansas.

December 4

For all have sinned and fall short of the glory of God. Romans 3:23, NIV

Of all the lessons taught to us by Dr. Leonard Werner, senior associate dean for medical student education for LLUSM, the most profound to me was the concept of unconditional, positive regard. Defined as "the acceptance of the patient as a person in need, regardless of what they have done," this term is used as a model for the physician/patient relationship.

As a first-year medical student without any clinical experience, this concept seemed like a noble aspiration and a logical position for a physician to take. However, I found this much more difficult to apply when faced with experiences, where the guilt is obvious and the consequences are painful.

During my intern years in general and orthopaedic surgery, I cared for many patients who chose to drive while intoxicated. We would always ask the paramedics who accompanied them for specifics about the auto accident. Many times, I was disturbed to hear that there was another car involved and that its innocent occupants had suffered some unspeakable trauma. After the excitement had passed and the patient was stabilized, my mind would invariably wander back to the concept of "unconditional positive regard" and what it really means.

I still cannot say I have reached an understanding of how to sincerely apply this concept in the trauma bay. One can literally smell the guilt; and yet, for us, work, personal risk, and even love are sometimes required to save these patients. How can one love a person who is so obviously guilty?

The breakthrough came for me as I began to see the parallels between the fallen state of humanity and the demonstration of unconditional positive regard given by Jesus Christ. Through his ultimate sacrifice, we received grace to live lives accepted before God. As my appreciation of this parallel has grown, so has my ability to care for these patients. No longer is it a mechanical compartmentalization of work and justice but a daily exercise of love and humility to care for these people.

Unconditional positive regard is grace exercised through love. It cannot be given expecting something in return. The demonstration of this principle by Christ on the Cross reminds me daily of my own need for a Savior. I pray that I may reach ever nearer to this noble goal.

Joseph Bowen, LLUSM class of 2004—for which he was sophomore class vice president and senior class president—is a resident in orthopaedic surgery at LLUMC. December 4 was chosen in memory of his father, Thomas M. Bowen, LLUSM class of 1976-A.

December 5

Before they call, I will answer. Isaiah 65:24, KJV

In 1964, I was a mission doctor at Kanye Medical Mission in Botswana. It was a 175-bed, two-door hospital on the edge of the Kalahari Desert. Every three months, one of us doctors would go out into the desert to visit and treat the bushmen. They lived in a half dozen villages, scattered over that hot, sandy desert that stretched over an area the combined size of Kentucky, Tennessee, Ohio, and Indiana.

Usually, we traveled in a five-ton, desert- and medically-equipped diesel truck, along with a nurse and three helpers. But one particular time, my friend, the British commissioner—knowing that I was well-acquainted with the desert—asked if I would try to find out about some ceremonial murders that had been reported out there.

Rather than taking the large truck, I decided to take a Chevy pickup, in order to go a little faster. The second day out, my wife and I found the sand scorching hot. My mercury thermometer ruptured at 120 degrees, and the truck got stuck "belly deep" in the sand. After digging for two hours and getting only more deeply buried, we felt hopeless and helpless. Being 150 miles from the nearest human being, we recognized that, short of a miracle, we were on death row.

My wife said, "We'd better pray." I wish I had a recording of her short, most-earnest petition. Only a miracle could save us. No one—and I mean *no one*—but myself or the other doctor ever went into the Kalahari.

But within ten minutes after her prayer, over a distant sand dune, appeared a brand new, spotless, red Massey Ferguson tractor! Can you imagine a dust-free, highly polished piece of machinery suddenly showing up in that sandy, hot, windy desert where no one ever ventured except us two doctors? It must have just descended from heaven, as it had not a speck of dust on it. And there was the driver, not a little bushman, but a tall, English-speaking person/angel. He said, "It looks like you need help." Was I dreaming? Surrounding us were no trees, no bushes, no people, no food, and no water—only hot, shifting sand for 200 miles in any direction.

"I'll pull you out, but don't try to drive out until morning," he said. "Tonight there will be heavy dew, and by daylight the sand will become firm. Let half the air out of your tires, and you will have no problems."

I asked, "Who are you? Where did you come from?"

"Very far from here," he said, and proceeded to pull me out of my pit and up onto an elevated dune. And then he left, driving back in the direction from whence he came.

Do you know what? I'm going to look for that angel when I get to heaven.

Sometimes, when I am wondering if God will ever get around to answer me as I pray beside my bed at night, I stop and reflect back . . . to when . . . and my faith is strengthened to press on.

Friend, let me assure you that there is a God in heaven, and He can find you and supply your need no matter how far away or hard to find you may be.

Ralph B. Moore, LLUSM class of 1953-A, is a general practitioner and resides with his wife, Earline, in Lebanon, Tennessee.

December 6

He heals the brokenhearted and binds up their wounds. Psalm 147:3, NIV

I t was a difficult time of life—losing a best friend to cancer, a 17-year-old family friend to a brain tumor, a grandfather to cancer, a grandmother to congestive heart failure, and my other grandfather to congestive heart failure and flu complications. These losses were the more difficult when placed on the shoulders of a 13-year-old boy who was still trying to figure out what life is all about. In the span of two years, I had lost some of the dearest people in my life.

During this very sobering time, I believe the desire to become a doctor started growing within me. It also created a concern in me for the interaction between physician and patient. As I overheard stories, both good and bad, of how these people I loved so much were treated by various medical personnel, I realized that in a profession that requires so much brain activity, it can be easy to let the heart activity slip.

As I became more interested in becoming a physician, I found myself delving more deeply into the Word. I searched for any Scripture that showed Jesus not only as a man who healed the sick, but also as a man with heart. And I found story after story about Jesus the Man, who did heal with a tender heart. He not only cleansed the sick of their afflictions, but also showed them complete love and acceptance. He stopped what He was doing on His important journey to heal, pray, hug.

The healing that Jesus offered went far beyond the physical. Rarely did souls leave the healing presence of Christ with only their sickness cured. They left as new persons, refreshed with love and the message of hope. It is in this light that I stepped into the premedicine program at Pacific Union College in Angwin, California, and later into the medical program at Loma Linda University.

Now, as I walk the wards at Loma Linda University Medical Center, I picture someone else's best friend or grandparent lying in that hospital bed; and I imagine how Jesus would interact with them and their loved ones. Would He hurry by on His busy morning, inquiring only about pertinent medical information as He rushed to the next patient? Or would He take the extra time, if even for a moment, to heal beyond the physical? As I continue my medical education, my prayer is that I do not lose sight of the Man who heals with a heart.

Brian Savino, LLUSM class of 2011, is from Rancho Mirage, California. December 6 is the birthday of his wife, Miljoy.

December 7

Well done, good and faithful servant. Matthew 25:23, KJV

He never won an award as a medical student. He never was the president of any prestigious medical society. He never published a scientific paper. Yet, in spite of all the things my father never did, he was an exemplary physician.

To his family, he was a hard-working, dedicated father and doctor. As a true internist, he made sure we took the full course of antibiotics prescribed, but only after strep throat had been diagnosed with a throat culture. He was compassionate and once allowed his children to bring a premature Shetland pony into the basement for several days. He then administered injections of antibiotics around the clock to the pony, in an effort to save what nature said was unfit to live. He was the consummate teacher to his two very young daughters, who would come to his clinic dressed in little white nurses' outfits ready to "assist" him.

To his community and his church, he was a passionate educator who enthusiastically conducted numerous Five-day Plan to Stop Smoking clinics. Because he had witnessed too many times what smoking had done to his patients, he became all the more passionate as an educator. At the nearby boarding academy, he was the "official" sex educator for years, much to the excitement of the students and the embarrassment of my sister and me! One of the highlights of his life was his "vacation" to South America as a "missionary doctor," traveling aboard the Luzeiro houseboat on the Amazon River and treating those who rarely, if ever, received healthcare.

To his patients, he was always available. House calls were a way of life, until the practice of medicine changed. Forty-eight hours before his death from metastatic cancer, a patient's elderly mother telephoned him. She had one last plea: "Please call the hospital and tell them my son doesn't tolerate the medication they are prescribing."

So, jaundiced and frail, my father called the hospital from his hospice bed and implored the staff to "listen to his mother as she has been taking care of her bedridden, unconscious son for years and knows his body better than anyone." As he hung up the phone, he looked at me with very dull eyes, his sclera the color of ocher, and said, "I'm so thankful I'm still able to help others."

He never made enough money to be a major donor to his alma mater; but, in his medical office for forty years, he had two pictures hanging. One was of his medical school class and the other was of Loma Linda University. Whenever the opportunity arose, he loved to tell his patients about the unique mission of "his" school.

One of his proudest moments was when his son was commissioned to paint the "Window of Hope" for Loma Linda University Children's Hospital. At the unveiling of the painting, just six months before his death, he told his son, "Your painting will give hope and healing to patients in ways that medicine is unable to give."

After Dad's funeral, we were handed a sympathy card from the local Catholic priest. His handwritten note read, "Dr. Olson practiced medicine like Christ would have." I can think of no earthly award that would have rivaled that in significance to my father.

Donna R. Hadley, LLUSN class of 1975, is volunteer chair of the centennial celebration committee for LLUSM. She and her husband, Roger, LLUSM class of 1974, reside in Redlands, California. This devotional is in honor of her late father, Rolland Olson, LLUSM class of 1946, who practiced at the same clinic in Wayzata, Minnesota, for forty-one years. December 7 was the wedding anniversary of her parents, Rolland and Rosella Olson.

December 8

Because of the LORD's great love we are not consumed, for his compassions never fail. They are new every morning; great is your faithfulness. Lamentations 3:22-23, NIV

O ne of the most memorable patients that I had the privilege of meeting in my third year of medical school was a man suffering from a malignant brain tumor. At the time of our encounter, it had only been a few months since the tranquility and stability of his life had been shattered with this diagnosis. While walking in the woods, he suffered a seizure and had to be medevaced to Loma Linda University Medical Center.

Following a battery of imaging tests, his diagnosis and grim prognosis were revealed to him—there was a tumor in his brain, and its rapid growth was responsible for the new onset seizure. He was told the lesion was inoperable and that he likely had less than a year to live. The perverse cruelty of my duty on the day of our meeting was to find out how his low-grade diabetes and hypertension were doing, the futility of which was pointed out to me by the patient numerous times during the course of his hour-long appointment.

Adding to the complexity of this interview was the fact that the patient would lapse into fits of inconsolable weeping whenever the conversation grazed some topic that reminded him of his impending death. While wrestling with one's finitude is never a light task, it was amplified for this man by the nature of where his brain tumor was growing. According to my attending physician, his mood and indeed his personality had been significantly altered in the brief time since his diagnosis.

Shortly into the interview, it became evident that the minor medical issues that had brought him in for his scheduled visit were under control and so we began to talk about his life history. The patient revealed to me how ten years previously he had been living a fast-paced, hedonistic life in a large, east coast city. Early one morning, after waking from a drunken stupor, God revealed Himself and showed him the vanity and uselessness of his wayward life. Following this event, the man gave up his old ways and submitted himself to Christ.

Deciding to devote his life to the Lord, he left his old line of work and went to a seminary, eventually obtaining a master's degree in theology. For many, this man's story would only enhance their skepticism that a good and gracious God existed. What I saw, however, was a counter intuitive stability that only the Holy Spirit could bring.

Despite the fact that he teetered on the brink of despair and faced an isolation exaggerated by the closeness of death, he never rejected his faith in Christ. While he questioned everything else, while his world collapsed around him, his faith was ensconced by the love of God. He yearned for a healing that this present age could not grant him—an eternal peace that medicine could not offer.

Alastair McKean, LLUSM class of 2009—for which he was junior class pastor—received a BA degree in theology from University of Oxford in Oxford, England, in 2005, and a BSc degree in biochemistry from University of Alberta in Edmonton in 2003. He and his wife, Michelle, are from Edmonton, Alberta, Canada. December 8 is his wife's birthday.

I no longer call you slaves, because a master doesn't confide in his slaves. Now you are my friends, since I have told you everything the Father told me. John 15:15, NLT

As a freshman medical student in 1973, I took Dr. Graham Maxwell's class. We read the sixty-six books of the Bible; and, after each book, Dr. Maxwell challenged us to ask ourselves, "What picture of God do you get from this book of the Bible?" My wife and I also regularly attended Dr. Maxwell's Sabbath School class at the Loma Linda University Church of Seventh-day Adventists.

This religion class and Dr. Maxwell's Sabbath School class were eye-opening and mind-expanding events in my Christian experience. I came to Loma Linda University with a picture of God that was not necessarily healthy. Some of the things I had learned during my childhood and academy and college education did not provide me with well-thought-out reasons for many of the things I believed spiritually.

Dr. Maxwell taught us to think for ourselves on the subject of what God is really like, what He expects from us in terms of behavior, and why. He specifically launched the idea that we could have assurance of salvation based on our relationship with God and His Son, not on what we did or did not do.

Dr. Maxwell frequently talked about the concept of being "safe to save." As I came to understand it, that phrase meant that God would not take to heaven people who would not want to be there for eternity. And because He would not take those who did not have a relationship with God, this would assure that sin would never rise again in the universe.

Another thing I learned from Dr. Maxwell was the idea, based on John 15:15, that Jesus no longer considered me His servant, but that He wanted me to be His friend. Talk about a new and reassuring view of God! Here's the God of the universe who wants to be my friend and have a relationship with me.

These experiences and the ideas that I learned from Dr. Maxwell have had a profound effect on my life and my spiritual beliefs. I am grateful for this aspect of my education and experience at the School of Medicine. I am sure his ideas and teaching have been a similar benefit and blessing to hundreds of LLU School of Medicine alumni.

Loran Hauck, LLUSM class of 1976-A, is an internist. He and his wife, Loretta, reside in Apopka, Florida. December 9 is his birthday.

December 10

Fear thou not; for I am with thee: be not dismayed; for I am thy God: I will strengthen thee; yea, I will help thee; yea, I will uphold thee with the right hand of my righteousness. Isaiah 41:10, KJV

During the five-and-a-half years that I wore the U.S. Army uniform as a medical officer during World War II, I had a number of providential experiences. Their effects have been long-lasting, both for me and for others.

One experience happened while I was executive officer of a portable surgical hospital on the island of New Guinea. Because the Japanese forces disregarded the red crosses on hospitals, all personnel in the Pacific were issued small weapons. One evening, the hospital's ordinance officer, Captain Harry Hill, said to me, "Sherm, you haven't come down to the ordinance tent to pick up your revolver and carbine." My reply was, "No, I haven't, Harry, and I won't be picking them up."

Though I outranked Harry, he blew his top. "Sherm, I don't understand you. You know the stories about military hospitals being overrun by Japanese forces. Suppose we get overrun, but you and I are still alive. A Japanese soldier aims his gun at me. You could probably kill him before he killed me. Wouldn't you do that?" That was a hard one to answer. I told him my trust was in the Lord's promises, not in armory.

From there we went to the Philippines. Between cases, I would flop down on a stretcher near the operating table and nap. Once, I was awakened when a bullet came through the roof and the operating table, and penetrated the floor. Had I been operating, the bullet would have gone through me and my patient! This is just one example of the numerous times that God marvelously protected my life.

The officers' accommodations there were only small tunnels dug into a hillside. One tunnel, just wide enough for two stretchers, was shared by Harry—also a surgeon—and me. Harry, unmarried, was two-to-three years younger than I. When he was off duty, he drank alcoholic beverages freely and smoked heavily. He seemed to me to be a person who showed no interest in religion.

Prayer had become meaningful to me, and I prayed each night. But I didn't want anyone to see me pray, so I usually found a secluded spot. One night, I decided to pray in our tiny hole, since Harry was gone. I was on my knees when Harry came in. Although caught, I wasn't going to insult God by jumping up; so I finished my prayer.

Harry, very polite, said nothing until I rose. Then he spoke words that, as long as I live, I will never forget. He said, "Sherm, I wish you would teach me how to pray." My conscience condemned me. I had been wrong in judging Harry's deep heart longings.

Though my own Bible knowledge was embryonic at that time, those words, "Teach me how to pray," opened a door that led to hours of Bible study with Harry. He survived the war, met a beautiful Southern gal, and they got married. They ended up joining a large Protestant congregation. Years later, my family visited them. He had invited to his home a number of his friends and physician colleagues to celebrate our visit. After a lovely meal, and out of the blue, Harry said, in his Southern drawl, "Sherm, I want you to tell my friends why you keep Saturday instead of Sunday." Another door, and only in eternity will we know about the seeds sown that night.

Sherman A. Nagel, LLUSM class of 1940, was an LLUSM Alumni Association 1964 Honored Alumnus. He and his wife, Edith, reside in Langley, British Columbia, Canada. They were married on December 10, 1940.

December 11

In everything, therefore, treat people the same way you want them to treat you, for this is the Law and the Prophets. Matthew 7:12, NASB

O f all the things learned during medical education and practice, the most important lessons often come from patients and their families. During my residency, I remember one particular night while on-call. I was called to see an elderly woman who was accompanied by her elderly husband. Due to her stroke, the patient was unable to provide the needed history; but her husband helped me with the details.

When asked about her current medications, he pulled out a piece of paper and the thickest magnifying glass I had ever seen. He proceeded to try to read the hand-written list of medications on the paper. It was still difficult for him to see, despite the magnifying glass. He looked up at me, with a smile, and said, "And these are the golden years."

As he sat next to his wife of decades and tried his best to help me help her, his love and commitment were obvious and impressive.

Ignoring my weariness, I sat down and talked with him for some time about their lives and learned how growing old together had offered many rewards and many challenges. He wanted the best care possible for his wife; and I was humbled by the opportunity to care for the most important thing in his life, his wife. Many times during training I had heard this question: How would you want your loved ones cared for or treated? My experience with this man impressed upon me that every patient is someone's treasured family member. Each person we interact with during that person's treatment deserves respect and a commitment from us to provide quality care.

Most doctors have knowledge; but, from the perspective of the patient, if that knowledge can't be transmitted with genuine concern for each patient, then the patient and family may not be satisfied with the treatment. My hope is that each patient and family I encounter will feel that I have genuine concern for them as I provide medical care. Little do they know they are teaching me as well.

Laura Nist, LLUSM class of 1995, is associate professor in LLUSM department of neurology. She is also clerkship director for neurology at LLUSM. She won the LLUMC Physician Customer Satisfaction Award in 2006.

December 12

Cast your bread upon the waters, for after many days you will find it again.
Ecclesiastes 11:1, NIV

I first met Roy S. Cornell, LLUSM class of 1946, at the Seventh-day Adventist General Conference meetings in San Francisco, California, in 1954. He, his wife, Alta, and their four sons had just accepted an invitation to serve in Benghazi, Libya, as the first pioneer medical missionaries in this newly liberated Islamic land. With the assistance of Pastor Neal Wilson, president of the Nile Union of Seventh-day Adventists, and Brother Ramses, our Seventh-day Adventist mission was welcomed into the new nation. In addition, we had the unusual privilege of actually purchasing Libyan land in the name of the Seventh-day Adventist Church on which to build a hospital.

Within a year's time, an old Italian hotel building was secured and remodeled into an attractive clinic and small hospital. As the building project was nearing completion, one major entity was lacking: furnishings. While many items had been ordered, the furnishings were absent. As Dr. Cornell busied himself with the oversight of remodeling and new construction, he also ingratiated himself into the limited medical community by volunteering his services at the major government hospital for the Province of Cyrene.

Dr. Cornell went to see the provincial director of medical services for Cyrenaica, an elderly British physician. He informed the director of the need for furnishings. The director took Dr. Cornell with him to the government warehouse where medical stores were kept and told Dr. Cornell to select anything he needed; he would have it delivered as a loan to our hospital. Thus, our hospital was fully furnished for the opening day.

The director further explained the reasons for his prompt and generous action. Many years previously, as a young British medical officer, he was assigned to a small, isolated bush hospital in East Africa. He was dismayed to find that the care demanded by the complicated surgical and gynecological problems presented at that hospital exceeded his training and abilities. Some miles away there was another bush hospital, a Seventh-day Adventist one. A young doctor at that hospital had the necessary surgical experience.

When this Seventh-day Adventist doctor discovered a colleague needed help, he arranged to drive once a week over the primitive roads to the government hospital and perform surgery for them. He also helped them with their emergencies. The director said that, after all these years had passed, he could now pay back the cost for the vital services our Seventh-day Adventist mission hospital and their surgeon, Jacob Janzen, LLUSM class of 1931, had so generously given.

Unfortunately, after a successful year in Benghazi, Dr. Cornell was stricken with acute bulbar polio. After treatment at a military hospital, a team of United States Air Force medics arrived, transferred Dr. Cornell into a portable "iron lung," and—in a specially equipped plane—carried him to the U.S. Dr. Cornell continued on respiratory assistance until his demise a few years later.

Our alumni leave deep marks along the way; and in so many lands, the pioneers in health and healing were our own faithful Seventh-day Adventist missionary physicians.

William Wagner, LLUSM class of 1944-B, is a surgeon in Loma Linda, California. He was an LLUSM Alumni Association 1964 Honored Alumnus, and received the LLUSM Distinguished Service Award in 2006. December 12 was the graduation day for the wartime class of 1944-B. It was also the day he married his wife, Kathleen.

December 13

But verily God hath heard me; he hath attended to the voice of my prayer. Psalm 66:19, KJV

While engaged in the practice of anesthesiology at St. Helena Hospital, in St. Helena, California, I conducted more than forty Bible study groups focused on Revelation in the evenings over a three-year period. These involved some 500 Seventh-day Adventists in the Napa Valley. In 1983, I also published the first of five books I have written about Daniel and Revelation, *Give Glory to Him* with the subtitle *The Sanctuary in the Book of Revelation.*

Subsequently, I was invited to hold weekend seminars at more than 125 Seventh-day Adventist churches on the west coast. A man who attended one of the seminars in southern California encouraged me to take my book to Moscow. He gave me a slip of paper with the name of a man, Ivanov, who was surreptitiously translating Seventh-day Adventist books into Russian and printing them on a press he had set up in the basement of his home. In addition to Ivanov's name was the Russian name of the district where he lived but not an address.

In 1984, when I arrived in Moscow, I checked into a large downtown hotel. I took to the concierge the slip of paper with the Russian name of the district and inquired about its location. He had not heard of the district but advised me to ask some of the taxi drivers on the street outside. There were fifteen taxis parked from the entrance of the hotel to the corner of the block. Not one of the drivers knew the location of the district.

At that point I was standing at the corner of a busy downtown intersection in a city of eight million people asking the Lord in prayer what I should do next, when, from the hundreds of people on the sidewalk, a short man who appeared to be of Arab descent walked up to me and asked, in perfect English, "Where are you going?" When I showed him the slip of paper, he said, "Oh, that is where I am going. Will you share a taxi with me?"

When we arrived at the district forty-five minutes later, he instructed the taxi driver, in Russian, to stop in front of a corner kiosk. He went inside and shortly returned to tell me that Ivanov lived just a few houses down the side street. He said he would instruct the driver to take me there, wait for me, and then take me back to my hotel. After speaking to the driver, he walked away from the taxi and around the corner. When the taxi driver turned the same corner, the man had disappeared.

You may believe that the events of this story were coincidence, but I remain convicted that the Lord sent an angel to provide the needed assistance. I found Ivanov, who agreed to translate and print my book, and then I went back to the hotel.

Did Ivanov actually do what I asked? More than twenty-five years later I still don't know the answer to that question, but I have experienced other miracles in my life that continue to convince me that my God answers prayer. Truly, I can agree with the Psalmist in Psalm 66:19 that "God hath heard me."

Robert W. Hauser, LLUSM class of 1954, is an anesthesiologist in Brookings, Oregon.

December 14

A friend is always loyal, and a brother is born to help in time of need. Proverbs 17:17, NLT

My alarm clock rudely jolts me awake at an incredibly early hour, warning me not to be late. I am a third-year medical student working on fulfilling my hospital rotations, which often translates into arriving early and leaving the hospital late. As I wearily walk onto the ward, my mind stops and I think, "Why am I here?" I am exhausted. What convoluted path have I chosen to lead me to this early morning?

It is a moment of contemplation, one of those existential moments. No doubt all of us have these from time to time. Why do we make conscious decisions to strive for such arduous goals? Why do some choose to work so hard? And how can I become one of those physicians, who, even in his seventies, is still full of passion and vigor?

This thought process quickly hits me with, "Why am I pursuing medicine?" Every medical student should have an answer to this question; and I suppose we all do, since we are, after all, studying in the library and running around the hospital exhausted. Yet I would like to propose that many of these conscious or unconscious "reasons" will leave some of us disillusioned early in our career. Often I hear a conglomeration of "I enjoy science," or "My parents encouraged me," or "I enjoy a challenge." These may be true; however, is there a core answer?

I recently had the privilege of taking a mission trip, traveling to the Dominican Republic with surgeons from Loma Linda University department of plastic surgery. The trip focused on cleft palate and hand repair. We arrived late on a Thursday, ready to work. As we walked into the hospital early Friday morning, the waiting room was already full. We set up the clinic and began seeing patients.

For me, all the studying, days in the library, and weekends spent on research projects so the surgeons could get to know me, rushed through my mind's eye in a single moment when a young mother handed me, a foreign "doctor," her most prized possession—her baby with a cleft lip and palate. She looked at me with anxious eyes, hoping that our team could help him. And we could!

We saw dozens more patients that day, but the young mother affected me immensely. Through her, I was able to experience the beauty of medicine. It allowed me to connect the question of why I am pursuing medicine to the answer. It gave purpose and meaning to the impersonal scientific knowledge that is stuffed in my head. This is the core of my answer. Medicine is too beautiful and exhausting for anyone to be in it for the wrong reason.

So, during that too early morning, walking down that dark ward, I suddenly return to reality. I am at peace. I have found my answer, which is to help my fellow brother. This must be the foundation upon which everything else is built. Each of us must find our own motive. What is yours?

Michael J. Matus, LLUSM class of 2010—for which he is the alumni association class representative—is from Grand Rapids, Michigan, and received a BS degree in biochemistry from Andrews University in Berrien Springs, Michigan.

December 15

Whatsoever ye do, do all to the glory of God. 1 Corinthians 10:31, KJV

As a medical military advisor to the Chinese army in Taiwan, I also cared for United States military families in the area. The United States military had a small hospital in Taipei, but I was stationed miles away in Taichung. I had access to Taiwan's Air Force planes at anytime, however, to transport those in need to Taipei and the American hospital. That arrangement included transporting pregnant women, who were delivered in the hospital in Taipei.

I remember an English lady, the wife of an American paratrooper, who was about to deliver. I called for the plane. We boarded the plane and were taxiing out to the runway, but it was too late. I told the pilot to stop and we would deliver the baby on the plane. That's exactly what we did!

I don't know what I said to the lady, either at that time or when seeing her earlier in her pregnancy. However, in those days, I was really anxious to make every attempt to reach people in a religious way.

Thirty years later, I had a series of meetings at the Oklahoma camp meeting. At this time, I also had the opportunity to speak to the ministers and other workers in the Oklahoma Conference of Seventh-day Adventists during the workers' meetings in the mornings. It was at one of those meetings that a minister in the Oklahoma Conference came to me and asked, "Did you ever deliver a baby on an airplane?" I had to think for a moment. "Yes, I remember I did that once." "Was it in Taiwan?" "Yes, it was." "Well, I was that baby!"

I learned that the father had left the mother; and she had relocated to Florida, where she reared her son. Their neighbor was a Seventh-day Adventist man, who became a good friend and like a father figure to this boy. The boy said to his mother that the neighbor man was a Seventh-day Adventist. The mother said, "You know, you were delivered by a Seventh-day Adventist doctor." As I said, I don't know what I had said to this man's mother, but she did know I was a Seventh-day Adventist.

The next day, the minister brought me the record of his birth with my signature, a picture of the airplane, and the signatures of all the Chinese crew members.

The mother and son had subsequently become Seventh-day Adventists. She was a strong worker in the local church's Dorcas Society; and, as noted, her son had become a minister. We never know how our influence, along with that of many others, will be used by God to bring people into close connection with Him. Therefore, at all times, do all to the glory of God.

John A. Scharffenberg, LLUSM class of 1948, was a faculty member in LLUSM department of preventive medicine. He also has an MPH degree and is adjunct professor in LLUSPH department of nutrition. He and his wife, Carmyn, reside in North Fork, California. December 15 is his birthday.

December 16

For you will be a witness for him to tell everyone what you have seen and heard.
Acts 22:15, TEV

Because of sin, it's hard for us to see and understand God directly. Thus, He needs to have ambassadors who will speak on His behalf. He needs spokespeople. Now, if I had to decide who would speak on my behalf, I would probably choose people better than myself, who would make me look good, people with good PR skills—good spin doctors.

However, God did just the opposite. He chose real-life people—you and me—who are often untrustworthy or wrapped up in ourselves, and more interested in making ourselves look good than in making God look good. Think about it: God made Himself vulnerable by giving us the responsibility and opportunity to be His spokespeople.

But I am convinced that the honor and responsibility of being God's spokespeople is even more serious for healthcare workers. Many of us hold positions of responsibility in the community and in the places where we work. We touch people in need every day during our patient care work. Patients see us at vulnerable times in their lives, when they are sick and in need. Because of this, they often listen to us when they won't listen to others. And they usually respect what we have to say.

The sad thing is that too many of us are wrapped up in ourselves or worried about the cares of life. Of course, we do things that are perfectly respectable: we try to make sure that we have a good reputation, and we struggle to get ahead in life. There is nothing inherently wrong with any of this. However, the problem is that while we have people listening to us, we spend most of our time talking about ourselves and trying to make ourselves look good.

Which brings me back to my point: whether we realize it or not, we are God's spokespeople. We WILL say something about God today, and it is likely that someone will listen to it. The only question is what will we say?

Let's say something good about Him today!

Mark Reeves, LLUSM class of 1992, is associate professor in LLUSM department of surgery. He is also director of LLUMC Cancer Institute. He and his wife, Michelle, LLUSM class of 1986, live in Grand Terrace, California. December 16 is the day of their wedding anniversary.

December 17

A word fitly spoken is like apples of gold in settings of silver. Proverbs 25:11, NKJV

I am the product of a threatened abortion. My mother had struggled to get pregnant. She finally became pregnant; but several weeks into her pregnancy, she began to bleed. Confident that she was pregnant, she went to see her obstetrician. After a cursory examination, the physician—irritated by her self-diagnosis of pregnancy—told her she couldn't possibly be pregnant and, if she were, the child would be "retarded." The bleeding stopped and two months passed.

She returned to her obstetrician, who now confirmed a four-month pregnancy. However, anticipating the possibility of the birth of a less-than-normal child, she requested termination of the pregnancy. Her physician convinced her to continue with her pregnancy, as things were progressing normally. But for the remainder of her term, my mother and father wrestled with visions of a "retarded" or malformed child and how this would impact the rest of their lives. It was a long five months. But, to their relief, they had a perfectly normal child.

My name bears the impact of this history. At minimum, my mother wanted me to spell my own name, and she thought I might struggle with the different "r" sounds in my first and last names. I was to be named Kirby Oberg, but they changed it to Kerby Oberg. I must say that my mother was very wise—I have never transposed the "r" sounds when writing Kerby or Oberg. Or, if I have, at least I couldn't tell.

My birth history reminds me to choose my words carefully and not to speak flippantly or in haste. We have unique opportunities to impact peoples' lives in moments of vulnerability, be it to elevate or diminish. I am reminded of my favorite text, Proverbs 25:11. I pray that today we can use words fitly spoken to bring peace, comfort, and healing to those in our care.

Kerby Oberg, LLUSM class of 1991, is associate professor in LLUSM department of pathology and human anatomy. He also has a PhD degree in anatomy. He was president of the Walter E. Macpherson Society from 2008 to 2009. December 17 is his birthday.

December 18

In all my prayers for all of you, I always pray with joy . . . being confident of this, that he who began a good work in you will carry it on to completion until the day of Christ Jesus. Philippians 1:4, 6, NIV

Loma Linda University was my last choice for medical school. I had every intention of staying near Pennsylvania, where my family and friends lived. But as the final year of college began, I had a growing sense that God wanted me to go to LLU to continue my education. This idea did not appeal to me at all; I "informed" God that if I were accepted at any other school, I would not go to LLU. Eventually, every east coast school sent a rejection letter.

My parents, two siblings, and I arrived at the Los Angeles, California, airport in July 2001, with twenty-three pieces of baggage, which we squeezed into a minivan and began our journey to Loma Linda. Within days of arriving, I felt like I belonged at LLU; this was the first of many wonderful surprises God had in store for me during my next few years.

I met my future husband during orientation week (a fellow 2006 alumnus). A mutual friend studied with us individually and informed each of us that we would make perfect study partners. We quickly became best friends and were married in 2003. We continue to have a relationship that has been richly blessed by God.

Additionally, I was befriended by a group of students that met for prayer before every test during our didactic years; this action focused each of us on the One whose strength is perfect in weakness. During second year, I also came to understand salvation by God's grace alone for the first time in my life. For a stressed medical student, it was a relief to learn that my eternal destiny was not dependent on my earthly failures or successes.

Lest any think me overly optimistic, I must admit that LLU is not heaven on earth. Just like any other institution, there are those who seem to be always competent and loving, a few who obliviously run roughshod over others, and many who are wounded or trying to find hope and purpose. Still, there remains a constant sense of God's presence at LLU. When I myself was struggling, God blessed me repeatedly with peers, faculty, and mentors, who listened to my doubts and reminded me that God brought me to LLU to do a good work in me, and He would be faithful to complete it.

These experiences have formed my personal perspective of viewing each peer, patient, staff, and student as a friend whom I have not yet met. As I listen to each individual's story—laughing with those who laugh, mourning with those who mourn, and trying to see Christ in each person—I feel satisfied that I am completing a small portion of the good work that God has purposed for my life. What a blessing that I was "rejected" elsewhere, only to find myself centered in God's will for my life at LLU.

April Wilson, LLUSM class of 2006, completed a residency in preventive medicine at LLUMC. In 2006, she received the Wil Alexander Whole-Person Care Award. December 18 is the birthday of her husband, Thad, LLUSM class of 2006. They both received MPH degrees from LLUSPH.

December 19

I thank my God every time I remember you. Philippians 1:3, NIV

Will you be remembered? If so, what type of mark will that remembrance have on those about you? Years after they have not seen you, what picture will come to mind when they recall your face?

My dad—Henry Stewart—was born in Manila, Philippines, on December 19, 1922. Dr. Montus, who delivered him, was an influence and role model throughout Dad's life. Dr. Montus, a devout Catholic, cared deeply for his patients and took care of all who needed help. In order to be seen, one needed only to come to his office. There, patients would move around in the chairs until they made it to the chair next to the examining room.

When a patient made it to the examining room, Dr. Montus would give that person his full attention and care. He never charged anyone; instead he left a bowl on a table where patients could leave whatever they could give. Dr. Montus' gift of compassion and his model of collecting for services became goals that Dad desired to emulate. Even though he left the Philippine Islands when he was thirteen years old, my Dad's vision of giving to everyone in need lived with him until his dying day.

Dad's life was not easy. When he was in high school, his father, a former army officer when in the Philippines, died and left him a farm in debt. During his first semester of college, World War II broke out. He joined the Navy Medical Corps. He served in five major battles on the attack hospital ship, *USS Pinckney*. After his ship was hit by a kamikaze attack, he felt blessed that he was not hurt, although 200 others on the ship died and many more were injured. This experience made him think his life had been spared for a purpose and increased his determination to become a physician.

Dad was blessed to have attended the College of Medical Evangelists so that he and Mom could be closer to their parents on the west coast. He said it did not matter that it was a "Christian" medical school. But he found out that it *did* matter that it was a Christian school!

Professors, fellow students, and the patient instruction of Pastor Robert Olson assisted Dad and Mom in committing their lives to being Bible-based, Seventh-day Adventist Christians. This commitment later bore fruit in the Carson City, Nevada, area where there was no Seventh-day Adventist church. However, while serving as a doctor there, my Dad, along with others, helped to start a church in Carson City, along with both a Black and a Hispanic church in Sparks, Nevada.

My dad died July 1, 2006. As I have read the stories in newspaper articles that individuals sent to the local paper or have listened to the stories people have told me—many of which I had never heard—I am reminded of the stories Dad told of Dr. Montus. One man, whom I had never met, recounted how he came to town without any money or a job and received the medical care he needed, with the words, "No charge."

Because I had worked for my dad during summers while in high school, I knew this happened on a daily basis. However, for the person without means who needed care, this kindness felt like his or her individual miracle. Dad did live his dream to emulate Dr. Montus, both in compassionate medical care and in charging only what a person could pay—even if it meant "no charge."

I have thought about Dr. Montus and Henry Stewart, LLUSM class of 1953-B. I wonder, will I be remembered? If so, what will I be remembered for in the future? If a man becomes like his God, will the people who know you and me remember our loving, living God? How will people remember you?

Sylvia Stewart is assistant professor in LLUSN. She received a PhD degree in education from Claremont Graduate School (now Claremont Graduate University) in Claremont, California, in 1993.

December 20

Mary treasured up all these things and pondered them in her heart. Luke 2:19, NIV

Clinical studies have shown that words spoken over and over in a person's mind reduce stress, build spiritual faith, and result in physical benefits. Spiritual phrases have a significantly greater positive impact than do nonspiritual phrases. (For example, see "Migraines and Meditation: Does Spirituality Matter?" by Amy B. Wachholtz and Kenneth I. Pargament in the August 2008 issue of *Journal of Behavioral Medicine*.)

This concept is not new to the Christian. Indeed, in several places in the Bible we are reminded of the value of keeping God's words in our minds. "I have hidden your word in my heart that I might not sin against you" (Psalm 119:11, NIV); "These commandments that I give you today are to be upon your hearts" (Deuteronomy 6:6, NIV).

With good intentions, I tried—but with poor success—to practice meditating upon a Scripture verse through my day—to remind myself to take a moment's time out. However, I recently discovered a way.

In 1999, when my hospital's medical records became computerized, I had to develop "strong" passwords, meaning they had to be at least eight characters, have capital and lower case letters, as well as symbols. Furthermore, I was forced to change them every ninety days. This seemed an unreasonable requirement; and I chaffed at the demand until, in a flash of insight, I thought back to a way I have used to memorize Scripture.

If I take a short phrase of Scripture and string together the first letters of each word and include punctuation or change a "to" to a "2," I can make a very strong password that is easy to remember. Furthermore, every one of the thirty or more times in a day that I log onto my computer, I recite the verse to myself. I suspect that God helps me choose the phrases that I use because often the words that I recite speak directly to the particular spiritual challenges I am facing during that ninety-day period.

Here are some of my passwords: J,SoD,hmom (Jesus, Son of David, have mercy on me); WmdmLh4hs? (What message does my Lord have for his servant?); HgitltFhlou, (How great is the love the Father has lavished on us,); Iw2kCatpohr (I want to know Christ and the power of his resurrection); TeGiyr,auatea. (The eternal God is your refuge, and underneath are the everlasting arms.). Here is one of my favorites that consoled me many times as I struggled with a difficult medical or ethical dilemma, or when I felt I had failed: Bth!Ihotw. (But take heart! I have overcome the world.).

As I look back on these passwords, a flood of God's grace washes over me when I think of how He has spoken to me through them. These words have become mine. How many times He has lifted me up to speak a little kinder, to be conscious of His presence in the exam room, to see an angry patient as His child, to know His hands are outstretched to help me!

Jim McMillan, LLUSM class of 1986, is associate professor in LLUSM department of medicine, division of nephrology.

December 21

I can do all things through Christ who strengthens me. Philippians 4:13, NKJV

Excellence is expected in healthcare. Unlike many other professions, it is not good enough to be "adequate" or even "above average" as a healthcare worker. Very few people would send their loved one to a medical professional who was known to be mediocre. We hope for, and expect, that our physician, nurse, dentist, or therapist will give us the best care possible.

Those outside the medical field may not realize how difficult it is to be truly competent, much less excellent, in our work. I write this, feeling exhausted and inadequate after my first day of internship. It is often said that all physicians remember their first day as a "real" doctor. There is a somewhat universal feeling of excitement, fear, accomplishment, and dread when one steps into a new role as a physician and assumes responsibility for the lives of others.

Despite the years of study, the hard work on hospital wards, and seemingly endless preparation, on this day my fellow interns and I felt like fish out of water, disoriented by new surroundings and besieged by new responsibilities. Within a few hours, I was challenged with questions and issues I had never confronted before. This experience reminded me of the sheer number of intellectual, technical, and interpersonal obstacles that must be overcome to achieve "excellence" in the work we do.

With the many challenges in professional and private life, how does one attain excellence? Christ left a lasting example of how one individual's devotion to a goal and a lifestyle can impact a life, an age, and a world. He was once challenged to name the greatest commandment. His response is a model for achieving excellence in our lives and in our work.

Christ said, "'Love the Lord your God with all your heart and with all your soul and with all your strength and with all your mind'; and, 'Love your neighbor as yourself'" (Luke 10:27, NIV). Christ's response reveals a singular, yet inclusive focus for us to emulate. If we can adopt a similar devotion and way of life in all we do, excellence will be the natural result; and all the "small stuff" will fall into place.

Football great Vincent Lombardi once said, "The quality of a person's life is in direct proportion to their commitment to excellence, regardless of their chosen field of endeavor." This commitment will nurture and produce excellence in your work, your church, and your home. Today, follow Christ's example to embody your calling as you use your skills and talents to serve those you meet.

Cody Chastain, LLUSM class of 2008, is a resident in internal medicine at Duke University in Durham, North Carolina. In 2008, he received the LLU Chancellor's Award. He and his wife, Jamie, were married on December 21.

December 22

I will not fail thee, nor forsake thee. Joshua 1:5, KJV

It was a beautiful, mild winter day as we sailed past the Statue of Liberty shining proudly in the evening sunset. New York Harbor seemed so calm and peaceful in comparison to the angry North Atlantic we had crossed in mid-December 1946.

As I stood alone along the railing of the Liberty ship admiring the sights, I was both happy and excited to be arriving in the United States for the first time. But there was also a growing sense of apprehension. Instead of docking in New York City, New York, the ship was heading for Newark, New Jersey. How would I get a taxi, find a place to stay overnight in New York City, catch the train to Washington, D.C., and eventually find my way to Washington Missionary College (now Columbia Union College) in Takoma Park, Maryland? I only had $100 to my name, and my command of the English language was far from perfect.

Suddenly, Rodney Pelton, a young member of the ship's crew, stood beside me and said: "I hear you are going to Washington Missionary College. I plan to be a student there myself as soon as my tour of duty on this ship is completed. I will help you find a place to stay in New York City and get you on the train to Washington, D.C." What a relief!

In 1946, the total membership of the Seventh-day Adventist Church was only about 500,000; and very few members were sailors on Liberty ships. So what was the chance of one appearing just at the right time? Some would say it was just a lucky coincidence. But I am convinced that the prayers of my devoted parents, family members, and friends had a lot to do with it.

As soon as the ship docked and the authorities had cleared us for debarkation, we all streamed ashore. I waited on the pier for quite a while, but my newfound friend was nowhere in sight. It was getting dark. Only one taxi and I were left on the pier, so I thought I better see if that taxi would take me to a hotel. Just as I was stepping into the taxi with my two small suitcases, my new friend came rushing down the gangplank and explained to the taxi driver that he would take care of me.

After a few phone calls and a thirty-minute wait, a car arrived; and we were on our way through the Holland Tunnel, across Manhattan and the Brooklyn Bridge, and on to a YMCA—which was right next to where Seventh-day Adventist evangelistic meetings were being held. My newfound friend from the ship introduced me to the young ministerial intern, who kindly agreed to help me get to Union Station and on the right train.

The following day I was on my way to Washington and Washington Missionary College. I was so thankful to God, who again showed me that He would not fail me or forsake me.

Trygve Opsahl, LLUSM class of 1954, is a surgeon in Sonora, California. He was an LLUSM Alumni Association 2004 Honored Alumnus. December 22 is the date when he arrived in the United States from Norway.

If you, then, though you are evil, know how to give good gifts to your children, how much more will your Father in heaven give good gifts to those who ask him! Matthew 7:11, NIV

"Santa, please hurry. I want a dolly. I've been good. Please, hurry."

As I recall, she was about 7 years old. I was making evening anesthesiology rounds before her surgery, which was scheduled for the following morning. I knew she was scheduled for a burn debridement. The chart told the sad story: Her older brother and friends had been playing in a garage with matches. Greasy rags nearby exploded into flames and quickly engulfed the garage and his youngest sister, the little patient.

I paused in front of the glass-enclosed room and admired the child's colorful artwork of Santa and his reindeer. His sleigh was piled high with toys, including a blond-haired beauty of a doll propped prominently at the top of the heap. The scrawled words beneath the picture implored, "Santa, please hurry. I want a dolly. I've been good. Please, hurry."

Bold red warning signs signaled she was in isolation. I wearily donned a gown, mask, and gloves and entered the twilight room, which revealed the small form of a child in a regular hospital bed. She looked so small, swathed in white sheets and white bandages about her head. As I came closer, I saw that the oxygen tubing had twisted away from her tiny nostrils and her skin was a pale gray. Her eyes were closed and her breathing was barely discernible. I repositioned her oxygen tube, ran from the room to the nurse's station, and gave the head nurse these orders, scribbled on her chart:

1. Cancel surgery
2. Call the surgeon
3. Blood gases STAT
4. One dolly STAT

The nurse looked at me with disdain. I'll never forget her expression, as if she were saying, "Don't bother me. Can't you see that I am busy?" She stammered something like, "Why would you cancel surgery?" I mumbled something like, "The baby is not going to live until surgery. Please get her a dolly, *STAT!*" The nurse shrugged and called the surgeon. No doubt she thought a young resident needed to be set straight.

I walked blindly into the hall, where the cloverleaf hospital wings join, and buckled over in agony with abdominal pain. The ward secretary in the opposite wing saw me and immediately offered leftover pudding and milk from food carts. How very kind that ward secretary was.

The little patient died shortly thereafter. I shall never forget her, that precious little girl whose life had been snuffed out by childhood mischief.

I hope to meet her in heaven and tell her I really tried to get her a dolly. How do I know she'll be in heaven? Because she told Santa, "I've been good"—and I believe her.

Linda Harsh Dixon, LLUSM class of 1972, also graduated from dental hygiene in 1967. She lives in Kailua, Hawaii.

December 24

Whatever you did for one of the least of these brothers of mine, you did for me.
Matthew 25:40, NIV

One Christmas season, my mother and I decided to go to South Coast Plaza in Costa Mesa, California, to do our Christmas shopping. They have every store imaginable, and we started out early to devote an entire day to this effort. Despite all the selection and the time we spent, in the end we only made one purchase. Early in our day I saw a huge package of white sport socks. My husband had needed a single pair, two pair at the most. I went ahead and bought the large bundle of socks at their bargain price.

My mother and I had a good laugh that, after all our effort, we had found only one suitable "gift." It was evening when we arrived back in Los Angeles, California. We decided to have dinner in Brentwood, California. As we approached our restaurant, we passed a homeless man.

He spoke to us as we passed. Both my mother and I stopped and looked at each other after walking by. I said to her, "What did that man just say?" She said, "I think he said, 'Ladies, do you have any socks?'" I turned around and confronted the man, who was quite startled to see me turn back and address him. I asked him, "What did you just say?" Sheepishly he repeated, "I said, 'Ladies, do you have any socks?'"

Looking down, I saw a pair of bare, swollen feet, covered with cracks and sores. My mother and I said nothing, turned around, went back to our car, and returned to hand this homeless man a huge package of white socks. He looked completely shocked by this response to what he must have felt was a futile request. What a wonderful Christmas gift for us to be able to fulfill such a simple request.

Monica McDonough was an anesthesia resident at LLUMC from 1987 to 1990. She received her MD degree from New York Medical College in Valhalla, New York, in 1982. Prior to her residency at LLUMC, she served as a flight surgeon in the United States Air Force. She resides in Marina Del Rey, California.

And the dead man came out, his hands and feet bound in graveclothes, his face wrapped in a headcloth. Jesus told them, "Unwrap him and let him go!" John 11:44, NLT

In the neonatal intensive care unit at Loma Linda University Children's Hospital during Christmas week, I watch a baby boy battle for his life. His eyes are closed, but he isn't asleep.

When he was born, his mother cut the umbilical cord. Then she brutally attacked him and left him for dead by a cold bathroom window. The hypothermia caused by the cold and the blood loss slowed his heart rate and, ironically, maybe saved his life. Someone came in to use the bathroom and heard a whimper.

His birth announcement was a crime report in the newspaper.

The veteran physicians who are treating the stabbed newborn are devastated at an occasion for joy turned to unspeakable evil and suffering, but around the clock they keep at their work of healing.

The third night of care, one of the physicians text-pages me, "I don't even know what to pray for."

"I do," I page back. "This is all or nothing for this child. If our Father in heaven anywhere in the world tonight sees one of His children who is torn and bleeding at the moment of birth by an act of unspeakable evil, I believe He would want that child in our neonatal intensive care unit with the skills and faith of our caregivers. I take that the baby is with us as a sign from God, and I pray to Him for the child's healing and life."

The child lives, whole of body and mind, thriving in a loving adoptive family. The hearts of the surgeons, physicians, nurses, technicians, and even lawyers, who prayed and cared for him are also renewed.

We serve a risen Savior. He is present. He lives in our hearts. It is He who raises the Lazaruses among us from the tombs of their futility but leaves it to us to unbind them from the wrappings of their bondage and to help them go healed and free.

This is the real Christmas story, and we who serve here at Loma Linda University and around the world in continuing the teaching and healing ministry of Jesus Christ are able to live it every day. Let's be thankful in this season of celebration for the blessings of Christ's love and our opportunities of service to minister to others in the liberating, restoring power of redeeming grace.

Kent A. Hansen is general counsel for LLUAHSC. He received his JD degree from Willamette University in Salem, Oregon, in 1979.

December 26

I wait for the Lord, my soul waits, and in his word I put my hope. Psalm 130:5, NIV

When the call came, I bolted out of my office and made it home as quickly as I could. As I rushed through the door, I knew that what my wife had said was true. My 7-year-old daughter, Hannah, had broken her arm. I'm pretty sure arms are supposed to be straight; and hers was not, by any means.

Hannah looked up at me with eyes full of trust: now that Daddy was home, things would be better. My problem was that I couldn't help her. (I'm pretty sure the look on my face was not comforting at all!)

We got Hannah into the car and off to the emergency room (emergency rooms fall under my domain). An hour later, the doctor walked in with the films and said Hannah would probably need surgery; but first the team was going to try to put the bones back in place. Through all of this, Hannah was a champ. I, however, was a wreck!

The thing about doctors is that they have all the information. While they can give hope, doctors can also confuse, comfort, or frustrate—simply by the attitude with which they choose to convey information. We were fortunate that night—Hannah's doctor and his team were great communicators. However, he was very clear that he was not sure setting the bone would work.

Let's fast forward past the setting of the bone, which was tough for me to watch. In fact, for all my big talk, I didn't watch a thing. After getting more x-rays, the doctor returned, with his team behind him. He had a big grin on his face. Now, I don't know which is more frightening, a doctor looking solemn or a doctor who is excited!

The doctor threw the films on the light board and said, "It's PERFECT!"

I must have had a look of disbelief, because he said it again. This time I saw his team all nodding, with looks of agreement and incredulity that they could have done such a great job. Perhaps they were surprised that what they were taught had actually worked!

Fortunately, Hannah's arm healed quickly and without incident and I was left with a couple of lingering thoughts regarding the whole ordeal. First of all, it was most enjoyable to watch a team of doctors become so excited about her treatment and subsequent healing process. Secondly, I now realize the impact physicians' words can have on a family going through a crisis. Yes, doctors have the ability, and, may I dare say the responsibility, to convey hope in some way, to all who come under their care.

Timothy Gillespie is pastor for young adults at Loma Linda University Church of Seventh-day Adventists in Loma Linda, California.

December 27

A new heart also will I give you, and a new spirit will I put within you: and I will take away the stony heart out of your flesh, and I will give you an heart of flesh. Ezekiel 36:26, KJV

As a slow interviewer and a stuttering presenter, my third year of medical school was a constant test. I consistently thought of rounds not as a chance to shine, but as a mine field to survive. No matter how thorough I thought I was during the patient interview, I would somehow fail to present some very pertinent information.

Several weeks into my first rotation, I was asked to interview a new patient being evaluated for a possible pulmonary embolism. I asked her the questions on my ever-present history and physical checklist. When I got to surgical history, she denied ever having had surgery before. Knowing that I'd been burned before when people forgot common surgeries, I asked again if she'd had tonsil, appendix, cesarean section, or gallbladder surgery. She admitted to having had two of those, but, when pressed, adamantly denied any further surgical history. Moving on to medical history, I asked if she'd ever had a heart attack. Her answer blew me away. "I had two before the transplant," she replied.

Initially, I was angry more than anything else, thinking of the possibility of presenting a morning case without having known she'd had a heart transplant. But since escaping the fear of morning presentations, the bigger picture has always amazed me. This woman had had a failing heart. She'd had a surgery where she'd been in the hospital for probably a week. She was constantly on medicines to protect her transplant. Someone had died and his or her heart kept this patient alive . . . and she completely forgot to mention it ever happened!

I constantly have to ask myself how many times that, even when pressed, I fail to mention how Someone gave His life for me, so I could have a new heart. Even beyond ignored opportunities to praise Him for His sacrifice, how many times do my words and actions deny His sacrifice before an unbelieving world? In the eyes of others, am I a new creation? Does my daily life tell others that I have a new heart? Do I, like the apostles, make others take note that I have been with Jesus? Or is my conversion experience simply a historical point in my life that I may or may not even remember to mention and no one would happen to guess on their own if they tried?

I pray that daily I will be given a new heart. I pray that I will always be ready with an answer for my faith, rather than ashamed and forgetful. But I also pray that I will always live a life that is congruent with the faith I express. May God help us all in this endeavor.

Brent Goodge, LLUSM class of 2000, was a resident in anesthesiology at LLUMC from 2001 to 2004. He and his wife, Synnova, were married on December 27, and live with their daughter, Madison, in Dalton, Georgia.

December 28

Look, he is coming with the clouds, and every eye will see him. Revelation 1:7, NIV

Due to stormy skies, my husband, "Dr. Sam," and I detoured from Cameron Highlands in Malaysia to stop at Phuket, Thailand, on our way back to our apartment near Bangkok Adventist Hospital in Bangkok, Thailand. Actually, it was a bit more than bad weather, for Dr. Sam was checking to see if his original building plan was being followed. He had designed a new thirty-bed Phuket hospital, where we would shortly be working with Paul Watson, LLUSM class of 1959.

But there was an even more important appointment for us that evening. We were to meet two Thai Air Force planes flying in there, loaded with thirty-two beds, bundles of new surgical instruments, equipment for my pathology laboratory, and some for the hydrotherapy department.

It came about this way: The old two-story shop house downtown used as the Phuket Mission Hospital had long been recognized as unsuitable, thus the need for a new hospital. But there was almost no equipment in it for use in the new building.

Recently, I had gone back to America to take my pathology board exams, but I was also constantly worrying about equipping the new hospital being built. The Lord knew I needed to concentrate on passing those exams, so He took over marvelously. Soon, I heard of a convalescent home due to close, and they offered thirty-two used beds of the old-fashioned crank style. These would be just right, for a mission hospital.

Also, a surgical supply-store manager opened his catalogs for me to pick out sets of instruments, which my husband would need for surgeries, for which he had just been trained in Bangkok Adventist Hospital's residency. Also, I would be able to use them in obstetrics and gynecology surgery. He also offered pathology lab equipment—all of these at greatly reduced prices. My generous mother and brother wrote the checks! We stored everything near Loma Linda, California, awaiting transportation.

Someone suggested asking if the nearby United States Air Force base in California would be willing to fly it all to Thailand. So I asked, not realizing how bold and impossible that was. To my surprise, the officer at the Air Force base simply said, "My pilots will be happy to transport this equipment, for a good purpose.

Back in Bangkok, we were told to meet the plane that would arrive at the Thai and United States Air Force base. I sat down with the officer in charge to discuss the equipment transfer to Phuket. I asked if we should get trucks and men to transfer it the 500 or so miles to Phuket. Raising his hand as if to stop me, he said, "Little lady! You leave that to me! The Thai Air Force owes us one; they can just transport it right to the Phuket Airport for you. After all, it's for that country's people's care!"

And so we were standing at the Phuket Airport with our two babies in our arms and tears in our eyes (literally), watching the skies as two Thai Air Force planes came in for a landing. (It took two planes to carry what one huge United States Air Force plane had transported across the Pacific Ocean to Bangkok!)

That evening we seemed to hear God's voice: "Friends, all of you who are Mine, I am coming to receive you, just as I promised, and all Heaven is with Me!"

Effie Jean Ketting, LLUSM class of 1954, is an anatomic pathologist and resides with her husband, Samuel, LLUSM class of 1960, in College Place, Washington. She was an LLUSM Alumni Association 2004 Honored Alumna.

"Surely I am coming soon." Amen. Come, Lord Jesus! Revelation 22:20, NRSV

Suzanne was 29 years old when she rolled the Jeep. It happened the day before Thanksgiving as she was on her way to the market. She remembered to secure the car seats for her three children, and they weren't hurt in the accident. But in the rush to get going, she forgot to fasten her own seat belt.

It happened quickly. Suzanne glanced away from the road for a second; and when she looked back, she saw an oncoming car. She turned the wheel too hard, and the Jeep turned over. Suzanne was pinned underneath. The accident broke her ribs, punctured her lungs, lacerated her liver, and crushed her spine. She was rushed to the hospital where surgeons heroically saved her life, but she would never walk again.

She'd come back to the operating room now, to repair a hole where tissue had been torn from her thigh. The pain medication that she'd received earlier was working, and Suzanne was sleepy. I put on the electrocardiogram (EKG) pads and the blood pressure cuff. I told her she was going to take a brief rest.

"I want to go and be with Jesus," Suzanne said.

"You'll do that someday," I replied, "but not now. You'll be waking up in a little bit; but if you like, you can dream about heaven while you sleep."

"Jesus has a mansion waiting for me," she said. "He has one for you, too."

Then the anesthetic took effect and Suzanne slept. She woke up peacefully when the surgery was finished. Her pain, for the moment, was gone. The night had fallen when I left the hospital. As I drove home, I listened to the radio and heard the news about the day's events: an 11-year-old had been killed in a drive-by shooting, fires had left scores of people homeless. The sorrow and misfortune went on, the same way it has for centuries. And I knew that someday, that sorrow would come for me and for those that I love.

At home I helped my wife read stories to our children. We said prayers before we put them to bed. "Jesus, help all the people in the world," my daughter requested. We kissed them goodnight, and then we also went to bed.

As the mists of sleep began to fall, I hoped I would dream about heaven. It would be good to be with Jesus.

David Hirst, LLUSM class of 1981, is an anesthesiologist in Corona, California.

December 30

The King will reply, "I tell you the truth, whatever you did for one of the least of these brothers of mine, you did for me." Matthew 25:40, NIV

As I walk through the wards of the Bere Adventist Hospital in Chad, I notice a crowd lounging around outside. Making a quick exit, I shout: "Rounds are starting! Everyone who is with a patient come in; all other visitors should leave." A few aggressive gestures later, most everyone clears out—leaving the hospital with a rare moment of relative peace.

Not for long. I find all the hospitalized children crammed into one small room because the pediatric ward has been vacated so that the leaky roof and moth-eaten ceiling can be replaced. At the end of my tour, I come to the last of the patients, a skinny 10-year-old boy with bulging eyes staring at me blankly. Suddenly the child goes crazy.

In one simultaneous gesture, the boy flips from his back to a kneeling position, thrusting his bottom up into the air. He reaches his hand around his back, sticks his fingers into his rectum, and releases a stream of urine that thrashes around like a fire hose out of control. All this time, he writhes around like a cat in a bag and screams as if someone is slowly skinning him alive.

I am shocked and unnerved. I quickly grab his arms—thus removing his hand from his anus—flip him over, and pin him to the urine-soaked mattress. I notice the urine is tinged with pus. I ask for his lab results as he moans and groans and futilely struggles. The only significant finding is white blood cells in the urine.

For some strange reason (perhaps years of being a resident and having surgeons drill it into my brain), I decide to do a rectal exam. I quickly call for a glove and feel inside the child's rectum. Where his prostate should be is a large, hard, smooth, somewhat oblong mass moving towards his bladder. An ultrasound check confirms a calcified mass in his bladder.

An hour later, as I stand poised with a scalpel over the boy's lower abdomen, I pause to pray. A few slices later, I am in his bladder. Despite expecting it, chills still run up and down my spine and my arm hairs stand on end as I reach a gloved finger into the bladder and touch the large urinary calculus.

The mass is so large compared to the small bladder that it is quite difficult to extract. I finally open the wound further, slip some forceps around the stone, and squeeze it out like a difficult childbirth. There on the table before me is a three-inch-by-one-inch-long kidney bean-shaped rock.

The next day the boy is smiling. For the first time in his life, he is without pain. After spending months and months of his life in many different hospitals, he found help in ours. Despite the fact that my first reaction was that he was crazy or demon-possessed, God gave me that small nudge necessary to help me diagnose and treat what turned out to be a rather simple but often missed problem.

James Appel, LLUSM class of 2000, is assistant professor in LLUSM department of family medicine and is serving at Bere Adventist Hospital in Chad. A deferred mission appointee, he and his wife, Sarah, were married on December 30.

December 31

Pure and genuine religion in the sight of God the Father means caring for orphans and widows in their distress and refusing to let the world corrupt you.
James 1:27, NLT

Following the path of Jesus Christ carries with it the practical imperative of serving others and helping our communities, in the context of our own life experiences and talents. Every single act of daily service helping those in need and healing those who are sick makes us better instruments of God's love in this world.

I was 14 years old when I began my first job. Working in a baseball stadium in San Juan, Puerto Rico, provided good pay; and the "fringe benefits" were great for an active teenager: free access to the stadium facilities and numerous opportunities to meet and hang out with the players—including such leading professionals as baseball Hall of Fame inductee Roberto Clemente.

Clemente had already achieved top honors in the game: four batting titles, National League Most Valuable Player, and a World Series championship ring. But it was his impressive skills and work ethic that made a long-lasting impression on my young mind. I saw an unstoppable dedication to improve his game through systematic drills, even while suffering chronic back pain. The constant executions of these drills were key in developing his throwing, running, hitting, and catching abilities.

Even more impressive were his admirable sportsmanship, his dedication to tutoring fellow players, his time spent doing charity work, and his visible voice for social justice to improve society. Clemente did not put on hold giving back to the community while traveling on his journey to be among the best in the history of the game. The real Clemente's life included not only outstanding defensive plays or producing a needed hit to win a game, but also an inspiring talk with a young kid or holding a free baseball clinic for a disadvantaged community.

Clemente reached the major landmark of 3,000 hits in 1972. In December of that year, he was part of a humanitarian-relief effort to help the people of Nicaragua who had been hit by a devastating earthquake. Clemente died December 31 of that year in a plane crash while carrying supplies to help the victims. His ultimate sacrifice was not an isolated event but part of his countless individual daily acts of service that enriched a lifelong commitment to service and excellence.

At times, we as Christians may feel that we have to make a choice between a life of service and a successful career. The exemplary life of humanitarians, like Roberto Clemente, shows that we can commit to daily acts of service and excel in our career of choice. James could have had this in mind when he wrote about the "pure and genuine religion." We may never be called to board a plane to help suffering communities in a distant land; but we are part of that same journey if we tutor a struggling student, coach a co-worker to succeed in his/her job, or provide for the needy among us.

Marino De Leon is associate professor in LLUSM department of basic sciences, division of physiology; and is director of LLUSM Center for Health Disparities and Molecular Medicine. He received a PhD degree from University of California, Davis, in 1987.

Index of Daily Scripture References

Index of Authors

Glossary
A layman's guide to many of the medical terms used in this book

ABSCESS: A collection of pus

ACCESSORY INSPIRATORY MUSCLES: Muscles other than the diaphragm that aid in breathing

ACUTE: Having a recent onset

ACUTE RESPIRATORY DISTRESS SYNDROME: Lung failure after shock or trauma

AEROSOLIZED EPINEPHRINE TREATMENT: Used to treat asthma

AMNIOCENTESIS: The removal of a small amount of fluid that surrounds a fetus, usually used to determine genetic disorders

AMNIOTIC FLUID: The liquid in which a fetus floats inside the womb

AMOXICILLIN: An antibiotic

ANENCEPHALIC: Absence of a brain at birth

ANGIOEDEMA: Rapid swelling under the skin or in the throat that, when severe, can cause difficulty breathing

AORTIC STENOSIS: A narrowing of the major artery of the thorax and abdomen

APGAR SCORE: A scale used to rate the condition of a baby immediately after birth

ARTERIAL LINE: A small tube in an artery, used to continuously monitor blood pressure or obtain blood-oxygen levels

ASCULTATE: To listen with a stethoscope for sounds within the body

ASYSTOLE: No heart beat

BACTRIM: An antibiotic

BALKAN FRAME: An over-the-bed pole or frame for supporting a fractured limb

BARBITURATE: A medication used as a sedative

BASILAR EFFUSION: Fluid around the lowest part of the lung

BIAXIN: An antibiotic

BRADYCARDIA: An abnormally slow heart rate

BLOOD GASES: A laboratory blood test to measure oxygen and acidity of the blood

BURN DEBRIDEMENT: Removal of dead tissue caused by a serious burn

BURSITIS: Inflammation, often painful, of a fluid-filled sac that otherwise allows layers of tissue to slide easily over one another

CALCIFIED MASS: A hard, stone-like lump either felt or seen on x-ray, ultrasound, or magnetic resonance image

CARDIOMYOPATHY: Disease of the heart muscle

CATHETERIZATION: Placing a tube in an organ of the body, usually the bladder or the heart

CELLULITIS: Infection of the skin

CLEFT PALATE: Failure of the roof of the mouth to close during fetal development

COAGULOPATHY: A disorder of blood coagulation

CODE BLUE: A phrase reserved to alarm those nearby of a life-threatening event that requires immediate medical attention

COLOSTOMY: A surgical opening of the large bowel (colon) through the skin

COMPUTERIZED TOMOGRAPHY (CT): A computer-assisted technique for making cross-sectional x-ray pictures

CONJUNCTIVA: A clear membrane that covers the white part of the eye and the inside of the eyelids

CONTRALATERAL: Refers to the opposite side

CORNELIA DE LANGE SYNDROME: Genetic disorder that leads to physical abnormalities and mental retardation

CORTICOSTEROID: A class of hormones produced in the adrenal glands

CYANOTIC: Having a bluish discoloration of the skin indicative of a lack of oxygen in the blood

DECADRON: A potent steroid used to treat life-threatening inflammation

DECOMPENSATE: Failure of the body to correct its failing systems

DEFIBRILLATE: To use electrical shock to reset the heart beat

DEHISCENCE: Unwanted separation of a surgical wound several days after surgery

DIASTEMA: In dentistry, a space between two teeth

DISSEMINATED INTRAVASCULAR COAGULATION: A serious condition in which the body consumes all of its clotting factors (often from overwhelming infection), which often leads to bleeding

DIURETIC (LASIX): A drug that increases urine output

ESOPHAGOGASTRODUODENOSCOPY (ECD): Passing a scope through the mouth to view the swallowing tube, stomach and duodenum

ECTOPIC PREGNANCY: A pregnancy that occurs outside the uterus

EDEMA: Swelling

EFFACEMENT: Used to describe the thinning of the opening of the womb during early labor

EFFEXOR XR: Modern antidepressant

EJECTION FRACTION: The percentage of blood in the final pumping chamber that leaves the heart with each of its beats

ELECTROCARDIOGRAM (ECG OR EKG): An electrical tracing of the heart used to diagnose irregular heart beats, heart attacks, or impending heart attacks

ELECTROENCEPHALOGRAM (EEG): Measurement of electrical brain waves that is used to understand seizure disorders, or to determine the presence or absence of brain activity

ENDOTRACHEAL: Within or passing through the trachea or windpipe

EPISIOTOMY: A surgical widening of the vaginal opening to facilitate the birth of a child

ETIOLOGIES: Causes or reasons for the patient's disease

FASCIA: Flat, sheet-like connective tissue layers throughout the body that surround the organs, muscles, and other structures

FECAL SPILLAGE: The loss of stool through a hole in the large intestine that if left untreated will cause acute generalized peritonitis

FIBROTIC TISSUE: Scar tissue

FOUL DISCHARGE: Bad-smelling things that come from any part of the body

FULMINATING: Severe, sudden onset

GASTROENTERITIS: Inflammation of the stomach and small intestine that may be caused by bacteria, viruses, chemicals, stress, etc.

GOITER: An enlarged thyroid that is most likely due to low thyroid hormone or low iodine in the diet

GRAM-NEGATIVE SEPTICEMIA: A blood infection from a specific class of bacteria found commonly in the gastrointestinal tract

hCG LEVEL: A pregnancy test

HELICOBACTER PYLORI ERADICATION: Elimination of the bacterium that causes stomach and small-bowel ulcers

HEMATOCRIT: The percentage of whole blood that is made up of red blood cells

HEMORRHAGE: Uncontrolled bleeding

HISTOLOGY: The study of microscopic structure of tissues

HISTOPLASMOSIS: Lung infection caused by a fungus inhaled from bird or bat droppings or from soil in the Ohio River Valley

HURLER'S SYNDROME: A rare, inherited disease of metabolism in which a person cannot break down long chains of sugar molecules. The disease is characterized by dwarfism, hunchback, and mental retardation.

HYPEREMESIS GRAVIDARUM: Excessive vomiting associated with pregnancy

HYPERTROPHY: Enlargement

HYPOPIGMENTED: Decreased amount of pigment in the skin

HYPOPLASTIC LEFT HEART SYNDROME: Underdevelopment of the left side of the heart

HYPOXIA: Low oxygen

ILEOSTOMY: A surgical opening of the small bowel (ileum) through the skin

INOTROPIC AGENTS: A class of medications used to improve the strength of each heart beat

INTERSTITIAL FLUID: Fluid between the cells of the body

INTRAVENOUS: Using a small tube or catheter to give fluids or medications via a vein

INTRAOCULAR PRESSURE: Pressure inside the eye

INTUBATE: To insert a breathing tube into the trachea

JUGULAR VENOUS PRESSURE: Pressure in the jugular vein located in the neck, measured by seeing how far the vein fills above the level of the heart

KETAMINE: Anesthetic agent that causes a dream-like state

LABILE: Opposite of stability

LACERATIONS: Slicing injuries to body tissues

LAPAROSCOPIC: Using a scope to look inside the abdominal cavity

LARYNGEAL-TRACHEAL RECONSTRUCTION: Surgery to repair the windpipe

LEUKOERYTHROBLASTOSIS: Numerous immature red and white cells in the blood stream

LPN NURSE: Licensed practical nurse

MARASMUS: Malnutrition from severe deficiency of calories

MAXILLARY SINUS CANCER: Cancer in the hollow space contained within the cheek bone

MEDIASTINAL FIBROSIS: A hardening of the tissues between the lungs that block the large blood vessels

MESOTHELIOMA: Cancer of the lining of the lung and chest wall

METASTIC CANCER: Cancer that has spread beyond the margin of its origin to surrounding sites elsewhere in the body

METHADONE: A narcotic given by mouth, usually to substitute for an addict's heroin

MISOPROSTOL INDUCTION: Medication used to start labor in a pregnant patient

MOLAR PREGNANCY: Abnormal pregnancy in which a mass of placenta tissue forms inside the uterus with no fetus

MYOCARDIAL INFARCTION: A heart attack

NASOGASTRIC (NG) TUBE: A tube placed into the nostril and passed into the stomach to drain the stomach of gastric contents or for instilling liquid food

NECROTIC: Dead tissue

NEPHRITIS: An inflammatory disease of the kidney, that may result in kidney failure

NEURONTIN: Medication used for chronic nerve pain or seizures

NEUTROPENIC: Low white blood cell count

NONLATEX AGGLUTINATED HORMONE: Hormone measuring technique

OPHTHALMOSCOPE: An instrument to look into the eye

OPTIC DISC: Blind spot at the back of the eye where the nerve enters the eye

OTOSCOPE: An instrument to look into the ear

OXY IR: Immediate-release narcotic medicine for pain relief

OXYGEN SATURATION: Used to describe the amount of oxygen carried by the red blood cells

PALLIATIVE MEDICINE: Emphasizes keeping a patient comfortable

PANCREATITIS: Inflammation of the pancreas where digestive enzymes digest the pancreas instead of digesting food

PARATHYROID GLAND: Four lentil-sized glands behind the thyroid that are important for the control of phosphate and calcium levels in the blood

PATELLAR BURSA: Small sac around the knee cap that can become inflamed and swollen

PELVIC INFLAMMATORY DISEASE: Infection of the female reproductive organs

PENROSE DRAIN: A flat piece of rubber protruding from the surgical site, temporarily delaying closure of the wound to allow fluids to escape

PERCUSS: A tapping technique that produces a sound revealing how hollow or solid a body part is

PERICARDIUM: The sac that surrounds the heart

PERINATAL: The time period before, during, and immediately after the delivery of a baby

PERINEUM: The area located in front of the anus

PERIOCULAR ECCYMOSIS: Bruises/bleeding in the superficial skin layers around the eye, commonly referred to as a "black eye"

PERIPHERAL SMEAR: A blood smear prepared for microscopic analysis

PERITONEAL CAVITY: The abdominal space that contains the stomach, intestines, liver, spleen, and other organs

PERITONITIS: Inflammation of the lining of the abdominal cavity and some of the organs it contains

PETHIDINE: Demerol—a drug used to control pain

PHLEBOTOMIST: One who draws blood from a patient for the purpose of laboratory tests or for blood donation

PLACENTA PREVIA: An abnormal position of the afterbirth where it blocks the fetus from entering the birth canal and causes severe bleeding as labor progresses

POORLY DIFFERENTIATED CARCINOMA: An aggressive cancer

PRESUMPTIVE NEOPLASTIC PROCESS: Thought to be cancer

PRIMIGRAVIDA: A female who is pregnant for the first time

PRODROME: Early symptoms indicating the start of a disease

PROLAPSED UMBILICAL CORD: In pregnancy, when the cord extrudes out of the womb before the fetus

PROTONIX: Medicine used to decrease acid in the stomach

PULMONARY EMBOLISM: Potentially fatal blockage of an artery of the lung by a blood clot that formed in a vein elsewhere and travelled to the lung

PULMONOLOGIST: A physician who specializes in diseases of the lung

PULSATILE: Repeated expansion and contraction of a vessel or organ

PURULENT FLUID: A body fluid that contains pus

RALES: Crackling sounds in the lungs caused by excess fluid or fibrous scar tissue

RECTUS ABDOMINUS FASCIA: Outer layer of the abdominal wall muscles

RETROPERITONEAL LYMPH NODES: Part of the lymphatic fluid-drainage system behind the abdominal cavity

RINGER'S LACTATE: Intravenous solution of balanced minerals that mimics the fluid in blood

SCLERA: The white of the eye

SEPSIS: Infection in the bloodstream or body tissues, most frequently caused by bacteria

SEPTIC: Infected

SMALL-BOWEL RESECTION: Surgical removal of portions of the small intestine

SOMATIZATION: Psychiatric term for a patient with many physical complaints

SQUAMOUS CELL CARCINOMA: A type of skin cancer

ST SEGMENT: Component of the electrocardiogram that may reveal abnormalities of coronary blood flow

STOKES-ADAMS SYNDROME: Sudden, irregular heart rhythm

SURGICAL SHUNT: Procedure to divert blood from one blood vessel to another or to drain excess spinal fluid from the brain

SYSTEMIC FUNGAL SEPSIS: Life-threatening fungal infection of the blood

TAMPONADE: Pressure surrounding an organ or tissue that prevents blood from flowing into that organ

TETANUS TOXOID: A vaccine used to prevent lockjaw

TETRALOGY OF FALLOT: Congenital disorder of the heart causing four abnormalities that are usually fatal if untreated

THORACENTESIS: Draining fluid from the chest cavity through a needle

THREADY PULSE: A weak pulse that often indicates a serious problem with low blood pressure due to bleeding or heart failure

THROMBOCYTOPENIA: An abnormally low count of the blood platelets that may lead to bleeding problems

THYROTOXIC STATE: Having too much thyroid hormone in the system

TONOMETER: A machine used to measure pressure in the fluid filling the eye

TRACHEA: The windpipe that can be felt just below the "Adam's apple"

TRACHEOSTOMY: A breathing tube placed through the skin into the windpipe just beneath the "Adam's apple"

TRIZYGOTIC TRIPLETS: Nonidentical triplets

TYMPANIC MEMBRANE: The ear drum

UREMIC FETOR: Urine-like odor of the breath

URINARY CALCULUS: A stone in the kidney, ureter, or bladder

VARICEAL BANDING: The tying off of a large vein around the esophagus to control bleeding

VASOACTIVE DRUGS: A classification of medications that alter blood pressure

VENTILATORY SUPPORT: Utilizing a machine to breathe for a patient

VENTRICULAR FIBRILLATION: A serious, life-threatening heart condition that will quickly result in death if immediate medical attention does not occur

VENTRICULAR SEPTAL DEFECT: A hole in the heart that is usually congenital, between the two major pumping chambers

WARFARIN: A drug used to prevent the clotting of blood

WELBUTRIN SR: The slow-release form of a modern antidepressant

School of Medicine Awards

Alpha Omega Alpha Honor Society

Alumni Association of Loma Linda University Herber Award

Chancellor's Award*
Presented in recognition of superior scholastic attainment and active participation in the student community, within the framework of Christian commitment. One recipient is selected from each school of the University.

Deferred Mission Appointment (DMA)*
Provides scholarship support to medical students who are committed to serve in a Seventh-day Adventist mission hospital after completing residency training.

Leonard Marmor Surgical Arthritis Foundation Award*
Presented on behalf of the Marmor Foundation to an outstanding student who has demonstrated academic excellence, leadership, and a desire to contribute to the medical profession.

Reynolds Compassionate Care Award

Wil Alexander Whole-Person Care Award*
Recognizes a senior medical student who has demonstrated to his/her peers and colleagues, during the clinical years, a growing excellence in the physical, mental, emotional, spiritual, and relational care of patients as part of the art of medical practice.

DEPARTMENTAL AWARDS

Department of Anesthesiology – **Bernard D. Briggs Award**

Department of Emergency Medicine – **Society of Emergency Medicine Award***
Awarded to the senior medical student who best exemplifies the qualities of an emergency medicine physician, as manifested by excellent clinical, interpersonal and manual skills; who is dedicated to continued professional development leading and to outstanding performance on emergency medicine rotations.

Department of Family Medicine – **Walter P. Ordelheide Award**

Department of Gynecology and Obstetrics – **Harold F. Ziprick Award**

Department of Medicine –
Daniel D. Comstock Award
Donald E. Griggs Award
Harold J. Hoxie Award
Varner J. Johns Jr. Award

Department of Neurology – **Guy M. Hunt Award**

Department of Pediatrics – **Robert F. Chinnock Award**

Department of Preventive Medicine –
  Distinguished Student in Preventive Medicine Award
Department of Psychiatry – Benjamin Kovitz Award
Department of Surgery – David B. Hinshaw Sr. Award
Department of Urology – Roger W. Barnes Award

*used in authors' bios throughout book